The best of Britain

D1589946

Edin

700036009877

and East Coast Scotland

Vivien Devlin

Contents

Themed Maps

Town/City Centre Maps

The Guide

Photo Essays

Foreword

Roy Brett

This travel guide offers a unique insight into Scotland's rich culture, landscape and life-style – all the distinctive characteristics of this country which bring me back here, no matter where I may travel in the world. In its descriptions of Edinburgh and the surrounding areas of East Lothian, Fife, Perthshire and the Borders there's a warm enticement, which should inspire people of all ages to get out and about, to see and do everything these fine places have to offer. Scotland is a world leader in too many areas to list here; and its fantastic scenery, outdoor pursuits and arts festivals, to name but a few, are vividly brought to life in these pages.

Within minutes of leaving Edinburgh's city centre, you can find yourself in beautiful countryside, on amazing sandy beaches and in friendly little fishing towns that are especially great for me when I'm looking to source the best fresh produce around. I gained invaluable experience when I worked with Rick Stein who shares my passion for fresh, quality food. One of our prime national assets is the food scene which is well worth boasting about, and though I have a personal vested interest, Scotland offers a wealth of culinary havens. We really are in a privileged position being able to access such high-quality natural ingredients. One of my favourite places to source seafood is at the traditional fishing port of Eyemouth on the Berwickshire coast where DR Collin and Sons presents an unrivalled selection which never fails to deliver on quality. The first thing that hits you on the arrival here is the harbour's distinct smell that brings back childhood memories of holidaying at the seaside.

The fishermen in the area still boast Eyemouth's ethic of hard work and toil and they deliver some of the most wonderful shellfish and seafood. At The Old Smokehouse 'Big Stuart's' fresh smoked salmon is simply delicious. When I leave Eyemouth to return to Edinburgh, I always travel via the coastal road. I make sure I have time to visit the Golf Tavern in Gullane; a warm friendly pub with great ales and fantastic fresh food.

Another one of these great little villages is right in the shadow of the Forth Bridge, very near to my restaurant, The Grill at Dakota Forth Bridge. South Queensferry has remarkably preserved buildings dating back to the 1600s, and spectacular views of the bridge and Fife over on the other side. I'd highly recommend the boat ride from Queensferry out to Inchcolm Island with its ancient abbey and beach. As you head back into Edinburgh, a stop off in Leith is essential. Bowman's the Butchers on Great Junction Street is renowned for their legendary Red Pudding.

Embarking on a journey around south-east Scotland will take you to so many places to eat and drink with the opportunity to sample, taste and buy regional specialiaties from our wonderful natural larder. This is a comprehensive travel guide which I hope will encourage readers to explore not only the city but further afield around the countryside and coastline. I am sure that this will become a well-thumbed book, used as a reference for visitors and locals alike.

Roy Brett has had a long, distinguished career as a leading chef around the UK, teaming up with Rick Stein as executive chef in Seafood, the flagship restaurant in Padstow and also opening Rick Stein's Fish and Chip Shop. Now working with Ken McCulloch at Dakota Hotels as Partner Chef, Roy Brett is Executive Chef at the destination restaurant, The Grill at Dakota Forth Bridge near Edinburgh. In 2008 The Grill was voted Best Hotel Restaurant in Scotland, Scottish Restaurant of the Year and Roy was honoured with the Silver Award at the Scottish Chef Awards.

Introduction

The first question to ask is: Why do nearly 16 million people choose to visit Scotland each year? Scenic beauty, ancient castles, the Edinburgh Festival, golf, whisky, seafood, hill climbing or perhaps its magical touch of romance. Scotland, especially in the imagination, is an artistic tapestry of proud historic cities, towns and villages, a rural landscape of lochs, glens, forested mountains and painterly seascapes of white sand beaches, clifftops and islands – everywhere coloured by its own distinctive heritage, character and culture. 'Scotland is indefinable', believed Robert Louis Stevenson, 'it has no unity except upon the map'.

The map for this travel guide covering southeast Scotland has been roughly drawn in the shape of a heart with Edinburgh in the centre, spanning out east, south and north to East Lothian, the Border country, the Kingdom of Fife and Perthshire. Whether you stay in the capital with a few day trips, or plan a two or three-location vacation, you can combine city attractions with a breath of fresh air in the country and beside the sea. The aim of this book is to take the reader on a richly illustrated journey to entice you to visit the very best historic sites, explore off-the-beaten-track treasures, indulge the taste buds and experience outdoor adventures.

Stevenson described Edinburgh as a 'profusion of eccentricities, this dream in masonry and living rock, not a scene in a theatre but a city in the world of every day reality'. Edinburgh Castle, standing defiant and indestructable above the rugged rockface, is an iconic trademark worldwide. The 'Athens of the North' is a city of architectural fascination and conservation, juxtaposing the medieval Old Town with the Georgian New Town. As the first ever Unesco City of Literature it proudly celebrates its long-standing literary tradition from classic writers Scott and Stevenson to present-day best-selling novelists, JK Rowling and Ian Rankin.

Edinburgh of the 21st century is an inspiring city of contrasts. Its Royal Palace and Castle, cobbled wynds, elegant crescents and gardens are complemented by its image today as a contemporary and cosmopolitan European capital. There are more restaurants per head of population than any other city in Britain, smart shopping boulevards, and a choice of designer boutique city-centre hotels and smart apartments. As well as the famous International and Fringe Festivals in August, you'll find a diverse and dynamic cultural scene year round with world-class museums, literary walks and ghost tours. Due to the huge university student population, expect a colourful nightlife in this lively party town.

From Easter to Christmas, visitors come season by season, from springtime to winter, for a feast of festivities, sporting events and family attractions – the Taste food festival, rugby internationals, Science and Film festivals, Winter Wonderland with outdoor skating rink, Ferris wheel and Hogmanay fireworks at New Year.

During your visit to Edinburgh, take time to tour further afield. You cannot afford to miss a trip to see the magnificent twin Forth Bridges, spanning the river between South and North Queensferry; stroll along a white sand beach in East Lothian; visit a whisky distillery; taste the freshest fish and chips at Anstruther in Fife; play golf on the famous Old Course, St Andrews; or be pampered at Stobo Castle Spa resort near Peebles in the Scottish Borders. The Border Country is a picturesque, tranquil region for golfing, fishing on the Tweed, mountain biking and long walks on the Southern Upland Way. Scotland is renowned for its breathtaking unspoilt scenery, and it's lochs, rivers, hills and seashore, and it's a natural adventure playground for a hike or bike ride. Go sailing, surfing and kayaking, while hill climbers should head to Perthshire to 'bag' another Munro mountain.

Wherever you travel, enjoy the opportunity to sample the local delicacies – Buccleuch beef, Eyemouth lobster, seafood and venison from Fife, Perthshire lamb, Loch Fyne kippers, artisan cheese. Follow the new Visit Scotland Café Trail to sample the best cup of tea or shortbread. Every region offers their own specialities, with smokeries, farmers' markets, and annual food and drink festivals. With the finest Scottish smoked salmon on your plate, when eating and drinking around East Coast Scotland, the world is, literally, your oyster.

Browse through this guide to find a fabulous wealth of experiences and excursions for all ages and interests. Here's the lowdown on everything you need to know to enjoy the romantic charm and cultural buzz of Edinburgh, to the get-away-from-it-all peaceful wilderness of green hills, lochside and coastline around the Lowlands of Scotland.

Unmissable highlights

01 Edinburgh Castle

This dramatic 11th century royal residence and military fort perched on the rugged volcanic rock, dominates the city skyline. p.87

02 The Royal Mile

The historic heart of the Old Town, links the Castle down the High Street and Canongate to the Palace of Holyroodhouse. p.91

03 Edinburgh Festivals

The largest cultural event on the planet. A spectacle of entertainment from opera, music, drama and comedy to jazz and street jugglers. p.30

04 St Andrews, Fife

This ancient university town is the international spiritual Home of Golf. There is a superb beach for kite flying and five-star golf and spa resorts. p.252

05 Queen's View, Loch Tummel

A peaceful Perthshire beauty spot with stunning loch views for photographers, artists and nature lovers. p.299

06 **The Scottish Borders**

The pretty towns of Peebles and Melrose, ancient abbeys, Abbotsford, River Tweed and green rolling hills. p.205

07 East Lothian
Quaint villages, sandy beaches, clifftop castles and Bass Rock bird sanctuary.
p.155

08 Forth Bridges
Visit South Queensferry for the best
view of the magnificent Forth (Rail)
Bridge and Forth Road Bridge. p.141

09 The Hermitage, Dunkeld

Enjoy a fantastic river walk, dramatic waterfalls and a forest of Britain's tallest trees. p.294

10 National Galleries of Scotland

Four distinctive galleries preserving the nation's collection of classical, contemporary and surreal art and sculpture. p.238

Secret
East Coast
Scotland
Local Recommendations

01 Seabird Safari
From North Berwick, take a high-speed rib boat ride to the Bass Rock bird sanctuary, p.159

02 Pitlochry Festival Theatre
The 'Theatre in the Hills' allows you to 'stay six days, see six plays', covering the classics, comedy, drama and thrillers, p.293

03 Edradour Distillery
Experience a classic dram with a chaser, followed by a pint of home-brewed Braveheart at the nearby Moulin Inn, p.301

04 Ghost Tour
Survive a seriously scary supernatural ghost-hunting walk around Edinburgh's Old Town, p.92

05 Yellowcraig Beach
With sand dunes and grassy banks, this beach is perfect for picnics and barbecues and the water is clean and safe for swimming. The Treasure Island adventure park will keep the children amused, p.166

06 Anstruther Fish Bar

Taste the best fish and chips in Scotland, if not the whole of the UK, p.273

07 Myres Castle

Stay in this luxury, 16th-century, restored, turreted mansion, which remains intact as a living museum, p.280

08 St Abb's

On the Berwickshire coastline, this tiny fishing port offers wild seas and stunning cliff-top walks, p.231

09 Museum of Flight

This East Lothian museum features vintage aircraft, wartime bombers and the chance to step on board Concorde, p.164

10 Arthur's Seat

For an energetic countryside ramble in the heart of Edinburgh and superb views, you can't beat a climb up Arthur's Seat, p.94

Factfile

01 Three of the world's best-selling novelists all live in Edinburgh.

02 East Lothian has more links golf courses in close proximity than anywhere else in the world.

03 Perthshire is Big Tree Country, with the world's tallest, and longest hedge, and many of the tallest trees in Britain.

04 The first game of rugby union between England and Scotland was played in Melrose in 1871, and the first golf club was founded in 1744 in Leith, Edinburgh.

05 The Edinburgh Festival Fringe is the largest arts festival in the world.

06 The clock on the Balmoral Hotel clock tower is kept three minutes fast to help passengers catch their trains at Waverley Station next door.

07 The Grassmarket in Edinburgh, a popular piazza of bars and restaurants, was once the site of the public gallows for hanging thieves and murderers.

08 The University of St Andrews was founded in 1413; the first university in Scotland. Elizabeth Garrett, the first female student in Britain, enrolled here in 1862 to study medicine; former rectors include JM Barrie, Rudyard Kipling and John Cleese; and Prince William graduated in 2005 with a 2:1 in Geography.

09 The Tweed is regarded as the best salmon fishing river in the world.

10 The Bass Rock near North Berwick is the largest rock gannetry and one of the wildlife wonders of the world.

THE FACTS

WHEN TO GO

As Billy Connolly once said, 'In Scotland, there is no such thing as bad weather – only the wrong clothes.'

As this guide will illustrate, it's the outdoor life and sporting activities which attracts the visitor to Scotland – whether to play golf, go hiking, biking, bird watching, fishing, nature rambling, or more extreme adventures such as white-water rafting. You can experience the majority of these activities from March to November, and some all year round. As for city life, culture, art galleries, museums, historic attractions and numerous festivals, Edinburgh can be visited at any time of year.

Spring

A fine time of year to explore the Scottish Borders, touring the Abbey towns, or taking wonderful fresh air walks or bike rides through the forests. From May onwards, the high cliffs along the Berwickshire coastline is the place to see the seabirds, and at Aberlady nature reserve in East Lothian, spring sees the arrival of migrant birds and the start of the breeding season for Skylark, Eider, Lapwing, Willow and Sedge Warblers – ospreys may also be seen here. Edinburgh is in a graceful mood from Easter to May, when the Castle and galleries are not packed out, and the city gardens are in bloom with snowdrops, daffodils or blossom.

Summer

Scotland's outdoor playground is truly open for business with visitors coming to enjoy all the traditional leisure activities of golf, hill climbing and the hunting, fishing and shooting season. Perthshire in summer is the centre for extreme adventure sports, white-water rafting, kayaking, canyoning and sphering, while the Pitlochry Festival Theatre runs from May to October. A season of arts and music festivals in the seaside villages along the East Neuk of Fife take place in July and August. Summertime along the East Lothian white sand beaches is great for families to paddle, take a picnic or fly a kite.

August is the month when it seems the world descends on Edinburgh for the annual arts and cultural bonanza. If you love music, theatre, comedy, dance, opera, books, and a carnival atmosphere on the streets, then come and join in to embrace the largest arts festival in the world.

Autumn

A visit to Perthshire, Big Tree Country, between mid-October to November is a must-see, when the woodlands at the Hermitage, Killiecrankie and Faskally turn a rich palette of crimson, gold and bronze. Enjoy fabulous long walks through forest trails watching out for red squirrels and roe deer. Scottish country house hotels as well as self-catering cottages offer superb autumn holidays and short breaks, so it's a perfect time to explore the lochs and glens of Perthshire, St Andrews and Fife and the wild coastline of the Scottish Borders.

Winter

November sees the annual launch of Visit Scotland's Winter White season to celebrate exciting outdoor activities for the young and active, as well as cosy country house romantic retreats. While men might prefer the golf course (winter discount green fees), women can be pampered at one of many superb spa resorts from Gleneagles to Stobo Castle. For good winter hotel deals from December to March, check out www. visitscotland.com/white. Edinburgh looks simply magical during the Winter Festival from the end of November to early January, with a wonderland of festive events.

GETTING THERE

By car

Instead of flying or taking the train direct to Edinburgh, the beauty of driving from England is that you can plan to stop off en route for a few days to explore the Scottish Borders, Berwickshire coast or East Lothian. This is such a forgotten corner of *south-east Scotland* and well worth a few days touring around. From the *south-west* or Birmingham area, the direct route is the M6 motorway north then the A74(M), which you leave at Junction 15 (Moffat) and take the A708 north to Selkirk and the gracious and relaxing Tweed valley. Alternatively, leave the M6 further north (J13 Abingdon) and drive cross country on the A702 to Biggar and on to Edinburgh, but this bypasses the central Borders.

From the south and east side of the UK, the A1 is the road north to Newcastle and Berwick upon Tweed, from where you cross the Border. You could stop off to explore the fabulous cliffs along the Berwickshire coastline or explore the great attractions of the local countryside. From Newcastle you could leave the A1 and take the A696 (then A68) which cuts diagonally across the Border country to Jedburgh and the Abbey towns of Tweeddale. The A697 from Newcastle goes directly north to Coldstream, Berwickshire and the neighbouring town of Kelso in the heart of the Scottish Borders.

A series of environmentally friendly **Park and Ride** schemes have been developed around the outskirts of Edinburgh offering free and secure car parking and regular bus services to the city centre. Although particularly aimed at commuters, visitors will find this service invaluable. Park and Ride areas, when travelling north from the Scottish Borders, can be found at Straiton (on the road from Peebles) and Sheriffhall (from Lauder, St Boswells, Melrose, Jedburgh). There are two other parks on the west of the city at Ingliston and Hermiston (☎ 0131 555 6363; www.lothianbuses.com/parkandride.php).

Newcraighall Park and Ride (off the A1 from Berwick) is linked by rail services to Waverley and Haymarket. Trains take just 11 minutes to reach the city centre and run about every half hour. Parking costs 50p for 24 hours.

By bus

Edinburgh Bus Station, St Andrew Square is the coach terminal for local and long-distance services. The bus companies are:

· Linking Edinburgh to England:
  National Express: ☎ 08717 818181; www.nationalexpress.com
· Linking Edinburgh to England and to cities across Scotland:
  Megabus: ☎ 0900 160 0900; www.megabus.com
· Linking Edinburgh to towns and cities across Scotland:
  CityLink: ☎ 08705 50 50 50; www.citylink.co.uk
  Stagecoach: ☎ 0870 608 2 608; www.stagecoachbus.com

By Train

The most comfortable way to travel from London and across the UK to Edinburgh is by train. You can't get a better introduction to one of the world's most stunning city centres than that which towers all around you as you leave Waverley Station. For the first-time visitor, emerging from the 'underground' station on to Waverley Bridge is an awesome view – the Castle straight ahead, the Old Town to the left and Princes Street and the New Town to the right. If you plan to spend a few days here, it is not essential to have a car as walking around the compact city (or taking the bus) is the most practical method of transport. For day or longer trips to East Lothian, Fife and Perthshire you can take the train and bus, or rent a car for the Borders and further afield.

National Express East Coast has taken over the former GNER line from London via York to Edinburgh. This is a wonderful journey, especially as you skirt the coastline north of Newcastle to Berwick upon Tweed, offering spectacular sea views. NXEC trains also travel via Perthshire and Fife to Inverness and Aberdeen (www. nationalexpresseastcoast.com).

Cross Country trains operate across three UK nations at 131 stations, with routes from Brighton, Bournemouth, Penzance and Birmingham to Edinburgh as well as further north to Aberdeen (☎ 0844 811 0124; www.crosscountrytrains.co.uk).

Virgin Trains travel across the midlands and have a west coast line to Glasgow and Edinburgh (☎ 08457 222 333; www. virgintrains.co.uk).

First Group Scotrail operates the regular Glasgow to Edinburgh route, trains to Fife, Leuchars (for St Andrews), north to Perth, Dunkeld and Pitlochry, and across East Lothian to North Berwick. Scotrail also manages **The Caledonian Sleeper** from London to Scotland, a fine way to travel overnight arriving in Edinburgh in time for breakfast (☎ 08457 550 033; www.scotrail. co.uk).

All trains arrive at Edinburgh's main station, **Waverley**, in the city centre just off Princes Street with a black cab rank in the station (National Rail Enquiries, ☎ 0845 748 4950; www.nationalrail.co.uk).

By air

Located 7 miles to the west of Edinburgh, close to the M8 motorway to Glasgow and M9 to Stirling, **Edinburgh International Airport** is a fast-expanding airport handling more than 40 airlines and over nine million passengers a year. Airlines serving destinations across the UK and Continental Europe include: British Airways, flybe, Ryanair, Air France, easyJet, Jet 2, SAS, Lufthansa, Aer Lingus, Aer Arann and Flyglobespan; Delta and Continental fly to and from New York.

The airport has numerous car hire companies and a regular Airlink bus service (£3 single, £5 return, children's fare) every 10–15 minutes to and from Waverley Bridge near the train station in the city centre. The **Airport Shuttle** is a minibus service for one to seven passengers, (£10 single and friends/family group rates; ☎ 0845 500 5000; www.edinburghshuttle.com). Lothian no. 35 bus has a route from the airport to the city centre and Leith Ocean Terminal (£1.10). Airport information: ☎ 0870 040 0007; www.baa.com.

By ferry

Norfolk Line start a new car and passenger route with three weekly sailings each way to and from Zeebrugge and Rosyth, Fife from spring 2009 (www.norfolkline.co.uk).

GETTING AROUND

In Edinburgh you'll find travelling around and finding your way is very simple, and as it's a compact city, the best way is explore on foot. City centre attractions across the Old and New Town are all within walking distance of one another and are also linked by the excellent tour buses which you can hop on and off.

Edinburgh buses

Edinburgh has two main bus services running throughout Edinburgh and Lothians. **Lothian Buses** travels around the city, Midlothian and outskirts (single fare £1.10, child 60p, any distance), or for a day's sightseeing take advantage of Lothian Bus Day Ticket (£2.50) which allows you unlimited travel in

10... places to avoid

1 Irvine Welsh's true-life Trainspotting territory is around the housing estates of Pilton, Muirhouse and Drylaw – known locally as MAD. Rather than walk around here, take Tim Bell's excellent Trainspotting tour in Leith (www.leithwalks.co.uk).

2 The Meadows, just south of the Old Town, is great for walk, a picnic or football by day, but don't risk taking a short cut across the park in the early hours of the morning.

3 Climbing to the top of Calton Hill is a top visitor attraction to catch that perfect Kodak moment of the city spread out below, but avoid coming here late at night unless you wish to join the cruising fraternity.

4 The Cowgate and Grassmarket is akin to Dublin's Temple bar area, lined with fine old pubs and lively, popular nightclubs. Friday and Saturday nights can be pretty wild around this area with hen and stag parties and young revellers.

5 Between North Queensferry and the charming East Neuk of Fife, there's a stretch of urban industrial hinterland around Kirkcaldy, Cowdenbeath, Lochgelly and the new town of Glenrothes. The former mining town of Lochgelly in recent years has had the lowest house prices in the UK.

6 Princes Street used to be a regally grand boulevard for supreme fashion, jewellers and my grandfather's luxury furrier, but today it's filled with familiar British brand stores and, towards the West End, some poor-quality tartan souvenir shops. A better option are the fine knitwear and tweed shops on Lawnmarket, High Street and Grassmarket.

7 Don't drive around Edinburgh city centre which is currently undergoing extensive road works for the construction of the controversial new tramline due to be completed in 2011. Road closures, traffic congestion and disruption have not been popular with residents and shop owners.

8 Galashiels. A report by Borders police revealed a high number of alcohol-related incidents around two nightclubs on Overhaugh Street, Galashiels after they close at 3am, when up to 1,000 people crowd the town centre.

9 The area from the foot of Leith Walk up the street to The Volunteer Arms (the pub in *Trainspotting* where Begbie plays pool with a hangover) can be a bit dodgy late at night. The Shore in Leith is a gentrified area of upmarket restaurants and bars.

10 Some lovely picnic spots or otherwise innocent car parks can play host to dogging action after dark – and we are not talking about Crufts here. Sites include Longniddry Bents car park (particularly number 3), East Lothian, Kinnoull Hill, Perth (on Wednesdays for some reason) and if you go down to the woods today at Tentsmuir Forest near St Andrews, prepare for a big surprise.

and around Edinburgh. A pack of 21 single tickets for £21 can be purchased from a Lothian Bus Travel shop (☎ 0131 555 6363; www.lothianbuses.com).

LOTHIAN BUS TRAVEL SHOPS

Waverley Bridge, corner of Market Street. Opening hours: Mon–Sat 8.15am–6pm, Sunday 9.30am–5.15pm.
Hanover Street (closed Sunday), Shandwick Place (closed Sunday)

First Buses operate around both the city centre and a wide region covering East Lothian and Borders. First Day and First Week zoned tickets for unlimited travel are ideal for the visitor wishing to explore further afield outside Edinburgh (☎ 08708 72 72 71; www.firstgroup.com).

A brand new, modern, efficient tram network is currently being created for Edinburgh and is scheduled to be running by 2011, linking Leith, Princes Street and the Airport.

Trains and buses across Scotland

For touring Scotland across a week or two involving different rail and bus companies, the **Freedom of Scotland Travel Pass** is a good deal. The Travelpass is valid on any First ScotRail, National Express East Coast, Virgin West Coast, First TransPennine Express and CrossCountry service within Scotland, as well as Stagecoach buses in Fife and First Buses in the Scottish Borders. There is a discount fare available on the Caledonian sleeper with this Travel Pass – which is valid as far south as Carlisle and Berwick upon Tweed.

The **Central Scotland Rover** is valid on all train services in Central Scotland between Edinburgh and North Berwick, Fife, Bridge of Allan, Stirling and Glasgow Queen Street (www.scotrail.co.uk).

The **One Ticket** is a multi-use ticket offering unlimited travel by bus and train, available for seven days, one month, or a year based on a number of zones in East Central Scotland. Valid for use on First ScotRail (between Edinburgh and North Berwick, Edinburgh and Newcraighall, Edinburgh and Curriehill, Edinburgh and Dalmeny) and National Express East Coast line (between Edinburgh and Dunbar) (www.oneticket.co.uk).

Car parking

There are NCP car parks at the west end of Princes Street (Castle Terrace) and the east end (St James Shopping centre) as well as short-term pay and display zones everywhere. Rates range from 70p to £1.80 per hour depending on the location. Central zones operate Mon–Sat; peripheral, Mon–Fri. Be aware of residents-only permit areas. There are parking restrictions in some areas on Sunday, but usually parking is free in pay and display zones and on single yellow lines. A visitor's quick guide to Edinburgh car parking is available on the Council website (www.edinburgh.gov.uk).

ACCOMMODATION

We have hand selected really special places to stay in each chapter of this book. For more comprehensive listings, a valuable online guide, packed with hundreds of professional, independent reviews is **Scottish Hotel Guide** (www.scottishhotelguide.com).

Hotels

The Townhouse Collection are four privately owned, classic-contemporary hotels across the West End and New Town of Edinburgh: **Channings, The Bonham, The Howard** and the **Edinburgh Residence.** These are all recommended for a fine blend of traditional furnishings and modern artistic design, award-winning restaurants, friendly staff and a subtle taste of quiet sophistication. (The Bonham ☎ 0131 274 7400; Channings ☎ 0131 274 7401; The Howard ☎ 0131 274 7402; The Edinburgh Residence ☎ 0131 274 7403; www.townhousecompany.com)

Apex Hotels are a group of cool and contemporary, family-friendly hotels with four hotels in Edinburgh, all with smart bars and restaurants: **Apex International** and **Apex City** (Grassmarket Old Town), **Apex European** (West End), and **Apex Waterloo** (☎ 0845 365 0000; www.apexhotels.co.uk).

The Eton Collection offers two distinctive chic, unique boutique hotels in the capital: **The Scotsman**, featuring a luxury spa, bar and brasserie, is located near the High Street, and nearby at the East End below Calton Hill is **The Glasshouse**, with fabulous glass-walled suites overlooking a rooftop lavender garden, voted one of the *world's coolest hotels and the sexiest hotel* in Scotland. (The Scotsman ☎ 0131 556 5565; The Glasshouse ☎ 0131 525 8200; www.theetoncollection.com).

B&B

- **Scotland's Best B&Bs** – a welcoming website listing the contact details and information on quality, four and five-star guest houses in Edinburgh, Fife, East Lothian and the Borders (www.scotlandsbestbandbs.co.uk).
- **Cotton Sheets** – with a name like this, it sounds homely and comfortable. B&B accommodation in Perthshire (www.cottonsheets.co.uk).
- **A Stay in Fife** – a network collection of the best B&Bs around Fife in towns, villages and hamlets (www.astayinfife.co.uk).
- **Farmstays** – stay on a farm with bed and breakfast or self catering (☎ 024 7669 6909; www.farmstayscotland.co.uk).

Unique places to stay

The National Trust for Scotland has many city centre and countryside historic houses and cottages, which can be rented as a holiday home for a week or weekend. These include Gladstone's Flat (sleeping two), Lawnmarket, Edinburgh and Harmony House, Melrose (which sleeps 12 for a family party) (☎ 0844 493 2108; www.ntsholidays.com).

The Vivat Trust saves and renovates important architectural properties for holiday homes and has some very special places to stay in the Scottish Borders, including Barns Tower, a rural retreat for just two people, near Peebles and Cloister House, Melrose (☎ 0845 090 0194; www.vivat.org.uk).

Coast Properties, based in North Berwick has some delightful beach-front East Lothian cottages and even a Lighthouse near Dunbar. They also offer Edinburgh city apartments (☎ 01620 671966; www.coast-properties.co.uk).

Luxury Scotland is a collection of fine hotels as well as exclusive-use castles and country houses, including Myres Castle, Fife and Greywalls, East Lothian. Perfect for golfing holidays, a small wedding, family gatherings or weekend house party (www.luxuryscotland.co.uk).

Luxury Edinburgh is an exclusive guide to the city's best and most romantic places to stay and eat (www.luxuryedinburgh.com).

Cottages and Castles is one of the largest self-catering companies in Scotland offering exclusive-use holiday castles, mansions, cottages and country lodges (☎ 01738 451610; www.cottages-and-castles.co.uk).

George Goldsmith offers an exclusive selection of prime sporting estates, lodges, castles, country houses, family holiday homes and small cottages in East Lothian, Scottish Borders and Perthshire (☎ 0131 476 6500; www.georgegoldsmith.com).

Large Holiday Homes offers a collection of castles, country mansions and some small cottages for small and large family holidays or groups of friends (☎ 01381 610496; www.lhhscotland.com).

The best... hotels

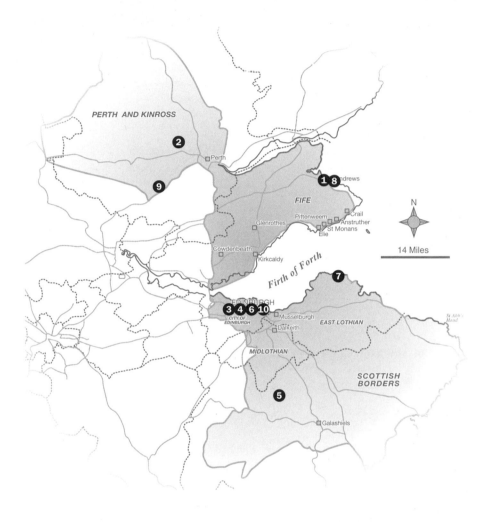

1. The Old Course Hotel, St Andrews – Seaview rooms, fine hospitality and prime golf, p.264
2. Kinnaird – Edwardian country house with the ambience of a private house party, p.306
3. The Glasshouse – smart glass and steel contemporary palace with roof garden, p.119
4. The Howard – Homely Georgian townhouse offering old-fashioned class and service, p.80
5. Peebles Hydro – visit the best family-friendly resort in Scotland for the perfect holiday, p.224
6. The Balmoral – the finest city accommodation, wining and dining since 1902, p.74
7. Macdonald Marine – a Victorian seaside resort, great for relaxation and leisure, p.168
8. St Andrews Golf Hotel – boutique, contemporary and stylish with fine dining, p.264
9. Gleneagles - world–famous golf resort perfect for country sports or sheer romance, p.325
10. The Bonham - a hidden city–centre gem with gorgeous design and superb food, p.80

Self-catering in Edinburgh

Apartments in Edinburgh offers a wide range of self-catering flats in the Old Town and Georgian New Town (☎ 0131 556 8309; www.apartmentsinedinburgh.com).

Scottish Apartments lists Edinburgh flats in every district for couples and families – from Leith penthouses to Old Town apartments (☎ 0131 240 0080; www.scottishapartment.com).

Festival Apartments offers a range of small and large city apartments and houses for festival lets, hen and stag parties, and family holidays (☎ 0131 222 9670; www.festivalapartments.com).

Dickins has dozens of Edinburgh flats in every area for festival accommodation, city breaks and holiday accommodation from £300 per week (☎ 0131 558 1108; www.dickins.co.uk).

Also worth a try are **Edinburgh Self Catering** (☎ 01875 341490; www.edinburgh-self catering.co.uk), **Festival Flats** (☎ 01620 810620, www.festivalflats.net) and **Edinburgh Accommodation** (www.edinburgh.org/accom).

Self-catering cottages

Taymouth Cottages offers a choice of traditional and modern holiday homes for couples and families (some with saunas, hot tubs and barbecues) beside Loch Tay. Leisure facilities, bar and restaurant nearby (☎ 01887 830226; www.taymouth.co.uk).

10... special holiday homes

1 Barns Tower, an ancient tiny castle just for two, p.224

2 Royal Mile Residence, two-bedroom apartments in the Old Town, p.106

3 Bell Tower Cottage, four-poster-bed and spa bath, near Loch Tay, p.321

4 Press Main cottage, luxury furnishings and a badger-watching webcam, p.242

5 Skippers Rest, 17th century seaman's cottage for family holidays, p.283

6 The Cottage on the Beach, garden, BBQ, gate to beach, sleeps six, p.168

7 Myres Castle, perfect for large family gathering or house party, p.280

8 28 Scotland Street, beautiful Georgian apartment near city bars, bistros, clubs, p.120

9 Old Admiralty House, St Andrews, dramatic clifftop setting near Old Course and castle, p.265

10 Green Craig, idyllic location on headland overlooking Aberlady bay, p.198

The best... visitor attractions

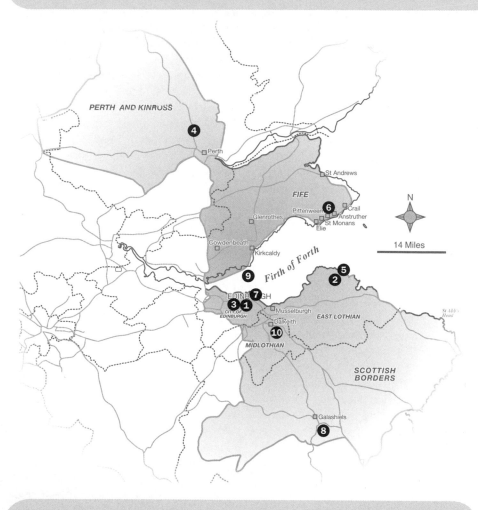

1. Edinburgh Castle – an iconic fortress on the volcanic rock with awesome views from the battlements, p.87
2. Museum of Flight – World War II planes, vintage aircraft and Concorde, p.164
3. National Galleries of Scotland – a treasure house of classical and modern art, sculpture, portraits and paintings, p.238
4. The Hermitage, Perthshire – a glorious, golden autumn riverside forest walk, p.294
5. Tantallon Castle – an ancient stronghold perched high on the clifftop, p.161
6. The Secret Bunker – an authentic British government nuclear shelter, p.280
7. Royal Yacht Britannia – a sleek, shining cruise ship now preserved for all to see, p.127
8. Abbotsford – the former home of Sir Walter Scott, untouched since his death in 1832, p.218
9. Inchcolm Island – take a boat trip to an ancient abbey, on a deserted island for summer picnics, p.144
10. Rosslyn Chapel – ancient carvings, secret symbols and the *Da Vinci Code* film set jet site, p.150

Eagleye Rentals has specially located cottages for the golfer, right beside several fine Scottish golf courses at Gleneagles, St Andrews and East Lothian (☎ 023 8087 3007; www.eagleeyerentals.com).

Unique Cottages has dozens of cottages, timber lodges and houses in the Scottish Borders (☎ 01835 822277; www.unique-cottages.co.uk).

The East Fife Letting Company, run by Peter and Sue Griffiths, offers a personal, friendly service to find your ideal accommodation in Fife from large family holiday homes and small cottages with great seaside locations (☎ 01333 330 241; www.eastfifeletting.co.uk).

FOOD AND DRINK

For a few uninitiated visitors to Scotland, food and drink is represented by the ubiquitous haggis, shortbread, porridge and whisky. But there is far more to experience from the traditional, locally sourced Scottish larder. Aberdeen Angus Beef is world famous and smoked salmon, lobsters and several crates of oysters are flown to Paris, the south of France and Hong Kong every week.

On your journey around East Coast Scotland you will have the opportunity to relish a gourmet feast of locally sourced food and drink. Scottish chefs are passionate and pedantic about real food, ensuring the best quality – from lobster, lamb, organic vegetables and wild venison to takeaway fish and chips – meaning dining out will surely be an education and an inspiration.

Edinburgh has several dozen exemplary restaurants, (including four Michelin star establishments) where chefs source their produce from Scottish farms, Perthshire estates and local fish markets. It would be invidious to pick out a couple of restaurants here, and the best places to eat out and buy food around town are listed in the five chapters covering Edinburgh.

The **Edinburgh Farmers' Market** takes place on Castle Terrace every Saturday 9am–2pm (☎ 0131 652 5940). This event came first in the National Farmers' Retail and Markets Association (FARMA) awards to find Britain's best farmers' market. While many butchers make their own haggis, **MacSweens** is world famous, an Edinburgh family business which began in 1953. To this day every batch of haggis, made to the original recipe, is tasted by the family and they also make a delicious spicy vegetarian haggis (☎ 0131 440 2555; www.macsween.co.uk).

Wherever you travel around south-east Scotland, you will experience the finest local produce and each region has their regional specialities. **East Lothian** is rich farming country renowned for fruit, vegetables, organic wild boar and Ballencrieff Rare Pedigree Pigs for prime bacon, sausages and cutlets (www.ballencrieffrppigs.co.uk). There are many excellent farm shops such as **Fenton Barns Farm Shop** (www.fentonbarnsfarmshop.com), selling fresh, local organic potatoes, asparagus, mushrooms, seasonal fruit, game, ostrich and chicken. You can also sample this delicious food at their café.

Down the **Berwickshire Coast**, the fishing port of **Eyemouth** lands the finest fish and shellfish with a Fish Market – taste a fresh crab sandwich or fish supper in one of several pubs, bistros and cafés in Eyemouth and St Abbs. **The Scottish Border** country is best known for salmon fished from the Tweed, superb lamb from the hill farms, as well as traditional homebaking. **Alex Dalgetty and Sons** makes traditional Black Buns, cakes and tarts but is especially famous for original Selkirk Bannocks. Alex worked in Selkirk at the bakery which produced the original bannock but left in the early 20th century to set up his own business in Galashiels. They are still making bannocks to the original recipe, now run by Alex's great granddaughter and her husband (☎ 01896 752508; www.alex-dalgetty.co.uk).

The best... country inns

1 **Moulin Hotel, Pitlochry** – a genuine 1695 roadside coaching inn with a fantastic old pub, p.306

2 **The Peat Inn** – an award-winning restaurant with cosy rooms and exquisite cuisine, p.286

3 **Kilspindie House** – a charming old pub, Michelin-rated restaurant, ideal for exploring East Lothian, p.198

4 **Ballathie** – a traditional, welcoming Perthshire country house on the River Tay, p.306

5 **Four Seasons** – located on the edge of Loch Earn, comfortable rooms, great food, superb views, p.329

6 **Killiecrankie** – hidden in a glorious forest, the perfect base to tour Perthshire, p.306

7 **Royal Hotel** – named by Queen Victoria after her visit, today it offers quiet luxury, p.226

8 **Windlestraw** – a charming Arts and Crafts house in the Borders with five-star cooking, p.228

9 **Dryburgh Abbey** – sample prime fish and game, homely comfort beside the Tweed, p.224

10 **Inn on the Tay** – on the banks of River Tay, popular with white-water rafters, p.321

For traditional tea and scones, coffee and cake, there's a useful collection of the best coffee shops and tea rooms around Scotland on the **Café Days Trail**, with a map to find the best place in the area you are touring (www.cafédays.visitscotland.com).

The coastal villages, **Crail**, **Anstruther**, **Elie** and **St Monans** along the **East Neuk of the Kingdom of Fife** are also famous for great seafood. Buy fresh and cooked lobster and crab from a wooden hut on Crail harbour wall, the **Lobster Store** (☎ 01333 450476). For fine dining and to sample the best locally sourced seafood from creel to plate, book a table at either of two Seafood Restaurants in St Andrews and St Monans, both with sea views (St Andrews ☎ 01334 479475; St Monans ☎ 01333 730327; www.thesea foodrestaurant.com). Alternatively stand in the queue to buy seriously good fish and chips at **Anstruther Fish Bar** (☎ 01333 310518; www.anstrutherfishbar.co.uk) as well as at popular fish bars in Pittenweem and Elie. The oldest bakery in the UK is **Adamson's Bakery** in Pittenweem, (☎ 01333 311336). Traditional Scottish oatcakes have won the bakery 200 gold medals over the four generations of the family. The Pollock

10... traditional pubs

1 **Kenmore Hotel,** the Poet's pub where Robert Burns wrote a poem, p.321

2 **Jolly Judge,** off Lawnmarket, fine whiskies, real crackling fire, p.110

3 **Ship Inn, Elie,** with beach-front terrace to watch the summer cricket, p.173

4 **The Old Clubouse, Gullane,** built 1890, cosy place, featured in the Good Beer guide, p.201

5 **The Cumberland Bar,** a true neighbourhood local with peaceful beer garden, p.126

6 **Carriers Quarters,** oldest unaltered pub in Leith with live music, p.139

7 **Café Royal,** ornate, original Victorian drinking hole with great booth seating, p.86

8 **Tibbie Shiels,** St Mary's Loch, historic literary pub in the Scottish Borders, p.212

9 **The Black Bull, Lauder,** an 18th century coaching inn rich in historic charm, p.188

10 **The Hawes Inn, South Queensferry,** with views of the Forth Bridges, p.147

The best... fresh local seafood

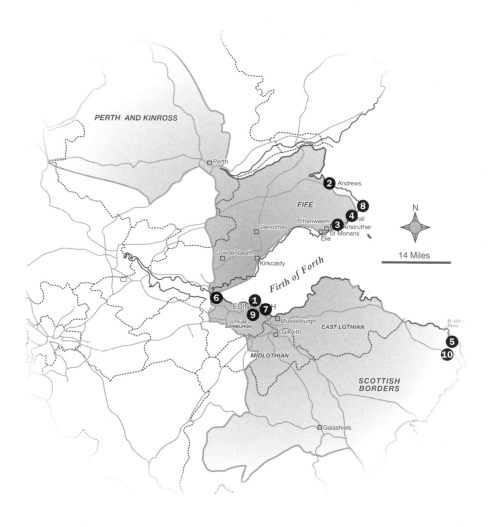

① Loch Fyne Restaurant, on Newhaven harbour – eat oysters as you watch the sunset, p.136
② The Seafood Restaurant, St Andrews – a glass box above the waves and tide rolling in, p.267
③ The Seafood Restaurant, St Monans – beach view terrace and intimate bistro, p.277
④ Anstruther Fish Bar – award-winning fish and chips, 'the Ritz could do no better', p. 284
⑤ Giacopazzi's, Eyemouth – try their gourmet Lemon Sole and chips, p.246
⑥ The Grill at Dakota Forth Bridge – Fruits de Mer straight from creel to plate, p.148
⑦ Fishers on The Shore, Leith – perennially popular, lively waterside diner, p.137
⑧ Lobster Store, Crail – harbour hut for takeaway fresh and cooked lobster, p.284
⑨ L'alba D'oro – reputedly the best fish and chips in Edinburgh, p.122
⑩ Craws Inn, Reston – crab sandwiches and platters of fresh Eyemouth fish

family has been farming in the East Neuk for over a century, and their **Ardross Farm Shop** near Elie stocks everything from fresh herbs, daily picked vegetables and beef from their ethically farmed herd, to rhubarb-infused vodka, homemade raspberry jam, pies and puddings.

Perthshire is the green heart of Scotland, and the land, rivers and climate provide the best meat, game, fish, fruit and vegetables as well as Highland Spring water and several malt whiskies. **Perth** became the first town in Scotland to join *Cittaslow*, an international network of 100 European towns where good food, local produce and traditional production methods ensure high quality. Cittaslow is Italian for Slow Cities, developed from the Slow Food Movement. **Perth Farmers' Market**, is held on the first Saturday of each month, 9am–2pm on King Edward Street with dozens of stalls and cookery demonstrations (www.perthfarmersmarket.co.uk). At Kenmore, near Loch Tay, the **Mains of Taymouth Courtyard Delicatessen** sells Rannoch game and meat, bread, cheese, fruit and vegetables, quality pâtés, chutney and preserves. Next door is the **Courtyard Brasserie** where you can sample 'Estate to Plate' beef, venison and blackface lamb, slow cooked on an indoor barbecue.

Scottish ales and whisky

For locally produced real ale, Traquair, the historic country house near Peebles, has its own private **Traquair Brewery**, making and selling Jacobite and Bear Ales (☎ 01896 830323; www.traquair.co.uk). The largest regional brewer in Scotland is the **Belhaven Brewery**, Spott Road, Dunbar (☎ 01368 869200) which produces a leading draught ale, Belhaven Best; the cask is conditioned with 80 Shilling, described a few centuries back by the Austrian Emperor as 'the burgundy of Scotland'.

Edradour distillery, 2 miles east of Pitlochry is Scotland's smallest distillery (the only original farm distillery) and the whisky is

---

FOODIE ROAD TRIPS

- **Wild Green Travel** offers eco-tours of Scotland on a trail to find wild food and wildlife. Meet local food producers, fishermen and take guided walks to gather wild herbs and mushrooms. See crabs landed and watch seals, otters and sea eagles (www.wildgreentravel.com).
- **McKinlay Kidd** offers two tours: Gastronomic Highlights designed to take you to some of the very best dining experiences in Scotland with tutored cookery demonstration and the Scottish Seafood Trail, featuring fish restaurants, hands-on cookery demonstrations, boarding a creel fishing boat and a taste of the day's catch (www.seescotlanddifferently.co.uk).

---

handmade today just as it was for over 150 years, with only 12 casks produced a week. Free distillery tours are given throughout the year (☎ 01796 472095; www.edradour.co.uk).

Also in Perthshire, **Dewars World of Whisky** is just outside Aberfeldy (☎ 01887 822010; www.dewarswow.com). The **Glenkinchie Whisky Distillery** is just outside Edinburgh at Pencaitland (EH34 5ET; ☎ 01875 342004; www.discoveringdistilleries.com).

FESTIVALS AND ANNUAL EVENTS

Edinburgh – City of Festivals

Hundreds of thousands of visitors come to Edinburgh during the summer months to experience the Edinburgh Festivals. When people talk of going to the Edinburgh Festival, this is a misnomer. There are in fact six international arts festivals taking place independently in the city between June and the end of August – covering music (from opera to jazz), drama, dance, literature, film, visual arts and the Military Tattoo.

The **Jazz and Blues Festival**, **Edinburgh International Festival**, **Edinburgh Fringe**, **Film**, **Book** and **Art Festivals** are all separately managed with their own distinctly different and inspiring programme. But in essence this offers a rich and stimulating cultural feast, with the freedom to move from one Festival to the other – theatre to concert hall, show to show – with a selection of events for every age, taste and interest.

The **Edinburgh International Festival** was founded in 1947, created as a post-war initiative to re-unite Europe, to enrich its cultural life and 'provide a platform for the flowering of the human spirit'. Rudolph Bing, founder and General Manager at Glyndebourne, was given the task of visiting several European capital cities to select which would be the most appropriate to stage a major festival. Bing was personally invited by Henry Harvey Wood, Director of the British Council in Scotland to visit Edinburgh. The story goes that while staying at the Caledonian Hotel on Princes Street, he looked up at the castle and was so impressed with the historic setting that he immediately decided that this was the perfect city for the Festival.

At that first Festival, eight university student groups, knowing there would be a large audience and media attention, decided to gatecrash this major international event, and turned up uninvited to perform their plays on the sidelines. They called themselves the Festival Adjuncts. The following year the term 'the Fringe' was coined by playwright, Robert Kemp in his article for the Evening News, 14 August, 1948:

'Round the fringe of official Festival drama, there seems to be more private enterprise than before...'

And so the Edinburgh Festival Fringe was created by enthusiastic amateur actors, growing from eight shows in 1947 to 2,088 shows in 2008. 18,792 performers, attracting international celebrity names in theatre, comedy and music, see it as the best platform to premiere a new show.

With so much choice across all the Festivals in August, you can divide your day moving from an early 'Shakespeare for breakfast' Fringe show, a relaxing International Festival morning concert, then an art exhibition, an inspiring Book Festival writers' debate in the afternoon, then off to the theatre, finishing with late-night jazz or comedy revue. It would take you around five years without a break to see every performance on the Fringe programme back to back. So as you can't see everything, pick what takes your fancy, read the media reviews and listen to the buzz about town for word-of-mouth recommendations. The last weekend in August is also when the **Mela Festival** celebrates the city's minority ethnic communities – a great family event of international music, food and entertainment.

The main thing is to experience the whole crazy, 'anything goes', innovative playground of live performance. There are dozens of free shows every year and do also join the crowds on the High Street for a colourful display of street theatre, jugglers, fire eaters and busking musicians. It's the largest arts festival on the planet – so come and enjoy the extraordinary range of shows and the unique atmosphere.

As well as a host of events in Edinburgh, many towns and villages across the Borders, Fife, East Lothian and Perthshire have their own traditional community fairs and arts festivals. Here is a calendar of the main events which may attract the visitor.

Calendar of Events

January

Loony Dook: New Year's Day swim in the Forth, South Queensferry

Burns Night dinners: on and around 25 January across Scotland

Winter Word's Festival: Pitlochry Festival Theatre

Turner Watercolours: free annual exhibition at the National Gallery, Edinburgh

February
Six Nations Rugby: tournament between Scotland, England, Wales, Ireland, France and Italy with home matches played at Murrayfield, Edinburgh

March
Hawick Reivers Festival: Scottish Borders
Stanza Poetry Festival: St Andrews

April
Beltane Fire Festival: 30 April at Calton Hill, Edinburgh

May
Perth Festival of the Arts: annual international music and theatre festival
Traquair Medieval Fayre: Traquair House
Pitlochry Theatre Festival: Repertory theatre season, May to October
Three Harbours Arts Festival: Port Seton, East Lothian
Jim Clark Rally: Kelso, Scottish Borders

June
Scottish Borders town festivals: Peebles Beltane, Hawick Common Riding, Selkirk Common Riding and Gala Braw Lads Festivals
Borders Book Festival: Melrose
Taste of Edinburgh: a food festival at the Meadows
Royal Highland Show: agricultural fair, show jumping, sheep shearing, food, crafts

July
Eyemouth Herring Queen: Berwickshire
Duns Summer Festival
Museum of Flight Air Show
Aberdour Festival: Fife
Crail Festival: Fife
East Neuk Music Festival: Fife

August
Pittenweem Arts Festival: Fife
Traquair Fair: Traquair House near Peebles
Festival by the Sea: North Berwick
Raft Race: North Berwick

10... festivals and events

1 Edinburgh Festivals, the whole jamboree lasts from June to August, p.30

2 T in the Park, the best summer weekend music bash in UK, p.302

3 Pittenweem arts festival, the whole village is a giant gallery, p.282

4 Perth Festival of the Arts, an international music festival, p.302

5 Pitlochry Theatre Festival, at 'the Theatre in the Hills', p.32

6 Scottish Borders, traditional Common Riding and Reiver festivals, p.222

7 Melrose Book Festival, a world-class literary event, p.222

8 Edinburgh Winter Festival, skating, a big wheel, markets, fireworks, p.75

9 St Andrews Festival, music, theatre, magic, art exhibitions, street events, p.260

10 Scotts Selkirk, magical family-themed Christmas celebration, p.33

September
St James' Fair: Kelso, Scottish Borders
East Lothian Food and Drink Festival

October
Perthshire Amber: Perth to Pitlochry area
Pitlochry Autumn Festival
The Enchanted Forest: near Pitlochry
Traquair Halloween festival

November
St Andrew's Festival: St Andrews
St Andrew's Day: events across Scotland
Borders Banquet: celebration of local food

December
Scott's Selkirk: a festive 19th century Christmas festival

Edinburgh is a year-round Festival City, from Easter to Christmas. In April there's the popular **Science Festival** with lectures for adults and workshops and fun activities for children. In late May the **Imaginate Theatre** festival is specifically staged for children.

The whole family will enjoy a visit to Edinburgh in the winter months for the fabulous **Winter Wonderland** in Princes Street Gardens, featuring a skating rink and the sky-high Big Wheel ride and Christmas markets. Experience the warmest welcome between November and early January for Christmas and Hogmanay celebrations with an exuberant programme of music, street theatre, outdoor markets, funfair and fireworks. One of the world's biggest New Year's celebrations takes place here as over 100,000 revellers join the world-famous street party. From candle-lit concerts to ceilidhs and rock-bands, Edinburgh is known for hosting the best party of the year, helping you to welcome the New Year in style.

EDINBURGH FESTIVALS

- **Science Festival**
  Early April
  www.sciencefestival.com
- **Imaginate Theatre Festival**
  End of May/early June
  www.imaginate.org.uk
- **The Edinburgh International Film Festival**
  Mid-June
  www.edfilmfest.org.uk
- **The Edinburgh International Jazz and Blues Festival**
  End of July to early August
  www.edinburghjazzfestival.co.uk
- **Edinburgh Festival Fringe**
  End of July to August Bank Holiday
  www.edfringe.com
- **Edinburgh International Festival**
  Early August for three weeks
  www.eif.co.uk
- **The Edinburgh International Book Festival**
  Early August for two weeks
  www.edbookfest.co.uk
- **The Edinburgh Military Tattoo**
  First three weeks of August
  www.edintattoo.co.uk
- **The Edinburgh Mela**
  Last weekend in August
  www.edinburgh-mela.co.uk
- **Edinburgh Winter Festival**
- **Edinburgh's Christmas**
  End of November to early January
  www.edinburghschristmas.com
- **Edinburgh's Hogmanay (New Year)**
  29 December to early January
  www.edinburghshogmanay.com

TRAVELLING WITH CHILDREN

Visitor attractions and festivals across Edinburgh and East Coast Scotland are becoming more and more geared up to welcome families and children. Edinburgh itself has many fine family-friendly attractions including the **Zoo**, the **National Museum of Scotland** with interactive exhibit and **Dynamic Earth**, an educational and informative exploration of geology and time around the world. **The Museum of**

2009 marks the 250th anniversary of the birth of Scotland's national bard and internationally renowned cultural icon, Robert Burns. This is the inspiration behind a year-long celebration of Scottish heritage, history, golf, whisky, arts, literature, culture and music as well as national innovation, invention and enterprise. A programme of around 100 festivals and events around the country has been created to entice people with Scottish ancestry, expat Scots or those who love Scottish landscape and culture, to visit Scotland for Homecoming 2009. The celebration begins on 25 January, Burns Night, and ends with a finale of traditional folk music concerts on and around St Andrew's Day at the end of November. For a complete list of planned events, visit: www.homecomingscotland2009.com

Childhood is stuffed full of old toys, and **Deep Sea World** in Fife is a great place for a wet afternoon, where the kids can see the sharks.

KidsEdinburgh is an inspiring website for families wanting to know what to do with children in and around Edinburgh. A 'what's on' guide and list of 500 activities, attractions, suggestions and events for children and families in and around Edinburgh can be found (www.kidsedinburgh.com).

The **Seabird Centre** at North Berwick has all kinds of exhibits and a webcam to spot the seabirds on the Bass Rock gannet colony. There are several **safari nature trails** suitable for children in Perthshire and on the Berwickshire coastline, accessed either walking or by Landrover. Outdoor sports are also geared for families, such as forest **bike rides** in the Scottish Borders and safe **canoeing** and **rafting** on the River Tay, Perthshire.

Throughout this guide there are suggestions for each region to highlight some fun indoor and outdoor adventures for all the family.

SPORTS AND ACTIVITIES
Golf

Scotland is undeniably the **Home of Golf**. The legend goes that golf was invented, many centuries ago, by a Scottish shepherd when he casually swung his crook to hit stones into rabbit holes. The word 'gowf' is the Gaelic for 'hit' and the game quickly developed into a popular sport. In 1457 the King's army preferred it to archery practice so much so that James II decided to ban it. However, golf was a favourite leisure activity for Scottish monarchs, especially Mary Queen of Scots who played at **Musselburgh**, now regarded as the most ancient course in the world. Queen Mary is reputed to have originated the use of the word 'caddy,' a derivation from the French *le cadet* (the boy), which was a local term for a water carrier or porter in Old Town Edinburgh. The **Gentleman Golfers of Leith** is regarded as the oldest club and first recorded official rules of the game in 1744. Through royal patronage the St Andrews Club was elevated to become the prestigious **Royal and Ancient Golf Club** (1834) and is recognised today as golf's international ruling association.

There are over 550 golf courses across Scotland, more per capita than anywhere in the world. It's that sense of tradition and heritage, and a choice of stunning seashore links and parkland courses, which makes a golfing destination par excellence. There are world-class Scotland resorts such as **Gleneagles** and the **Old Course**, as well as numerous fine courses across Fife, East Lothian, Perthshire and the Borders. A series of Golf Passes are available to the visitor in order to tour around several clubs in one region.

Visit Scotland publishes a *Golf in Scotland* brochure and has a website listing all regional golf passes, golfing events, golf

The best... things to do with children

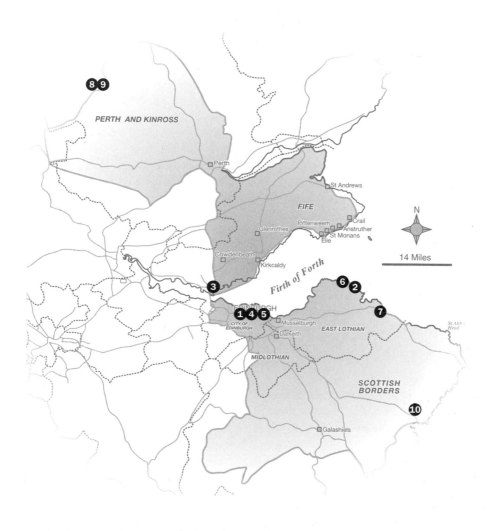

① Dynamic Earth – educational but fun science and geology centre, p.101
② Seabird Centre – learn all about seabirds and see them nesting on webcam, p.158
③ Deep Sea World – amazing aquarium where you can swim with the sharks, p.279
④ Edinburgh Zoo – penguins, new chimp house, lions, tigers and bears, oh my!, p.73
⑤ Museum of Childhood – nostalgic old toys for parents, fun for kids, p.101
⑥ Yellowcraig Beach – Treasure Island pirate-themed rope climbing park, p.159
⑦ East Links Family Park – farm animals, go carts, flying fox, trampolines etc, p.181
⑧ Highland Safari – family adventure to spot red deer, grouse, mountain hare and golden eagles, p.319
⑨ White-Water Rafting – family rafting trips with picnic down the River Tay, p.292
⑩ Bowhill House – adventure play park, ranger trails and children's activities, p.221

operators, accommodation and golf trail itineraries (www.visitscotland.com/golf).

For those planning a visit to St Andrews a ballot system operates for the **Old Course.** Phone the **St Andrews Links Trust** on the morning of the day before you wish to play to enter the daily ballot.

- **St Andrews Links Trust:**
  ☎ 01334 466666;
  www.standrews.golf.org
- **Fife Golf Pass:** ☎ 01592 267775;
  www.firstinfifegolf.com
- **Fife Fairways Discount Card:** Wilkinson Golf and Leisure; ☎ 01383 629940;
  www.wilkinsongolf.com/golfpass
- **Golf East Lothian:** ☎ 01620 892197;
  www.golfeastlothian.com
- **Scottish Borders Freedom of the Fairways:** ☎ 0870 608 0404;
  www.visitscottishborders.com
- **Perthshire Green Card and Golf Ticket:**
  ☎ 01577 861186;
  www.perthshire.co.uk

Adventure sports

Scotland is also renowned as the **Adventure Capital of Europe** offering an extraordinary choice of sports and activities from hill climbing, kite buggying, diving, surfing, canyoning, white-water rafting, kayaking, water skiing, sailing, sphereing, mountain biking, hiking and motor racing, as well as indoor rock climbing.

With hills, fast-flowing rivers, lochs and rugged countryside, **Perthshire** is the county for extreme outdoor watersports with a high adrenaline rating. For all information, locations and activity companies, check out **www.visitscotland.com/adventure**. Children can join too – see **www.visitscotland.com/adventure/familyfriendly**.

White-water rafting and kayaking

There are numerous rafting companies based around the River Tay, Braan and Tummel near Dunkeld, Pitlochry and Aberfeldy, listed in the Perthshire chapters.

- **Nae Limits**
  Ballinluig PY9 0KG; ☎ 08450 178177;
  www.naelimits.co.uk
- **Activ8s**
  The Coachyard, Aberfeldy PH15 2AS;
  ☎ 01887 829292; www.activ8s.com
- **Dunolly Adventures**
  Taybridge Drive, Aberfeldy PH15 2BP;
  ☎ 01887 820298;
  www.dunollyadventures.co.uk
- **Ace Adventures**
  Grampian Road, Aviemore PH22 1RH;
  ☎ 01479 810 510,
  www.aceadventures.co.uk

Sailing

- **Legend @ Loch Tay Highland Lodges**
  Nr Killin, Perthshire FK21 8TY;
  ☎ 01567 820 051;
  www.legendsailing.co.uk

Water skiing and knee boarding

- **Active Scotland**
  Lochearnhead Watersports Centre,
  Lochearnhead FK19 8PU;
  ☎ 01567 830321;
  www.activescotland.com

Sphereing

- **Nae Limits**
  Ballinluig PY9 0KG;
  ☎ 08450 178177; www.naelimits.co.uk

Surfing

Dunbar boasts the best surfable waves in the area, with wave faces as high as 12ft at Belhaven, the most exposed beach in East Lothian.

- **Coast to Coast Surf School**
  ☎ 01368 869734;
  mobile: 07971 990361;
  www.c2csurfschool.com

10... golf courses

1 Muirfield, Gullane, home to the Honourable Company of Edinburgh Golfers, the oldest club in the world, p.192

2 Gleneagles, choice of three pristine, championship courses in a glorious setting, p.325

3 Gullane no. 1 course, from no. 6 and 7 green, a splendid 360 degree panorama across East Lothian and the Forth, p.192

4 Old Course, the famous St Andrews course, open to all by ballot, p.257

5 Kilspindie, a short but perfect links course, p.192

6 Roxburghe, a distinctively beautiful, rolling course in the Scottish Borders, p.217

7 The Torrance, a new, challenging course at Fairmont St Andrews, p.258

8 Taymouth, 'the best course in Scotland, beats St Andrews' says the US Embassy in London, p.313

9 Eyemouth, superb links course, sea views, club house fish and chips, p.234

10 Dunbar, established in 1856 and one of the best seaside links courses in the country, p.176

Mountain biking

The **Scottish Borders** offers fantastic forested hills for serious mountain biking and it is now seen as Scotland's other national sport apart from golf. The country's flagship centre is at Glentress, near Peebles and there's the 7stanes network of trails from Innerleithen to Dumfries and Galloway across the south of Scotland (www.7stanes.gov.uk). Check out www.visitscotland.com/mountainbiking

- **The Hub in the Forest**
  Glentress EH45 8NB; ☎ 01721 721 736; www.thehubintheforest.co.uk

Land yachting and X-sailing

The wide open beaches at **St Andrews** are the place for kite flying as well as land yachting and kite buggying.

- **St Andrews Traction Kites**
  Balmullo, St Andrews; ☎ 07714 214667; www.standrewstractionkites.co.uk

10... sporting and leisure activities

1 Golfing in Scotland, with 550 courses to choose from, p.34

2 Adventure sports, rafting, kayaking, canyoning in Perthshire, p.36

3 Country walks, Perthshire and the Borders, p.235

4 Rent a classic car, weekend-break driving an open-top vintage car, p.39

5 Wildlife trails, ranger-led walk or 4x4 drive at St Abb's Head, p.39

6 Mountain biking, world-class trails at Glentress, p.37

7 Diving, scuba diving at Marine Reserve, Berwickshire, p.176

8 Hill climbing, whether at Arthur's Seat or Ben Y Vrackie, p.36

9 Rugby 7s, festival of 7-a-side rugby matches in the Borders, p.222

10 Fishing, salmon and trout fishing on the Tweed and Tay, p.217

ACE SPORTS

Scottish world-class tennis champion **Andy Murray** selects his grand slam of inspiring places for sport around Edinburgh and east Scotland:

- **'Craiglochhart Tennis Centre,** Edinburgh: the only clay court in Scotland and where I won my first Scottish junior title.
- **Golf at Gleneagles:** where I learnt to play on a 9 hole par 3 course when I was tiny.
- **The Himalayas putting green** on the seafront at St Andrews: this is a great course, which is really challenging.
- **Knockhill Motorsport Centre,** near Dunfermline, Fife: go karting at this great racing circuit.'

- **Team X Sail**
  ☎ 077853 50843; x-sailevents@hotmail.co.uk

Indoor climbing

The world's largest indoor climbing wall is at the **Edinburgh International Climbing Areana** and a great place to learn all the ropes.

- **EICA**
  ☎ 0131 333 6333; www.eica-ratho.com

Country sports

From the Highland game estates in Perthshire to the River Tweed in the Borders, the east of Scotland is renowned for grouse shooting on the heather-clad moors, stalking over isolated hills and fishing in the best salmon rivers of the world. 'The Glorious Twelfth', 12 August, is the start of the grouse season;

partridge and pheasant shooting is from Septtember to February. Salmon fishing begins on 15 January on he River Tay and 1 February on the Tweed through to autumn with the peak season in July to September.

- **Fish Tweed**
  ☎ 01573 470 612; www.fishtweed.co.uk
- **Tweed Guide**
  ☎ 07962 401770; www.tweedguide.com
- **Kinnaird – Perthshire shooting and fishing estate**
  ☎ 01796 482440; www.kinnairdestate.com

ORGANISED HOLIDAYS, COURSES AND OUTDOOR ACTIVITIES

Touring by car, coach, train and bike

- **McKinlay Kidd** (☎ 0844 804 0020; www.seescotlanddifferently.co.uk): specialist Scottish holiday company which offers a personal service to plan your trip to Scotland with a choice of self-drive touring packages, romantic breaks, classic and sports car hire, tailor-made family holidays, wildlife and whisky-themed tours.
- **Rabbies Trail Burners** (☎ 0131 226 3133; www.rabbies.com): environmentally friendly coach tours from Edinburgh which include the *Da Vinci Code*, the Scottish Borders and St Andrews and East Neuk of Fife.
- **Caledonian Classics** (☎ 01259 742476; www.caledonianclassics.co.uk): weekend breaks and touring holiday packages in a classic vintage car.
- **Edinburgh Cycle Tours** (☎ 07966 447 206; www.edinburghcycletour.com): an entertaining and informative guide to Edinburgh. All cycling equipment is pro-vided including the easy riding Trek Bicycles and tours are suitable for children over 10.

- **Trike Tours** (☎ 0800 056 7779; www.triketoursscotland.com): city tour by chauffeur-driven trike. Also fun trike trips to East Lothian Perthshire, St Andrews or Peebles.
- **Scottish Borders Tours** (☎ 07900 030 666; www.scottishbordertours.co.uk): personally guided tours by eight-seater people carrier visiting Scott Country, Abbey trail, stately homes and reiver trails across Tweeddale.
- **Afternoon Tea Tours** (☎ 07873 211 856; www.afternoonteatours.com): genteel afternoon tour by car visiting several visitor attractions, castles and gardens around Edinburgh, Cramond and Midlothian, followed by tea at an elegant country house hotel in the Scottish Borders.
- **Glyn Farrer – Hail the Cabbie** (☎ 07747670123; www.hailthecabbie.com): born and bred in Scotland's capital and with 28 years' experience of driving Edinburgh taxis, Glyn is the owner of hailthecabbie.com which offers personally tailored tours of Edinburgh and the Lothians to all the attractions.
- **Royal Scotsman Train** (☎ 0845 077 2222 (UK only); www.royalscotsman.com; www.orient-express.com): a choice of two, three, four, five, and seven-day different itineraries depart from Edinburgh between April and October. Experience five-star comfort, cuisine and service on the most memorable house party on wheels.

Walking holidays

- **Walkabout Scotland** (☎ 0845 686 1344; www.walkaboutscotland.com): guided walks for day hikes, weekend breaks and walking holidays all graded for ability and experience.
- **Rob Roy Tours** (☎ 01620 890 908; www.robroyytours.com): walking, cultural and activity holidays for single travellers, couples and families.
- **Make Tracks** (☎ 0131 229 6844; www.maketracks.net): Make Tracks will

plan your walking holiday in Scotland, providing quality B&B or hotel accommodation, written guides and maps, door to door luggage transfers.

· **Contours** (☎ 017684 80451; www. contours.co.uk): self-guided walks in Scotland. Guided tailor-made walking tours can also be arranged.

Sports holidays

· **Trailbrakes** (☎ 07922 653327; www. trailbrakes.co.uk): two-day trips, weekend mountain bike training courses and week-long adventures, such as the world-renowned 7stanes trail with accommodation (choice of camping hostel, B&B, hotel), and baggage transfers arranged.

· **Scottish Cycle Holidays** (☎ 01250 876100; www.scotcycle.co.uk): based in Perthshire, they plan biking trips on quiet roads to explore hills, glens, lochs, seashores and historic places. Two-day, week and fortnight tours for adults and children include selected accommodation, airport/rail collection, luggage transfers, maps, routes, touring and mountain bike hire.

· **Coast to Coast Surf School** (☎ 01368 869734; mobile 07971 990361; www. c2csurfschool.com): based in Dunbar, offers surf lessons and courses for adults and children. Water temperatures are very comfortable for lessons from late March through to early November. The C2C Whitewater weekend package is an ideal introduction for beginners and includes beach games and barbecues.

· **Splash White-Water Rafting** (☎ 01887 829 706; www.rafting.co.uk): journey by river, exploring the natural environment and scenic beauty around Loch Tay. Short breaks and holidays include accommodation in either bunk houses, hotels or self catering.

· **Fishing at East Haugh Country Hotel** (☎ 01796 473121; www.easthaugh. co.uk): East Haugh in Pitlochry specialises in fishing breaks with expert tuition on the beat and equipment hire. Good dinner, B&B rates, BBQ and packed lunches, clothes drying and larder facilities.

· **Shooting and fishing at Kinnaird** (☎ 01796 482440; www.kinnairdestate. com): located near Dunkeld, this is one of the finest private sporting estates in Scotland for excellent shooting experiences from beginner to experienced. Five miles of private beats along the River Tay for salmon fishing and trout fishing on the Millpond loch.

· **Gleneagles Resort** (☎ 01764 662231; www.gleneagles.com/activities): the famous golf resort also has a world-class shooting school, fishing on the estate trout loch and an Equestrian centre.

Art courses

· **The Four Seasons Hotel** (☎ 01764 685 333; www.thefourseasonshotel.co.uk): four to six-night seasonal tutored painting holidays in St Fillans, Perthshire with great dinner, B&B rates.

· **Art in Crail** (☎ 01333 450842; www. artincrail.co.uk): weekly painting courses under the tutorship of professional artist, Gerry Pine, from the end of May to mid-September; weekend courses during May, September and October.

FURTHER INFORMATION

Scottish tourist boards

Useful advice and information can be found at **www.visitscotland.com** and **www. scotland.org.** Further advice is available from the following local tourism authorities:

· **Edinburgh and south east Scotland Tourism:** ☎ 0845 225 5121; www.edinburgh.org

The best... beaches and seashores

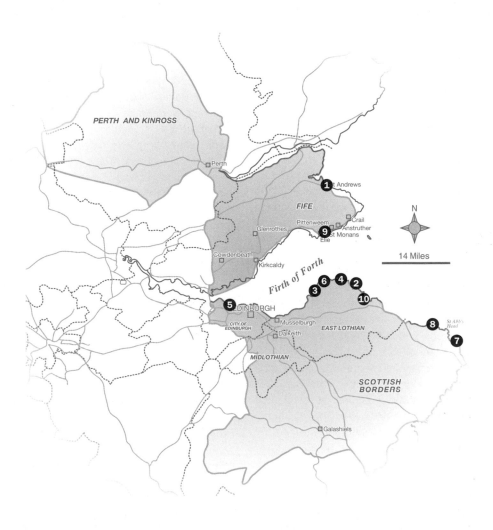

1. St Andrews – the West Sands where *Chariots of Fire* was filmed, p.256
2. North Berwick – two fabulous sandy beaches for sandcastles and games, p.158
3. Longniddry – for children, walkers and beach combers, p.189
4. Gullane – for board surfers, wind surfers, barbecues and family fun, p.189
5. Cramond – a beach near Edinburgh city centre for a good day out, p.142
6. Aberlady Nature Reserve – seashore rambles to see birds and flora, p.189
7. St Abb's Head – exhilarating clifftop walk above seabird colony, p.232
8. Coldingham Bay, the place to learn to surf on the high rollers, p.232
9. Elie – wide sandy beach where cricket matches are played in summer, p.272
10. Tyninghame – a secret little bay and beach for lazy-day picnics, p.177

- **East Lothian:** ☎ 01620 827282; www.visiteastlothian.org
- **North Berwick TIC:** ☎ 01620 892197
- **Scottish Borders:** ☎ 01750 20555; www.visitscottishborders.com
- **Melrose TIC:** ☎ 01896 822283
- **Fife:** ☎ 01334 472021; www.kftb.net
- **St Andrews TIC:** ☎ 01334 472021
- **Perthshire:** ☎ 01738 450600; www.perthshire.co.uk

Useful passes

- **Historic Scotland** (☎ 0131 668 8800; www.historic-scotland.gov.uk/explorer): if you plan to visit a few Historic Scotland castles, towers and properties, purchase an Explorer Pass for three, seven or 10 days (adult, child and family passes) giving free entry to all attractions. There is also a regional Explorer Pass for the Scottish Borders.
- **National Trust for Scotland** (☎ 0844 493 2100; www.nts.org.uk): members of the National Trust in England and Wales have free entry to NTS properties in Scotland. For non-member visitors, a good-value three, seven or 14-day, individual and family Discovery Pass can be purchased from tour operators, such as Holiday in Britain (www.holidayinbritain.com).
- **Edinburgh Pass** (www.edinburghpass. com): a one or two-day ticket giving free access to numerous city attractions and discounts on restaurants, tours and car hire.

Media and magazines

The *Scotsman* newspaper and *Evening News* will give all Scottish and local news, weather and arts reviews and listings. *The List* magazine, published fornightly, is the main 'what's on' guide in and around Edinburgh, available at all newsagents. *The List* also publishes an annual **Eating and Drinking Guide** for Edinburgh and Glasgow, published every April.

Instant and Artmag is two magazines in one, available free in cafés, restaurants and bars with topical features, restaurant reviews and full listing of art exhibitions at Edinburgh galleries. *Ion magazine* is the local style bible for fashion, beauty, restaurants, bars and cafés, free in boutiques and bars.

Useful websites

- **www.edinburghfestivals.co.uk**: dates and information on all the festivals.
- **www.scotsman.com**: Scotland's online newspaper.
- **www.list.co.uk**: what's on entertainment and going out-and-about city guide.
- **www.rampantscotland.com**: Scottish history, travel and cultural features.
- **www.edinburghguide.com**: entertainment, travel and visitor attractions.
- **www.luxuryedinburgh.com**: for the best hotels, restaurants, shopping and lifestyle.
- **www.cityofliterature.com**: Edinburgh's writers, festivals and events.
- **www.wild-scotland.org.uk**: Scottish wildlife and nature tourism.

THE BACKGROUND

HISTORY

Edinburgh

Edinburgh was forged by volcanic action and almost continuous border warfare. Set amongst several volcanic hills, the most westerly of these with a mile-long ridge, became the site of a fort that led to the formation of Edinburgh. A Bronze Age settlement as far back as 850BC, in the second century AD it was Probably '*Din Eidyn*' (fortress on the rock), the home of the Celtic tribe of **Votadini**, whom the Romans encountered as they advanced north.

In the seventh century the **Angles** captured this part of Scotland and called it 'Eiden's burgh' (burgh is an old word for fort). Around 960 AD it was captured by **Malcolm II**, King of Scotland. The marriage of King Malcolm III (son of Duncan, murdered by Macbeth) brought about the building of a royal residence on the rock.

During most of the 13th century, Scotland was at peace with England and Edinburgh developed rapidly. But with the establishment of the alliance with France, the Castle was seized by **Edward I** and it was destined to change hands again and again under attack and counter attack. With the English occupying the castle, there followed the rise of **William Wallace** and **Robert the Bruce** and the liberation of Scotland following the battle of **Bannockburn** in 1314. A charter was granted by Bruce to allow Edinburgh the use of the port of Leith and Edinburgh's importance grew.

Edinburgh prospered and became the Scottish capital during the reign of James III. But when Henry VIII invaded France, **James IV** invaded England due to the 'Auld Alliance'. The population of Edinburgh feared invasion and so a defensive wall was built – parts of the Flodden Wall can still be seen off the Royal Mile at the junction of The Pleasance and the Cowgate. This wall formed the city boundary and the edge of the citizens' world. Today, there's a pub on the Royal Mile called The World's End near where one gate stood. As the population grew inside the city walls, the only way to build was up and soon buildings of seven or more storeys became characteristic, with the wealthier residents living on the upper floors.

James V entered the city with his army in 1528 to assert his right to rule and Palace of Holyrood was built for him. When he died, Henry VIII wanted his son Edward to marry James' daughter, Mary. In a move known as 'The Rough Wooing' Henry sent the Earl of Hertford with 10,000 men to set fire to the town, the palace and the abbey. Mary's short reign contributed little to Edinburgh and by the time **John Knox** preached at St Giles' Cathedral on the Royal Mile, the Reformation of the Church was under way. John Knox's house can still be seen on the Royal Mile.

In 1560 the **Treaty of Edinburgh** was signed, ending the warring between Scotland, England and France and paving the way for a Protestant nation and union with England. **James VI** was on the throne of Scotland, and again Edinburgh enjoyed prosperity with the founding of **Edinburgh University** in 1583. When Queen Elizabeth I died he became **James I of England** leading to the **Union of the Crowns** in 1603.

Throughout this period, Edinburgh had continued to grow upwards with consequent overcrowding and disease. The High Street had been paved with open sewers for drainage, which did little to help the unsanitary

43

conditions, and in 1654 there was the largest outbreak of the plague. In 1681 running water was piped to wells down the High Street; some of the well heads can still be seen. This meant that the street could be washed down, but there were still 30,000 chamber pots being emptied out of windows in the space of a square mile every night at 10pm to the call of 'Guardez l'eau'.

The Lord Provost, George Drummond recognised the need for expansion and in 1766 a young architect, **James Craig**, won a design competition for the **New Town**. The first house was completed in 1767 and much of the gentry soon moved to their new Georgian mansions. A second phase of the New Town was built between 1804 and 1820 and today much is still preserved. Edinburgh became an important centre of 'the enlightenment' and its wealth and middle classes continued to grow throughout the 18th and 19th centuries. Notable figures included philosophers David Hume and Adam Smith, authors Robert Louis Stevenson, Sir Arthur Conan Doyle and Sir Walter Scott – statues of whom can be seen in the city.

In the first half of the 20th century Edinburgh went from being a merchant to a financial centre. Many of the financial centres and other businesses have in recent years moved to new offices in the west of the city, and a number of the old financial headquarters around **George Street** are now upmarket glamorous hotels, restaurants, pubs and wine bars. Edinburgh has lost many of its traditional industries, such as printing, publishing and brewing and the port of Leith has been gentrified with residential and retail developments.

In 1995 the Old and New Town areas were listed as a Unesco World Heritage Site and after great debate and a public referendum, the **Scottish Parliament** was re-established – the first since 1707. The opening of the Scottish Parliament by The Queen on 1 July 1999 instilled renewed energy and innovation in the nation. 'This is about more than politics and laws', said First Minister Donald Dewar at the time, 'This is about who we are. The past is part of us but today there is a new voice in the land to shape Scotland. A voice for the future.' And history has gone full circle, the controversial new Scottish Parliament building next to the Palace of Holyroodhouse is a (royal) mile from where the history of Edinburgh began on the Castle Rock.

The visitor to Edinburgh today will understand a great deal of the city's history by walking around the medieval Old Town and by visiting the Castle, the Palace of Holyroodhouse, St Giles' Cathedral, Mary King's Close, John Knox House, Greyfriars Kirk, the Grassmarket, Gladstone's Land and the Georgian House.

South-east Scotland

To the east of Edinburgh along the fertile coastal farmlands is **East Lothian**, bordered by the beaches of the Forth, with the Lammermuir hills and Border country to the south. Haddington was the birthplace of John Knox, a leader of the Protestant Reformation who is considered the founder of the Presbyterian denomination.

There was royal intrigue near North Berwick in 1590 when the Earl of Bothwell summoned 200 witches to cast a spell on **James VI** as he travelled back by ship from Denmark, but the black magic failed to cause a shipwreck and the King survived. **Tantallon Castle** perched high on the cliffs here was the almost impregnable stronghold of the Red Douglases clan, which withstood 300 years of attack before become beseiged by Cromwell in 1651. Tantallon Castle today is owned by Historic Scotland and is a great place to visit. During the **Jacobite Rising** of 1745, **Bonnie Prince Charlie** and his band of Highlanders defeated the English army at Prestonpans – although it was a short-lived victory for the Prince Charles Edward Stuart.

The **Scottish Borders**, with its ruined abbeys, castles, isolated moors and forested dales, is regarded as Scotland's most romantic and unspoilt region, assisted mainly by **Sir Walter Scott** waxing lyrical in poems and novels about his beloved country. The Anglo Saxons and the Anglo Normans settled here, and through English feudal land boundaries became quite separate from Lowland and Highland Scotland. The River Tweed marked the border with England from 1018 and in order to show his authority over the Border region, King **David I** built four great abbeys in Melrose, Jedburgh, Dryburgh and Kelso, which brought great prosperity and trade. But this debatable land between the two countries also saw the brunt of English and Scottish family feuds, arson and attack by the infamous **Border Reivers**. By the mid-16th century, as the Reformation took hold, the great abbeys were attacked and partially destroyed. Many of the Border towns continue the tradition of The Riding of the Marches or Common Riding festivals every year which links back to the marking out of land boundaries checked by horseback.

The Borders' landscape is ideal for sheep farming, from which the textile industry developed, with knitting and weaving flourishing in the Industrial Revolution in the woollen mills along the Tweed. The woollen cloth, tweed, was invented by the weavers of **Jedburgh** experimenting with different wools. The river however may not have given tweed its name, but 'tweel', a Borders word for woollen fabric could have. The charming town of **Melrose** has a rich folklore history, where legend claims King Arthur and his knights lie under a spell deep within the **Eildon Hills**. The heart of Robert the Bruce is believed to be buried at Melrose Abbey, and Walter Scott is buried at Dryburgh Abbey.

The Picts laid claim to and named the **Kingdom of Fife** in the fourth century. Dunfermline was the former capital of Scotland and six Scottish monarchs are buried at the Abbey. Built as a country residence for the Stuart monarchy is the rather grand French chateaux-styled, **Falkland Palace**, which features the oldest tennis court in Britain, built in 1539 for James V. The East Neuk of Fife villages and fishing ports of Culross, Crail, Anstruther and Pittenweem still retain much of the medieval-to-16th-century architecture of old merchant townhouses and church towers inspired by trade with the Low Countries. St Andrews has a history all to itself, as a significant place of religious and educational history, with the founding of its world famous university in 1412, as well as being the home of golf and the Royal and Ancient Golf Club.

The city of **Perth** became the capital of Scotland in the 12th century, adjacent to the nearby **Stone of Scone** – crowning place of the Scottish Kings. This coronation **Stone of Destiny** had been brought here by King Kenneth MacAlpin in the nineth century and it remained at Scone until 1296 when Edward I removed it during the Wars of Independence. In 1950 a group of young Scottish Nationalists stole the stone back from Westminster Abbey and brought it (briefly) home to Scotland. On St Andrews Day, 1996, the Stone of Scone arrived officially at its new resting place, Edinburgh Castle.

GEOGRAPHY AND GEOLOGY

For its size, Scotland has the most varied geographical landscape on the planet, and much of its natural scenic beauty is located around south-east Scotland. Here you will find the dramatic valleys of Perthshire and the Borders, volcanoes rising from glaciated plains, rugged seashore cliffs and rounded hills rising from the floor of a long-vanished ocean.

Around 420 million years ago when the land mass of Scotland collided with England, Scotland came out on top. The Lowlands were a Sahara-like desert, but as the continent drifted near the equator, lush forests grew, forming peat bogs and then coal. The area was rocked by volcanoes: **Arthur's Seat** erupted about 400 million years ago and the rocks around **Salisbury Crag** are sandstone, formed in warm shallow seas with layers of volcanic ash and lava. The cores of these volcanic vents cooled and solidified to form basalt volcanic plugs such as **Edinburgh Castle Rock**. During the ice ages, glaciers were forced over and round these volcanic hills, carving out hollows (Princes Street Gardens, Grassmarket), exposing rocky crags and creating the distinctive crag and tail ridge – today, the Royal Mile, running from the Castle down to the Palace.

The Scottish landscape was eroded, shaped and reshaped as glaciers moulded U-shaped glens, the **Ochil Hills**, the **Eildons**, **North Berwick Law**, the seven hills of Edinburgh and volcanic cliffs at **St Abb's Head**. Fluctuating sea levels left behind raised beaches with wind-formed dunes along the coasts of East Lothian and St Andrews – later developed as iconic links golf courses. About 13,000 years ago, the sea would have reached inland as far as Scone Palace, Perth, and lapped at the site of the Scottish Parliament at Holyrood. Rivers channelled out valleys, their plains providing flat, fertile agricultural land and giving rise to riverside settlements such as Haddington and many Border towns. The sandstone along the A9 road through Perthshire shows that the ancient river was of a similar scale to the Mississippi.

This diverse and ancient topography of Scotland led to many important developments in the understanding of the Earth. Louis Agazziz used evidence from Blackford Hill, Edinburgh to support his research to propose his scientific theory of the Ice Ages. It was James Hutton's field work on Salisbury Crags in the 1780s, where he studied multicoloured rock formations, and at Siccar Point on the Berwickshire coast, that he found his 'Unconformity' – the junction between folded rock and sedimentary rock. Hutton's *Theory of the Earth* was the first to challenge the conventional view of the planet's age (at that point 4004 BC) and to recognise the true forces of nature, which credited him as father of modern geology.

Today, this region has a temperate maritime climate which is relatively mild despite its northerly latitude. The proximity of the sea prevents any large variation in temperature or extremes of climate. South-westerly winds are associated with warm air from the Gulf Stream and the annual rainfall is lower than most UK cities outside south-east England.

WILDLIFE AND HABITATS

The South-East of Scotland is home to a great diversity of habitats and species as well as stunning landscapes.

Woodland

The area would have originally been mainly forested in oak, elm and birch, but much has been cleared for farming. The remains of these ancient woodlands, such as at **The Hermitage** in Dunkeld, Perthshire, have great biodiversity, with bluebells, wild garlic, wood anemones, dog's mercury and lesser celandine. Birch and rowan are the most common tree species on the hills, with oak and hazel lower down, and willow, alder, ash and wych elm in wetter areas and river valleys. The woodlands also support bats, a huge variety of birds, beetles, fungi, lichens and mosses.

Moorland and hills

Moorland and grassland have been created by sheep grazing and by the burning of heather to encourage the growth of new shoots on red grouse moors. The planting of parts of the moorland with conifers has reduced some species but has encouraged the rare goshawk. The hills provide breeding sites for wading birds such as the curlew, and are home to the mountain hare. Heather moorland is found in the Scottish Borders and Perthshire.

Grassland

When the ancient woodlands were cleared for farming, meadows rich in wildflowers, butterflies and birds such as skylarks and partridges were created. However, with more intensive farming these have often been pushed to the edges or roadsides out of reach of cultivation or grazing.

Freshwater

There are a number of natural, large lochs and plenty of reservoirs and smaller ponds. Many are home to large numbers of waterbirds, including wintering geese and breeding gulls, ducks, grebes and teal. Smaller ponds, both in farmland and in urban areas, provide important habitats for species such as dragonflies and newts. The larger rivers support salmon, trout, otters, herons and wagtails.

Bogs and fens

Wet areas formed in the hollows left by the last Ice Age support plants like waterlilies, horsetails, orchids, birch-willow carr, cranberry and scarce mosses and sedges. Where mosses have accumulated over thousands of years, peat bogs have been created. Bogs and fens support dragonflies, damselflies, butterflies, moths and water beetles. A good example are the **Whitlaw Mosses**, four wetland jewels tucked into troughs in the landscape 2 miles east of Selkirk in the Scottish Borders. The best time to visit is mid-May to late August.

Coast

The coast is rich in wildlife, with internationally important populations of wintering waders such as golden plover, bar-tailed godwit, oystercatcher, redshank and dunlin, and waterfowl including pink-footed geese, eider ducks, shelduck, divers and grebes. The offshore islands, and a few coastal sites such as **St Abb's Head**, support huge numbers of breeding seabirds such as puffin, gannets, guillemots, razorbills, shags, kittiwakes and fulmars. Grey seals are abundant on the islands. The Voluntary Marine Nature Reserve off St Abb's has a vast variety of marine life including soft corals, dead men's fingers, anemones and sea cucumbers.

Some notable fauna

- **Adder:** Scotland's only wild snake. Adders can be about 65cm long with very obvious dark zig-zag markings (anything without markings will be a Slow Worm). They will bask in the sun but are not aggressive and will usually hide if disturbed. One place to see them is at **Loch of the Lowes**, Perthshire.
- **Badgers:** Scotland has about 10% of the British badger population. Usually their underground homes (setts) are in woodland, typically with pasture for foraging nearby. Active throughout the year (less so in winter), they are primarily nocturnal but can be seen around dusk during summer. All young are born between mid-January and mid-March, after which they can emerge to the warmth of spring. Badgers can be seen at **Fleecefaulds Meadow**, Ceres, Fife, in **Elibank** and **Traquair** forests; or watch badgers in your bedroom at **Pressmains Cottages** near Coldingham, Scottish Borders.
- **Bats:** **Pipistrelle** bats are small, no bigger than a mouse and with a wingspan of about 20cm. Less common is the **Daubenton's** bat, which hunt by skimming low over water, catching insects close to the surface. Both can be seen at **The Hermitage**, Dunkeld.
- **Crossbill:** Found particularly in coniferous plantations, this large finch is a neighbour of the red squirrel. Males are orange-to-

brick-red and the females greenish-grey and slightly streaked. There is a Scottish Crossbill but it is only found in the Highlands – however, some experts still consider it the same species.

· **Eider:** The UK's heaviest duck and its fastest flying, they can be seen round rocky coasts where they require suitable islands or low-lying land with access to the sea for nests, which are lined in the famous eiderdown. The male is white with a black crown and the female brown with darker barring and a distinctive long forehead.

· **Freshwater pearl mussels:** One of the reasons the Romans invaded Britain. Now extremely endangered, very few rivers still have them, yet Scotland has half the world's breeding population.

· **Gannet:** A large white seabird with black wingtips, a long profile and pointed beak. The world's largest single rock gannetry is on the **Bass Rock** off North Berwick, East Lothian with an estimated 50,000 pairs.

· **Goshawk:** Conifer planting in the Borders has encouraged the rare Goshawk. It became extinct as a breeding species in Britain in the 1880s, but was re-established from captive birds. The female is almost the size of a Buzzard at 62cm; the male smaller at 48cm. It is elusive but can be seen soaring over its nest site in early spring. When displaying it will sky-dance – flying slowly and eventually rising and falling dramatically.

· **Grouse:** Found on the heather moors of the Borders and Perthshire, the **Red Grouse** is medium sized with reddish-brown plumage and red combs over the eyes. The birds form pairs in the autumn and eggs are laid in April to May. They are considered a game bird and are shot in considerable numbers during a season starting on 12 August – 'The Glorious Twelfth'. The larger **Black Grouse** males have glossy black feathers and a red wattle over the eyes; the females are grey-brown

with darker freckles or bars. They are at home around the edges of moors and in young forestry plantations or the edges of ancient pinewoods. Research has shown that their numbers are diminishing. If you are very lucky you might see one on a Landrover safari in Perthshire.

· **Osprey:** **Ospreys** are magnificent fish-eating birds of prey with an impressive 1.45–1.75m wingspan. Possibly the best place to see them is at the **Loch of the Lowes**, near Dunkeld. A breeding pair return from Africa in early April and are at the Loch until late August. They can be viewed from a hide 200m away. There are also two **Tweed Valley Osprey Watch** centres at Glentress Forest and Kailzie Gardens in the Scottish Borders where, in season, you can see live footage of ospreys and other wildlife.

· **Otter:** A terrestrial mammal, otters spend much of their time in water, particularly when feeding – mainly on fish. More common in the north-west of Scotland, you may still come across them. For example, they are present but unpredictable at Loch of the Lowes, Perthshire, and you can look for them at **The Hirsel Visitor Centre**, Coldstream in the Borders.

· **Pine marten:** This dark brown, cat-sized member of the weasel family is found in North and West Perthshire. Nearly extinct at the end of the 19th century, they are now on the increase.

· **Puffin:** One of the most recognisable of birds around the coast. There are large colonies on the islands of **Craigleith** and **Fidra** off the East Lothian coast where there is an ongoing Operation Puffin to remove invasive vegetation from their burrow breeding grounds. They arrive in March and April and leave in mid-August.

· **Red squirrel:** Scotland has 75% of Britain's red squirrel population. However, they remain one of the rarest and most threatened of the native species. They live in a number of woodland habitats and are most abundant in Scots pine or mixed conifers. There are opportunities to see them from Glentress in the Borders, north through Fife and particularly at the Hermitage, Dunkeld in 'Big Tree Country', Perth and Kinross. Autumn is the peak time. At **Killiecrankie House Hotel**, north of Pitlochry, there is a feeding station near the garden – so there is a chance that you will see a red squirrel having breakfast while you are having yours.

· **Roe deer:** Part of the Scottish landscape since prehistoric times, they are mainly found in woodland, but in recent years a rise in numbers has seen them colonise heather and scrub areas. The male is identified by short antlers and markings on the head. The female is smaller. In summer, the adult coat will be rich red and in winter, a greyish fawn, flecked with yellow. They can be seen in the forests of the Scottish Borders and from the hide at Loch of the Lowes, Perthshire.

· **Salmon:** Good places to see the salmon leap are the fish ladder at Pitlochry and the falls at The Hermitage, Dunkeld. Famous salmon and trout fishing rivers are The Tweed in the Borders and The Tay in Perthshire.

Some notable flora

· **Creeping Lady's-Tresses:** Of all the British orchids, this is the species most strongly associated with pinewoods, and can be found in drier, shaded woods throughout the area. One of the later-flowering orchids, the sweetly scented flowers are produced in July. It was discovered in 1767 by James Robertson, a gardener at the Royal Botanic Garden Edinburgh.

· **Douglas Fir:** Not a native species, but notable all the same. Named after David Douglas, the famous plant collector who was born in Scone, near Perth, the one to see is at The Hermitage, Dunkeld. At around 212ft (64.5m) it's one of the tallest trees in Britain.

· **Dropwort:** This beautiful plant is rare in Scotland but can be found in the south-east, up the coast from the Borders, around Edinburgh, through Fife and into mid-Perthshire. It is a perennial, growing to 60–80cm tall with fern-like leaves and white flowers from late spring to mid-summer. A good place to find it, along with bloody cranesbill and lesser meadow-rue, is on the **Fife Coastal Footpath** from North Queensferry, which cuts through the nature reserve at Carlingnose Point.

· **Heather:** Immortalised in song and verse, it's hard to think of Scotland without conjuring up the 'Bonnie Bloomin' Heather'. Common to the moors of the Borders and Perthshire, this low perennial shrub grows in open locations on acidic soil. Heather was an ingredient in beer in the middle ages and is now used in some modern Scottish varieties. It is also home to the Emperor Moth.

· **Purple Oxytrpis:** One of the most attractive of the native species, this rare plant can be found at Ben Vrackie in Perthshire. The leaves are covered with silky hairs and the purple flowers are seen May to July.

· **Scots Lovage:** A Scottish speciality found right around the coastline, it was first recorded in 1684. In 1688 botanist John Ray gave its first exact location 'on a certain sandy and stony hill six miles from Edinburgh towards Queensferry'. This leathery-leaved plant, divided into three stalked leaflets and lobes, is generally confined to more sheltered cliff ledges. It flowers in late June to August with seeds ripening in October and November.

· **Sticky Catchfly:** An upright perennial growing to about 60cm high with pink/purple flowers. So-named because its sticky stems trap insects to prevent them eating the plant or laying eggs on it. It is said to improve the disease resistance of surrounding plants. It was first discovered in Edinburgh nearly 400 years ago and became the favourite flower of King James VI of Scotland. It can still be found in Holyrood Park, surrounding the Royal Palace.

· **Yew:** While the yew tree is native across Europe and beyond, the specimen at Fortingall, Perthshire is distinguished by being the oldest known tree in Europe. The lower end of the estimates put its age at 2,000 years old and there have been claims that it is up to 5,000 years old. According to legend, Pontius Pilate was born in its shade. Important in the ancient Celtic world and often associated with mystical powers, the yew is mentioned in literature from Shakespeare's *Titus Andronicus* to JK Rowling's *Harry Potter*.

CULTURE

Edinburgh: Unesco World City of Literature

Few people may realise that, outside of London, Edinburgh has more literary associations than any other part of Britain—spanning 300 years of poetry, fiction and biography, from Walter Scott to Robert Louis Stevenson, Arthur Conan Doyle to Muriel Spark. In October 2004 Edinburgh was appointed by Unesco as the first World City of Literature.

Contemporary literature

Three of Britain's most successful and internationally acclaimed writers, JK Rowling, Alexander McCall Smith and Ian Rankin, all live and write in Edinburgh, living within a mile of each other on the southside of the city.

JK Rowling is named the world's best-selling author for her seven *Harry Potter* books (275 million sold). Edinburgh is where the *Harry Potter* series was mainly conceived and written, the original manuscript sent from a post box in Leith. She recently commented: 'Edinburgh has been my home since 1994. It was the place that Harry Potter took shape...I used to sit in the Old Town cafés scribbling as my daughter slept in her pushchair. I'm proud to be known as a Scottish writer, albeit by adoption... it's impossible to live in Edinburgh without sensing its literary heritage everywhere.'

In September 2008, she was presented with the **Edinburgh Award** by the City Council, as a prestigious civic and national recognition of her outstanding contribution to her services to literature and to the city. Further information on JK Rowling can be found on p.97.

Ian Rankin was born in Fife and attended Edinburgh University to study English literature. On graduation, while researching the works of Muriel Spark for a PhD, Rankin began writing a thriller instead. It was a good career move. He is now regarded as the number one crime writer in the UK and is a commercially successful writer. Amongst numerous awards over the years for his very popular *Inspector Rebus* novels, he was presented with the CWA Cartier Diamond Dagger Award 2005 for lifetime achievement, one of the world's foremost crime awards.

Edinburgh is a major character in the *Rebus* books. He describes the culture, history and the age-old duality and contrast between affluent New Town residents and the unseen, seedy housing estates with vivid detail. Rankin transcends the conventional crime novel by infusing the plot with a literary chronicle of the city's changing social scene and Scotland's political identity over the past 20 years. 'I wrote the first Rebus novel because I wanted to write about contemporary Edinburgh,' he once commented. 'I wanted to explain Edinburgh to myself, and later on, once I was confident about my abilities, I decided to try explaining Scotland to the world, and to people living in Scotland, too.'

Alexander McCall Smith has lived most of his life in Edinburgh, working as an academic (Professor of Medical Law and Bioethics)—but with the major success of his books, (translated into 42 languages), he now concentrates on writing his popular series of novels: *The No. 1 Ladies Detective Agency* (with a TV series currently being filmed), *44 Scotland Street, Sunday Philosophy Club, Von Igelfeld* and other books. The *Scotland Street* novels began as a daily serialisation in *The Scotsman* newspaper, an idea sparked by a meeting between McCall Smith and Armistead Maupin, the author of *Tales in the City*, originally serialised in the *San Francisco Chronicle*. This revival of the Victorian tradition was inspirational and *The Scotsman* decided to give McCall Smith the challenge of writing one himself.

Scotland Street is a real street, although no. 44 is fictional. You can wander around the New Town visiting many of the cafés, galleries and pubs mentioned in the stories: Cumberland Bar, Café St Honore restaurant, Drummond Place and Valvona & Crolla Italian delicatessen. Likewise, **Isabel Dalhousie** lives in the leafy district of Merchiston and visits her niece's café nearby in Bruntsfield, and often takes a walk to the Scottish Gallery, Dundas Street and down the hill to Stockbridge.

Classic literature and poetry

Scotland's capital city has inspired over 500 novels ranging from *Dr Jekyll and Mr Hyde* to *Trainspotting*. **Percy Bysshe Shelley** came to stay for a few weeks in George Street in 1811, before his marriage to his young bride, 16-year-old Harriet, later living with his family in Frederick Street. A few years later, **Mary Wollstonecraft Shelley**, his second wife, describes its fine architecture in her novel, *Frankenstein*: '*I visited Edinburgh with languid eyes and mind... the beauty and regularity of the New Town, its romantic castle and its environs, the most delightful in the world, Arthur's Seat, St Bernard's Well and the Pentland Hills.*'

Charles Dickens had strong Edinburgh connections and *The Pickwick Papers* is partly set here. **Kenneth Graham**, author of *The Wind in the Willows* and **Arthur**

Conan Doyle were both born here. From 1876 to 1881, Doyle studied medicine at the University of Edinburgh and modelled Sherlock Holmes on his professor Dr Joseph Bell, who developed the practice of 'close observation' in medical diagnosis as an early pioneer of forensic science. A statue of Sherlock Holmes stands on Picardy Place, at the top of Broughton Street, to commemorate his association with the city.

Compton Mackenzie and **Thomas de Quincey** spent their last years here – you can visit De Quincey's grave in St Cuthbert's Church cemetery. **RM Ballantyne**, who wrote the children's classic *Coral Island*, was educated at the Edinburgh Academy just before **Robert Louis Stevenson** became a pupil. **Rebecca West** was educated at George Watson's Ladies College while Ian Fleming's character **James Bond** was sent to the public school Fettes, after an indiscretion with a ladies maid at Eton. *St Trinians*, immortalised in Ronald Searle's cartoons and films, was based on an Edinburgh girls' school of the same name.

The best-known Edinburgh novel, *The Prime of Miss Jean Brodie*, was based on **Muriel Spark**'s experience at James Gillespie's School for Girls, where a favourite teacher, Miss Christina Kay, a lover of Italian art and travel, was a powerful, inspirational figure in her life.

Sir Walter Scott: What other city in the world has a railway station and a towering gothic monument dedicated to a poet! Edinburgh's Waverley Station is named after Sir Walter Scott's series of novels and the Scott Monument dominates Princes Street Gardens – which you will see immediately as you walk out of the station. Scott was born on 15 August 1771 in College Wynd, Old Town. In 1779 he attended Royal High School, and this child prodigy began studying classics at Edinburgh University aged just 12 years old

His famous works include *Ivanhoe, Rob Roy, The Lady of the Lake*, the *Waverley* novels, *The Heart of Midlothian* and *The Bride of Lammermoor*. A very popular and admired novelist and poet throughout his life, Scott did a huge amount to promote Scotland to visitors, highlighting the romantic history of the Borders, Edinburgh and the Highlands, and he is now seen as the founder of modern Scottish tourism. Scott lived with his wife Charlotte at 39 North Castle Street, for 28 years, which today has a plaque outside his beloved home. He then moved to his beautiful mansion house, Abbotsford, near Melrose, which you can visit (see p.208).

Robert Louis Stevenson: Poet, novelist and world travel writer, Robert Louis Stevenson was born in Edinburgh in 1850, into a family which for the previous three generations had established the tradition of being notable lighthouse engineers. Aged 17, Stevenson entered Edinburgh University to study engineering, but soon discovered that his interest was more inclined towards

10... fictional characters born in Edinburgh

1 Sherlock Holmes: Conan Doyle based the detective on his medical school tutor

2 Harry Potter: his wizardry adventures imagined by JK Rowling in Old Town cafés

3 Detective Inspector Rebus: crime novels by Ian Rankin, probably written in the Oxford Bar

4 Mma Precious Ramotswe: the No. 1 Ladies Detective agent by Alexander McCall Smith

5 Frankenstein: Gothic Edinburgh and the grisly murderers Burke and Hare inspired Mary Shelley

6 Long John Silver: from the mind of Robert Louis Stevenson

7 Begbie, Sick Boy, Renton and Spud: Irvine Welsh's *Trainspotting* guys

8 Miss Jean Brodie: based on Muriel Spark's artistic teacher

9 Isabel Dalhousie: McCall Smith's charming philosopher and sleuth

10 Dr Jekyll and Mr Hyde: Stevenson's character based on the real Deacon Brodie

literature instead. His father however forced Stevenson to continue his studies and he went on to graduate with a degree in law. His passion for adventure, combined with his poor health, meant that Stevenson spent the rest of his life travelling the world to find a climate more suitable for his health. He died on the Pacific Island of Samoa in December 1894 aged only 44. His famous novels include *A Child's Garden of Verses*, *Treasure Island*, *Kidnapped* and *The Strange Case of Dr Jekyll and Mr Hyde*. His family home was at 17 Heriot Row, New Town, which now features a commemorative plaque.

Robert Burns: The Scottish Bard is an internationally renowned writer of romantic, sentimental poems such as *Red, Red Rose*, *Ae Fond Kiss* and *Auld Lang Syne*. Born in Alloway, Ayrshire, the self-educated intellectual Burns was inspired by Scottish folklore and traditional songs. He moved to Edinburgh on the publication of his first volume of poems in 1786, hailed by the literati as a natural genius and a 'heaven-taught ploughman poet'. Initially it was felt that his work was the result of his rural upbringing, away from the artificialities of civilized life and culture. Across the world on Burns Night, 25 January, his life and work is celebrated at formal dinner parties featuring haggis, whisky and poetry recitation.

Visit **The Writers' Museum**, Lady Stair's House, Makar's court, off the Lawnmarket to learn more about Burns, Scott and Stevenson and Edinburgh's contemporary writers. Free admission, Mon–Sat 10am–5pm. Sunday (August only) 12–5pm; ☎ 0131 529 4901; www.cac.org.uk

Art

Scotland's first major painter, **Allan Ramsay** (1713–1784) was born in Edinburgh and trained in London and Italy to become the leading British portrait painter of the late 1730s and 1740s, until he had to compete with Joshua Reynolds. Ramsay returned to Edinburgh in the mid 1850s as Court Painter to George III. Ramsay's reputation faded somewhat in the 19th and 20th centuries, but he is now regarded as one of the pre-eminent artists of the 18th century.

Sir Henry Raeburn's (1756–1823) precocious talents as a portrait painter were

---

EDINBURGH LITERARY TOURS

· **Rebus Tours** (☎ 0131 553 7473; www.rebustours.com): Ian Rankin's best-selling Inspector Rebus books have brought Edinburgh alive in the minds of millions of readers. A choice of Rebus tours with guide Colin Brown, visit real city locations, such as the Royal Oak, Oxford Bar and St Leonard's police station. The tours were launched in 2000 following close consultation with Ian Rankin and his publisher. Rankin has been spotted on the tour a couple of times, so it must be good! Advance booking is essential: £10.

· **Trainspotting Tours** (☎ 0131 555 2500; www.leithwalks.co.uk): Follow expert guide Tim Bell through the landscape of Leith, the setting of Irvine Welsh's contemporary classic *Trainspotting*. The tour explores some key locations from the book and the movie, starring Ewan McGregor.

· **Edinburgh Book Lovers' Tour** (www.edinburghbookloverstour.com): Starting outside The Writers' Museum this tour takes you through Edinburgh's closes, and through time, as you walk in the footsteps of literary greats such as Scott, Stevenson and Burns. Led by Allan Foster, author of *The Literary Traveller in Edinburgh*, the tour is full of entertaining stories and commentary.

· **Edinburgh Literary Pub Tour** (☎ 0800 169 7410; www.edinburghliterarypubtour.co.uk): Departing from The Beehive Inn, this award-winning, entertaining evening walking tour led by professional actors takes you through 300 years of literary history and in and out of some old pubs associated with Edinburgh's great writers.

quickly recognised and he swiftly developed a distinctive style characterised by detailed brushwork. He opened his own studio in 1798, attracting rich and influential patrons including Highland chieftains and Sir Walter Scott. A famous portrait 'Rev. Robert Walker skating on Duddingston Loch' is often used as the image on Christmas cards and a perennial favourite. The graceful figure elegantly clad in black is silhouetted against a luminescent, late-afternoon sky. Raeburn is regarded as the principal Scottish portrait painter of his age.

The Scottish Colourists were a group of four artists, SJ Peploe, FCB Cadell, Leslie Hunter and JD Fergusson, formed during the early 20th century, who were inspired by the strong and vibrant colours of French Impressionism to develop their own distinctive Scottish painterly idiom and style. Their individual paintings depicted still life, island lansdcapes, Edinburgh interiors and portraits of fashionable women. They enjoyed some commercial and popular success when they were actually exhibiting, but latterly they are now highly regarded internationally. A new world-record price was set in October 2008 when the Scottish Colourist painting, *Roses* (1922) by the artist Samuel Peploe sold for £529,750. Examples of their work can be seen at the Scottish National Gallery of Modern Art, Kirkcaldy Art Gallery and the JD Fergusson Gallery in Perth.

Eduardo Paolozzi (1924–2005) was born of Italian parents in Leith, Edinburgh. He studied at St Martin's School of Art and at Slade School of Fine Art before moving to Paris to become inspired by Dadaism and Surrealism. His work as a sculptor and print-maker and pioneer of Pop Art is world renowned. The Scottish Gallery of Modern Art holds a large collection as well as a recreation of his studio at the Dean Gallery.

John Bellany was born in Port Seton and trained at the Edinburgh College of Art and the Royal College of Art, London.

During the late 1960s he developed a mythological-figurative style–at a time when abstract art was the mode. He is regarded as one of Scotland's leading artists for his iconic seascapes and portraits. His work is exhibited for sale at the Open Eye Gallery, Edinburgh and the Harbour gallery, Port Seton and in permanent collections in Scottish National Gallery of Modern Art, Tate Britain, and Museum of Modern Art and Metropolitan in New York.

Jack Vettriano was born in 1953 in St Andrews and spent his childhood in Fife. As a self-taught artist, Vettriano's paintings, reproduced wildly on greetings cards, posters and prints, are miniature stories of seduction and betrayal, with a romanticised style of Sickert and Hopper and influences from the Scottish Colourists. His new paintings sell out at London gallery exhibitions and reach high prices at the auction houses.

Contemporary music

The Kingdom of Fife is proud to have two contemporary music stars who were brought up a few miles apart. **KT Tunstall** spent her childhood and formative years in St Andrews and it was her close family life here which influenced her music and poetic, romantic song lyrics. She describes her home town as 'beautiful but sheltered; a little bubble'. Along the coast, **Edith Bowman**, Radio 1 DJ and TV presenter was born and brought up in Anstruther, moving to Edinburgh to study media and communications, where she cut her music Dj-ing teeth at Radio Forth.

Shirley Manson began her career in Edinburgh in the early 1980s, fronting Angelfish while signed as a solo artist. Having seen Manson in an Angelfish video on MTV, Garbage invited Manson to record with them as the band's lead singer. After four successful studio albums, one greatest hits compilation and over 14 million record sales, Manson has embarked on a solo career.

10... galleries and art exhibitions

1 Scottish National Gallery of Modern art: inside and in the gardens, p.69

2 National Gallery of Scotland: magnificent world-class collection, p.71

3 East Neuk of Fife: artists' studios and galleries along the coast, p.282

4 The Watermill, Aberfeldy: Pop Art, contemporary prints and bookshop, p.319

5 Open Eye, Edinburgh: monthly changing exhibitions of leading Scottish artists, p.67

6 Scotland Art, Stockbridge: inspiring modern art at affordable prices, p.112

7 Greens and Blues: North Berwick gallery promoting fine local artists, p.167

8 Scottish Gallery: fine art, contemporary paintings, crafts and sculpture, p.69

9 Peter Potter, Haddington: paintings, prints, jewellery, glassware, ceramics, p.182

10 Scottish Borders Art Trail: a collection of art galleries across the Border towns (www.crossing-borders.org.uk), p.223

LOCAL HEROES

The shaping of 'The Athens of the North'

Edinburgh is sometimes called 'The Athens of the North' in reference to its intellectual history, the role played by the ridge of the Old Town (the Greek 'acropolis' literally meaning 'city on the edge'), and its wealth of neoclassical buildings and monuments. Two local architectural heroes are Robert Adam and William Henry Playfair

Robert Adam

Considered by many as the greatest architect of the late 18th century, Adam shaped many of the neoclassical buildings throughout the area and his work influenced architecture both in Europe and North America. Born in 1728 in Linktown of Abbotshall in the district of Kirkcaldy, Fife, Robert his family moved later that year to Edinburgh. He joined his elder brother John as apprentice to his father, William, who was Scotland's foremost architect at the time and assisted on projects including extensions to Hopetoun

10... local heroes (past and present)

1 Alexander Graham Bell: the best name to invent the telephone

2 Sir Sean Connery: born and educated in Edinburgh and a proud Freeman of the City

3 JK Rowling: who inspired children to read again with her magical tales

4 Chris Hoy: Olympic star and fastest cyclist in the world

5 Adam Smith: father of economics, author of The *Wealth of Nations*

6 Ronnie Corbett: TV comic star and loves to play golf at Gullane, East Lothian

7 KT Tunstall: best-selling singer and song writer from St Andrews

8 David Hume: the greatest philosopher the world has ever known

9 Mark Beaumont: cycled the world in 195 days to beat the record

10 Eduardo Paolozzo: world-renowned sculptor and pioneer of Pop Art

House near South Queensferry. Significant works include the northside of Charlotte Square, Register House and Edinburgh University Old College; Gosford House, near Longniddry, East Lothian; and Mellerstain House, Kelso, Scottish Borders.

William Henry Playfair

Born in London in 1790, the son of Scottish architect James Playfair, **William Henry Playfair** moved to Edinburgh to live with his uncle, Professor John Playfair, the scientist and mathematician. He made his neoclassical mark on Edinburgh in the 19th century, not only in his plans to complete Edinburgh University College, but also in landmark buildings.

Perhaps the most obvious is an apparently unfinished one – The National Monument on Calton Hill to those who died in the Napoleonic Wars. Modelled on The Parthenon in Athens in collaboration with Charles Robert Cockerell, it was started in 1822. It may be that there were not sufficient funds or political will to complete it, or perhaps it was never intended to build a complete replica – whatever the reason, it was destined to be known as 'Edinburgh's Disgrace'. His elaborate designs for the Royal Scottish Academy and National Gallery added to the 'The Athens of the North' epithet.

Other works of Playfair's include St Stephen's Church, Stockbridge (1828) (which has been called one of Scotland's best churches) and The Royal College of Surgeons and New College, Mound Place. In the Scottish Borders he was responsible for

St Ronan's Wells, Innerleithen, and carried out alterations to Floors Castle, Kelso. He died on 19 March 1857 and was buried in Dean Cemetery. The National Gallery was opened two years after his death.

The Age of Enlightenment

Edinburgh was a major centre of The Scottish Enlightenment, a remarkable outpouring of thought and learning that lasted for most of the 18th century with great advances in philosophy, science and economics of significance to Europe, America and beyond. Members of the intellectual Select Society included James Burnett (Lord Monboddo), Adam Ferguson, David Hume and Adam Smith.

James Burnett, Lord Monboddo

Born in 1714, **James Burnett** came to Edinburgh University to study law, and later became a judge in the Court of Session. He is famous for his theories on the evolution of language skills in response to changing environment and social structures. Based on linguistic evolution, he was the first to suggest that all humankind originated from a single region of the earth. Some scholars credit him with anticipating the idea of natural selection which was developed by Charles Darwin. For all his genius he was considered eccentric. Keen on the ancient Greek ideas of health, he once walked home in a rain storm while sending his wig back in his sedan chair. He held 'learned suppers' at his home in the Old Town where his theories would be discussed – guests included Robert Burns, Dr Samuel Johnson and James Boswell. While he was close for some time with Boswell, he would snipe at Johnson, not considering him a model for a scholar or polite writer. He died in 1799 and is buried in Greyfriars Kirkyard. Appropriately for a sociable patron of the arts, his name lives on in two Edinburgh bars—Monboddos Bar (Mercure Point Hotel, 34 Bread Street) and Lord Bodos (3 Dublin Street).

Adam Ferguson

Born at Logierait, Perthshire in 1723, **Adam Ferguson's** insights have been seen as the origin of the subject of sociology. He was appointed Professor of Natural Philosophy at Edinburgh University in 1759 and of Moral Philosophy in 1764. He nearly lost the post due to his prolonged absences in Italy and France, where he met Voltaire. His (anonymous) pamphlet on the American Revolution sympathised with the British legislature. In 1783 he published *History of the Progress and Termination of the Roman Republic,* believing that history could form a practical illustration of ethical and political doctrines. His lectures were published in 1792 as *The Principles of Moral and Political Science.*

He lived at Neidpath Castle, near Peebles, and at South Street in St Andrews, where he died aged 93. He is buried at St Andrews Cathedral where his monument has an insciption composed by Sir Walter Scott. A portrait of him by Sir Joshua Reynolds is in the National Gallery's collection.

David Hume

Born in 1711 in the Lawnmarket, Edinburgh, **David Hume** would become one of the greatest philosophers the world has ever known. He was sent to Edinburgh University at the age of 12 and encouraged to take up a career in law, but his thoughts soon turned to philosophy. At the age of 28 he wrote his groundbreaking and now classic work, *A Treatise on Human Nature*, a bold attempt to introduce scientific reasoning into moral subjects. It was not initially a success, and only his later re-workings of it into shorter, more attractive essays first won him recognition. It was to be his *History of England* which assured his fame and fortune.

His mausoleum (designed by Robert Adam) is in the Calton Old Burial Ground, Edinburgh. There is a modern bronze statue of Hume by Alexander Stoddart on the High Street near its junction with Bank Street.

Adam Smith

Adam Smith was born in Kirkcaldy, Fife, in 1723 and he is known as 'the father of economics'. He went to school in his home town, and at the age of 14 attended Glasgow University. He won a scholarship to Oxford to study moral philosophy and was there for six years before returning to Kirkcaldy. He had the opportunity of giving a series of public lectures in Edinburgh from 1748 to 1751 and this led to the offer of a teaching post at Glasgow University and the following year the Chair of Moral Philosophy. He might have stayed but for the offer in 1764 of a job as tutor of the Duke of Buccleuch. They travelled to the continent where he met physiocrats and philosophes including Voltaire. While travelling, he began writing a book 'to pass the time'. He returned to Kirkcaldy and continued working on his most famous book, the bible of modern capitalist economics, *An Inquiry into the Nature and Causes of the Wealth of Nations*, which was published in 1776.

He was profoundly interested in not only how money was made but in what kind of society free trade would be created, believing that economic change would make everyone richer in real terms. He saw society as evolving and slavery as an economically backward stage in that process. He advocated an end to the American War of Independence, arguing that Britain would be better served by trading with America than having it as a servile colony and was in the delegation which negotiated peace.

In 1778 Smith was appointed as commissioner of customs in Scotland and went to live with his mother at Panmure House, Lochend Close, off the Royal Mile in Edinburgh. He died there in 1790. It is said that on his death bed he expressed disappointment that he had not achieved more. There is a bronze statue of him by Alexander Stoddart in the High Street (opposite the City Chambers) looking down towards his burial place of Canongate Kirkyard and over to his birthplace of Fife. There is a commemorative plaque on the site of his home in Kirkcaldy.

19th-century heroes

Perhaps The Enlightenment paved the way, or perhaps there was something in the water, as the south-east of Scotland continued to be the cradle of progress and innovation throughout the 19th century and beyond. Heros of the period include **Andrew Carnegie** (1835–1919), industrialist, businessman and philanthropist, born in Dumfermline, Fife; **Alexander Graham Bell** (1847–1922), scientist and prolific inventor, widely credited as the inventor of the telephone, born in Edinburgh; **James Young Simpson** (1811–1870), Edinburgh doctor and discoverer of the anaesthetic properties of chloroform; **James Clerk Maxwell** (1831–1879) developer of a unified theory of electromagnetism, born in Edinburgh; and **Elsie Inglis** (1864–1917), innovative Edinburgh doctor and suffragist.

Modern-day heroes

The area continues to be home to innovation and development (from the first cloned animal 'Dolly the Sheep' to the *Grand Theft Auto* video games) and to political life (former Prime Minister Tony Blair was born in Edinburgh and Prime Minister Gordon Brown was educated in Fife and Edinburgh, represents a constituency in Fife and has his family home there), but perhaps its current most famous sons are stars of track and screen.

Sir Chris Hoy

Chris Hoy was born in Edinburgh in 1976 and is a multiple world champion track cyclist, Scotland's most successful Olympian and the most successful Olympic male cyclist of all time. Inspired by the 1982 film *ET The Extra-Terrestrial,* he started to compete in BMX cycling and between the ages of seven and 14 he was Scottish Champion, British No. 2, European no. 5 and World no. 9 and raced all over Britain, Europe and USA. In 1994 he joined the most successful track club in Britain, The City of Edinburgh Racing Club. He collected his first World Championship medal, a Silver in the Team Sprint event in 1999 and his first Olympic title in 2004. At the 2008 World Championship he became the first British man to win the sprint title in 52 years and and at the 2008 Olympics in Beijing he became the first Briton in 100 years to win three gold medals at one games. He took part in a number of celebrations throughout the country, including one in Edinburgh. He said, 'I was overwhelmed when 50,000 people lined Edinburgh's Royal Mile to welcome me home. It was an amazing feeling.' In November 2008 he was named 'Sportsman of the Year' by the Sports Journalists' Association of Great Britain and the Glenfiddich Spirit of Scotland 'Top Scot'. Along with Sir Sean Connery and other stars he took part in a campaign to invite anyone with a love of Scotland to 'come home' to enjoy the Homecoming Scotland 2009 programme.

Sir Sean Connery

Born in Edinburgh in 1930, **Sir Sean Connery** is an Academy, Golden Globe and BAFTA award-winning actor and producer, perhaps best known for his portrayal of James Bond.

He grew up in the Fountainbridge area of Edinburgh. He remembers the area with affection but recalls it as 'something of a grim no-man's-land far away from Edinburgh's historic Royal Mile and the classical crescents and squares of the New Town'. He left school early and his first job was delivering milk before joining the Royal Navy at the age of 16. His career was cut short after three years by a stomach ulcer, and returning to Edinburgh he took up various jobs, including bricklayer, lifeguard and coffin polisher. His pastime of bodybuilding would lead him to third place in the 1950 Mr Universe title—and ultimately to work as an artist's model and in small theatrical parts and chorus appearances. He considered being a footballer, but realised that an acting career would have more longevity, later saying 'it turned out to be one of my more intelligent moves'.

It would not be until 1958 that he would be cast opposite Lana Turner in *Another Time, Another Place* and it would be a further four years before his breakthrough role as secret agent, James Bond. It's said that that the character's creator, Ian Fleming, didn't initially think he had the right look, but filmgoers have often cited him as the definitive Bond. Over the next decade he would make six Bond movies. He broadened his career in films such as *Murder on the Orient Express* (1974), *The Man Who Would Be King* (1975), and *Outland* (1981) before reprising a more mature Bond in *Never Say Never Again* (1983). He extended his range further with *The Name of the Rose* and *Highlander* (1986), *The Untouchables* (1987) and *Indiana Jones and the Last Crusade* (1989). The 1990s saw more movies from *The Hunt for Red October* to *Entrapment,* and in 2000, what many have said to be one of his best films, *Finding Forrester*. Following *The League of Extraordinary Gentlemen* (2003) he took a break from acting to co-write his book, *Being a Scot* (Weidenfeld & Nicolson, 2008) and subsequently confirmed his retirement. A supporter of many charities, he donated his entire salary (well over $1 million) from the Bond film *Diamonds Are Forever* to establish the Scottish International Educational Trust.

Connery has received many industry and national honours for his work, was named Scot of the Year in 1991, made Honourary Doctor of Letters by both Heriot-Watt and St Andrews Universities, awarded the Freedom of the City of Edinburgh in 1991 and was knighted by the Queen in Edinburgh in 2000. Edinburgh being close to his heart, he said 'to become a Freeman of Edinburgh was one of the greatest honours of my life'.

The City of Edinburgh

a. The New Town
b. The Old Town
c. Edinburgh's Urban 'Villages'
d. Leith and the Waterfront
e. South Queensferry and Cramond

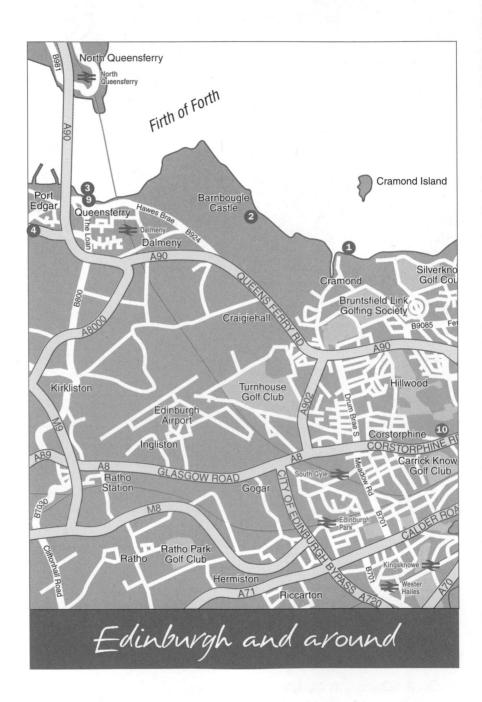

Edinburgh and around

Things to see and do

1. Cramond – waterfront village with beach and Island
2. Dalmeny House
3. Forth Bridges
4. Hopetoun House
5. Leith – The Waterfront on the Shore
6. Scottish National Gallery of Modern Art and Dean Gallery
7. Portobello Beach
8. Royal Yacht Britannia, Leith
9. South Queensferry, historic village
10. The Zoo

Unmissable highlights

01 Edinburgh Castle, Calton Hill or Scott Monument for the panoramic views, p.87

02 Take an open-top bus tour around the city, p.90

03 Visit Royal Yacht Britannia moored at Ocean Terminal, p.90

04 Experience a few pints in a traditional Old Town 'howff', p.110

05 Relax in the tranquil green Royal Botanic Garden, p.113

06 Walk along the river from Stockbridge to the Gallery of Modern Art, p.111

07 Head down to The Shore, Leith for superb seafood, beside the sea, p.137

08 Experience the magic of the Edinburgh Fringe, the largest arts festival on the planet, p.75

09 Join 100,000 revellers to see in New Year at the world's most famous street party, p.76

10 Stroll along glamorous George Street for fashion and wine bars, p.76

THE CITY OF EDINBURGH

'Edinburgh is obviously regal. She is plainly a capital. She has the superiority complex of a capital city. The air seems to demand a viceroy – you feel there should be a throne somewhere. Edinburgh is one of the few cities which cannot be exaggerated'

H. V Morton, *In Search of Scotland*, (Methuen, 1929)

Edinburgh, indeed, has attitude and an identity like no other British city. It is, undeniably, an extraordinarily popular destination year round for millions of UK and international visitors. Renowned as one of the most elegant cities in Europe, its status as a World Heritage Site is defined by its historical architecture and its cultural and literary sense of place.

When you first arrive, to get your bearings, take an open-top bus tour around town, jumping on and off at all the famous sites. The best way to appreciate the architecture is to explore on foot: stroll down the medieval Royal Mile from Castle to Palace and the Scottish Parliament; browse the Old Town for fine Scottish cashmere, antiques and whisky; wander around the New Town for designer fashion stores, art galleries and café society. Families will enjoy all the visitor attractions such as Our Dynamic Earth, the Royal Britannia ship in Leith, the Zoo, and a fun climb to the top of Arthur's Seat for a bird's eye view over the city.

Summer in the city is a magical and inspiring time when, it seems, the rest of the world comes to town. In August the population more than doubles – around 850,000 visitors attend the Edinburgh International Festival, a showcase of opera, music, theatre and dance; the Fringe; Book and Jazz Festivals; while the free street theatre, jugglers and buskers bring a colourful, carnival atmosphere.

Expect a warm and cheery welcome during the autumn and winter, a quieter time of year to experience museums, galleries, fine dining and the Winter Wonderland, featuring fairground rides, a big wheel and a skating rink in Princes Street Gardens. The compact, pedestrian-friendly city centre means you can easily walk everywhere – from the Old Town over the Mound to the New Town then downhill to the urban village of Stockbridge and Botanic Gardens. Wherever you wander you'll find quaint Victorian pubs, cool wine bars and pavement cafés for a pitstop. Above all, Edinburgh just oozes with style and romance. Shopping, entertainment and historic attractions: it's a sexy, sassy city with something unique to see and do for all ages.

THE NEW TOWN

'New Town: everywhere else in Scotland it meant the likes of Glenrothes and Livingston, places built from nothing in the 1950s and 60s. But in Edinburgh, the New Town dated back to the eighteenth century. That was about as new as the city liked things.' Ian Rankin, *Dead Souls* (Orion, 1999)

Edinburgh is a city of stark contrasts, where Princes Street Gardens separates the medieval Old Town from the elegant Georgian New Town. It's this unique blend of ancient and modern architecture, which frames the awe-inspiring city landscape. When the architect James Craig won the competition to map out major city development in 1767, it was his stroke of genius to design Princes Street, the wide Parisian-style boulevard with buildings on one side only with magnificent gardens spread out below Castle rock opposite. The New Town is considered to be a masterpiece of city planning, built in an artistic, neo-classical grid of grand squares, gardens and palatial pillared townhouses.

Today, the New Town is the smart casual backdrop for the city's café society and fashionable lifestyle. This is the place to explore the best designer clothes shops, art galleries, snazzy boutique hotels, restaurants, wine bars and nightclubs. The focal point for retail therapy heaven begins at Harvey Nichols on St Andrews Square and the luxury stores around the pedestrianised Multrees Walk.

Princes Street is regarded as the most picturesque shopping street in the world and the extraordinary setting for the Hogmanay (New Year) street party with fireworks set off from the Castle at midnight. The street is closed for special events and pipe band processions throughout the year, such as the Cavalcade to mark the start of the Edinburgh Festivals in August. Princes Street Gardens is simply stunningly beautiful year round, a city centre park to wander through and relax with its grassy lawns, avenue of trees, and colourful flower borders. Office workers and visitors alike will flock here on warm summer days for a picnic. Between November and January, the Gardens transform into a Winter Wonderland fairground for family fun. The cultural, European style of the New Town highlights the city's contemporary image as a truly romantic, classic and classy city. 'Edinburgh', said Robert Louis Stevenson, 'is what Paris ought to be.'

WHAT TO SEE AND DO

Walk around to admire the amazing architectural design of the New Town, with **St Andrews Square** at one end of George Street and **Charlotte Square** at the other. St Andrews Square Garden has recently been landscaped with an ornamental lake, flower borders and a café with patio seating. Charlotte Square Gardens is a private garden for residents, but opens up in August as the calm tree-lined oasis for the Book Festival.

As you stroll around, take note of the royal and imperial street names: George Street, after the king at the time, George III; Queen Street named after his wife;

and Princes Street after his sons. **Thistle Street** (Scotland's emblem) is a charming cobbled street between George Street and Queen Street, and **Rose Street** (England's emblem) is a narrow lane between George Street and Princes Street. Charlotte Square and Castle, Frederick and Hanover Streets linking George and Princes Street, represent the castle view and royal family names. From Princes Street take a look up at that fantastic higgledy-piggledy skyline of the Old Town. Its jumbled layers of towering tenements, the majestic **Ramsay Garden**, and towering church spires, create a painterly view which, whether silhouetted in a soft morning mist or rose-tinted sunset, will surely make your heart skip a beat. Dominating East Princes Street Gardens, is the unmissable 200ft tower – reminiscent of a *Star Wars* space ship – the **Scott Monument** built in 1846

The imposing Gothic tower, the Scott Monument

to commemorate one Scotland's foremost poets and novelists, Sir Walter Scott. A fine example of Gothic architecture, the architect was George Meikle Kemp who, sadly, never saw it completed. One foggy night in 1844 he fell into the Union Canal and drowned. You can be one of the 46,500 (or so) people who climb the 287 steps every year if you have enough puff. The £3 admission fee is cheaper than the Arc de Triomphe in Paris, which has fewer steps!

THE SCOTT MONUMENT: East Princes Street Gardens EH2 2EJ; ☎ 0131 529 4068. Entry £3; open Apr–Sept, Mon–Sat, 9am–6pm, Sun 10am–6pm; Oct–Mar, Mon–Sat, 9am–3pm, Sun 10am–3pm.

Princes Street is famous for many British high-street brand stores; while **George Street** has a relaxing and genteel ambience for sophisticated designer shopping. This is a broad boulevard of funky boutique hotels, pavement cafés, stylish wine bars, leading fashion, men's tailoring and jewellery stores.

Galleries

Hanover Street leads down the hill to Heriot Row and the top of **Dundas Street**. This is the Cork Street of Edinburgh. For a couple of blocks on either side of the street, as well as several upmarket fashion boutiques, you'll find a fascinating range of small commercial art galleries – quiet, inspiring havens of culture. Each specialises in Scottish, British and international artists, from new talent to well-established artists, with regularly changing monthly exhibitions. Start at the **Open Eye** and **Eye Two** (34 Abercromby Place, corner of Dundas Street; ☎ 0131 557 1020; www.openeyegallery. co.uk), which showcases Scottish contemporary art, ceramics and jewellery. The gallery

Edinburgh New Town

Things to see and do
1. Edinburgh Dungeon
2. Georgian House
3. National Gallery of Scotland
4. Royal Scottish Academy
5. Scott Monument .

Shopping
6. Art Galleries, Dundas Street
7. Harvey Nichols
8. Jenners
9. Multrees Walk: Designer store district
10. William Street boutiques, West End

Places to Stay
11. The Balmoral Hotel
12. The Bonham
13. The Howard
14. The Roxburghe
15. Tigerlily

Eat and Drink
16. Café Royal
17. Centotre
18. The Dogs
19. Fishers in the City
20. Oloroso
21. The Rutland
22. Scotch Malt Whisky Society
23. Vin Caffe

Visitor Information
24. Tourist Information Centre

Some of the art galleries found in Dundas Street

SCOTTISH NATIONAL GALLERY OF MODERN ART: 75 Belford Road EH4 3DR; ☎ 0131 624 6200; www.nationalgalleries.org. Free admission except for special exhibitions; open daily 10am–5pm (6pm in August).

is also a specialist dealer in European and American printmaking. **Bourne Fine Art**, at 6 Dundas Street, presents fine Scottish paintings and sculpture dating from the 17th century to the present day. **The Scottish Gallery**, 16 Dundas Street, established in 1842, showcases 20th-century and contemporary Scottish artists, international crafts, glass, textiles and sculpture. For what's on, check the free *Artmag* magazine.

It would be advisable to visit the **Modern Art Gallery**, in the West End on a fine day, to enjoy a coffee or lunch at the charming garden café. The gallery's collection includes contemporary Scottish and international art from 1900 with superb temporary exhibitions of major artists. You can also appreciate the stunning parkland and Landform geological hill and lake sculpture, which won the Gulbenkian prize in 2004. Across the road is the

The Open Eye Gallery

The Scottish National Gallery of Modern Art

Dean Gallery, surrounded by magnificent gardens, which has a world-class collection of Dada and Surrealism, including Dalí, Miró, Ernst, Magritte, and Picasso and Eduardo Paolozzi.

> DEAN GALLERY: 73 Belford Road EH4 3DS; ☎ 0131 624 6200; www.nationalgalleries. org. Free admission except for special exhibitions; open daily 10am–5pm (6pm August).

Calton Hill

Edinburgh is not called 'The Athens of the North' for nothing. With its wild grass and gorse-covered slopes and windswept ruggedness, many people climb Calton Hill for the spectacular cityscape and sea views. But the jumble of historic towers and structures at the top are very important architecturally, dating from the Enlightenment era and of classical Grecian design. Designed by CR Cockrell and William Playfair, the **National Monument**, featuring 12 giant Greek Doric columns, is inspired by the Acropolis in Athens and built to commemorate the loss of lives during the Napoleonic Wars. This National Monument is known locally as 'Edinburgh's Disgrace' due to the fact that it was never completed.

> NELSON MONUMENT: Calton Hill EH7 5AA; ☎ 0131 556 2716; www.cac.org.uk. Entry £3; open 1 Apr–30 Sept, Mon 1pm–6pm, Tue–Sat 10am–6pm; 1 Oct–31 Mar, Mon–Sat 10am–3pm.

But is a city landmark all the same and you'll have fun clambering all over the steps. Located on the southern edge of Calton Hill, the (former) Royal High School is based on the Temple of Theseus. The 106ft **Nelson Monument** was designed like an upturned telescope as a look-out

The Greek Doric columns on Calton Hill

signal tower. If you are energetic and don't suffer from vertigo, you can climb the 143 steps of the spiral staircase to the viewing platform. There used to be a time ball in the tower's mast which dropped at 1pm to assist ships out at sea to check the time. It is now being renovated. Also on Calton Hill is the old **City Observatory**, dating from 1818, which provided accurate time readings for ships' captains.

In August, Calton Hill is the site for unusual outdoor Fringe shows and also the best place to see firework displays from the castle. On the last day of April this is the theatrical setting for the **Beltane Fire Festival**, which began 21 years ago as a revival of the ancient Celtic fertility festival. Celebrating the blossoming of spring, it attracts around 12,000 people each year. With a festival spirit of revelry, music, drummers, performance art and flaming torches, a spectacular procession leads the crowd anti-clockwise around Calton Hill up to the Acropolis where the sacred Neid Fire is lit to reveal the May Queen. The whole colourful event is a ritualistic performance by druid spirits and white warrior women who conquer the spirits of the underworld to awaken the elements of Air, Earth, Water and Fire. The horned god loses his winter coat to be crowned by the May Queen as the Green Man, the symbol of summer.

Wet weather

The New Town is home to all the National Galleries, the **National Gallery of Scotland** complex on The Mound, the **Scottish National Portrait Gallery**, Queen Street (closed

The National Gallery of Scotland

Spring 2009–2011 for refurbishment) and, as listed above, the modern art galleries at the West End. Spend a wet afternoon touring the National Gallery to see the magnificent permanent collection of classical works from the Early Renaissance to the 19th century. It features artists such as Raphael, Botticelli, Titian, Monet, Van Gogh and Scottish artists like Raeburn and Ramsay. There are also seasonal special exhibits of major international artists.

NATIONAL GALLERY OF SCOTLAND: The Mound EH2 2EL; ☎ 0131 624 6200; www.nationalgalleries.org. Free admission to permanent collection; entry fee for special exhibitions; open daily 10am–5pm (6pm August).

The National Gallery complex has a bookshop, educational events, talks and the Gallery café and restaurant. This links through to the **Royal Scottish Academy**, a magnificent Playfair landmark building with Queen Victoria's statue on the roof. There is an annual calendar of exhibitions, including art graduates, the annual summer exhibition and major seasonal National Gallery of Scotland exhibitions.

ROYAL SCOTTISH ACADEMY: The Mound EH2 2EL; www.royalscottishacademy.org. Free admission; entry fee for special exhibitions; open Mon–Sat 10am–5pm; Sun 12–5pm

On your travels around the New Town, to have a clearer understanding of the architecture, middle and upper-class society and culture during the 18th and 19th century, a fascinating attraction is the **Georgian House** on Charlotte Square. This National Trust of Scotland property, designed in 1791 by Robert Adam featuring a classic Palatial façade, is a beautifully preserved townhouse, rich in original antiques, period furnishings, silver, porcelain and paintings. There is an excellent background information documentary film, as well as children's activities and knowledgeable guides.

THE GEORGIAN HOUSE: 7 Charlotte Square EH2 4ET; ☎ 0844 493 2100; www.nts. org.uk. Entry: adult £5; family £10/14; concession £4; free for National Trust members; open daily: 1–30 Mar, 11am–4pm; 31 Mar–30 Jun, 10am–5pm; 1 Jul–31 Aug, 10am–6pm; 1 Sep–31 Oct, 10am–5pm; 1–30 Nov, 11am–3pm; last admission 30 minutes before closing.

➜ What to do with children...

Children (over seven) will enjoy the Georgian House (see above) where they can try on period costumes as they explore the house and are given a fun quiz to do. For something more exciting, the very scary **Edinburgh Dungeon,** which features special effects, live actors and a Disney-style boat ride on a journey through Scotland's bloody history. It's worth noting that you can book online for fast-track discount price tickets.

THE EDINBURGH DUNGEON: 31 Market Street EH1 1QB; ☎ 0131 240 1000; www. thedungeons.com. Entry: adult £13.95/£12.95, child £9.95; discounted family tickets; open daily: Mar–June, 10am–5pm; July–31 Aug, 10am–7pm; 1 Sept–2 Nov, 10am–5pm; 3 Nov–20 Mar, weekdays, 11am–4pm; weekends, 10.30am–4.30pm.

Further afield to the west of Edinburgh is **Edinburgh Zoo,** which receives over 600,000 visitors a year, and is Scotland's second most popular paid-for tourist attraction, after Edinburgh Castle. As well as a great day out for families, the Zoo is renowned for its valuable academic research, breeding of endangered animals, studies of animal behaviour and global conservation programmes. The aim of Edinburgh Zoo is 'to excite and inspire our visitors with the wonder of living animals, and so to promote the conservation of threatened species and habitats.'

Set in 82 acres of sloping parkland, the Zoo features 180 species of animals, birds, mammals and reptiles. Highlights include the penguin field station–a vast naturalistic 'ice-flow' waterpark where dozens of King, Rockhopper and other penguins breed every spring. You can see the grey fluffy chicks being kept warm by their mother while dad fetches stones for the nest and food. The Zoo also features the only koala bears and polar bear in Britain. There are Indian rhinos, jaguars, a breeding pair of rare Amur tigers, Asian lions, sealions, flamingos, pygmy hippos and baboons. A major new attraction is the Budongo Trail,

EDINBURGH ZOO: Corstorphine Road EH12 6TS; ☎ 0131 334 9171; www. edinburghzoo.org.uk. Entry: adult, £11, child £8, under 3s free family tickets £31–£36; open 365 days of the year, Apr–Sept, 9am–6pm; Oct–Mar, 9am–4.30pm.

a purpose-built, state-of-the-art, £5.65 million chimpanzee house. With an outdoor adventure playground and indoor living pods, the Trail has been designed on a model of the Budongo Forest in Uganda to recreate a natural conservation habitat for up to 40 chimps. Another new enclosure is Living Links, a primate research centre for different species of monkeys.

... and how to avoid children

Take time out for a few hours and visit a **luxury spa** to relax mind, body and soul. Edinburgh has several to-class urban spas to indulge in a sensual health, wellness and beauty experience.

THE BALMORAL HOTEL SPA: 1 Princes Street EH2 2EQ; ☎ 0131 622 8880; www.roccofortecollection.com.
Prices: luxury spa day package from £115; Ytsara signature treatment £95; open Mon–Fri 6.30am–10pm, Sat–Sun 7am–10pm.

The **Balmoral Hotel** was voted Scotland's top Urban Day Spa (2007) by *Conde Nast Traveller* and welcomes non-residents for a spa day to its relaxing, candlelit, lazy-day, health and leisure centre. There is a swimming pool, gym, Finnish and Turkish saunas and range of ESPA treatments for men and women. Highly recommended is the Balmoral Ytsara signature package for an authentic Thai-style ritual. Using organic, exotic ingredients this is a truly calming luxurious experience.

One Spa at the Sheraton Grand won the Destination Hotel Spa award from 2003 to 2006 (British Beauty awards). Book a day pass (£65) to enjoy the rejuvenating thermal suite, with hammam steam room, laconium and rock sauna, 19m swimming pool and

The Balmoral Hotel

fabulous outdoor hydropool with body jets. There are 17 tranquil treatments rooms with an extensive programme of ESPA facials, massages and therapeutic treatments.

ONE SPA: Sheraton Grand Hotel, Lothian Road, EH3 9SR; ☎0131 221 7777; www.onespa.com.
Prices: spa day in thermal suite £65; tranquility spa day package £215; hot stone therapy £135; open 9.30am–10pm; Sat–Sun 7am–9pm.

SERENITY IN THE CITY: 9a Castle Street EH2 3AH; ☎ 0131 226 7459; www.serenityinthecity.com.
Prices: serenity lime and ginger experience £130; Reiki £70; Elemis facial £75; open Mon–Wed 10am–6pm; Sat 9am–6pm; Thur 9am–8pm; Fri 9am–7pm.

Serenity in the City has Japanese-inspired single and double treatment boudoirs, a candlelit Buddha lounge and a Zen water bed relaxation room. The spa offers Elemis facials, hot stone therapy, Serenity wellbeing massage, detox aroma wrap and a men-only grooming programme.

Entertainment

The city's main theatres and concert halls are on the southside of Princes Street, with the **Traverse**, housing world-class contemporary drama, and the **Royal Lyceum Theatre**, which has a monthly changing programme from September to May, as well as the **Usher Hall**, a short walk from the West End. **The Filmhouse** is an excellent independent Arthouse cinema (88 Lothian Road; ☎ 0131 228 2688; www.filmhousecinema.com), which celebrates global cinema year round with several special European and international film seasons. Just down the road, a new music venue and club has opened in the former Caley cinema. Now called the **Picture House,** it presents a top-class programme of singers and band. (31 Lothian Road EH1 2DJ; 0844 847 1740; www.themamagroup.co.uk/picturehouse)

For something completely different check out **The Stand Comedy Club** (5 York Place; ☎ 0131 558 7272; www.thestand.co.uk) for year-round top live acts and raw talent: 'The Stand is different…where else would they appreciate my particular brand of psychology?' Johnny Vegas asked.

Events

The Edinburgh Festivals (International, Fringe, Book, Jazz and Film) take place throughout the city across the summer. (See p.30 for details.) Summer in the city during the August Arts Festivals is exhilarating and a little bit manic, but the New Town in winter is simply magical.

Enjoy festive fun during **Edinburgh's Winter Festival**, which attracts around 500,000 visitors between the end of November and early January. The Castle creates a fairytale backdrop for the **Winter Wonderland**: a giant Christmas tree, fairy lights, a magnificent outdoor skating rink, a bungy dome, a funfair, a carousel, German and Highland Village Christmas Markets and the Big Wheel – an exhilarating 108ft skyride above Princes Street Gardens. After a whirl on the wheel or an icy skate, keep warm with some hot mulled wine at the German market, browse the craft and gift stalls, and you are sure to be glowing with the festive mood. See www.edinburghschristmas.com for details.

The city sparkles and fizzes with Christmas spirit for six weeks leading up to Edinburgh's famous New Year celebrations. On 30 December (the day before New Year's Eve), there is the must-see **Night Afore Fiesta**, a major street theatre spectacle beneath the Christmas trees and twinkling lights all along George Street.

The Edinburgh Winter Wonderland

On New Year's Eve, experience one of the world's largest and best-loved parties, the **Hogmanay Street Party** (www.edinburghshogmanay.com) with live music (including top bands and acts such as Blondie, Scissor Sisters, KT Tunstall, Texas and Groove Armada), ceilidh dancing and spectacular fireworks at midnight. Add cool shopping, cosy pubs, gourmet dining, ghost tours, lively nightlife and a feast of entertainment for a unique, fun and romantic festive treat for all ages.

Nightlife

From the 18th century, **George Street** has been the hub of High Society and today it's famous for its glittering row of glamorous wine bars and clubs for the cocktail set. A great night might include **Le Monde** (16 George Street EH2 2PF; ☎ 0131 270 3900; www.lemondehotel.co.uk), a global-themed hotel featuring Paris and Vienna bars and the Shanghai nightclub, open every night till 3am. Stroll on to the **Opal Lounge** (51a George Street EH2 2HT; ☎ 0131 226 2275; www.opallounge.co.uk), a subterranean hot spot for cool drinks and cooler DJs, specialising in VIP table packages to skip the queue, and along to the glitzy **Lulu** club below the **Tigerlily** hotel (125 George Street EH2 4JN; ☎ 0131 225 5005; www.tigerlilyedinburgh.co.uk) till the wee small hours. The Lulu cub is free after 10pm and Tigerlily hotel guests have complimentary entry.

For something rather different to usual clubbing, the place to drink and party the night away is at **El Barrio**, (119 Rose Street EH2 3DT; ☎ 0131 226 4311; www.elbarrio.co.uk), a Latino bar for Cuban cocktails and Salsa dancing.

At the West End of Princes Street the **Rutland Bar** (1–3 Rutland Street; ☎ 0131 229 3402) has a sophisticated lounge club, **The One Below**, for the perfect nightcap. Comfortable seats, cool music and full waiter service creates a real New York ambience. The main attraction of this 'iBar' is the high-tech video projection as well as private booths with iPod docks for personal music choice.

Sport

For rugby fans, **Murrayfield Stadium** (www.murrayfieldexperience.com) is the home of Scottish Rugby Union. It held the record for the largest ever attendance for a rugby union match, with 104,000 watching Scotland play Wales in 1975. Its all-seater capacity is 67,800, the largest stadium in Scotland, and has been host to the Rugby World Cup. The home matches in the Six Nations Championship are played here between February and March. Like Wembley, it's a prime venue for major rock and pop concerts.

Scotland playing South Africa at Murrayfield

🛒 Shopping

'Sasha was sitting down for morning coffee with her daughter Lizzie. Sasha had chosen Jenners' tea room because Jenners made her feel secure, and had always done so. Other shops might come and go… but she, quite rightly, remained loyal to Jenners.' Alexander McCall Smith, *44 Scotland Street*

Princes Street is where you'll find all the familiar British high street shops and it's also home (until recently) to the oldest independent department store in the world. **Jenners** has occupied the same site at 48 Princes Street since 1838. Now part of the House of Fraser group, the magnificent store has had a £3 million investment to bring the Victorian building into the 21st century, and is well worth a visit. This is the Harrods of Edinburgh with a superb Valvona and Crolla Italian-Scottish food hall, coffee shop, world-class designer fashion boutiques for men and women, a beauty hall, handbags, accessories and Hamley's toy department.

The Knightsbridge-style designer district radiates along George Street to the West End, beginning at **Harvey Nichols** which overlooks the tree-lined park of St Andrews Square. This landmark store is a stunning glass box with four spacious, elegant floors stuffed with beautiful bags, accessories, cosmetics and high fashion. Next door is **Louis Vuitton** at the start of Multrees Walk, an L-shaped pedestrianised precinct lined with all your top shops from Armani to Mulberry. Then head right, along George Street, Edinburgh's Bond Street, and one of the premier shopping streets in Britain. Here's Cruise, the cutting-edge boutique for men and women, Brooks Brothers,

Designer shopping on the Multrees Walk

Hardy Amis, Phase Eight, Coast, Hamilton & Inches and Lime Blue. And all the shops are interspersed by cafés and wine bars for a speedy pit stop or leisurely lunch. Just off George Street, an award-winning lingerie boutique, **Le Boudiche**, is on Frederick Street – a treat for ladies, or men should visit for birthday, Valentine and Christmas gifts.

One street down the hill (walking away from Princes Street) is **Thistle Street**. This block between Hanover and Frederick Street is a hidden haven of wee shops: Pam Jenkins Shoetique, Jane Davidson for fashion, and Joseph Bonnar's Aladdin's cave of jewellery. Over at the West End, **William Street** features **Helen Bateman, Sam Thomas** and **Arkangel**, three quality boutiques on this quiet cobbled row of individual boutiques for clothes, shoes, accessories and gifts. Round the corner on Stafford Street, is **Guilty**, one of three boutiques in Scotland, with a unique range of glamorous sexy clothes for women.

LOCAL KNOWLEDGE

Alexander McCall Smith has lived most of his life in Edinburgh, working as an academic (Professor of Medical Law and Bioethics). He is the internationally acclaimed writer of several best-selling series of novels, including *No. 1 Ladies Detective Agency*, *44 Scotland Street*, the *Isabel Dalhousie* stories and *Von Igelfeld*.

Favourite Edinburgh view: One of my favourite views is from Dundas Street, looking out over the Firth of Forth to the hills of Fife. This view has so many moods – at any moment the light may change and give the hills a totally different complexion: blue fading into white, green, the brown of ripe fields.

Favourite museum: The National Museum of Scotland, Chambers Street with its Great Hall and magnificent atrium. The museum has a fascinating collection of the artefacts of our past.

Best countryside drive: As you leave Edinburgh to the south, the Pentlands loom up on one side and the road snakes off and you see the hills of Peebleshire in the distance.

misty, blue, and so inviting as the countryside opens up in its soft beauty.

Most historic street: The Cowgate in the Old Town is deeply atmospheric. As one walks along the lower street and looks up, one realises what a feat of engineering the old town was. Building is stacked upon building, all imbued with that strong sense of history that pervades this part of Edinburgh.

Most stylish café: Glass & Thompson (2 Dundas Street) offers the perfect latte and an equally perfect window seat from which to watch those who inhabit and visit Edinburgh's New Town, pass by.

Best places to eat and drink: There is no shortage of establishments in the Old Town. The most traditional pub is the Jolly Judge in James Court just two minutes walk from the Castle but if you are looking for a latte and a scone, then walk down the Royal Mile to the Scottish Storytelling Centre (43–45 High Street). A much loved haunt by university staff is Caffe Sardi, an Italian restaurant (18 Forrest Road) near the Museum of Scotland.

The best... **PLACES TO STAY**

BOUTIQUE

The Bonham

35 Drumsheugh Gardens EH3 7RN
☎ 0131 226 6050
www.thebonham.com

Conde Nast Traveller magazine named The Bonham one of 21 Coolest Hotels in the World for its 'relaxed conviviality'. This grand townhouse juxtaposes classic features with modern artistic design in bold colours. Add stylish dining – ambience and food – for a cosmopolitan, seriously cool hotel in the West End.

Price: from £130, room with breakfast.

The Howard

34 Great King Street EH3 6QH
☎ 0131 315 2220; www.thehoward.com

With its discreet front door, authentic period features, antiques and touch of tartan, it's like an exclusive private club oozing quiet sophistication and gracious hospitality. Butler service, valet parking. 15 gorgeous rooms plus garden suites with private patio for relaxing hideaway.

Price: from £165, room with breakfast.

Le Monde

16 George Hotel EH2 2PF
☎ 0131 270 3900
www.lemondehotel.co.uk

This globally themed hotel has 18 suites designed around international cities. Sleep in lavish, luxury style in Havana, Rome, New York or Sydney; drink and eat in Paris, Vienna, Milan; dance in Shanghai. A fashionable, fun and funky place to stay.

Price: from £135 pp pn, B&B.

The Balmoral

1 Princes Street EH22 2EQ
☎ 0131 556 2414
www.thebalmoralhotel.com

Rocco Forte's classic, classy European capital hotel, this grand old lady originally opened in 1903 and has always boasted superior star quality. Sophisticated, elegant interior design, Michelin-star dining, tranquil ESPA spa and leisure club. Expect exceptional hospitality.

Price: from £360 (standard room) to £520 (deluxe), £690 (suite) per room.

HOTEL

Tigerlily

125 George Street EH2 4JN
☎ 0131 225 5005
www.tigerlilyedinburgh.co.uk

More of a bar/restaurant/nightclub with rooms, the design is stunningly glamorous and sexy – perfect for a romantic weekend. Lavish luxury suites with top-notch facilities like iPods, Wi-Fi and hair straighteners. Buzzing cocktail bars, cosy lounges, smart fusion food in the classy restaurant and Lulu nightclub.

Price: £195–£375 pr B&B.

Macdonald Roxburghe

38 Charlotte Square EH2 4HQ
☎ 0844 879 9063
www.macdonaldhotels.co.uk/roxburghe

Built as a grand hotel in 1881, this welcoming city centre hotel has recently had a complete face lift for 'the glorious return of the Roxburghe.' Classic and contemporary, superior, family, executive and castle view rooms and suites. Courtyard bar and smart brasserie. Leisure centre, pool, gym and spa treatments.

Price: £128–£399 double room with breakfast.

The best... **PLACES TO STAY**

SELF-CATERING

Royal Garden Apartments

York Buildings, Queen Street EH2 1HY
☎ 0131 625 1239
www.royal-garden.co.uk

Stay in a city centre luxury apartment for the price of a hotel room! One/two-bedroom apartments (sofa bed for extra guests), deluxe penthouse. Smart, spacious self-catering accommodation for couples, friends, families, children. Five-star guest facilities, breakfast coffee and muffin, bathrobes, DVDs, beauty spa, and local health club.

Price: £130–£220 (one bed), £205–£295 (2 bed), £295–£415 (penthouse).

10 Glenfinlas Street

EH3 6AQ (off Charlotte Square)
☎ 0131 225 8695
www.edinburgh-holidays.com

Elegant, comfortable s/c flat on ground floor of Georgian Townhouse beside Charlotte Square Garden. Drawing room, quietly located double bedroom, kitchen/diner (breakfast goodies and cooking essentials supplied); bathroom, utility room, with daily cleaning service. This is a beautiful home from home at the West End.

Price: £90–£160 pn, two-night minimum stay.

26 Abercromby Place

EH3 6QE; ☎ 0131 624 0084
www.26abercrombyplace.co.uk

Ideal holiday accommodation for friends or family – two double bedrooms with extra fold-up bed. Cable television, broadband, washing machine, dishwasher, pay telephone, DVD/CD. Welcome breakfast pack. Five minute walk to city centre restaurants, bars, Sainsbury's, Harvey Nichols, railway station and airport bus.

Price: £80–£120 pn, two night minimum stay.

GUEST HOUSE

Ingrams

24 Northumberland Street EH3 6LS;
☎ 0131 556 8140
www.ingrams.co.uk

David and Theresa Ingram are your welcoming hosts in their distinguished Georgian Townhouse (1812) stuffed with period furnishings. Three charming, restful pink, green and yellow double/twin bedrooms, Classic Scottish breakfast (porridge, gourmet sausages) served in grand dining room.

Price: £50 per person per night.

Four Hill Street

4 Hill Street EH2 3JZ
☎ 0131 225 8884
www.fourhillstreet.com

Magnificent New Town home with five richly furnished romantic boudoirs, (four double, one twin) all with digital TV, tea and coffee tray, quality linen and toiletries. Classic drawing room and gourmet Scottish breakfast: eggs, bacon, smoked salmon, homemade bread and marmalade. Superior hospitality.

Price: £100–£150 per room.

B&B

Moray Place

11 Moray Place EH3 6DT
☎ 0131 226 4997
www.morayplace.com

Experience this tranquil classic New Town square in the heart of city centre. Superior accommodation in this grand townhouse: luxury suite with private lounge (or child's room); two spacious double/twin rooms. Exceptional breakfast menu. Guest access to Lord Moray's Pleasure Gardens. Short stroll to restaurants, bars and shops.

Price: £40–£65 pppn, £50–£100 (single occupancy).

The best... FOOD AND DRINK

Edinburgh city centre has hundreds of restaurants for both Scottish (traditional and inventively modern) and global dining experiences, meaning that it is impossible to list them all or indeed recommend all the very best, but wherever you wander throughout the New Town, there will be a smart gourmet restaurant, brasserie, pub and café to suit your taste, appetite and pocket.

▶ Staying in

For the best food shopping, the finest food stores in the centre of town are **Harvey Nichols** food hall (30–34 St Andrews Square EH2 2HD; ☎ 0131 524 8350), **Marks and Spencer** (54 Princes Street), the **Valvona and Crolla Food Hall and Deli** in Jenners (47 Princes Street EH2 2YJ; ☎ 0131 225 2442) and **Sainsbury's** (9–10 St Andrews Square, behind Jenners). **Henderson's Farm shop** (94 Hanover Street EH2 1DR; ☎ 0131 225 6694) sells organic bread, locally grown fruit and vegetables, and vegetarian cheese. **Glass and Thomson** (known locally as G&T) is an upmarket deli and café (2 Dundas Street EH3 6HZ; ☎ 0131 557 0909).

The Eating Place Food Market takes place on Castle Street, which has been recently redesigned and laid out to create an attractive pedestrianised piazza – perfect for local office workers at lunchtime, shoppers and visitors to the city wanting to find a quiet spot to sit down in the city centre. Taking place on the second and last Thursdays of every month from 12pm to 6pm, the Eating Place aims to offer some of the best produce from the city region and other fine food. The market also reflects the rich cultural diversity of the city and provides an accessible shopping experience in Edinburgh's food and drink scene. A seasonal French and wide-ranging continental food market takes place on Castle Street on selected dates through the year. For information on food events see www.edinburghcc.com.

EATING OUT

FINE DINING

Fourth Floor, Harvey Nichols
30–34 St Andrews Square EH2 2AD
☎ 0131 524 8350
www.harveynichols.com

Harvey Nichols restaurant is the perfect mixture of sophisticated style and artistic fashionable food to match the designer clothes downstairs. Located on the fourth floor with large glass windows and an outdoor terrace for fantastic views of the castle and Firth of Forth. Two-course lunch £20. Dinner from £32.

Oloroso Bar and Restaurant
33 Castle Street EH2 3DN
☎ 0131 226 7614
www.oloroso.co.uk

This roof terrace restaurant is famous for incredible views and cool, minimalist décor. A la carte contemporary cuisine and grill menu: Highland beef, seafood and veal are specialities. There is a bar snack menu for a more relaxed lunch or pre-dinner canapés with bottle of wine. Two-course lunch £15. Dinner main course £22.

Number One, Balmoral Hotel
1 Princes Street EH2 2EQ
☎ 0131 556 2414
www.thebalmoralhotel.com

Under executive chef, Jeff Bland, this is one of Scotland's best Michelin-star restaurants. Using only the finest Scottish ingredients, expect classic French cuisine and superior service in romantic surroundings. Foie gras, rare venison, Skye scallops, apple tarte tatin. Three-course dinner £55. Chef's tasting menu £60 (plus £50 for wine pairings).

RESTAURANT

Centotre
103 George Street EH2 3ES
☎ 0131 225 1550
www.centotre.com

This bright, light, spacious ballroom restaurant takes to heart its philosophy of: 'Fresh. Simple. Italian.' High-quality fresh Artisan products imported from Milan for all-day dining: breakfast, coffee, pastries, lunch and dinner. Homemade pastas, fresh salads, chicken, seafood, Italian sausage with polenta. Two-course lunch £14. Dinner £24.

Fishers in the City
58 Thistle Street EH2 1EN
☎ 0131 225 5109
www.fishersbistros.co.uk

Specialises in contemporary seafood dishes: 'Fishers Favorites' – oysters, chunky fishcakes, mussels. Inventive Asian dishes: steamed crab in Thai green curry sauce, Monkfish, whole grilled Dover sole and market specials. Good selection of wine by the glass. Always busy, with a lively atmosphere. Two-course set lunch £12. Dinner from £21.

Scotch Malt Whisky Society
28 Queen Street EH2 1JX
☎ 0131 220 2044
www.smws.co.uk/thediningroom

The SMWS was founded in 1983 by a group of whisky-loving friends; the intimate Dining Room offers exquisite contemporary French cuisine: whisky-cured smoked salmon, Ballotine of rabbit, armagnac prunes, foie gras. Warm ambience, first-class service, fine wines, exclusive single malt cask strength whiskies. Lunch £11, two-course dinner £25.

EATING OUT

BISTRO

The Dogs
110 Hanover Street EH2 1DR
☎ **0131 220 1208**
www.thedogsonline.co.uk

With church pews, bentwood chairs and quirky decor, this award winning wine bar and restaurant has a unique, eccentric charm. As does the owner David Ramsden. Great value menu celebrates British dishes. Poached coley with colcannon, mushroom barley risotto, goat's cheese and beetroot. Gluggable wines. Two course lunch £8. Dinner £13.

The Rutland Restaurant
Rutland hotel, 1 Rutland Street EH1 2AE
☎ **0131 229 3402**
www.therutlandhotel.com

Glittering, glamorous new hotel with three floors for decadent drinking and dining at the West End. Elegant Brasserie overlooking Princes Street has intimate tables for two and round party booths. Designer food to match the look: Shellfish platter, Scotch Lamb, Steak Frite, Lemon sole, Chocolate fondue. Two course dinner £20.

Café Marlayne
76 Thistle Street EH2 1EN
☎ **0131 226 2230**

Enjoy an intimate eating experience in this tiny nine tabled restaurant tucked away on Thistle Street. The hand written menus offer fantastic no fuss French food with a Scottish twist. Quail, king scallops with black pudding and perfectly cooked seabass and lamb cutlets. Two course lunch £12. Dinner £20.

GASTROPUB

Tigerlily
125 George Street EH2 4JN
☎ **0131 225 5005**
www.tigerlillyedinburgh.co.uk

Design and Style awards galore for this maze of glamorously theatrical rooms and courtyards for drinking and dining. Sit in a Bedouin-style booth to taste modern European cuisine with touch of Eastern spice, prepared with passion. This is not just food, this is Tigerlily food. Two course lunch £12. Dinner £21.

Ricks
55a Frederick Street EH2
☎ **0131 622 7800**
www.ricksedinburgh.co.uk

Of all the gin joints, Rick's is the place. Sip a sexy Vesper, the original James Bond Martini, order a seafood platter to share (scallops, langoustines, prawns), followed by tuna steak or Porcini and truffle ravioli, with a bottle of plummy Pinotage. Smooth service, party atmosphere – a cool place for cocktails and dinner. Two courses for £20.

The Dome Grill Room
14 George Street EH2 2PF
☎ **0131 624 8649**
www.thedomeedinburgh.com

Originally the site of the old Physicians Hall in 1775 the Dome features the most beautiful classic architecture with a huge glass dome, pillars and central bar. French/Scottish fusion cuisine - chicken breast with black pudding.

Beautiful lighting and decorations at Christmas time. Two course lunch £22. Dinner £26.

EATING OUT

CAFÉ

Henderson's Salad Table
94 Hanover Street EH2 1DR
☎ **0131 225 2131**
www.hendersonsofedinburgh.co.uk

This vegetarian country kitchen is an Edinburgh institution, established by Janet Henderson in the 1960s, featuring organic produce from the family farm. Open all day for nutritious meals of fresh salads, delicious, homely stews, spicy curries and pasta dishes, cheese and homebaking. Wine bar and farm shop next door. Two courses £10–£15.

Vin Caffe
11 Multrees Walk EH1 3DQ
☎ **0131 557 0088**
www.vincaffe.com

Vin Caffe is located in the trendiest shopping district near Harvey Nichols and Louis Vuitton. Downstairs, a café serving coffee, paninis and fabulous cakes, whilst upstairs the stylish restaurant offers fresh, tasty Italian food: buffalo mozzarella salad, calamari, antipasti platters: peppers, aubergine, marinated beef, lemon tart. Two courses £22.

Glass and Thompson
2 Dundas Street EH3 6HZ
☎ **0131 557 0909**

Well established and beloved neighbourhood deli and coffee shop, frequented by local residents, Dundas Street art gallery browsers and visitors exploring New Town. An elegant ambience for a good cappuccino and platters of cheese, pâté, cold meat, quiche, hummus, salads, fresh bread. Around £12 for two courses.

🥂 Drinking

The New Town boasts a variety of drinking holes to suit every age and taste. The **Guildford Arms** (EH2 2AA; ☎ 0131 556 4312), off St Andrews Square at 1–5 West Register Street, an historic pub built in 1898, is beautifully decorated with original Victorian features and a Jacobean ceiling. Renowned as one of the best real ale pubs in the city centre, 'a bad pint is unheard of' says a regular. The **Café Royal** (EH2 2AA; ☎ 0131 556 1884) next door is ornately decorated in French baroque style, with a huge circular bar, carved mahogany, corniced ceiling and decorative painted tiles. It's a unique setting for pint of ice cold Guinness, Deuchars IPA, wines and good pub grub.

Along the pedestrianised **Rose Street** (a narrow cobbled lane between Princes Street and George Street) you'll find loud and lively wine bars and traditional pubs favoured by hen parties and stag nights for a cracking Saturday night out. Recommended is **The Brewery** (55–57 Rose Street EH2 2NH; ☎ 0131 220 1227) which used to have a brewery for **Auld Reekie Ale** on the second floor, now the Brewhouse Restaurant. Downstairs is an attractive pub serving Caledonian Deuchars IPA and guest ales. And for a taste of Latin America, there's **Tequila Joe's** (47 Hanover Street, ☎ 0131 220 6818); its sister bar nearby, **El Barrio** (119 Rose Street EH2 3DT; ☎ 0131 226 4311) serves Mexican beers, Peruvian Pisco, Caribbean tequila and rum cocktails.

For a more sophisticated drinking experience a series of cocktail-style bars line **George Street**. Winner of several design awards, **Tigerlily** (125 George Street) creates a glittering, opulent setting in the Black bar, Champagne bar and Lulu nightclub. The **Living Room** (113–115 George Street EH2 4JN; ☎ 0870 442 2718) offers a New York piano bar, lively ambience and a unique Raw Juices cocktail menu for non-alcolohic, freshly squeezed pineapple, watermelon and pear drinks. On the other side of George Street is **Tempus bar** (25 George Street EH2 2PA; ☎ 0131 240 7197) with stylish bar stools, spacious booth seating, a superlative cocktail list and is the fashionable meeting place for Edinburgh socialites.

Just off George Street is **Rick's** (55 Frederick Street; ☎ 0131 622 7800), a friendly welcoming clubby kind of cocktail bar to meet friends. Classic New York and Paris cocktails from the 1920s, Rick's own minty Mojiito and Vesper, the original James Bond martini as created by Ian Fleming, are all on offer to hit the spot. Winner of both Scottish Classic Bar and Bartender of the year awards is **Tonic** (34a Castle Street) which has real class, a jazzy vibe and bottle-juggling mixologists.

One of Ian Rankin's favourite pubs (and also where Detective Inspector Rebus drinks), the **Oxford Bar**, is hidden away off the main drag, one street down from George Street (8 Young Street EH2 4JB; ☎ 0131 539 7119; www.oxfordbar.com). One block over is Thistle Street where **The Bon Vivant** (55 Thistle Street EH2 1DY; ☎ 0131 225 3275) has a truly laid-back mood serving affordable champagne (£6 glass), tiny tapas, good food and music – DJs Fri/Sat night. Head a little further down the hill towards Stockbridge to find **Kay's Bar** (39 Jamaica Street West EH3 6HF), a cosy snug off Heriot Row/India Street with 50 fine malts, cask conditioned beers and guest ales. Round the corner is **The Standard** (24 Howe Street EH3 6TG; ☎ 0131 225 6490), a contemporary, classy American-style bar which still has the warmth of a good old local, Deuchars IPA, and fine wines by the glass. Try a spicy Bloody Mary with Sunday brunch and TV sports.

THE OLD TOWN

The Old Town around the Castle and stretching down the Royal Mile to the Palace of Holyroodhouse is the ancient heart of Scotland's capital city. Today it's a World Heritage Site and simply oozes a lingering sense of history, character and cultural heritage around every corner. Explore on foot this labyrinthine, medieval Manhattan maze of high-rise tenement flats, (very) steep steps and narrow winding alleyways, each named after the old trades, professions and residents – Fishmarket Close, Advocates Close, Grassmarket, Boswell's Court, Bell's Wynd. Walking over these worn cobbled stones in and out of this warren of wynds and courtyards is like taking a journey back through time.

The Royal Mile (in fact 1 mile, 107 yards) was described by Daniel Defoe as the 'largest, longest and finest street in the world.' It's divided into different street names – Castlehill, Lawnmarket and High Street – leading on down the hill to the Canongate. The Old Town is the dark soul of the city where ghosts of its seedy past still linger in the shadows. An entertaining way to experience both the architecture and dark secrets is to take a walking tour. Literary and historical walks by day and ghost tours by night venture down dark, sinister closes and spooky kirkyards rich in mystery, myths and legends.

As well as the Castle, all the major city museums and visitor attractions are located around here including Mary King's Close, the Scotch Whisky Experience, the National Museum of Scotland, the Palace of Holyroodhouse and the Scottish Parliament. The Old Town is a charming area to browse around the myriad of shops for souvenirs, cashmere and Celtic jewellery, with quaint old pubs for a pitstop wherever you may wander.

WHAT TO SEE AND DO

Edinburgh Castle

While there are numerous museums and exhibitions to visit on the Castle Rock, it would be best to choose a dry day to enjoy an exhilarating walking tour around **Edinburgh Castle**. And where better to start your exploration of the city than with the Castle, where the origins of the city began? As you walk up and around the steep curving hill, you'll hear stories of Scottish Kings and Queens, the prisoners of war and ancient history of this military stronghold and former royal residence dating back to the Middle Ages. Due to centuries of attack, damage and destruction by the besieging English armies, the castle has been rebuilt and developed with contrasting styles of architecture. In 1566, this was the birthplace of Mary Queen of Scots' son James, who later became James VI of Scotland, James I of England.

The oldest building is the 12th-century **St Margaret's Chapel**, popular today for weddings. Highlights include the 17th-century Royal Palace, Great Hall, dungeons,

Edinburgh Old Town

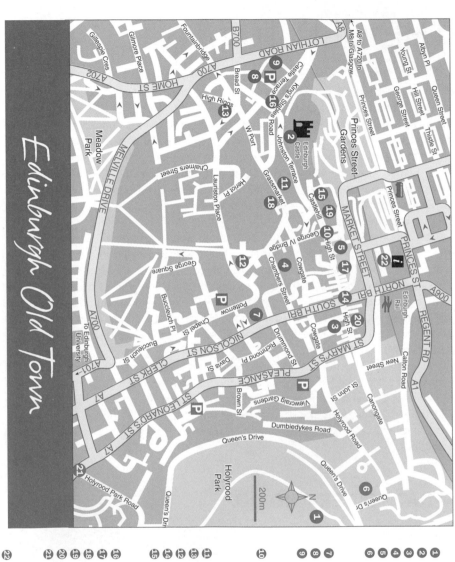

Things to see and do

1. Arthur's Seat
2. The Castle
3. Museum of Childhood
4. National Museum of Scotland
5. The Real Mary King's Close
6. Our Dynamic Earth

Entertainment

7. Festival Theatre
8. Royal Lyceum
9. Traverse Theatre

Shopping

10. High Street – (Scottish cashmere, tweed and whisky)

Places to Stay

11. Apex International and Apex City
12. Hotel du Vin
13. The Mercure Point
14. The Scotsman
15. The Witchery

Eat and Drink

16. Abstract
17. Albanach
18. The Beehive
19. Jolly Judge
20. Whiski
21. Rhubarb @ Prestonfield House

Visitor Information

22. Tourist Information Centre

The Esplanade of Edinburgh Castle

National War Museum, and the Crown Room where the Scottish Crown Jewels – the oldest in Europe – are on display. Stand on the battlements beside the vast cannons for a breathtaking view across Princes Street Gardens, over the New Town, across the Forth of Firth to the Kingdom of Fife. At 1pm daily (except Sunday) the one o'clock gun is fired – and even long-time residents will still jump at the sound of the blast. Throughout the year there are occasional entertainments and performances by costumed storytellers.

Over a million visitors flock here every year as one of Edinburgh's must-see attractions. Queues get very busy in summer so you'll save a lot of time by booking tickets in advance through the Edinburgh Castle website (www.edinburghcastle. gov.uk). Allow a few hours for your visit and wear comfortable shoes. For those with mobility problems, a courtesy car will take visitors up the steep hill. As well as guided tours, there are audio guides in eight languages, a children's trail, gift shops and two café-restaurants.

During August, an outdoor arena of tiered seating is built on the Castle Esplanade for the dramatic setting of the Edinburgh Military Tattoo. This is a phenomenally popular event for international and UK visitors, with tickets often selling out well in advance. The Esplanade is also used for music concerts, attracting top bands and singers, in the summer.

> **EDINBURGH CASTLE:** Castlehill (top of Royal Mile); ☎ 0131 225 9846; www.edinburghcastle.gov.uk.
> Entry adult £12/9.50, child £6, seasonal discounts available; last ticket sold 45 minutes before closing; open all year, 21 Mar–30 Sept 9.30am–6pm; 1 Oct–31 Mar, 9.30am–5pm; parking for disabled visitors only.

Edinburgh City bus tours

Edinburgh has five open-top sightseeing bus tours visiting the famous attractions on a choice of routes. Tickets are valid for 24 hours, just hop-on and hop-off when you want to visit a particular place of interest. Edinburgh bus tours leave from Waverley Bridge, opposite Waverley Station.

- **Edinburgh Tour:** a knowldegeable tour guide gives an entertaining talk on the history and culture of the Old Town and New Town.
- **City Sightseeing:** has a recorded multi-lingual commentary available in English, French, German, Italian, Spanish, Dutch and Japanese. A children's channel offers a Horrible Histories version for kids.
- **MacTours:** is on a vintage bus with a guide, visiting all the sites, including the Palace, Parliament, Dynamic Earth, Royal Mile, the Castle and the New Town.
- **Majestic Tour:** travels to the Botanic Garden, Royal Yacht Britannia, the Palace and Castle.
- **Bus and Boat Tour:** a journey down to South Queensferry to take a boat trip to see the Bridges and islands on the Forth.
- **Royal Edinburgh Ticket:** this special all-inclusive ticket is valid for two days on all bus tours with entrance to the Castle, Palace and Royal Yacht Britannia.

> EDINBURGH BUS TOURS: ☎ 0131 220 0770; www.edinburghtour.com.
> Prices: adult £10 individual tour; £13 valid any tour; children aged 5–15; £5; student and family tickets available. Bus tours depart Waverley Bridge, every 20 minutes.

> ROYAL EDINBURGH TICKET: www. royaledinburghticket.co.uk.
> Prices: adult £36, children £16.

Bus tours are a great way to see the sights in the city

Walking around

Spend a fine morning or afternoon exploring the old wynds and closes down the **Royal Mile** from Castlehill to the Canongate and the Palace.

At each turn, around a corner or a glimpse through an archway, you'll see stunning images down narrow wynds over the chimney pots to Princes Street and the New Town to the north. For instance, walk down **Advocates Close** opposite St Giles' Cathedral to see a picture-postcard image of the Scott Monument. Further down the Canongate, look out for many fascinating buildings and hidden gems, such as **John Knox House**, the turreted **Tolbooth** (1591), the former prison featuring an impressive clock, and also venture down **Dunbar's Close**, to find a tranquil and charming garden for a welcome rest on your tour around the Old Town.

The view of the Scott Monument from Advocates Close

Beside the Edinburgh Castle Esplanade, **Ramsay Garden** is not a garden at all but a collection of 18th and 19th-century whitewashed houses with steeply pitched red roofs. The apartments are named after the poet Allan Ramsay, whose Goose-pie

The red roofs of Ramsay Garden

The Grassmarket with its outdoor restaurants

house is an octagonal shape. The best view of Ramsay Garden is on Princes Street, from where the distinctive fairytale houses and surrounding church steeples are a prominent landmark on the Old Town skyline.

Another recommended walk is from the top of the Lawnmarket beside St Columba's Church. Take the steps down to **Victoria Terrace** on the upper level and immediately below, to the charming, curving **Victoria Street** with its row of multi-coloured shops. As you stroll down the hill, look up at the curiously contrasting styles of tall townhouses and tenements featuring an architectural blend of Gothic turrets, crow-step gables and Dutch-style architecture. Victoria Street leads down to the **Grassmarket**, which has recently been renovated to create a Parisian-style piazza with outdoor canopied restaurant tables around an avenue of trees. Located in the shadow of the Castle towering above, the Grassmarket was originally the city's cattle market (1477–1911) and is steeped in history. You can visit the site of the scaffold, opposite **The Last Drop** Tavern, from where dignitaries would stand at the windows to witness thieves and murderers hang as crowds gathered outside to watch the spectacle as a popular entertainment of the time.

Ghost walks

Edinburgh ghost tours are among the most popular walking tours of the city and the gothic Old Town is the perfect setting to hear gruesome folklore tales. The German film producer Joachim von Mengershuausen believed it must have been built by the set designers of *Dracula* for Hammer Horror films. Visitors of all ages will enjoy a ghost walking tour, combining history, architecture and spine-tingling entertainment. Some

Notorious graverobbers: Burke and Hare

In the early 1800s, Edinburgh University was at the forefront of anatomy teaching and the lecturing surgeons needed a supply of bodies. The demand led to a market for grave robbers who would enter a cemetery at night, dig up a recently buried body then sell it to the medical school, no questions asked. These body snatchers were known as 'resurrectionists'. Given a substantial fee of £10 per body by Dr Knox, Burke and Hare had to find another way to obtain 'fresh' bodies more easily; in a word, murder. In 1827 Burke and Hare went on a killing spree around Edinburgh. It is not known exactly how many of their victims arrived on Dr Knox's table but it is estimated at around 30 bodies. Finally, the body of Irish immigrant Mary Docherty was linked back to Burke and Hare, who were arrested. Hare agreed to testify in exchange for his own freedom; while Burke confessed to 16 murders but always denied having robbed a grave. Burke was found guilty and hanged in January 1829 with his body given, inevitably, to the university for medical research. Hare was released and is said to have died living in poverty in London.

are more fun and suitable for children, especially the daytime tours, while others are rather more near the knuckle in terms of spooks. **The City of the Dead Tour**, for example, is a seriously scary, supernatural ghost-hunting walk around a graveyard with a potential encounter with a poltergeist! There are dozens of professionally guided tours to choose from, all departing on or near the High Street. The guides are masters of their art, dramatic actors with sound knowledge of Edinburgh's dark and dangerous history; they enrich your imagination and instil the perfect, creepy mood for brilliant storytelling about witches, body snatching and grisly murder.

GHOST AND WALKING TOURS
- **MERCAT TOURS:** Mercat Cross, High Street; ☎ 0131 225 5445; www.mercattours.com. History and Underground Vault Ghost tours. Prices: adult £8.50, children £5, family tickets. Seasonal and year round; day and evening tours.
- **AULD REEKIE TOURS:** Tron Kirk, Royal Mile; ☎ 0131 557 4700; www.auldreekietours.com. Prices: adult £7–£10; children £6–£9. Day and evening, underground, ghost and terror tours. Complimentary whisky/beer.
- **THE CADIES & WITCHERY TOURS:** 84 West Bow (Victoria Street); ☎ 0131 225 6745; www. witcherytours.com. Prices: adult £7.50, children £5. Very popular Murder, Mystery and Ghost tours led by Adam Lyal.
- **CITY OF THE DEAD TOUR:** St Giles' Cathedral, High Street; www.blackhart.uk.com. A scary, supernatural ghost-hunting graveyard tour. Prices: adults £8.50, student £6.50, child £5. Halloween to Easter, 8.30pm and 9.30pm; Easter to Halloween, 8.30pm and 10pm.

A climb up Arthur's Seat

*'I didn't realise Edinburgh was so beautiful. I love that
whole mountain in the middle of the city thing.'* Dido

Surrounding the Palace of Holyroodhouse is the wonderful green and grassy Highland
landscape of Holyrood Park, also known as the Queen's Park. This was originally the royal
hunting ground and was later used for grazing sheep and cattle. In the centre, dominating
the city skyline is 'that whole mountain': the extinct volcanic mound of **Arthur's Seat** (250m
high) and the dramatic sandstone cliffs of **Salisbury Crag**, which resemble the Australian
desert cliffs in the sunshine. Escape to this countryside-in-the-city for fresh air and exercise,
a bracing walk, kite flying, a game of football or great cycling. There are well-designated
hiking paths like the twisting, dusty paths of the Inca trails of Peru over various routes right
to the summit. Explore further to find the ruins of 15th-century St Anthony's Chapel, and
three lochs (St Margaret's, Dunsapie and Duddingston)–all of which are nature reserves for
swans, ducks and geese. Walking routes and (free) rock climbing licences are available from
the Holyrood Information Centre, Holyrood Lodge, Horse Wynd (weekdays 10am–3pm). You
can also drive through Holyrood Park along the Queen's Drive which circles Arthur's Seat in
a single-track one-way route. Closed to traffic Sundays.

The extinct volcano Arthur's Seat towers over the city

Mary King's Close

After walking around the Royal Mile, absorbing a hint of its history and social life centuries ago, it's an exciting experience to enter the dark, underground street and houses of the old **Mary King's Close,** which was closed off after the Plague and completely built over in 1753. This unique – allegedly *haunted* – site is an underground time capsule, recreated as a five-star visitor attraction. Costumed character guides (based on real people) tell their stories of 16th and 17th-century life here. The Close was expected to attract 60,000 visitors a year, but over the past year alone, over 170,000 people have descended into the subterranean maze.

THE REAL MARY KING'S CLOSE:
2 Warriston's Close, High Street; ☎ 08702 430 160; www.realmarykingsclose.com. Prices: adult £10/£9, children £6 (over 5s only); open 21 March–31 October 10am–9pm; August only 9am–9pm; 1 Nov–31 March, Sun–Fri 10am–5pm; Sat only 10am–9pm.

Go on a tour of the old Mary King's Close with a costumed guide

Other attractions

Opposite Mary King's Close and dominating the top of the High Street is the imposing **St Giles' Cathedral** (www.stgilescathedral.org.uk), originally founded as a small church in the 12th century when the Scottish royal family made strenuous efforts to spread Catholic worship throughout the Lowlands. In 1385, a larger Gothic church was built and over the next 150 years, many more chapels were added, until the 16th century when there were 50 altars in the church. Interesting architectural features include medieval stone work, a beautiful stained glass window designed by Edward Burne-Jones and a Robert Louis Stevenson memorial. Admission to the Cathedral is free (donations welcome) and volunteer guides are on duty each day to welcome visitors and conduct guided tours on request. St Giles is Church of Scotland and has a renowned Cathedral Choir presenting regular lunchtime and Sunday evening concerts.

NATIONAL MUSEUM OF SCOTLAND: Tower entrance, Chambers Street; ☎ 0131 220 4819; www.nms.ac.uk. Free entry; daily tours.

For a broad perspective of the history of Scotland, the excellent **National Museum of Scotland** features extraordinary exhibits to illustrate the history of the nation, arts, science and natural history. The main Chambers Street entrance and sections of the Royal Museum are closed until 2011 for a £46 million refurbishment project.

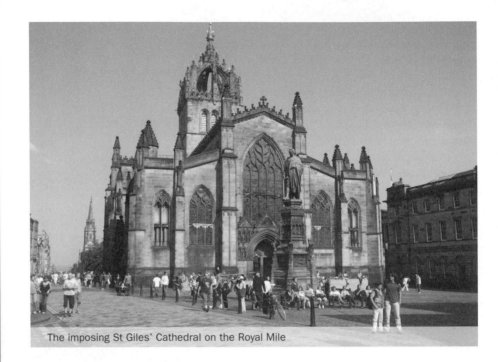

The imposing St Giles' Cathedral on the Royal Mile

THE SCOTCH WHISKY EXPERIENCE: 354 Castlehill, the Royal Mile; ☎ 0131 220 0441; www.whisky-heritage.co.uk. Prices: adult £7.50, children £3 (13–17); 12 and under free; open 7 days, 10am–6.30pm (last tour 5pm).

A visit to the **Scotch Whisky Experience** on Castlehill will answer all your questions about Scotland's national drink and major export – but have been afraid to ask. Take a

Disney-style barrel ride through the history of whisky making, with whisky tastings, café and Amber restaurant.

The literary city

To find out more about the city's literary heritage (see *The Background*, p.50), Lady Stair's House (1622) just off the Lawnmarket, is the unique setting for the **Writers' Museum**. The courtyard immediately out-side has been designated as Makers' (Poets') Court where inscriptions and quotations have been carved in the paving stones commemorating Scottish writers from the 14th century to the

The Writers' Museum has exhibits about famous literary names associated with Edinburgh

THE WRITERS' MUSEUM: Lady Stair's Close, Makar's Court, Lawnmarket; ☎ 0131 529 4901; www.cac.org.uk. Admission free; open Mon–Sat 10am–5pm; Sundays (August only) 12–5pm.

present. The Writers' Museum is dedicated to the lives and work of Robert Burns, Sir Walter Scott and Robert Louis Stevenson as well as contemporary Scottish writers, with important manuscripts, books, original furniture and personal ephemera.

CELEBRITY CONNECTIONS

A few years ago **JK Rowling** revealed that she instantly fell in love with Edinburgh when she first arrived. Having left her home and work in Portugal, coping as a single mother back in the UK, Joanne Rowling received a phone call from her sister Di, then a law student, who suggested the move to Scotland. She travelled north with her baby daughter, Jessica, and the first pages of a manuscript, the first Harry Potter story in her suitcase. This was the start of her classic rags-to-riches story – living on state benefits in a flat which was expensive to heat all day in winter. She would spend hours scribbling away at her children's story in two favourite coffee shops as her daughter slept in a pram. **The Elephant House** café on George IV Bridge claims to be the 'birthplace' of Harry Potter, as Rowling spent much time writing in the cosy back room overlooking the Castle. A sign at the entrance now reads: '*Experience the same atmosphere that JK Rowling did as she mulled over a coffee, writing the first Harry Potter novel.*'

Rowling would also also go to Nicolson's café nearby: '*I would go to Nicolson's because the staff were so nice and so patient there*' she recalls. '*They allowed me to order one espresso and sit there for hours, writing until Jessica woke up. You can get a hell of a lot of writing done in two hours if you know that's the only chance you are going to get.*' The co-owner Dougal McBride remembers this regular customer in the café. '*She would just rock the pram back and forward with one hand and write away with the other.*'

Nicolson's has since changed to a Chinese restaurant but a plaque has been placed outside the Black Medicine coffee shop (2 Nicolson Street) to commemorate the association with the former café upstairs: '*JK Rowling wrote some of the early chapters of Harry Potter in the rooms on the first floor of this building.*'

In January 2007, Rowling checked into room 552 at the Balmoral Hotel, Princes Street to complete the final chapters of *Harry Potter and the Deathly Hallows*. Now the hotel is honouring this literary episode, by renaming the room, the JK Rowling Suite, available to guests for £965 per night. The room contains a marble bust of the Greek God Hermes which Rowling signed after she finished the final book on 11 January 2007. The suite also includes the desk she used during her stay. A brass plaque is now on the front door and the door knocker has been replaced by a brass owl.

Greyfriars Cemetery is one of many locations which JK Rowling visited when she was writing the Harry Potter books. It is possible to find several gravestones with names which Potter fans will recognise: Tom Riddle, Crookshanks, McGonagall… to name a few. George Heriot's School, with its castellated towers and turrets overlooking the Cemetery, is said to be an inspiration for Hogwarts School.

Year round, day and night, there are several entertaining **Literary walks** and **Pub Tours** around the Old and New Town exploring the lives and work of Scottish writers. (See Entertainment below, and City of Literature section in *The Background,* p.50.)

The real Dr Jekyll

The original idea for Robert Louis Stevenson's novel, *The Strange Case of Dr Jekyll and Mr Hyde* comes from the true story of Deacon William Brodie (1741–1788), a professional man who was a master cabinet-maker and a member of the Town Council. But he enjoyed a lifestyle beyond his means, through gambling and mistresses and began to use his knowledge as a locksmith to copy keys, returning at night as a thief. Brodie was eventually caught when duplicate keys were found at his home. On 1 September 1788 he was sentenced to death on the gallows which, ironically, he had designed himself. It was this double life which Stevenson used to create his character of Dr Jekyll. You can visit the site of Brodie's home in Brodie Close off the Lawnmarket, directly opposite the Deacon Brodie pub which commemorates his infamous life and times.

Wet weather

A short walk from The Writers' Museum, the **National Library of Scotland** is not only a world-class library, but offers the visitor excellent permanent and temporary exhibitions on all manner of Scottish and international writers, books, manuscripts and maps. A major attraction is the John Murray Archive collected by John Murray Publishers, London, established in 1768. Over seven generations the firm grew to become one of the world's greatest publishers. The firm's historical archive of over 150,000 items is now housed at the National Library of Scotland. These items represent the lives and works of many writers of literature, science, politics and travel with private letters, manuscripts and mementoes, including Lord Byron, Jane Austen, Charles Darwin and David Livingstone, as part of a colourful and interactive presentation.

> NATIONAL LIBRARY OF SCOTLAND: George IV Bridge EH1 1EW; ☎ 0131 623 3700; www.nls.uk. Free admission; open Mon–Fri 10am–8pm; Sat 10am–5pm; Sun 2pm–5pm.

Greyfriars Bobby

You might be familiar with this wee dog through books and the 2006 film relating the story of Bobby the Skye terrier. A statue of the dog stands at the top of Candlemaker Row on the corner with George IV Bridge, leading down to the Grassmarket. In February 1858, John Gray, a nightwatchman with the city police, died and was buried in Greyfriars Churchyard and for 14 years his bereaved and faithful dog kept constant watch and guard over the grave until his own death in 1872. As the cemetery was consecrated ground, he could not be buried here, but was buried just outside the churchyard near his beloved master. A red granite stone was erected on Bobby's grave by The Dog Aid Society of Scotland, and unveiled by the Duke of Gloucester on 13 May 1981. It reads: *'Greyfriars Bobby, died 14th January 1872 aged 16 years – Let his loyalty and devotion be a lesson to us all.'*

The statue of the devoted Greyfriars Bobby

Huntly House at 142 Canongate down the bottom of the Royal Mile, is home to the **Museum of Edinburgh** with important collections relating to the city's history. If you know the story of Greyfriars Bobby you will be interested to see his collar and feeding bowl, along with also silver, glass, and decorative art. Open daily with free admission.

At the foot of the Royal Mile is the **Palace of Holyroodhouse**, former home

PALACE OF HOLYROODHOUSE: Foot of Royal Mile; ☎ 0131 556 5100; www.royalcollection.org.uk.
Prices: adult £9.80/£8.80, children £5.80 (ages 5–17), under 5s, free; open Nov–Mar 9.30am–4.30pm (last admission 3.30pm); Apr–Oct 9.30am–6pm (last admission 5pm); closed during royal visits. Check opening hours before visiting.

The Palace of Holyroodhouse

of Scotland's Kings and Queens and the official Edinburgh residence of HM The Queen and members of the royal family when visiting Scotland. A regular programme of exhibitions of the royal art collection is shown at the Queen's Gallery. There is also an attractive courtyard café.

Opposite the Palace is the new **Scottish Parliament**, which opened in 2004 and since then has received numerous awards for its controversial artistic design by Catalan architects, the late Enric Miralles and Benedetta Tagliabue.

For art lovers there are two very interesting galleries on Market Street at the foot of Cockburn Street, which leads down from the Royal Mile:

The City Arts Centre (2 Market Street; ☎ 0131 529 3993) is managed by the City Council and presents free exhibitions of paintings, portraits, landscapes, and photographs taken from the City collection of contemporary Scottish art. During the summer months, special exhibitions (admission fee) are curated to appeal to international visitors, such as James Bond book design, rare Egyptian antiquities, Michelangelo drawings and Star Trek.

The **Fruitmarket Gallery** (45 Market Street; ☎ 0131 225 2383) opposite the City Arts Centre shows cutting-edge international contemporary artists in a magnificent old warehouse building. There is free entry and a superb arts bookshop and the excellent Gallery café-bistro for coffee, cake and seriously good, healthy lunch dishes.

🏃 What to do with children

Children will enjoy the **National Museum of Scotland** (see p.95) with fun educational activities, science and discovery zones. Just down from the Castle is the black and white-domed **Outlook Tower Camera Obscura**, a family-oriented attraction for a panoramic view of the city and a World of Illusions magic gallery.

Further down the High Street is a place described as 'the noisiest museum in the world', the world's first **Museum of Childhood** and perennial favourite with adults and children alike – a treasure house of toys, games, books, dolls, teddies and train sets from the past century to present day.

Designed as a science museum for families to educate and entertain children aged 5–15, **Our Dynamic Earth** is a world-class high-tech museum in the shape of a giant white tent, telling the story of the natural world from 15,000 million years ago.

Take an interactive journey around volcanic mountains, polar landscape, oceans and tropical rain forest.

CAMERA OBSCURA: Castlehill; ☎ 0131 226 3709; www.camera-obscura.co.uk. Prices: adult £7.95/£6.50, children £5.50 (5–15 years), under 5s free; open daily 9.30am–6pm (7.30pm July/August); Nov–Mar 10am–5pm.

MUSEUM OF CHILDHOOD: 42 High Street, Royal Mile; ☎ 0131 529 4142. Free admission; open Mon–Sat 10am–5pm; Sun 12–5pm.

OUR DYNAMIC EARTH: Holyrood Road; ☎ 0131 550 7800; www.dynamicearth.co.uk. Prices: adult £9.50/£7.50; children £5.95; under 3s free; open daily Apr–June, Sep–Oct 10am–5pm; Jul/Aug 10am–6pm; Nov–Mar Wed–Sun 10am–5pm.

The Museum of Childhood, 'the noisiest museum in the world'

🎭 Entertainment

The Old Town is a focal point of the **Edinburgh Festival Fringe** (see p.75) every August, when the High Street is closed to traffic and a spectacular display of street theatre, buskers, stilt walkers, cyclists, jugglers and fire eaters entertain the crowds – in return for a small gratuity in their hat. Actors from Fringe companies will wander the street to advertise their show in person, handing out flyers. This is a must-visit attraction with daily performances on temporary stages as well as street theatre day and night. It's very useful to meet costumed actors, comedians and musicians who are advertising their show so that you can find out exactly what a show might be all about.

The busy Royal Mile during the Fringe

The Fringe box office is located here on the High Street. The **Edinburgh International Festival** (see p.75) have their headquarters just up the road at The Hub, a towering gothic old church at the foot of Castlehill. Here you'll find the Festival Ticket desk, information leaflets and the Hub café with outdoor terrace for great people watching.

Year round the **Festival Theatre** nearby, on Nicolson Street, offers a superb programme of contemporary dance, ballet, opera and theatre, and the **Queens Hall** is a small concert hall for chamber music and jazz.

This whole area between the Royal Mile, Grassmarket and Cowgate has pubs featuring music entertainment: **Ensign Ewart**, Lawnmarket, for traditional folk music, the legendary **Sandy Bells** on Forest Road has informal fiddle sessions, and a popular folk music pub is the **Royal Oak**, Infirmary Street. Catch a local Indie rock band at **Bannerman's** on the Cowgate and cocktails and DJ sounds at **Assembly**, Lothian Street.

EDINBURGH LITERARY PUB TOUR: Departs Beehive Inn, 18–20 Grassmarket; ☎ 0800 169 7410; www.edinburghliterarypubtour. co.uk. Prices: adult £9, concession/student £8.50; tours run Jan, Feb, Nov, Dec, Friday, 7.30pm; Mar, Apr, Oct, Thu–Sun, 7.30pm; May–Sept, seven days, 7.30pm.

The Grassmarket is famous for its old pubs (but beware the wild hen and stag parties on Saturday nights!), such as the quaint old White Hart which dates back to 1516 and is reputedly Edinburgh's oldest pub. (See Drinking below). Almost next door is the **Beehive Inn** with a sunspot beer garden. The Beehive is the starting point (and where you buy tickets) for the award-winning and very popular **Edinburgh Literary Pub Tour** for a great night out.

LOCAL KNOWLEDGE

Claire Askew *is an award-winning poet, editor-in-chief of arts magazine* Read This *and is the creator of One Night Stanzas, a blog to promote young writers. Claire lives in the Old Town and is currently studying for an MSc in creative writing at Edinburgh University*

Favourite café: The Forest (3 Bristo Place) is a café you must visit – an ethical, veggie-and-vegan-friendly establishment run by volunteers. Massive selection of teas and enjoy the music playlist, piano recital or poetry reading.

Favourite restaurant: The Lot on Grassmarket. The food is simple, delicious and affordable, with a bias towards traditional Scottish dishes. They host great ceilidhs and jazz events in their upstairs venue.

Best bookshop: It's easy to spend hours in Word Power on West Nicolson Street, and emptying your wallet at the counter. It's full of stuff you don't get anywhere else – Scottish literature, politics, philosophy and environment.

Favourite pub: The City Café is a funky bar just off the Royal Mile, and if you're looking for fantastic pub food, this is the place. But for the ultimate Edinburgh pub experience, try The Halfway House (24 Fleshmarket Close), Edinburgh's smallest pub and undoubtedly the best for Real Ales, with an impressive selection of whiskies and home-cooked Scottish food served till closing time.

Best tourist attraction: Camera Obscura & World of Illusions, Castlehill is a great attraction for visitors of all ages with a whole floor of interactive gadgetry, a hall of mirrors and a machine that turns you into a monkey.

Favourite street: Cockburn Street has something for everyone: The Baked Potato Shop (number 56), Avalanche Records (number 63) and Beyond Words bookshop (number 42–44), and independent galleries, antiques, quirky clothes and gift shops.

Best shop: Wm Armstrong's Vintage Clothing Emporium (81–83 Grassmarket) is a favourite of Debbie Harry and the Kaiser Chiefs, this massive store boasts everything from as-new Scottish cashmere and kilts to one-off vintage wear for men and women.

The party nightlife happens around the bars and clubs along the Cowgate. Check *The List* entertainment and lifestyle guide for all dance club nights, music gigs and events. One of the top venues is **Cabaret Voltaire** (www.thecabaretvoltaire.com) on the Cowgate, for hot dance music, club nights and live music gigs. For a lively, cool place to enjoy the best jazz music, check out **The Jazz Bar** (1 Chambers Street, ☎ 0131 220 4298).

🛒 Shopping

The Old Town has an extraordinary, eclectic mix of traders – kiltmakers, antique shops, whisky shops, woollen mills outlets, craft shops and cutting-edge fashion boutiques– all cheek-by-jowl with traditional pubs, cafés and restaurants. The Lawmarket is stuffed with tourist souvenir bazaars selling tartan tammies, scarves, sweaters and shortbread, but look carefully for quality knitwear, bags and accessories such as **Ness Scottish Clothing** (336 Lawnmarket) and **Marchbrae** (375 High Street). For traditional Highland dress and contemporary fashionable kilts visit **Geoffrey (Tailor) Kiltmaker** (57 High Street).

In contrast, there are funky fashion boutiques, jewellery, design and art galleries down the colourfully painted Victoria Street and around Grassmarket. Check out **Totty Rocks** for retro styles and accessories designed by retro chicks, Holly and Lynsey, (40 Victoria Street) and **Godiva** (9 West Port), run by a sassy lady called Fleur who displays cool and eccentric clothes by young, talented designers and vintage chic. If you want something original, spend time browsing at **Armstrong's** famous vintage clothes emporium (83 Grassmarket). Just along the road is **Anta** (73 Grassmarket) for beautiful homeware, bags and Scottish crafts, and next door **Hawick Cashmere** (71 Grassmarket), for the purest quality Scottish designer knitwear. Browse around several second-hand book shops such as **Armchair Books** on West Port and book collectors and children will love the **Old Children's Bookshelf** (175 Canongate).

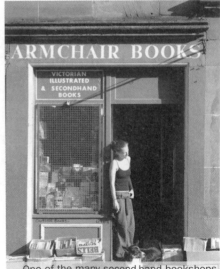
One of the many second-hand bookshops in the city, Armchair Books

The best... **PLACES TO STAY**

BOUTIQUE

The Witchery by the Castle

Castlehill EH1 2NF; ☎ 0131 225 5613; www.thewitchery.com

Seven luxurious and decadently sexy suites; secret hideaways lavishly furnished with French antiques, velvet drapes, wood-panelled walls and roll-top baths for two. Reserve a suite well in advance for a Gothic-inspired indulgent romantic weekend with gourmet dinner at Witchery Restaurant. '*The perfect lust den*' says Danni Minogue.

Price: from £295 per suite.

Scotsman Hotel

20 North Bridge EH1 1YT ☎ 0131 556 5565 www.theetoncollection.com

Five-star chic boutique hotel housed within the former *Scotsman* newspaper building. Themed rooms and Penthouse suites, all with luxury guest facilities. Enticing, contemporary menu at the hotel's North Bridge Bar, and relax in the leisure centre and Spa.

Price: £325 per night.

HOTEL

Hotel du Vin Edinburgh

11 Bristo Place EH1 2QN ☎ 0131 247 4900 www.hotelduvin.com

This sparkling new luxury Hotel du Vin offers 47 bedrooms and suites, bistro, chef's table, whisky snug, mezzanine bar, courtyard for alfresco dining and cigar shack. Located on the site of the old Bedlam asylum.

Prices: £140/£375 standard suite

Missoni

George IV Bridge, EH1 www.hotelmissoni.com

A super-stylish new boutique hotel, a joint partnership between Missoni and Rezidor hotels. Missoni's first hotel in Europe has 136 bedrooms and suites, Cucini Missoni bar and restaurant and fitness centre featuring their iconic décor and furnishings in bold, colourful patterns.

Price: Opens summer 09, check website.

Apex International

31–35 Grassmarket EH1 2HS ☎ 0131 300 3456 www.apexhotels.co.uk

The smart contemporary design is bright, fresh and fashionable. Sleep well in deluxe rooms (with bathrobes), superior (with a balcony) and eat well at Metro brasserie and Heights rooftop restaurant. Fabulous Castle view location, with a swimming pool and gym and hearty breakfasts. Families welcome with kids stay/eat free package.

Price: from £65 pppn B&B.

Apex City

61 Grassmarket EH1 2JF ☎ 0131 243 3456 www.apexhotels.co.uk

If the Apex International caters well for families, the chic sleek City hotel is for weekender/short-break cultural couples and business travellers. Stylish rooms, walk-in power showers, quiet library, fashionable bar and Agua seafood brasserie serving the very classic oysters and champagne.

Price: from £60 pppn B&B.

The best... PLACES TO STAY

The Mercure Point Hotel

34 Bread Street EH3 9AG
☎ 0131 221 5555
www.point-hotel.co.uk

Located a short walk from Grassmarket, between West End and Old Town, this is a chic, sleek design hotel with Parisian brasserie and cool cocktail bar. Colourful, stylish bedrooms, and suites, some with Castle view. Children (up to 11) stay free sharing parents' room.

Price: £75–£125 room, £155–£250 suite.

B&B

2 Fingal Place

The Meadows EH9 1JX
☎ 0131 667 4436

Your hostess is Gillian Charlton-Meyrick, who is a multi-lingual Blue Badge guide, with a long career in the tourism and hospitality profession. Two pretty twin en suite bedrooms, with private entrance, are located in this 1825 townhouse situated on the Meadows parkland with views of Arthur's Seat.

Price: £75–£90 prpn.

SELF-CATERING

Royal Mile Residence

219 High Street, Royal Mile EH1 1PE
☎ 0131 226 5155
www.royalmileresidence.co.uk

Central address in the heart of the Old Town for a weekend break with friends, a romantic break, or a family holiday. One/two-bed luxury apartments, stylish design, daily maid service, homely comfort, cook in/eat out, and complimentary use of local health club.

Price: £150–£175 pn.

Gladstone's Land Apartments

477B Lawnmarket, Royal Mile EH1 2NT
☎ 0844 493 2108
www.ntsholidays.com

An extraordinary, unique apartment within Gladstone's Land, the 17th-century townhouse museum owned by the National Trust of Scotland, which is open to the public. Two private one-bedroom self-catering flats upstairs have a kitchen, lounge and bathroom.

Price: from £350 weekend, £500 week.

5/6 Ramsay Garden

EH1 2NA; ☎ 0131 558 1108
www.dickins.co.uk

Spectacular location beside the Castle, overlooking Princes Street towards the Firth of Forth. The apartment is on two levels, with three double bedrooms, two bathrooms, a spacious living room with large dining table. There is cable TV, DVD and CD players, as well as a balcony and shared garden.

Price: £600–£960, three nights, £600–£1,200 week.

HOSTEL

Smart City Hostel

50 Blackfriars Street EH1 1NE
☎ 0131 524 1989
www.smartcityhostels.com

More a modern budget hotel than hostel, for backpackers, families, friends and couples, with en suite bedrooms for two, four, six, eight and 10 guests. Located just off the Royal Mile with excellent facilities (laundry, self-catering kitchens) and a stylish café bar.

Price: £50–£65 pp (two sharing), £20–£27 (four sharing), £18–£25 (six sharing).

The best... FOOD AND DRINK

As a central area for visitors, the Old Town has dozens of cafés, coffee houses, restaurants, pubs (with good home cooking), bistros, bars, and several quality delis and food and spirit merchants selling artisan local food and, of course, Scotch whisky.

▶ Staying in

The weekly **Edinburgh Farmers' Market** takes place on Castle Terrace every Saturday, 9am–2pm (☎ 0131 652 5940; www.edinburghfarmersmarket.com). Featuring 35 food producers, this is Scotland's largest market and was voted Britain's best farmers' market by National Farmers' Retail and Markets Association (FARMA) and it also scooped a national award in *Country Life* magazine.

Victoria Street is the place for foodies and imbibers of fine drink. The very best cheesemonger in town is at 30a Victoria Street, **I J Mellis**, an absolute gourmet shop selling the finest farmhouse and artisan cheese from around Scotland and UK. You will find it easily by the strong whiff drifting up the street! **The Whisky Shop** nearby at no. 28 has a huge selection of single malts and blended whiskies for every budget. They stock famous brands, independent bottlings, miniatures and rare single malt whiskies in barrels. These are bottled to order for customers looking for something truly different. Up the road at no. 32 is **Demijohn**, specialising in Scottish Blackwood dry gin, liqueurs and olive oil. For a fabulous range of fine tea and coffee, visit **Cuttea Sark**, at no. 26.

Takeaways

The Baked Potato Shop (56 Cockburn Street; ☎ 0131 225 7572) around the corner from the High Street, is the best in town, with every conceivable filling from veggie chilli to haggis. For traditional fish 'n' chips **The Clamshell** is at 148 High Street (☎ 0131 225 4338), and also **Bene Fish Bar** (162 Canongate; ☎ 0131 557 1092) where Princes William and Harry reputedly ordered a takeaway when staying at the Palace.

For authentic huge, thin-base pizzas, head to **Mammas American Pizza Company** (30 Grassmarket; ☎ 0131 225 6464). For a healthy snack try **Hula** (☎ 103 West Bow; ☎ 0131 220 1121) for fruit smoothes, juices and wraps. Up the road, **Oink** is an innovative hog-roast café and takeaway (34 Victoria Street; ☎ 0131 220 0089). It sells only two rolls: a hog roast with sage and onion, apple sauce or chilli, and hog roast with crackling.

EATING OUT

FINE DINING

Abstract
33 Castle Terrace EH1 2EL
☎ 0131 229 1222
www.abstractrestaurant.com

This serious, sophisticated, smart European restaurant is stylish with a capital S. Dining here is not just about eating – there's a touch of theatre about it. Exquisite, exciting cuisine, in a glamorous setting with piano bar. Sample the seven-course chef's menu (£55).

Price: £12.95 (lunch), or a la carte two, courses £25.

Rhubarb
Prestonfield House,
Prestonfield Road EH16 5UT
☎ 0131 225 1333
www.rhubarb-restaurant.com

Within the wonderfully baroque Prestonfield House Hotel, treat yourself to a romantic, opulent dining experience. Try an aperitif in a velvet-draped salon then taste foie gras with roast fig, lobster thermidor, rhubarb parfait. You can also stay overnight in a decadently deluxe bedroom.

Price: expect to pay £16.95 (lunch), £39 for two-course dinner.

RESTAURANT

Santini
Sheraton Grand Hotel & Spa,
8 Conference Square EH3 8AN
☎ 0131 221 7788
www.santiniedinburgh.co.uk

Hidden beside the One Spa complex, Santini is the 'Dolce and Gabbana' of fashionable, stylish Italian cuisine. First sip a chilled flute of Prosecco in the glamorous bar. Try carpaccio di tonno, linguine ai frutti di mare or vitello alla milanese.

Price: set lunch/dinner, £9.50/£16.50; a la carte two-course dinner £21.

Monteiths
57–61 High Street EH1 1SR
☎ 0131 557 0330
www.monteithsbar.co.uk

Hidden away down an alleyway, there's a courtyard patio, cosy bar and romantic candlelit Highland lodge ambience with stag heads and purple leather armchairs. Inventive modern Scottish cooking – scallop ravioli, venison, smoked haddock with black pudding.

Price: Two courses and half a bottle wine, around £28.

North Bridge Brasserie
Scotsman Hotel,
20 North Bridge EH1 1YT
☎ 0131 556 5565
www.theetoncollection.com

Within the stunning Victorian wood-panelled reception hall of the former *Scotsman* newspaper building, this is a buzzing, busy bar and brasserie. Romantic, cosy booths or mezzanine-level tables. Inventive, contemporary cooking using fine Scottish produce: Perthshire lamb, Loch Tarbert scallops, salmon with truffled salt cod.

Price: Two courses around £20.

Agua at the Apex City
61 Grassmarket EH1 2JF
☎ 0131 243 3456
www.apexhotels.co.uk

Exciting new dining concept, very popular with hotel guests and non-residents. Cool bar for cocktails, wine, oysters, smoked salmon, seafood platter. Restaurant menu offers seasonal variation on superb quality fish and seafood, organic Shetland creamy white Salmon, seabass, halibut. Also offers steak, chicken and vegetarian dishes.

Price: set price menu £19.95.

EATING OUT

Nile Valley
**6 Chapel Street EH8 9AY
(near Bristo Square).
☎ 0131 667 8200**

A well established, beloved favourite for laid back ambience, authentic North African cuisine and smiling staff. Eat in the upstairs café or the cosy candle-lit, romantic basement. Speciality lamb, chicken, fish, veggie bean and okra chilli. BYOB at no charge.

Price: £5.99 set lunch, two course dinner £16.50.

BISTRO

Olive Branch Bistro
**44 George IV Bridge EH1 1EJ
☎ 0131 226 4155
www.theolivebranchscotland.com**

Well established Edinburgh chain of smart, lively neighbourhood bistros, serving quality freshly prepared sandwiches, salads, burgers, fish, meat, pasta dishes. Open all day, from breakfast, weekend brunch to dinner.

Price: Starters £5, main courses under a tenner. Reservation essential at this popular place. And check out the Deli upstairs.

David Bann
**56 St Mary's Street EH1 1SX
☎ 0131 556 5888
www.davidbann.com**

Award winning and well established gourmet vegetarian restaurant. Sophisticated setting with stylish and imaginative good food. Menu includes salads, soup, risotto, crepe, chilli and Vegan dishes. And to drink? An exciting choice of beers - Kelpie seaweed ale (as well as wine and cocktails).

Price: two courses £15. All day weekend brunch £6.

GASTROPUB

The Albanach
**197 High Street EH1 1PE
☎ 0131 220 5277**

The name means 'Scottish' in Gaelic. This cosy stone walled pub has a dining room upstairs. Modern Scottish cuisine with hearty good food to feed you up – cullen skink, smoked salmon, mussels, stews, gourmet sausages, haggis (veggie haggis too), with mash and whisky sauce. Friendly service.

Price: two courses only £12.

CAFÉ

Always Sunday
**170 High Street EH1 1QS
☎ 0131 622 0667
www.alwayssunday.co.uk**

This is a very special hideaway, a 'feel good' place where you can relax over breakfast, coffee, leisurely lunch or afternoon tea, where the mood *is* always Sunday. Quality of homemade healthy savoury dishes, fabulous, fresh salads and wheat/sugar free cakes is exceptional.

Price: two courses around £8.50.

The Elephant House
**21 George IV Bridge EH1 1EN
☎ 0131 220 5355
www.elephanthouse.biz**

'Harry Potter was born here; a literary café where JK Rowling wrote, with views of the Castle for magical inspiration. Charming tea and coffee house, open for breakfast, cakes, salads, sandwiches, beer, wine. Live jazz evenings. Also does takeaway too.

Price: average snack £7.

⬧ Drinking

The Old Town is the place to sample a good pint or dram of whisky in some atmospheric old pubs – howffs – such as the historic **Jolly Judge** on James Court with its old oak beams and log fire. The very traditional wood-panelled **Bow Bar** on Victoria Street has won an award for best drinkers' pub in Britain, with staff who know their whisky (150 malts) and an interesting mix of English and Scottish cask beers.

The **Whiski** pub, High Street, claims to have 250 single malts and also speciality whisky cocktails, plus hearty pub grub served till late. **The Canon's Gait** down the Canongate has a fine reputation for having a good range of beers, comfy seats, quiz nights and lively ambience.

At the foot of Cockburn Street is **Ecco Vino**, a casual, laid-back all-day wine bar with extensive global list, vintage labels and discounted bin-end bottles. The **Half Way House** (off Cockburn Street on Fleshmarket Close) is a tiny wee place, like someone's living room and an award-winning Camra pub serving real ales from small Scottish breweries.

The Grassmarket boasts some of the oldest pubs in the city, all in a row along the northside of the street, dating back to the days when men used to go visit the market wearing swords and pistols and then have a few drinks in the taverns. This market square today is a popular place for the weekend revellers and stag and hen nights. This is also a great area during summer months with tables and chairs right along the pavement outside all these pubs for lunchtime and evening drinks.

The **White Hart Tavern** (34 Grassmarket) which dates from 1516, claims to be the oldest pub in Edinburgh and offers regular live folk, blues and country music.

Maggie Dickson (92 Grassmarket) is named after the pub's 18th-century landlady who had been sentenced to death for concealing the body of a still-born child. She went to the gallows here on 2 September 1726 but actually survived and was heard banging from inside the coffin. Known as 'half-hangit Maggie', she lived another 40 years. **The Beehive Inn** (18–20 Grassmarket) is from where the Edinburgh Literary Pub Tour departs.

EDINBURGH'S URBAN 'VILLAGES'

If the New Town is smart, grand and gracious in its architecture and lifestyle, just stroll down the hill from George Street and you enter the cool, casual and cultural world of **Stockbridge**. This quiet, prosperous residential neighbourhood (similar to London's Hampstead) has long attracted artists, historians and writers—notably the artist Sir Henry Raeburn who owned two adjoining estates, Deanhaugh and St Bernard's, which he developed with architect James Milne to create curving crescents, grand streets of tall townhouses and private gardens.

Today this is a distinctive, fashionable urban village, yet it is only a 10-minute walk up the hill to the New Town. The Bohemian ethnic culture of the 1950s and 1960s has gentrified into a laid-back, arty ambience of galleries, wine bars, bistros and delis and is famed for its eclectic range of homeware, fashion, jewellery and vintage clothes boutiques. Stockbridge was indeed shortlisted by The Academy of Urbanism for the award 'Great Neighbourhood of the Year: 2009' chosen from a selection of 10 UK neighbourhoods as one of three finalists.

An enchanting 'rural' walk takes you from Stockbridge through **Dean Village** along the river to the National Gallery of Modern Art and the Dean Gallery. Nearby is the Royal Botanic Garden—an absolute must-visit attraction any time of the year.

The eastern side of the New Town and **Broughton Street** district is another arty, lively, cosmopolitan, multi-cultural neighbourhood with quirky fashion studios, Polish cafés, a tattoo parlour and health food stores. It's affectionately known as 'the pink triangle' due to the many stylish residents and gay bars and clubs. Bordered by Leith Walk and the New Town, it's sassy, edgy and vibrant. This is the street for seriously cutting-edge trends in fashion and style. Around Stockbridge and Broughton Street there's a fascinating range of niche shops, making these city villages a great place for a day out. You can shop and get fed and watered at the many eateries, then pick up some fine food and drink from the specialist booze and food shops.

WHAT TO SEE AND DO

It's an easy walk down from George Street in the centre of town, down Frederick Street, which leads to Howe Street where you'll see St Stephen's Church, designed by William Playfair in 1828, featuring a most imposing palatial structure with its landmark square 162ft tower. From here, bear left onto **St Stephen's Street,** at the far end of which (past a curving cresent of modern apartments and over Clarence Street) you'll find yourself in the heart of Stockbridge.

'I was in quite a groovy street the other day. The doors were all painted different colours and there was this strange old shop that sold the most amazing old clothes.

"Stockbridge", said Matthew, "It must have been Stockbridge, St Stephen's Street, probably".' Alexander McCall Smith *Love Over Scotland*

Along this colourful, cultural, buzzing street is a rich art and café-bar scene with an attractive row of independent galleries – **Scotland Art, Laurel Gallery, Rosie McKenzie** art, **Lucie Fenton, Studio Art,** as well as **Flaubert Gallery** round the corner on **NW Circus Place** and **Alpha Art** (52 Hamilton Place) further on. You could spend hours browsing the affordable art exhibitions for paintings, prints, sculpture, crafts, cards and contemporary jewellery. Around here too there is a plethora of small fashion, gift and distinctive homeware boutiques, vintage clothes stores, quirky antique

Street in Stockbridge

shops as well as beauty salons, cafés, restaurants, pubs, bars. A tiny cul de sac beside Scotland Art gallery (2 St Stephen's Place) features a charming old archway with faded letters reading 'Stockbridge Market'. Dating from 1824, this was the site of fish, poultry, fruit and vegetable stalls, and while the market has gone, the sign

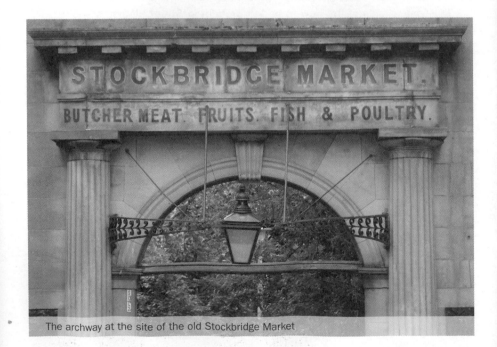
The archway at the site of the old Stockbridge Market

The best of... EDINBURGH

LIKE A THEATRICAL SET DESIGN, DOMINATED BY THE CASTLE ROCK, EDINBURGH PRESENTS A ROMANTIC EXPRESSION OF ITS FINE ARCHITECTURAL HERITAGE. EXPLORE THE MEDIEVAL OLD TOWN, GEORGIAN NEW TOWN, CHARMING URBAN VILLAGES AND THE WATERFRONT, TO EXPERIENCE THE RICH HISTORY OF THIS GRACIOUS CAPITAL CITY COMBINING CLASSICAL DESIGN WITH A CONTEMPORARY, COSMOPOLITAN LIFESTYLE.

Top: Victoria Street; Bottom: Edinburgh Sunset

Top: Ramsay Garden from Princes Street;
Middle: Scott Monument and Gardens; Bottom: Edinburgh Winter Skyline

Top: Ramsay Statue and Castle;
Middle: Hogmanay Fireworks; Bottom: Stockbridge

Top: Arthur's Seat; Middle: High Street Fringe Performers; Bottom: Dean Gallery

The Royal Botanic Garden

still remains, while contemporary design shops and galleries have taken the place of vendors selling cod and carrots, oysters and apples.

NW Circus Place leads down to the Stock Bridge (1830) spanning the Water of Leith, the pretty river which flows from the south-west of the city down to the port of Leith. Along **Deanhaugh Street** and **Raeburn Place**, you'll find more great shopping, bars, cafés and superb local restaurants.

A 10-minute stroll from Raeburn Place, along St Bernard's Row following the curving river is the **Royal Botanic Garden** located beside Inverleith Park, between Inverleith Row and Arboretum Road. Surrounding a Georgian mansion, Inverleith House (now a stylish art gallery), the Garden features some superb sculptures by Andy Goldsworthy dotted amongst the Californian redwoods and monkey puzzle trees.

This beautifully tranquil 72-acre park features a world-class display of exotic trees, plants and flowers, rhododendron bushes, specialist Chinese zen garden, rock garden, woodland, Palm houses dating from 1850, a beech hedge, herbaceous border and the Queen Mother's garden. There are suided tours available, as well as wheelchair access, a shop and a café.

ROYAL BOTANIC GARDEN: Main East Gate: 20a Inverleith Row EH3 5LR; ☎ 0131 552 7171; www.rbge.org.uk. Free entry, £3.50 for Palm houses; open Apr–Sept 10am–7pm; March and Oct till 6pm; Nov–Feb till 4pm. West Gate: Arboretum Place re-opens summer 2009.

From **St Bernard's Bridge** off Dean Terrace you can take a leisurely stroll along the pathway (which has a good cycle track) beside the **Water of Leith** to the Dean Village. On the way you'll see the classic 'pagoda' of **St Bernard's Well**. Architect Alexander Naismyth (1788) based the design on Sybils's Temple at Tivoli with 10 columns in a circle surrounding a statue of Hygeia in Coade stone. The interior has a mosaic floor in terracotta and white, with an ornate mosaic domed ceiling and gilded sun-face. The mineral water from the well was regarded to be of great medicinal value and on payment of five shillings for a season, subscribers could partake of a cup or two of water each morning followed by an exercise regime. St Bernard's Well is open on the first Sunday of each month during the summer, April to July, every Sunday during August, and on Doors Open Day in September.

From the well, it's a short walk along the river and under the impressive span of the Dean Bridge to the Dean Village, which, despite some modern tastefully designed apartments being built around the periphery, is well preserved. As you walk through the cobbled streets you'll see the dates of buildings and the original names of streets such as Miller Row and Bell's Brae, denoting the old flour water Mills. Follow the path down on to the riverbank again with signposts along the way to the **Dean Gallery** and further down the river, the **Scottish National Gallery of Modern Art**.

SCOTTISH NATIONAL GALLERY OF MODERN ART AND DEAN GALLERY: 75 and 73 Belford Road EH4 3DR; ☎ 0131 624 6200; www.nationalgalleries.org. Free admission except for special exhibitions; open daily 10am–5pm (6pm August).

It would be advisable to visit the Scottish Gallery of Modern Art on a fine day, to enjoy a coffee or lunch at the charming garden café. You can also appreciate the stunning parkland and Landform geological hill and lake sculpture, which won the Gulbenkian prize in 2004. Children love running up and down the hill and around the lake. The Gallery houses a prime collection of international and Scottish contemporary art dating from 1900. This is a stunning classically designed building. Formerly an orphanage, it still retains the original high banisters up the curving staircase, designed to protect the children.

If you are walking around the Broughton area, near the corner of York Place, outside St Mary's Cathedral are three grand bronze sculptures by the famous Edinburgh artist, **Eduardo Paolozzi**. Called *The Manuscript of Montecassino* the sculptures commemorate the Italians who fought during the Second World War. Paolozzi was a founder of Brtish Pop Art, an extraordinary sculptor of huge powerful works and overall an artistic collossos. A permanent display and reproduction of his studio is housed at the Dean Gallery. As writer JG Ballard said of him, 'If the entire 20th century were to vanish in some calamity, it would be possible to reconstintute a large part of it from Paolozzi's work.'

Madame Doubtfire

A well-known Stockbridge resident was Madame Doubtfire, aka Mrs Annabell Coutts, a pawnbroker and money lender during the 1920s depression. She owned a rag and bone shop on South-East Circus Place and her name remained in large faded-gold letters above the door for years after her death. The novelist and Children's laureate Anne Fine used to live nearby and borrowed the name for her novel, later adapted into a film about a Scottish nanny, played by Robin Williams. Madame Doubfire's favourite saying apparently was 'the walls have ears'.

Nearby on Picardy Place is a fine statue of **Sherlock Holmes** by Gerald Laing. Sir Arthur Conan Doyle was born and lived in the area and there's also a Conan Doyle pub nearby on the corner of York Place. Look at the statue carefully and you'll notice that on his pipe is the inscription 'This is not a pipe', a tribute to the surrealist artist Magritte's 1929 painting, *La Trahision des Images*. Stand on a ledge on the plinth and feel around beneath Sherlock's feet – you'll feel the paw prints of the Hound of the Baskervilles!

Wet weather

At the foot of Broughton Street, the corner of East London Road is the **Mansfield Traquair church**, a former Catholic Apostolic church. This historic building is now preserved by a trust due to its magnificent murals by Phoebe Traquair. Phoebe Anna Traquair (1852–1936) was the leading artist in the Arts and Crafts movement in Edinburgh. She worked in a wide range of media – painting, manuscript illumination, book cover tooling and mural decoration. She exhibited in Chicago, London, Turin and St Louis, but the decoration of the Mansfield Church helped to confirm her international recognition. The church is used for weddings and special events and is open to the public on the second Sunday each month and extra days during the Festival.

What to do with children

Children will love a walk around the Botanics (as the Royal Botanic Garden is locally known), running across the lawns, hiding behind bushes, chasing squirrels and feeding the swans. Look out for regular kids' events. Opposite the West Gate is **Inverleith**

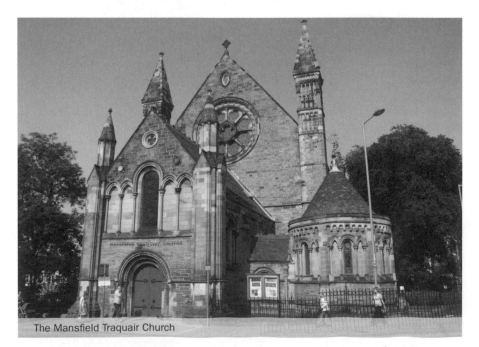
The Mansfield Traquair Church

Park, a haven for families with a toy boating pond, football and cricket pitches and a playground with swings and a slide.

⛻ Entertainment

Theatre and cinema

An extraordinarily diverse range of shows for all tastes is staged throughout the year at **The Playhouse Theatre** (18–22 Greenside Place EH1 3AA; ☎ 0870 606 3424). The programme includes touring musicals (heading for the West End in London), opera, classical and contemporary dance, kids shows, top singers and bands.

A popular Fringe and year-round venue is the **Theatre Workshop** (34 Hamilton Place, Stockbridge EH3 5AX; ☎ 0131 226 5425), which offers Seasonal Community shows and touring productions. The theatre's aim is to be all inclusive and accessible for actors and audience alike.

The **Omni Centre** (28 Greenside Row EH1 3AJ; ☎ 0131 524 7770) is an entertainment superstore, with an excellent Vue cinema complex, Virgin leisure centre and restaurants and bars.

Entrance to the Omni Centre

Nightlife

Two clubs worth a visit in this area are **CC Bloom's Club** (23 Greenside Place; ☎ 0131 556 9331), a welcoming and friendly gay bar and nightclub (no entry charge; Mon–Sat 6pm–3am/Festival till 5am) and **Luna** (14 Picardy Place; ☎ 0131 556 3553; www.lunaedinburgh.co.uk). This is the city's best loved nightclub. A dancehall since 1918, the glamorous ballroom creates a fabulous dance space offering indie/punk, tech-house, underground, gay and burlesque club nights.

🛒 Shopping

You could spend an enthralling afternoon browsing the independent fashion, gift, homeware, antique and curio shops around Stockbridge. **St Stephen's Street** is an Aladdin's cave of small shops selling art, jewellery and fashion; check out Elaine's vintage clothing and Gramophone Emporium for vinyl records and 78s. Just around the corner at 22 NW Circus Place, make time to visit **Diana Forrester**, a fabulous

LOCAL KNOWLEDGE

Susanna Beaumont is the passionately creative entrepreneur, founder and director of the Doggerfisher Art Gallery and agency, promoting the work of leading contemporary artists, based in Scotland and beyond, exhibiting work at Venice Biennale, Frieze and other major art fairs. The gallery is within a former tyre garage at 11 Gayfield Square. Susanna lives and works in the Broughton district of the New Town.

Best bar: The Cumberland Bar with a fine willow tree in a small garden, a friendly bar, good wines and importantly a pub that does not attempt to masquerade as a style bar or a fancy eatery.

Favourite food shops: On Broughton Street, Broughton Deli for gorgeous home cooking, wonderful lemon tart and hearty bread to takeaway or eat in. Also, Real Foods is an emporium of nuts, pulses and every imaginable grain and herbal tea. This is a place to browse and study obscure and familiar ingredients and tasty treats.

Best place to sit or walk the dog: Hopetoun Crescent Garden is a small remnant of what was once the Botanic Gardens, before they moved to their current location in Inverleith back in the 19th century. Still partially run by the Botanics, it is a delightful enclave of greenery and fine trees.

Most interesting visitor attraction: Mansfield Church is now a venue for hire for weddings, fashion shows and social events but still quite an extraordinary place with stunning murals by the 19th century artist Phoebe Traquair.

Best walk: Calton Hill is an easy-to walk-up hill with brilliant views of the city, the Forth and Arthur's Seat. Studded with monuments and a one-time observatory it gives a splendid sense of Edinburgh's wonderful typography.

117

French homeware and accessories boutique. Immediately opposite is **Anta** which has the most beautiful contemporary Scottish fabrics, bags, rugs and accessories. Across the bridge over the Water of Leith, at 8 Deanhaugh Street is **Chic and Unique**, a magical salon for gorgeous Art Deco, 1920s–1960s jewellery. Keep walking along the main road from here to Raeburn Place, where there's a wonderful collection of upmarket charity shops (clothes, records, books), galleries, jewellery, fashion and gift boutiques. **Bliss** is a delightful gift, accessory and baby clothes shop at 5 Raeburn Place (there is also another branch at 111 Broughton Street).

For beauty advice and professional cosmetic treatments, **Dolly Leo** (22 Raeburn Place; ☎ 0131 315 2035) is a stylish apothecary with an exclusive range of niche skin care products. Look for the gold velvet chaise longue in the window.

A 20-minute walk from Stockbridge is **Broughton Street** with its laid back multicultural buzz. **Concrete Wardrobe** (50a Broughton Street) is a fantastic gem of shop specialising in clothing by young, new Scottish designers whose work is quality, affordable and often exclusive to this boutique. **Joey D** (54 Broughton Street) is a genius craftsman who deconstructs vintage tweed, leather and denim to create extraordinary, unique, urban clothes and accessories for men and women. A few doors down is **Threadbare** (66a Broughton Street), an amazing little place, well worth visiting, with lovely staff and lots of well-picked vintage pieces and new garments made in the shop. It specialises in eclectic and unusual clothes.

For an inspiring artistic environment, check out **Doggerfisher**, a short stroll from Broughton Street at 11 Gayfield Square (☎ 0131 558 7110). Susanna Beaumont founded this contemporary agency to promote established and new generation artists (Turner Prize winners) through exhibitions at her gallery and international art fairs.

For Ian Rankin fans, **Gayfield Square police station** is just up the road, where the fictional detective Inspector Rebus worked in his final years.

The quirky clothing store, Threadbare

The best... **PLACES TO STAY**

BOUTIQUE

Channings 🛌 🍴

15 South Learmonth Gardens EH4 1EZ
☎ **0131 332 3232**
www.channings.co.uk

Former home of Sir Ernest Shackleton, Arctic explorer, this hidden gem is simply charming, with a tranquil patio garden, classic bedrooms and bold, colourful suites. Dine well with a casual bar meal, romantic dinner or indulgent Boozy Snoozy lunch. Friendly and attentive staff. Sean Connery, David Coulthard and Elton John are all former guests.

Price: from £120 per room with breakfast.

The Glasshouse 🛌

Greenside Place EH1 3AA
☎ **0131 525 8200**
www.theetoncollection.com

21st-century, five-star chic, unique, boutique, recent winner of Most Stylish and Most Sexiest hotel awards. Luxurious, lavish suites, fabulous bathrooms and ultra-modern design, with entertainment system, private balconies or door to rooftop garden. Snug Bar for hotel guests only, creating a private club ambience.

Price: £110–£295 B&B (double room). Suites £295–£500.

Christopher North Hotel 🛌 🍴

6 Gloucester Place EH3 6EF
☎ **0131 225 2720**
www.christophernorth.co.uk

More like a country house hotel, experience its opulent, sophisticated black and gold design, tall draped windows, inspired by Coco Chanel's Paris apartment. Stunning bedrooms feature soft velvet throws, romantic lighting and jacuzzi baths with views over Dean Village and Stockbridge. Dine in European style at the Mozart Kaffe Haus.

Price: double £98–£170; executive £148–£198; suite £188–£298.

HOTEL

Broughton Hotel

37 Broughton Place EH1 3RR
☎ **0131 558 9792**
www.broughton-hotel.com

A hidden gem just off Broughton Street, owned and personally run by Freddie and Fiona. Smart modern accommodation with six en suite bedrooms, colour TV, tea tray, large towels, power showers and free parking. Breakfast includes Full Monty fry up, waffles, porridge and kippers.

Price: £25–£50 pp sharing double. £40–£75 single occupancy.

B&B

Six St Mary's Place

6 St Mary's Place EH4 1JH
☎ **0131 332 8965**
www.sixmarysplace.co.uk

Vegetarian, environmentally friendly, welcoming and homely townhouse. Immaculately clean en suite bedrooms with flexible accommodation – single, double and family (sleeps six), cosy lounge, peaceful garden and scrumptious healthy breakfast served in conservatory. Cyclists and walkers are particularly well cared for with a bike store and clothes dryer.

Price: from £95 double room; £150 family room.

The best... **PLACES TO STAY**

21 India Street

EH3 6HE (off Heriot Row)
☎ 0131 225 4353
www.twenty-one.co.uk

Zandra Macpherson, a member of Clan Macpherson chieftains, is a well-known writer of books on Scottish history and culture. Her home, filled with family portraits, fine art and antiques, offers two classically furnished guest suites. Traditional Scottish breakfast is served in the elegant, crimson dining room.

Price: £95–£125 per room. Discounts for short breaks.

24 Saxe Coburg Place

EH3 5BP (off Henderson Row, Stockbridge)
☎ 0131 315 3263
www.saxecoburgplace.co.uk

Peaceful, tree-lined square with a private front door to the garden flat of owners' Georgian (1827) townhouse. Luxury double (7ft bed), twin and single bedrooms, with en suite, TV/radio. Homemade continental breakfast with organic fruit, cereal, porridge, croissants, honey, served in dining hall or patio. A real homely touch is the guest kitchen/fridge.

Price: £45–£60 pp. Single occupancy rates available.

Bouverie

9b Scotland Street EH3 6PP
☎ 0131 556 5080
www.edinburghbedandbreakfast.co.uk

Ideally located between the New Town and Broughton, local and city centre restaurants, bars, shops and attractions are within a 10-minute walk. Two double and two twin rooms overlooking a quiet garden offer homely accommodation cared for by your hosts, the Bouverie family. Farmhouse-style breakfast cooked on the Aga.

Price: £35–£50 pp. Minimum two night stay weekends; four nights at New Year.

SELF-CATERING

20a Dean Terrace

EH4 1NL (in the heart of Stockbridge)
☎ 0131 225 9225
www.20adeanterrace.com

Like a country cottage, this is a charming, artistically furnished, bright, sunny flat situated beside the Water of Leith. Four-poster bedroom and twin room. Quality linen, towels and Molton Brown toiletries provided. There is a drawing room (with a sofa bed), fully fitted kitchen catering for eight guests and a private garden. Deluxe, relaxing, holiday haven.

Price: £160–£200 per night (two-night minimum). £1,000–£1,400 per week.

28 Scotland Street

EH3 6PX
☎ 0131 554 4944
www.luxuryapartments.com

Sumptuously furnished, blending contemporary design with Georgian grandeur. Double bedroom with luxury bathroom (jacuzzi), drawing room with sofa bed. Home-from-home kitchen facilities, cable TV and CD/DVD. Easy staggering distance from Broughton Street pubs, restaurants and local food shops.

Price: £110–£150 per night (seasonal variation).

The best... FOOD AND DRINK

▶ Staying in

Stockbridge is renowned for a gastronomic treasure trove of dozens of delis, superior food stores, coffee and sandwich shops and takeaways.

Herbie's has two shops in the district, 66 Raeburn Place (deli) and 1 NW Circus Place (deli-café). It is reputed to stock the 'Best Bread in Edinburgh', unpasteurised artisan cheeses, olives, salami, pâté, parma ham and smoked salmon. Le Brie de Meaux by Richard Gillard is a specialty. Fallachan, made from whey, one of the oldest Scottish alcoholic drinks, is stocked exclusively at Herbie's.

Down the hill from NW Circus Place is **Mellis Cheesemonger** (6 Baker Place), famous in Scotland for supplying fine-dining restaurants. The pungent smell as you step inside is mesmerising; a paradise for cheese lovers.

Next door is an Italian bakery and round the corner at 39 St Stephen's Street, **Sprio** is an Italian café and deli serving quality pastries, gluten-free breads, cheese, salads and good coffee. **Peckhams** (48 Raeburn Place) is a five-star grocer, deli and café selling an extraordinary range of fine food and wine. It's open all day to 11.30pm/midnight at weekends, so you need never run out of good food and drink. Opposite at

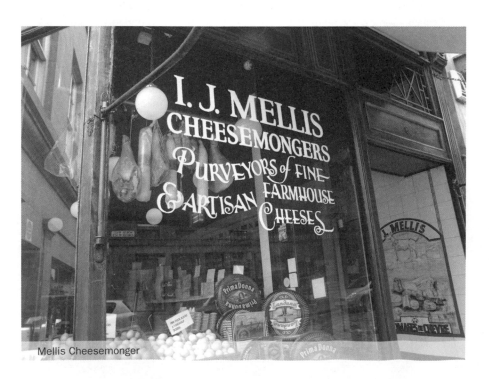

Mellis Cheesemonger

27 Raeburn Place is **Red Sugar**, specialising in superfoods, smoothies, quality coffee and raw chocolate cake.

Check out **Armstrongs** fishmonger (80 Raeburn Place) for a feast of seafood, and the legendary **Bowers Butcher** (75 Raeburn Place) for excellent bacon, poultry, beef, duck and game. **The Store** (13 Comely Bank Road) is a farm shop in the city, selling high-quality poultry, eggs, field grown seasonal vegetables, cheeses, bread and homebaking.

Around Broughton Street

If self-catering in the Broughton district, you don't have far to go to buy excellent fresh food. **Real Foods** (37 Broughton Street; ☎ 0131 557 1911) is the place to shop for vegetarian, vegan, natural, organic and Fairtrade produce.

Villeneuve wines (49a Broughton Street; ☎ 0131 558 8441) is one of the finest wine and whisky retailers in the UK. **Crombies** at 97 Broughton St (☎ 0131 556 7643; www.sausages.co.uk) is a five-star butcher for quality meat, game, homemade gourmet sausages (lamb, garlic and rosemary) and haggis (halal version too). If you are planning a Sunday roast or barbecue, this is the place to come. To illustrate the multicultural community, down the road from Crombies is **Pani Solinska** (73 Broughton Street; ☎ 557 6900), a Polish bistro and deli, where you can sample Haggis Pierogi, as well as traditional Polish fare.

The fishmonger, **Something Fishy** (16a Broughton Street), is great for fresh tuna, monkfish and their own smoked salmon. The wonderfully named **Sejuiced** (36 Broughton Street) is the place for healthy fruit juices, booster shots and smoothies with special berries and ingredients for certain ailments and hangover cures. A short walk away at 19 Elm Row is **Valvona and Crolla**, an Italian deli which first opened in 1934 and is stuffed with luscious deluxe produce.

Takeaway

In Stockbridge, for quality baked potatoes take a trip to **Take It Away Spud** (31 NW Circus Place; ☎ 0131 225 2004) which has an exceptional range of fillings, including veggie curry, lentil bolognaise and haggis, stuffed into fat, chunky, tasty tatties. They offer friendly service and the perfect healthy meal in a box. **L'Aquila Bianca** (17 Raeburn Place; ☎ 0131 332 8433) has a good reputation for fresh fish and crispy batter. **L'Alba D'Oro** (5–7 Henderson Row; ☎ 0131 557 2580; www.lalbadoro.com) is an award-winning fish and chip shop which serves traditional fish and chicken as well as prawns and squid, pies, haggis, burgers vegetarian dishes and chunky chips. Wine and champagne are also available for a sophisticated fish supper. And for a quality contemporary Indian feast, **Shanas** (45 Raeburn Place; ☎ 0131 332 6606) has an enticing menu for all tastes.

Many of Broughton's restaurants offer takeaway, such as **Siam Thani** (14 Broughton Street), where you can pick up an entire three-course Thai meal to go.

Try **The Bakehouse Co**, (32c Broughton Street) and **The Globe** (72 Broughton Street) for delicious snacks and gourmet sandwiches.

Local legend: Pierre Levicky

Pierre Levicky is a French chef and restaurateur who has lived on and off in Edinburgh for over 20 years. Brought up near Lyon, by an Italian mother and Ukrainian father, Pierre Levicky began cooking as a boy because his mother only cooked a meal at lunchtime. After training as a chef, he was given the opportunity to run a restaurant at a small hotel in Belfast – the Pierre Levicky French Restaurant became a destination dining room. Wanting a change of scene and new start he moved to Edinburgh: *'I arrived with a small battered suitcase and £70 in my pocket. The year was 1986 and everything was just beginning.'*

After working in two leading city restaurants and gaining serious recognition, he opened his own restaurant, Pierre Victoire in 1988, the first of several in the city, based on his concept of a modern French Brasserie serving high-quality French country cuisine at good-value prices. In less than 10 years the Pierre Victoire chain developed across the UK and Europe with around 150 restaurants in Galway, London and Brussels with a global turnover of over £40 million. But Levicky's empire had grown too big too fast and the bubble burst. In 1998 the company went into receivership with debts of £6 million. But the ever-ebullient chef bounced back, moving to Paris before creating the Chez Pierre brand in Andalusia. Twenty years since opening his first restaurant in Edinburgh, Monsieur Levicky is back in town and in July 2008 he opened a new brand of bistro, Chez Pierre (18 Eyre Place; ☎ 0131 556 0006), serving great European food at friendly, affordable prices.

 EATING OUT

FINE DINING

The Stockbridge Restaurant
**54 St Stephen Street,
Stockbridge EH3 5AL
☎ 0131 226 6766
www.thestockbridgerestaurant.co.uk**

Descend into a grotto beautifully decorated with fairy lights and flowers, the perfect place for a romantic meal. First-class cuisine in a modern European style, using the finest quality Scottish seafood and meat. Best value on Sundays with a varied set menu and the option to bring your own wine (£3 corkage). Lunch £12.95; two-course, dinner, £26.

RESTAURANT

La Concha
**18–24 Deanhaugh Street,
Stockbridge EH4 1LY
☎ 0131 332 0414
www.laconcharestaurant.co.uk**

This attractive wee basement trattoria offers classic Italian cuisine. Family-run business with a maximum of 18 covers ensures chef Richard Morana provides high-quality cuisine and freshly prepared dishes. 80% of its customers are repeat diners. Closed Sunday and Monday. Two courses from £18.

EATING OUT

Sabor Criollo
**36 Deanhaugh Street,
Stockbridge EH4 1LY
☎ 0131 332 3322**

This Latin American restaurant
transports you to a sunnier climate
through its colourful, exotic décor of
seascape mural and a huge tree. Run
by Chef Mohammad and his South
American wife Mercedes, the food is
inspired by Peru, Chile and Mexico, but
at its heart Sabor celebrates Venezuelan
cooking. Two-course dinner under £15.

Bella Mbriana
**7-11 East London Street EH7 4BN
☎ 0131 558 9581**

From the Neapolitan phrase meaning
'Soul of the House', Bella Mbriana
specialises in authentic homely
southern Italian cuisine: pasta with
juicy lobster, mussels, Italian sausages
cooked on the charcoal grill. Finish
with tiramasu and coffee. Good choice
of wine by the glass. Set lunch £9.95.
Dinner (two courses) £20.

Chez Pierre
**18 Eyre Place EH3 5EP
☎ 0131 556 0006
www.pierrelevicky.co.uk**

Pierre Levicky is a legendary Edinburgh
restaurateur. His new brasserie offers
a contemporary French menu of 'tiny
playful dishes' like large tapas. Seared
tuna, shellfish soup, lamb meatballs,
garlic chicken and ripe cheese are all on
offer. Open all day for drinks and light
dishes. Le Complets Lunch £6, a la
carte dinner around £23.

Siam Thani
**14 Broughton Street EH1 3HR
☎ 0131 477 2724
www.siamthanirestaurant.co.uk**

Awarded the 'Thai Select Seal of
Approval' by the Ministry of Commerce
in Thailand, celebrating chef Kaoswri's
authentic Thai cuisine. Seafood tom kha
soup with creamy coconut milk and tang
of chilli and lemon grass and spicy stir
fried beef. BYOB (£5), house wine £14;
two courses £20.

BISTRO

Iglu Bistro and Bar
**2b Jamaica Street EH3 6HH
☎ 0131 476 5333
www.theiglu.com**

The ethical philosophy behind this
intimate bistro above a pub, is wild,
organic, meat, game and fish from
boutique Scottish farms and local food
producers. Sample Shetland mussels,
boar burger, ethically reared salmon,
venison steak, slow braised lamb, hearty
vegetarian dishes, vanilla rice pudding
and Scottish cheeses. Three courses
costs around £20

Olive Branch
**91 Broughton Street EH1 3RX
☎ 0131 557 8589
www.olivebranchscotland.co.uk**

Very popular all day neighbourhood diner
serving fresh, wholesome, homely food
from breakfast to dinner: goats cheese
and Mediterranean vegetables, grilled
seabass, venison casserole, fat chunky
chips. Fabulous Sunday brunch. Booking
essential any time of the day. Two
course lunch £12; dinner £16.

Smoke Stack
**53–55 Broughton Street EH1 3RJ
☎ 0131 556 6032
www.smokestack.org.uk**

Smart-casual, unpretentious, retro
setting for American-style dining serving

EATING OUT

chargrilled steak and real burgers, seafood, Tex-Mex, pasta, 'Boston cut' rump steak, fajiitas, surf and turf platter, Cajun chicken salad and white chocolate cheesecake in Stateside portions! Hip hop kind of place for two, or a crowd of friends. Dinner £16 (two courses).

Pani Solinska
73 Broughton Street EH1 3RJ
☎ 0131 557 6900

The name means Mrs Solinska, (the owner); the chef comes from *Gessler*, a leading Warsaw restaurant, guaranteeing traditional Polish food. The speciality is grilled Polish sausages served on rye with mustard; or try Zragy - beef and gherkins with mash. Coffee, cakes and Polish whisky-vodka cocktail. Lunch £9; dinner, £13.

Urban Angel
1-9 Forth Street EH1 3JS
☎ 0131 556 6323
www.urban-angel.co.uk

Urban Angel functions by the motto 'Refresh and revive with food and drink that doesn't cost the earth.' Ingredients are all locally sourced, organic and free range; homemade soups, haggis, neeps and tatties (veggie haggis too), hummus and pitta bread, pork belly and scallops. Also does brunch and tapas. Dinner (two courses) £20.

GASTROPUB

Hamilton's Bar and Kitchen
16–18 Hamilton Place EH3 5AU
☎ 0131 226 4199
www.hamiltonsedinburgh.co.uk

Contemporary but cosy, the design is 'home from home'. Roy Lichtenstein inspired décor gives the place a trendy edge and relaxed atmosphere. Menu changes every month and all the food is natural local produce. All day breakfast on Sundays. Free Wi-Fi. Lunch dishes around £6, dinner mains £15.

Hectors
47–49 Deanhaugh Street EH4 1LR
☎ 0131 343 1735

A real neighbourhood bar/café/bistro for all day drinking and eating, established for around 14 years. This quirky, cosy place blends comfy sofas and coffee tables with dining area. Contemporary European fusion food. Brunch on Sunday, DJ on Thursdays and Sundays. Meals around £12.50.

CAFÉ

Zanzero
15 NW Circus Place EH3 6SX
☎ 0131 220 0333
www.zanzero.com

This cheerful, citrus yellow Italian café prides itself on high quality, organic food. Their motto is 'Slow Food Served Quickly' where *slow food* is great food nurtured from seed to plate. Fresh salads, tasty antipasti, authentic pizza, pasta, meat and fish. Patio alfresco dining. Two courses from £12–£20.

The Bakehouse Co.
32c Broughton Street EH1 3SB
☎ 0131 557 2012
www.thebakehousecompany.co.uk

This charming, old fashioned café is reminiscent of the days of the Lyons tea-rooms. Fresh, locally sourced, Fairtrade and free range ingredients. Soups, pies, sandwiches pastries and cakes, all made from scratch on the premises. Sit in and takeaway. Tea and cakes for two costs £12.

125

🍸 Drinking

Stockbridge

In the heart of Stockbridge, **St Stephen Street** is lined with art galleries and boutiques as well as several traditional pubs such as **The Antiquary** (72–78 St Stephen Street). This basement bar is stuffed with old oak furniture and paintings with a cosy coal fire in winter. Part of its charm comes from the stories of a resident ghost, quiz nights and live folk music on Thursdays. **The Bailie** (2–4 St Stephen Street) is a community-oriented pub with regulars who have been coming here since the 1960s. One of the most charismatic features is a large island bar which is perfect for encouraging banter and debate. The pub specialises in cask ales.

A short walk up the hill between Stockbridge and New Town is **The Standard** (24 Howe Street). Slick, chic and comfortable with leather armchairs, this is a Freehouse serving Deuchars IPA, Belhaven Best, continental beers, several wines by the glass. Funky music and sports TV attracting a lively mix of drinkers.

The Iglu Bar round the corner has draught and bottled beers such as Black Isle Organic Blonde Lager, an extensive wine list including organic, premium spirits, organic and Fairtrade juices, artisan coffee and organic teas. Drink healthily to the background of Iglu's eclectic taste in music.

Around Broughton Street

Whatever the ambience and mood you seek for your drinking pleasure, you'll find it here. Traditional old pubs with bar stools and bentwood chairs or chic cocktail bars and leather sofas abound. Mingle with the locals at **The Barony** (81 Broughton Street), with Belgian and guest beers, log fire and Bert's band on Sundays. **Mathers** (25 Broughton Street) has 110 whiskies, and is a popular sports bar for football and rugby. **The Cask and Barrel** (116 Broughton Street) is a real favourite by those who prefer a traditional 'boozer' rather than the trendy bars on George Street, to sample Caledonian Deuchars IPA and other guest ales.

The Basement (10a Broughton Street) is a lively, studenty, happening place with great music. It was named as one of the top 50 bars in Britain, together with **The Outhouse** (on Broughton Street Lane). **Mezz** (49 London Street) is stylish and mellow for a chill-out evening for wine, beer and cocktails.

Sunday breakfast is a tradition around here. Head to Broughton Street from around noon till mid-afternoon for a classic fry up and Bloody Mary at **Mathers**, **The Outhouse**, **Baroque** and **The Barony** or to **The Basement** for a Tex Mex Brex.

At the top of Broughton Street, round the corner at 12 Picardy Place, is **Hawke and Hunter**, formerly the private Hallion club but now open to all. This has the ambience of a smart, fashionable gentleman and gentlewoman's club with stylish bar, lounges and patio garden for a sophisticated drink. The champagne list is for the connoisseur, with Krug, Veuve Clicquot and Dom Perignon, as well as a long wine list. Eat well here too with a food menu themed around game and fish from the Scottish Highlands. A short walk towards Stockbridge, the **Cumberland Bar** is a charming Camra Real Ale pub with an attractive beer garden under the trees (1–3 Cumberland Street).

LEITH AND THE WATERFRONT

Just like the London docklands, Liverpool, Gateshead and Salford, the docks at Leith underwent severe decline in the period after the Second World War with the last shipbuilding yard closing in 1984. Major investment in recent years has brought significant and attractive development, with the transformation of disused warehouses and whisky bonds into restaurants and high-tech design offices for TV, PR and advertising companies. Deluxe high-rise apartments with seaview balconies now line the water-front. The port is visited by world cruise liners and is the home of the Royal Yacht Britannia, a five-star visitor attraction. The curving cobbled street called **The Shore** is now thriving with smart pubs, wine bars and seafood bistros amidst charming waterside surroundings. This is 'Michelin Mile' due to the high number of Michelin-star fine-dining restaurants.

Historically, the major shipping Port of Leith and Edinburgh were separate town burghs, but with growth over the centuries, Leith was swallowed up into the city of Edinburgh. The old town border even divided a pub, The Boundary bar, down the centre where, due to local licencing laws, you could drink later on the Leith side of the bar than on the Edinburgh side. The story goes that Edinburgh police tested drunkardness with the tongue twister, 'The Leith Police dismisseth us'. Even today, long-time residents, or 'Leithers', still feel they live in a distinct and separate town. And it is, oozing a real sense of gritty, working class character and maritime history, despite the upmarket gentrification over the past 10 years.

The seafront stretches west along the River Forth to the pretty harbour with a lighthouse at Newhaven. Once a major fishing and shipbuilding port, it's now a conservation village striving to retain its architecture and sense of heritage. Heading along the east coast from Leith, **Portobello** is Edinburgh's seaside. The resort started as simply one house when a seaman built his seafront cottage here in 1742 in memory of his service in Puerto Bello, Panama. It gradually grew as a separate town until 1896 when it became part of Edinburgh.

WHAT TO SEE AND DO

The Waterfront in Leith along The Shore, with its bars, bistros and art galleries, is the place for sitting outside a pub with a glass of wine, a pint or a plate of seafood. Wander along The Shore to no. 65 to find the attractive blue-painted **Leith Gallery** (☎ 0131 553 5255; www.the-leith-gallery.co.uk), showing monthly changing exhibitions of paintings by Scottish artists, an impressive collection of Scottish Contemporary Art Limited Edition Prints, as well as jewellery, ceramics and crafts.

A short walk away round the corner is **The Corn Exchange Gallery** (Constitution Street; ☎ 0131 561 2300; www.cornexchangegallery.com), housed in a magnificent

The waterfront in Leith

Victorian building, now a design studio, presenting cutting-edge, diverse art and photography exhibitions.

Visiting the Waterfront means you can take a boat trip out to the Forth. Along the seafront from Leith is **Newhaven**, formerly an important fishing port with a thriving oyster trade. The village is connected to the birth of photography and forever preserved in the early photographs by pioneers David Octavious Hill and Robert Adamson, who took numerous studies of the Newhaven fishwives. Now the huge high hangar of the old fishmarket has been transformed into two excellent restaurants, Loch Fyne seafood and Prezzo, Italian trattoria – a fine place to eat and drink overlooking the pretty harbour.

SEAFARI ADVENTURES FORTH: ☎ 0131 331 4857; www.seafari.co.uk. Boat trips take place daily from Newhaven Harbour but must be booked in advance.
Prices: adult £20, child £18; Incholm Express £22/£18.50. Waterproof jackets and lifebelts are provided.

From Newhaven you can take a **Seafari boat trip** on board an 11m RIB (Rigid Inflatable Boat) for a cruise around the Forth. These are the all-weather rescue boats as used by the RNLI and the Royal Navy, so don't worry, you will be safe! Seafari offers a range of exciting eco-tours to see the wildlife up close and in their natural habitat around the rocky islands of the Firth of Forth. It's a superb opportunity to capture those Kodak views of seals, puffins and seabirds. There's also a thrilling high-speed ride over to the island of **Inchcolm**, home to a fine, old, ruined abbey, sandy beach and high cliffs. It's a wonderfully wild atmosphere with the seagulls screeching and swooping overhead. On this trip you go ashore with time to explore this tiny 'desert island', visit the abbey then sit on the beach with a picnic before being picked up again by the Seafari boat.

On a fine day take a 20-minute bus trip from Edinburgh city centre down to **Portobello Beach**; or as the locals would say, Porty. Get off at the High Street and walk down Bath Street to the Promenade. As long ago as 1795 there were bathing machines installed for the Edinburgh middle classes to experience the healthy mineral springs, water baths, sea and sand. From the mid-19th century to 1964 Portobello had a railway station to bring holidaymakers from near and far to this fashionable bathing resort. The Marine Gardens Pleasure Park had a ballroom, theatre, amusement park, and Lido with figure-of-eight roller coaster. There were summer variety shows on the pier, a fairground, donkey rides and an outdoor heated seawater swimming pool, which could hold 1,000 swimmers. Sean Connery once worked here, a job which indirectly led to his acting career: '*I worked as a lifeguard at Portobello outdoor swimming pool... I made good use of the high boards and was invited to join a troupe of demonstration divers and asked to dress up for a walk on part in Anna Neagles'* Glorious Days *show at the Empire Theatre.*'

Today there's still the old promenade running along its extensive, clean, sandy beach. The fairground has gone, but there are two entertainment arcades, a children's playpark, cafés and bars. The water may be rather cold for swimming but children will love the sea and sand – the Promenade is perfect for a bracing walk or cycle ride breathing in the salt sea air, year round. Yes, it's old fashioned and a bit shabby chic in places, but it has a soul, authenticity and good dash of magic. From the beach you can see over to Fife and along the East Lothian coastline to North Berwick. If you like fish suppers and ice cream (there's organic ice cream at the Beach Café), dogs, eclectic gift boutiques, old ladies in hats, and don't need the Blackpool lights or razzmatazz of Brighton, you'll have a fun day out at Porty.

The Promenade at Portobello Beach

CELEBRITY CONNECTIONS

In 1993, a debut Scottish novel entitled *Trainspotting* by **Irvine Welsh** quietly hit the bookshops with little media hype. Welsh's portrait of Edinburgh was not the Old and middle-class New Town as depicted by Stevenson and Spark. He wrote about *his* Edinburgh: Leith and the neighbouring housing estates of Muirhouse and Granton. This bold and blisteringly bleak portrait of a group of young Leith heroin addicts captured the voice and attitudes of the city's disaffected, working-class youth. Its darkly cynical tone tinged with black humour creates genuine empathy for its characters. Begbie, Renton, Tommy and Sick Boy are as unforgettable a clutch of junkies and nutters as you will ever encounter. *Trainspotting*, with its glamorisation of drug addiction and streetwise dialogue (adapted into a stylishly graphic movie) was seen as completely original and became a cult-hit novel and international best-seller.

The Proclaimers, aka Craig and Charles Reid, shared a musical passion during a childhood spent in Edinburgh and Auchtermuchty, Fife. Their hits include *Letter from America* and *Life with You*. They topped the UK singles chart in March 2007 with a new rendition of their classic anthem *I'm Gonna Be (500 Miles)*, with comedians Peter Kay and Matt Lucas for Comic Relief. They are supporters of Hibernian Football club, or Hibs, and their song *Sunshine on Leith* is regularly played before home matches.

And finally, world-renowned computer game developers **Rockstar North** had their first office in Leith next to Leith Links. This park is honoured in the fourth Grand Theft Auto game, Vice City, where the local country club is called Leaf Links.

Trainspotting tour

The best way to experience Irvine Welsh's colourful Leith landscape is to take the **Trainspotting tour** to visit the famous sights and haunts of Begbie, Renton, Tommy and Sick Boy. Tim Bell is your personal and extremely knowledgeable guide as you explore the real-life locations featured in Irvine Welsh's cult novel and the movie: Sick Boy's pub, Central Station, flats, streets, police station et al. Welsh was extremely chuffed to hear of his own literary walking tour, 'You feel you should've been dead 100 years before that kind of thing happens', he commented. 'I'm flattered, but I'm no Rabbie Louis Stevenson!'

TRAINSPOTTING – THE TOUR: ☎ 0131 555 2500; www.leithwalks.co.uk.
Prices: adult £8 (no children allowed). Book in advance or pay on the day. Choice of walking, walking/bus tours available.

Wet weather

At **Ocean Terminal** the sleek, intimate, ocean-going liner, the **Royal Yacht Britannia** is moored as a five-star visitor attraction. With many interior apartments, bedrooms, drawing room, banquet hall and crew quarters to see, as well as outside decks, you can experience the ship in all weathers, rain or shine.

ROYAL YACHT BRITANNIA: Ocean Terminal Leith EH6 6JJ; ☎ 0131 555 5566; www. royalyachtbritannia.co.uk.
Prices: adult £9.75, concession £7.75, child £5.75, under 5s free, family £27.75 (two adults and three children). If visiting in August to avoid queuing it is best pre-book. Open Jan–Mar, Nov, Dec 10am–3.30pm; Apr–Jun 10am–4.30pm; Jul–Aug 9.30am–4.30pm.

For over 40 years The Royal Yacht Britannia served the royal family as the perfect floating royal residence for glittering state visits, official receptions, royal honeymoons and relaxing family holidays. Now moored at the Ocean Terminal, Leith, the most famous ship in the world will surprise and delight all the family. An excellent audio guide gives a fascinating history and leads you on a journey around five decks of this magnificent yacht visiting the bridge, sumptuous drawing room, state dining room, the Queen's small and homely bedroom, sun lounge and the Admiral's and staff quarters.

The period design and furnishings have been carefully preserved, while the commentary describes the history and anecdotes about royal life at sea. Everything is just as it was in Britannia's heyday between the 1960s and 1980s. You can imagine the Queen Mother sitting in an armchair with a G&T, Noel Coward performing some romantic songs on the piano after dinner or recall the image of Princess Diana on deck rushing with her arms open wide to greet William and Harry as they arrived on board. The ghosts of the past still linger with the sound of laughter and music around this unique ship. There is an audio guide in 21 languages as well as a version for children.

What to do with children

Alien Rock was created in 1994 inside a disused church opposite Newhaven harbour as Scotland's first dedicated indoor climbing centre and has over 200 roped climbs and everything to cater for climbing fun and skills for all ages. The children's weekend sessions (ages 8 and over) allow kids to learn how to climb and look after themselves and others in an exciting, energetic environment.

ALIEN ROCK: 8 Pier Place EH6 4LP; ☎ 0131 552 7211; www.alienrock.co.uk.
Prices: adult £7.50(summer)/£6.80(winter), child £4.50; open May–Sept, Mon–Fri noon–10pm, Sat–Sun 10am–7pm; Oct–Apr, Mon–Fri 12noon–10pm, Sat–Sun 10am–9pm. Kid's club Sat–Sun 10am–12noon, 1pm–3pm.

PORTOBELLO SWIM CENTRE: The
Promenade EH15 2BS; ☎ 0131 669 6888;
www.edinburghleisure.co.uk.
Prices: adult swim, £3.30, child £1.90.
Family tickets available; open Mon–Fri,
7am–9pm, Sat–Sun, 9am–3.30pm.

Edinburgh has its own seaside at **Portobello beach,** where kids can build sand castles, and enjoy the play parks and the entertainment arcades with the usual suspects of slot machines and games. The **Portobello Swim Centre** is in a traditional Victorian building but with modern fitness facilities, situated right on the beach. It includes a swimming pool, state of the art gym, Turkish Baths, steam room, a plunge pool as well as a café.

And after a swim or walk along the Promenade, **Reds** (254 Portobello High Street; ☎ 0131 669 5558; www.reds4families.com) is a specifically child-friendly bistro with soft play area.

Entertainment

The annual **Leith Festival** (www.leithfestival.com) in early June is a major local community event expanding year by year. It's a colourful jamboree of music (100 gigs), comedy (50 performances), club nights, art exhibitions, gala day, markets and special *Trainspotting* tours.

LOCAL KNOWLEDGE

In 1998 **Tony Borthwick** opened his restaurant The Plumed Horse in Dumfries and Galloway. After receiving the accolade of a Michelin star and Scottish Chef of the Year, Borthwick and The Plumed Horse relocated to Leith, Edinburgh. Tony's unique style of cooking is inspired by his love for European cuisine, combining traditional techniques with light, individual flavours.

Favourite pub: The Malt & Hops is a pub, not a trendy wine bar: it's a proper pub. I like it because the seven or eight real ales served are lovingly tended by Callum, who is a partner in the business. Lisa, the other half of the business is a larger-than-life character who heads up a team of friendly and enthusiastic bartenders. Very good selection of whiskies at reasonable prices too.

Best bistro: The Kings Wark is a great pub for food. Sunday brunch is not to be missed, and the food in both the bar and the restaurant qualifies as my favourite bistro.

Best restaurant: Anyone looking for something special or a celebration should try Restaurant Martin Wishart, fine Michelin-star dining (and needless to say, The Plumed Horse!).

Favourite shops: George Campbell the fishmonger. There is also a veritable Princes Street in the form of Ocean Terminal Shopping Mall right alongside the Royal Yacht Britannia. A few delicatessens are springing up around here which is very encouraging.

Best gallery: The Leith Gallery is a great place to browse, showing some very unusual pieces from Scottish artists.

Best thing about living here: I like to walk around Leith at night – sounds a bit dodgy but it's a safe enough place. Just ambling around The Shore and along to Rennie's Isle where I live is a nice relaxing thing to do, dropping into various places that take one's fancy along the way. It's like living in a small town yet only a 10-minute bus ride from Edinburgh.

The best... **PLACES TO STAY**

HOTEL

Malmaison Edinburgh

1 Tower Place, Leith EH6 7DB
☎ **0131 468 5000**
www.malmaison.com

Housed in the grand old Seaman's Mission on the waterside, this ultra-chic design hotel offers luxury on a budget. 100 individually styled bedrooms (with desirable minibar goodies), fabulous café/cocktail bar, piazza tables and a Parisian brasserie serving modern European cuisine with smart, sophisticated ambience.

Price: from £150–£295 per night.

Premier Inn Edinburgh

51/53 Newhaven Place EH6 4TX
☎ **08701 977 093**
www.premierinn.com

If you fancy a waterfront setting at Newhaven harbour with nearby attractions at Leith, this is the ideal base. 10-minute bus ride to city centre. Good value tariff for spacious, well-designed bedrooms.

Price: from £65 per room per night.

SELF-CATERING

Harbour Apartments

Western Harbour, Leith EH6 4PB
☎ **0131 240 0080**
www.theharbourapartments.com

Selection of apartments and luxury penthouses on waterfront: two double bedrooms (one ensuite), sleeping four to six guests. Lounge with dining area, Plasma TV/DVD/Wi-Fi. Bath and shower, fully fitted kitchen, open-plan design with wood flooring. Superior apartments have sea views.

Price: standard £50–£200 per night. Penthouse £200–£250 per night.

The Moorings

144 The Moorings
☎ **01573 224 171**
www.themooringsinedinburgh.co.uk

Self-catering holiday apartment beside Ocean Terminal, Leith, this cosy flat is within a modern warehouse conversion. Sleeps six guests comfortably with a double bedroom with en suite shower and two twin rooms, with bathroom. The living room also has double sofa bed. The kitchen is fully fitted with washer/dryer, dishwasher and microwave.

Price: £450–£750 per week.

B&B

Ardmor House

74 Pilrig Street EH6 5AS
☎ **0131 554 4944**
www.ardmorhouse.com

Colin and Robin welcome you to their beautiful Victorian home. Five spacious bedrooms, kingsize beds, flat screen TV, power showers and crisp white linen. Scottish breakfast available in the dining room or continental feast in bed after a late night.

Price: £85–£125 per night.

Pillars House

125 Constitution Street EH6 7AE
☎ **0131 555 1517**
www.pillarshouse.co.uk

Grand, pillared B-listed Victorian house offering homely accommodation in double, twin and family rooms. You can expect a sincere greeting from your hosts Edna and Forbes and a friendly, international house-party atmosphere.

Price: £25–£60 pppn (low/high season).

The best... FOOD AND DRINK

This is the gastronomic quarter of Edinburgh, catering for every taste and budget with bars, pubs, bistros, seafood diners (check out The Shore, Fishers, Skippers, Ship on The Shore, Loch Fyne), pizza houses, Indian, Mexican and French cuisine, as well as a cluster of Michelin-star-fine-dining restaurants.

▶ Staying in

Along with some of the best places to eat out in town, Leith has some excellent food shops and delis all within a five-minute walk of The Shore.

- **Fleur** (52 The Shore) is great for cooked meats, bread, cheese, soups and a huge menu of freshly made sandwiches and lunchtime gourmet snacks to takeaway.
- **Relish** (6 Commercial Street) is a grocer, delicatessen, wine merchant and off-licence.
- **The Clock** (35 The Shore) offers coffees, sandwiches and homebaking.
- **The Globe** (23 Bernard Street) and **Beets** (49 Bernard Street) are both delis, with takeaway sandwiches and snacks.
- **Rocksalt** (46 Constitution Street) is a café and deli with a takeaway service for homemade soups, burgers and stews.
- **Porto and Fi** (47 Newhaven Main Street) is a café and deli with freshly prepared good food.

Takeaway
The best pizza in the UK can be sampled from **La Favorita** (325–331 Leith Walk EH6 8SA; ☎ 0131 554 2430) up the hill from Leith. For the third year running PAPA, the Pizza and Pasta Association, has voted this Edinburgh Italian restaurant the UK's best pizzeria and best delivery service.

EATING OUT

FINE DINING

Restaurant Martin Wishart
54 The Shore EH6 6RA
☎ 0131 553 3557
www.martin-wishart.co.uk

The ultimate Michelin-star dining experience amidst glamorously chic interior design dressed in white, gold and mahogany. A la carte (£50, three courses) or indulge in the divine six course tasting menu (£60) celebrating classic and modern French cuisine. Faultless professional service without fuss. Treat yourselves!

The Kitchin
78 Commercial Quay EH6 6LX
☎ 0131 555 1755
www.thekitchin.com

Tom Kitchin is the youngest Scottish chef to receive a Michelin star, six months after opening his restaurant. He has perfected the unique marriage of seasonal Scottish produce with classical French technique and inventive flair. Intimate, cool minimalist setting in converted whisky bond warehouse. Lunch £20; dinner £38.

The Plumed Horse
50 Henderson Street EH6 6DE
☎ 0131 554 5556
www.plumedhorse.co.uk

Having received a Michelin star in 2001 for his restaurant in rural SW Scotland, chef Tony Borthwick relocated to Leith. A gracious drawing room, the design is simple white and cream elegance. Taste foie gras, scallop, salmon, avruga caviar, twice-baked parmesan soufflé, and a truffle and herb salad. Two courses £32.

RESTAURANT

The Brasserie at Malmaison Hotel
1 Tower Place, Leith EH6 7DB
☎ 0131 468 5000
www.malmaison.com

Waterfront location with classic Parisian brasserie design rich in dark wood and leather banquette seating. French country cooking, with a menu of Toulouse sausages, lamb, pork, salads and favourite comfort food (Mal burgers and pasta); 'home-grown and local' Buccleuch beef and Scottish fish. Relaxed mood and kids menu on offer. Two courses: lunch £14, dinner £20.

Loch Fyne Restaurant
25 Pier Place,
Newhaven Harbour EH6 4LP
☎ 0131 559 3900
www.lochfyne.com

The original Oyster Bar and Smokehouse on Loch Fyne has grown into a nationwide collection of seafood restaurants. This attractive old fish market building has a fabulous setting beside the pretty harbour with sunset view decking. Loch Fyne oysters, smoked salmon, fish pie, crabcakes and market specials. Two courses £10–£20.

E.S.I.
46 Queen Charlotte Street,
Leith EH6 7EX
☎ 0131 555 3103
www.esibrasserie.com

E.S.I. stands for Englishman, Scotsman, Irishman, namely Richard, Jon and Paul, who run this artistically smart glass and white brick brasserie. Exciting, good-value modern food with seasonal British and Irish classic dishes. Steak served three ways – with fried egg, Stornoway black pudding or colcannon mash. £15–£25 for two courses.

EATING OUT

GASTROPUB

The Rose Leaf
23 Sandport Place EH6 6EW
☎ 0131 476 5268
www.roseleaf.co.uk

Run by Lyn and Jonny, this fabulously eccentric pub is furnished with vintage furniture, collectables and floral teapots. Gourmet brunch is served 10am to 5pm, supper till 10pm. Home cooked, homely fusion cuisine - Cullen Skink, pure beef burgers, veggie burgers, fish pie, spicy fajitas, as well as Sunday roasts. Two courses, £10.

The Shore
3 The Shore,
☎ 0131 553 5080
www.theshore.biz

Popular cosy, timber walled bar and restaurant serving classy British food such as steak and kidney pie, Borders Lamb, liver and bacon, haddock and chips and treacle tart. A good idea is to have a late supper dish, which is served till midnight. Live folk and jazz music Tuesday and Thursday add a lively ambience £18 (two courses).

The Espy
62–64 Bath Street, The Esplanade, Portobello
☎ 0131 669 0082
www.the-espy.com

Beach front location for this homely, friendly pub-diner. (Espy is Australian for Esplanade). Menu includes homemade pure beef burgers, veggie burgers, cheese platters, Breakfast, High Teas and huge wholesome 'hangover cure' brunches. Offers table service, candle lit tables or you can relax on a comfy sofa. Kids welcome. Two courses £14, bottle of wine £12.50.

BISTRO

Fishers Bistro
1 The Shore EH6 6QW
☎ 0131 554 5666
www.fishersbistros.co.uk

Casual, chilled out diner, wood panelled walls and designed like a ship with mezzanine level and views over the harbour. Long established and perennially popular. Daily selection of exceptional quality fresh seafood, oysters, lobster, halibut, wild seabass, salmon, tuna as well as a vegetarian menu. Two courses, £21. House wine from £12.

A Room in Leith
1c Dock Place EH6 6LU
☎ 0131 554 7427
www.aroomin.co.uk

One of three city restaurants, this cosy pub and conservatory restaurant has an unbeatable waterside location, with a pontoon deck for alfresco drinking/ dining. Serious Scottish cuisine with an extensive menu: scallops, Shetland salmon, beef, rabbit; haggis (and veggie haggis) neeps and tatties followed by luscious puddings. Set lunch £12, dinner, £22 (two courses).

CAFÉ

Café Truva
77 The Shore
☎ 0131 554 5502
www.cafétruva.com

This hidden gem of a place is no ordinary tearoom. Step inside to find colourful Mediterranean décor and sample authentic Turkish food: mezze, moussaka, salads, olives, grilled peppers, couscous, pitta bread, feta cheese, delicious cakes and strong Turkish tea. Licensed. Excellent value, two courses around £10.

The Malmaison Hotel

🍸 Drinking

The Leith Waterfront is renowned for its row of fascinating old pubs and lively wine bars, and you can enjoy a good pub crawl along The Shore. **The King's Wark** has a rustic country inn feel about it with real fire, cask ales and great pub grub too. **The Malt and Hops** has eight cask ales, dozens of malt whiskies and cask-conditioned cider (not for the faint hearted). Decorated with beer mats and old mirrors, and featuring a roaring fire and low-beamed ceiling this is an attractive, cosy pub. **The Shore** is a lively old wood-panelled pub with regular live music on Tuesday and Thursday night. It also does good food.

For a different drinking environment, you can actually board the ship moored on the harbour wall. This old steamer, **Ocean Mist**, was built in 1919 and used as a trawler, mine sweeper and pleasure yacht. Now revamped and renamed **Cruz**, it's a floating bar and restaurant with an outdoor top deck and a chic, sleek cocktail bar inside where you can sit and look out the portholes for a true seaview. The **Malmaison Hotel** at the very end of The Shore has a smart café bar (outdoor patio) for all-day coffees, wine, beer and bistro menu.

Teuchters Landing, just over the river at 1 Dock Place, has an amazing history. Teuchters Landing was the waiting room for steamship passengers who used to embark at Leith Docks for the ferry to Aberdeen. With wood-panelled walls and original port artefacts, it retains a sense of heritage. Good wine list and beers- (Deuchars IPA, Landlord, Ossian, Guinness) and 80 whiskies. Almost next door is **Sirius** (7–10 Dock Place), a trendy, lively bar with good music and a popular local reputation as 'the place' to hang out for a few beers.

The Roseleaf (23 Sandport Place) is a welcoming, friendly, fun old pub revamped with vintage curios and funky attitude. **Carriers Quarters** (42 Bernard Street) is your traditional Leith pub, which has a plaque outside stating it is 'Leith's oldest unaltered public house, 1785'. The front room is so small that the bar takes up most of the space but there's a cosy back room with comfy seating and tables.

Another famous Leith drinking hole is the **Port o' Leith** (58 Constitution Street), open from early morning for shift workers and sailors from the docks. This wee pub has a big reputation for its lively ambience and for making everyone welcome. Offering one cask ale, half a dozen malts and a standard range of bottled beers. The decor has a nautical theme littered with authentic artefacts donated by worldwide sailors and the ceiling is draped in ship's flags. **The Harbour Inn** (4 Fishmarket Square) at Newhaven has a prime spot overlooking the Firth of Forth. The oldest free house in Newhaven, it's located near Ocean Terminal and the Royal Yacht Britannia.

SOUTH QUEENSFERRY AND CRAMOND

South Queensferry, 10 miles from Edinburgh city centre, is a little harbour town on the Firth of Forth – a hidden gem located directly between the iconic two bridges – the Forth Bridge and the Forth Road Bridge. Today the ancient cobbled streets, quaint little antique and arts and craft shops, cafés, pubs and bistros are a great place to browse, enjoy a seafood lunch, or a waterfront drink. And it's a quiet wee place to stay away from the city hustle and bustle. The town is named after Queen Margaret of Scotland who frequently visited 'Queen's Ferry' to cross over the Forth to Dunfermline where she had founded a church and priory. She died in 1093 and made her final journey by ferry to Dunfermline Abbey. Her son, David I of Scotland awarded the ferry rights to the abbey. A ferry service continued and developed for 900 years, with passenger and car ferries between South and North Queensferry operating until 1964 when the Forth Road Bridge opened.

Just along the coast towards Edinburgh, the charming coastal village of **Cramond** sits at the mouth of the River Almond and looks out over the wind and waves of the Forth estuary. This relaxed corner of the capital has a proud Roman past and graceful appearance; rows of whitewashed houses descend steeply down the Almond's east bank to a small harbour of swans and sailing boats. The leafy neighbourhood that lies alongside, belted between the river and two golf courses, stretches from the Forth in the north to Barnton in the south. These two faces of Cramond, of a village and a city, are bound by a welcoming community and a strong sense of local identity.

A unique New Year's Day event at South Queensferry is open to all: if you are brave or mad enough to take part. The 'Loony Dook' is a crazy ritual on 1 January when people paddle or even swim in the icy waters of the Firth of Forth (see p.128). This colourful spectacle attracts many visitors from all over the world visiting Edinburgh to celebrate New Year.

WHAT TO SEE AND DO

South Queensferry was a favourite haunt of Robert Louis Stevenson which he used as a prime location for his hero, David Balfour, in his novel *Kidnapped*: '*The Firth of Forth narrows at this point to the width of a good-sized river, which makes a convenient ferry going north... on the south shore they have built a pier for the service of the ferry. On the other side of the road, and backed against a garden of holly trees and hawthorns, I could see the Hawes Inn.*'

Wander through the pretty village and find a seat on the promenade to admire the two Forth Bridges, standing side by side. As long as it's not too windy, then take a walk across the **Forth Road Bridge**. You can also cycle on a dedicated track.

At 1.5 miles, the towering suspension Forth Road Bridge was the longest in Europe when it was opened by Queen Elizabeth II in 1964. From here you will have a fabulous view of the **Forth (Rail) Bridge**. Built 74 years apart, the two bridges make a magnificent double act and complement each other with their contrasting design styles. The Forth Bridge, known locally as 'The Brig', was the world's first major steel Cantilever bridge, with gigantic girder spans of 1,710ft, and ranks as one of the great wonders of civilization and a masterpiece of engineering. Building began in 1883 and was completed on 4 March 1890 when Edward, Prince of Wales tapped into place a golden rivet. Today around 200 train journeys cross the Bridge every day, en route north to Fife, Perthshire and the Highlands. Driving over the Road Bridge or taking the train over the Forth Bridge are also great experiences.

The suspension Forth Road Bridge

PORT EDGAR MARINA AND SAILING SCHOOL: Shore Road, South Queensferry EH30 9SQ; ☎ 0131 331 3330; www. edinburghleisure.co.uk. Open daily 9am–4.30pm.

Port Edgar Marina and Sailing School is a watersports complex and marina. The sheltered South Queensferry Bay offers an excellent area for dinghy sailing and the watersports centre, offering all kinds of tuition, is one of the largest in the country. For those wishing to race, Port Edgar Yacht Club has an active yacht racing programme from April to December.

Dalmeny Estate

The extensive **Dalmeny Estate** has public access along the shore from South Queensferry to the boating marina at Cramond. This is an exhilarating 4.5-mile walk and takes you past several old piers, used centuries ago by the boats and ferries traversing the river. It is worth taking a detour to **Hound Point headland**, which allegedly is haunted by a dog owned by Sir Richard Mowbray, who died on the Crusades. The views from Hound Point are magnificent, looking out to Inchcolm

DALMENY HOUSE: Near South Queensferry EH30 9TQ;☎ 0131 311 1888; www. dalmeny.co.uk. Entry: adult £6(summer)/ £5(winter), children 10–16 £4; open July and August, Sun–Tue 2pm–5.30pm (last entry 4.30pm).

Island with its old abbey and the Forth Bridge. Nearby are relics of First World War naval gunnery defences. Along the walk you will pass Barnbougle Castle used by the prime minister, the fourth Earl of Rosebery to practice his speeches. Across the Dalmeny Golf course you will catch a glimpse of Dalmeny House. Enjoy encounters with wonderful wildlife and seabirds along the seashore here and look out for Eagle Rock thought to have the eagle of a Roman Legion carved into it.

The walk ends at the River Almond, on the opposite side of the river from Cramond. Since the 19th century there has been a ferryman, rowing people across for a few pence. The ferryman who served for 40 years from 1951, was Rudolph Badura, a Czech who came to Scotland after serving in the Scottish army during the Second World War. He lived in Ferryman Cottage on the Dalmeny Estate and reputedly swam out to and around Cramond Island every day. The ferry boat crossing closed in 2000.

Dalmeny House itself is the historic home of the Earls of Rosebery and contains world-renowned collections of art and furniture from the Rothschild and Rosebery families. Built in 1817 to a Tudor Gothic design, this magnificent house features fine paintings and portraits (Gainsborough), French antique furniture, Sevres porcelain, Napoleonic art and personal artefacts.

Cramond beach and Cramond Island

For a great day or afternoon out, take a trip to the historic village of Cramond beside the river Almond. Lothian buses 24 and 41 from the city centre stop at the top of Cramond Glebe Road and it is a short walk from there down the hill to the village. Cramond also has a large public car park off the main village street. The ancient ferry service that once crossed the river between the Dalmeny Estate and Cramond is to be revived in the form of a chain-ferry (a platform tied to both shores by cables and guided by a ferry operator), due to open by 2010.

You could start with an amble along a stretch of the 2-mile beachfront promenade to **Silverknowes** to take in some sweeping views of the Forth. The sandy beach is a haven for metal-detectives, kite flyers and picnickers, and an ice cream van caters for the many joggers, cyclists, couples and families. The tide at Silverknowes can come in swiftly up the wide beach, so be prepared to paddle if you are marooned on a sandbank.

If the tide is out, the more adventurous will want to cross the 1-mile causeway to **Cramond Island** with its treasure-trove of abandoned Second World War military buildings. Don't forget to check tide times first on the noticeboard at the start of the causeway or with the Forth Coastguard (☎ 01333 450666) lest you be stranded when the sea rushes in; several people have been stranded on the island overnight. A welcome sense of seclusion rewards those who make the journey across. Take a picnic to enjoy your own Robinson Crusoe experience with deserted sandy beaches, grassy hills and rocks for *Famous Five* adventures around the island.

After a bite to eat at the Cramond bistro or the inn, leave the village harbour and take a stroll along the River Almond walkway. En route, you'll pass the **Cramond Boat Club** (www.cramondboatclub.org.uk) which organises sailing activities such as the annual Cramond Regatta (the clubhouse is only open to members). This tree-lined path winds upstream beside alternately fast and slow rapids: be aware that the walk features a section of steep wooden steps, not suitable for children's buggies or the elderly. The path passes under a large brick archway beside some mill ruins from the river's industrial past. Here, the **Almond Weir** is a small but loud, splashing, crashing waterfall, jumped by salmon in spring and local kids in summer. Continue on for half a mile or so to arrive at **Cramond Bridge**. Cross the bridge and end the day with a visit to the **Cramond Brig** bar and restaurant.

Houses in Cramond

Cramond's history

To appreciate a sense of history about the village, it's worth learning about Cramond's history. **The Maltings** by the harbour is a good place to start. This former brewery has an interesting exhibition run by the Cramond Heritage Trust on 'Cramond's Story'.

For a full and truly authentic introduction to the village visit **Cramond Kirk** located up the hill a little way up past the car park. The Kirk belongs to the Church of Scotland and remains at the heart of the community. The church tower dates from the 1400s, but the main part of the building was completed in 1656. If that's not old enough, there are Roman ruins in the kirkyard grounds through the gate in the graveyard's north-east wall. Finally visible after undergoing excavations and landscaping in early 2009, Cramond's fort is remarkably complete, virtually an intact Roman relic and boasts a garrison, a gatehouse and a bathhouse. Lying adjacent to the site are the 17th-century Cramond House and the medieval Cramond Tower (not open to the public).

> THE MALTINGS: ☎ 0131 312 6034; www.cramondheritagetrust.org.uk. Free entry; open Jun–Sept, Sat and Sun 2pm–5pm; open daily during August.

Lauriston Castle

Lauriston Castle is a four-storey 1590s stone-tower house, with a circular stair tower and two turrets complete with gun loops. It was built for Sir Archibald Napier, father of the mathematician and inventor of Logarithms, John Napier. In 1926 the resident owner, Margaret Reid, left the castle in Trust to the Nation. The interior has been preserved just as it was and illustrates the typical leisured and wealthy Edwardian way of life before the Great War. The castle has a wonderful collection of paintings, tapestries, textiles, porcelain, Sheffield-plate, Blue John, British and continental furniture and many objets d'art. There are lovely gardens to explore including the Edinburgh-Kyoto Friendship Garden, one of the largest Japanese gardens created in the UK. There are guided tours available but it's best to phone to check seasonal times.

☂ Wet weather

Hopetoun House is one of the most splendid examples of Georgian architecture in Britain, designed by Scottish architects Sir William Bruce and William Adam. The home of the Earls of Hopetoun, it's surrounded by 150 acres of rolling parkland with woodland walks, breathtaking views over the River Forth and a deer park. It has

a superb collection of paintings, antique furniture and Aubusson tapestries, an ornate red drawing room and ballroom and George IV once dined in the state dining room. There are gardens and shore walks, the Stables tearoom, ranger wildlife tours, theatre events, and summer and Christmas fairs.

The **Queensferry Museum** at South Queensferry commands superb views of the two great bridges spanning the Forth. Its collections trace the history of the people of Queensferry and Dalmeny, the historic ferry passage to Fife, the building of the road and rail bridges, and the wildlife of the Forth estuary.

ᕗ What to do with children

Take a boat trip from South Queensferry out to Inchcolm Island and sail under the Forth Bridge. The **Maid of the Forth** from Hawes Pier (opposite Hawes Inn) offers day and evening cruises on the Firth of Forth. You can go ashore on Inchcolm Island known as the 'Iona of the East' due to its 12th-century medieval abbey. There's also a visitor centre, pretty beach and picnic areas. The on-board cruise commentary tells you about the

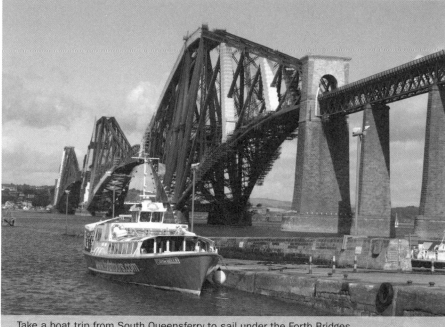
Take a boat trip from South Queensferry to sail under the Forth Bridges

castles and maritime history of the Forth as well as allowing you to experience the great natural sealife – seals, dolphins and porpoises, puffins, cormorants, gannets, guillemots and terns. There is also the High Speed Seafari Inchcolm Express trips from Newhaven Harbour and South Queensferry (see p.128).

MAID OF THE FORTH: ☎ 0131 331 5000; www.maidoftheforth.co.uk. Operating Easter to the end of October, several 90-minute and three-hour cruises. Weekly evening jazz trips with optional BBQ supper also available.

🎭 Entertainment

Events

The **Ferry Fair** (www.ferryfair.co.uk) takes place each August, a community festival of entertainment when the town is decorated with flags, bunting and banners. Events include the crowning of a schoolgirl as the Ferry Fair Queen, pipe bands and the appearance of the Burry Man. The name probably derives from the fruits of the Burdock plant or alternatively from 'Burgh Man', as the town was formerly a Royal Burgh. On Festival Friday, a local man, wearing a costume covered in sticky burrs and a floral hat, parades around the town for nine hours visiting the Lord Provost and several pubs to be fortified by whisky. The likely reasons behind this ancient pagan custom are to invoke good fortune in harvesting the land and sea or to drive out evil spirits.

Loony Dook

If you visit Edinburgh at New Year, you can celebrate the first day of January by taking a cold and cleansing dip in the Forth at South Queensferry. Or just come and cheer on the brave souls. It's a bizarre and very popular tradition with locals and visitors raising money for charity. To take part, sign up in advance and meet at the Moorings Pub (☎ 0131 311 2555) beforehand. Afterwards enjoy a hot toddy and soup to warm the blood. Wetsuits are not allowed but fancy dress is encouraged.

The week-long celebration includes processions, music, sport and entertainment especially for children.

🛒 Shopping

The old cobbled High Street in South Queensferry, featuring pretty flower-bordered terraces on a 'mezzanine' level, is an attractive row of antique, jewellery, accessory and gift shops, tearooms, pubs and restaurants. Next door to the Hawes Inn in a courtyard setting is **Scotia Tartans and Kilts**, the ideal place for all your Scottish heritage scarves, ties and souvenirs and next door the wonderful **Curiosity Shop**, sells second-hand books, paintings, pottery and all kinds of nick nacks. Definitely worth a good browse.

The best... PLACES TO STAY

BOUTIQUE

Orocco Pier

17 High Street, South Queensferry EH30 9PP
☎ **0131 331 1298**
www.oroccopier.co.uk

'Dining, Drinking, Dreaming' is the motto of this contemporary-designed hotel, located literally on the beach between the two Forth Bridges. Modern, minimalist bedrooms have TV/DVD and goodie chest mini bar. There is a lively ambience in the bar and brasserie.

Price: £110 –£140 double room with breakfast.

HOTEL

The Dakota Forth Bridge

South Queensferry EH30 9QZ
☎ **0870 423 4293**
www.dakotaforthbridge.co.uk

Sophisticated, New York loft-style living designed by hotelier Ken McCulloch for the 21st-century traveller who will find comfortable beds, soft towels (tiny shower room), funky furnishings and art work, TV with 65 channels, and all for a budget tariff. There are cosy guest lounges, a sexy cocktail bar and the Dakota Grill. Winner of the Scottish Hotel Restaurant award 2008.

Price: from £99 room only.

COUNTRY HOUSE

Norton House

Ingliston EH28 8LX
☎ **0131 333 1275; www.handpicked.co.uk**

Winner of the AA Hotel of the Year in Scotland, 2008–2009, in recognition of a smart refurbishment for this Victorian mansion, with impressive fine dining and luxury spa and health club. Located near the airport and Forth Bridge within lush parkland, escape the city at this hidden gem. The new wing features romantic suites with balconies.

Price: £110–£480 per double room (B&B).

COUNTRY INN

The Hawes Inn

7 Newhalls Road, South Queensferry EH30 9TA
☎ **0845 11 26 001**

You can eat but also sleep at the Hawes Inn, where Robert Louis Stevenson stayed when writing *Kidnapped*, with room 5 named after him. Several bedrooms overlook the breathtaking sight of the Forth Bridge and across the river to Fife. Good-quality pub food and drink.

Price: £65–£69 B&B per room, per night.

GUEST HOUSE

Priory Lodge

8 The Loan, South Queensferry EH30 9NS
☎ **0131 331 4345**
www.queensferry.com

Four-star comfort is guaranteed with Calmyn and Gordon's supreme hospitality. Five homely bedrooms with robes, fridge and tea tray. Gourmet breakfast includes porridge with Drambuie, kippers, full Scottish, smoked salmon and haggis. Ideal location to take day trips to Edinburgh, Fife or Perthshire.

Price: £35–£45 pp, £50–£70 single.

B&B

Hawthorne House

15 West Terrace (High Street), South Queensferry EH30 9LL
☎ **0131 319 1447**
www.hawthorne-house.com

Charming, traditional Victorian cottage on a quiet lane above the High Street. Modern comfortable accommodation: double, twin, single and family ensuite rooms. Hearty Scottish breakfast of porridge, bacon and eggs, kippers, vegetarian breakfast. Local bars, restaurants. Luxury New Year 'Loony Dook' packages available.

Price: £50–£55 double room, £25 single.

EATING OUT

FINE DINING

Dakota Grill
Dakota Forth Bridge Hotel EH30 9QZ
☎ 0870 423 4293
www.dakotaforthbridge.co.uk

Under leading chef Roy Brett (formerly at Rick Stein, Padstow), the fabulous fresh and classy seafood menu offers Eyemouth crab, lobster, oysters, fish curry, steak and chicken. Winner of two awards, the Scottish Restaurant 2008 and Hotel Restaurant 2008. High-style décor with low-cost dining. Starters £8, mains £12–£15.

RESTAURANT

Orocco Pier
17 High Street,
South Queensferry EH30 9PP
☎ 0870 118 1664
www.oroccopier.co.uk

This cosmopolitan bar and brasserie (with rooms) is the place for cocktails at sunset looking out over the river and two bridges, and then to enjoy contemporary, freshly prepared Scottish and Mediterranean cuisine. The menu includes roast lamb, langoustines, salads, pasta etc. Very popular day and night with a fabulous outside decking above the beach. A dinner bill of around £ 22 for two courses.

The Boat House
22 High Street,
South Queensferry EH30 9PP
☎ 0131 331 5429
www.theboathouse-sq.co.uk

This whitewashed boathouse perched above the beach has pine tables, antique curios and fishing ephemera. There's a casual bistro for mussels and tapas, a smart restaurant for seafood bisque, local oak-smoked salmon, scallops with truffles, as well as an outdoor patio and daytime café and deli. Bistro mussels £4.85, two-course restaurant dinner £22.

BISTRO

Cramond Gallery Bistro
4–5 Riverside,
Cramond Village EH4 6NU
☎ 0131 312 6555

This delightful harbour bistro is known as 'the oldest restaurant in Edinburgh' as it stands on the foundations of the Roman boathouse. Have a browse around the gallery of local art before sampling tea and scones by day or a seafood dinner of smoked salmon, haddock, sea bass, mussels and scallops. Two courses £12.50.

Cramond Brig
66 Queensferry Road,
Cramond Bridge EH4 6DY
☎ 0131 339 4350
www.cramondbrig.com

Comfortable bar/restaurant with cavernous sofas and armchairs, log fire and widescreen TV. Italian-Scottish cuisine including pizzas, spaghetti, risotto, steak, burgers, chicken, mussels, scampi, salmon. There's a separate family area where kids can make their own pizzas and an activity room. Two courses £15.

EATING OUT

TRATTORIA

Bella Vista
23 Edinburgh Road, South Queensferry EH30 9HR
☎ 0131 331 4727

Popular Italian food served by friendly staff in this aptly named restaurant. You get the feeling that you actually are in the water from some of the tables! Good food with great views of the Bridges. There's also a lounge bar and garden. Starters £6–£8, pasta and pizza £12, steak £20.

CAFÉ

Craigie's Farmhouse Café
West Craigie Farm, South Queensferry EH30 9TR
☎ 0131 319 1048
www.craigies.co.uk

Scandinavian style barn beside a working farm with views to the Forth and Pentland Hills. Well established family run, bright and spacious licensed café with a deli counter and grocery shop. Offers breakfast and lunch, and wholesome, rustic dishes such as a ploughman's lunch or pork burger around £5–£8.

TEA ROOM

Picnic Coffee Shop & Gallery
5 Mid Ter, South Queensferry EH30 9LH
☎ 0131 331 1346

Located on the High Street, this is a traditional tearoom owned by Geraldine serving all the goodies you will love, Cream Teas, coffee, cakes, homemade soup, jacket potatoes, paninis and sandwiches, as well as kid's picnics. Open Mon–Sat, 9am–4.15pm and Sun (May–Oct), 11am–4.15pm. Lunchtime snack costs £5–£8.

The best... FOOD AND DRINK

▶ Staying in

Craigie's Farm Deli and Café near South Queensferry (see under Eating Out) is great for local farm produce, fresh vegetables and summer strawberries, homemade Granny Sinclair's jam and chutney. They have been nominated for the Glenfiddich Spirit of Scotland award for excellent food. Along Queensferry High Street, **The Picnic** has a takeaway service for homebaking, sandwiches and snacks and you'll find a couple of fish and chip shops along the High Street.

🍸 Drinking

South Queensferry has several wonderful inns, pubs and contemporary wine bars. **Hawes Inn** is a quaint vintage pub dating back to the 17th century, opposite the harbour, and is a member of the Cask Marque Trust in recognition of its excellent real ale.

In contrast **Orocco Pier** is a contemporary, classy cocktail bar for beer, wine and spirits, leather sofas, soft lighting, and outside decking. **The Boathouse** has recently created a cocktail and champagne bar, to complement their seafood bistro and restaurant. **The Moorings** pub is a popular local, hosting the Loony Dook on New Years day. The **Ferry Tap** is an attractive pub decorated with flower baskets on the High Street, and near the Hawes Pier is **The Rail Bridge**, a bar and bistro with outside seating. Over at Cramond, the **Cramond Inn** is the village local and popular with visitors after a walk along the promenade or a trip to Cramond Island.

FURTHER AFIELD

Midlothian

ROSSLYN CHAPEL: Roslin, Midlothian EH25 9PU; 0131 440 2159; www.rosslynchapel. com. Entry: adults £7.50(summer)/£6 (winter),children free up to 16; open 1 Apr–30 Sept, Mon–Sat 9.30am–6pm, Sun 12–4.45pm; 1 Oct–31 Mar, Mon–Sat 9.30am–5pm; Sun 12–4.45pm.

To the south of Edinburgh beyond the southside residential suburbs, the city is surrounded by a greenbelt, the rural region of Midlothian, which is dotted with historic villages, battlesites, castles, magnificent countryside and the Pentland Hills. Midlothian has some superb visitor attractions which are ideal for an afternoon visit or day trip and easily accessible by buses from the city centre.

LOCAL KNOWLEDGE

Born and bred in Edinburgh and with nearly 30 years' experience of driving Edinburgh taxis, **Glyn Farrer** of Hail the Cabbie (www.hailthecabbie.com) offers personally tailored tours of Edinburgh and the best attractions around Midlothian and East Lothian.

Best tourist attractions: Our world-famous castle, home of the world's oldest crown jewels, a military museum and the one o'clock gun; a unique insight into the history of Scotland. Rosslyn Chapel famous for The Knights Templar, *The Da Vinci Code* and the visit by Tom Hanks to film the movie of Dan Brown's novel.

Best place to take children: The Dynamic Earth is a joy, as well as the Museum of Childhood for children young and old and the Seabird Centre, North Berwick.

Best sport and leisure: For golfers, East Lothian has dozens of courses ranging from links, public and championship courses.

Best walk: The walk I most enjoy with my wife and sons is the Roman village at Cramond, from the mouth of the river Almond to the Old Mill at the waterfall, where, if you are lucky enough, you might catch site of an otter.

Best view: Edinburgh is built on seven hills and the view from Calton Hill inspires awe at such a magnificent city. Walk towards the house at the top of the and gaze at the panoramic views of south Edinburgh, Old Town, New Town and the Fife coast.

Best beach: Portobello is called Edinburgh's Victorian seaside, a good place for families with games arcades and fish and chip shops.

Best parks and gardens: Holyrood Park, home to Arthur's Seat, an extinct volcano and three Lochs: St Margaret's which was once a boating pond, Dunsapie which was created by Prince Albert and Duddingston which has a bird sanctuary visited in summer by Canadian and Greylag geese.

Rosslyn Chapel

Rosslyn Chapel was founded in 1446 by Sir William St Clair as a Collegiate church to spread intellectual and spiritual knowledge; but the chapel was still not complete by William's death in 1482. Those interested in architecture, religion, freemasonry and history have long visited the chapel to admire its extraordinary, intricate symbolic stone carvings and sculptures depicting biblical, masonic, pagan and Knights Templar themes. Dan Brown's best-selling novel, *The Da Vinci Code,* which weaves together the legends of the Holy Grail, the mysteries of the Knights Templar and Priory of Sion, features a plot finale at Rosslyn Chapel. The movie based on the

The Rosslyn Chapel contains beautiful and intricate stone carvings

novel starring Tom Hanks was partly filmed here and this too has enticed thousands of set jetters and Grail seekers to visit the ancient church.

Rosslyn Chapel is an Episcopalian Church and holds regular services on Sundays, such as the 10.30am Family Eucharist and 5.00pm Evensong. On Tuesdays and Fridays there are brief prayer sessions in the Chapel at noon.

Rosslyn Revealed

Imaginative fiction aside, in a recent non-fiction book, *Rosslyn Revealed* by Alan Butler and John Ritchie, the Chapel is described as 'the secret library in stone'. John Ritchie lives nearby in the village of Roslin and knows the history and artistry of the chapel inside out and this is his description of what is probably the most unique medieval building in the world.

'Rosslyn chapel is not a Notre Dame or a Westminster Abbey – it is a small unfinished collegiate chapel, but which probably contains more arcane knowledge than both of these august buildings. Rosslyn was built to be a guide and tutor to be understood by people of all languages and also by the illiterate, all of whom could read its messages and stories through its exquisite sculpted figures and friezes. These multitudinous carvings hold information from medieval manuscripts, biblical phrases, references to astronomy and all the religious philosophies of the period. This library in stone is a jewel of the Mason's Art and the repository of the Templar's Knowledge; it is paralleled only by the great cathedrals of Chartes or Santiago de Compostella, paralleled but not surpassed. From the time it was built, Rosslyn Chapel has always been a sacred site of pilgrimage where visitors over the centuries to the present day are undoubtedly moved, mystified and mesmerised by this magical place.'

Other Midlothian attractions

If you have no interest in industrial buildings or coal mining, this attraction might not seem worth a trip, but you would be mistaken. **The Scottish Mining Museum** provides a great day out for all the family; it's particularly entertaining as well as educational for children. This five-star tourist attraction, attracting 40,000 visitors a year, was created within the former Lady Victoria Colliery, founded to preserve Midlothian and Scotland's mining heritage. There are superb interactive exhibits, film footage, audio recordings, photographs, old lamps and machinery, allowing you to trace the history of mining and its social community. A few of the guides are former miners so that you can hear the true stories of the experience, working life down the pit. There is a café and a gift shop.

SCOTTISH MINING MUSEUM: Newtongrange, Midlothian EH22 4QN; ☎ 0131 663 7519, www.scottishminingmuseum.com. Entry: adult £5.95 (summer)/£3.95 (winter), child £3.95; open Mar–Oct 10am–5pm; Nov–Feb 10am–4pm.

Another attraction nearby is **Butterfly and Insect World** where you can learn, close up, all about the creepie crawlies. As well as caterpillars and butterflies, there are spiders, tarantulas and snakes, which you can touch (if you dare!).

BUTTERFLY AND INSECT WORLD: Dobbies Garden Centre, Midlothian EH18 1AZ; ☎ 0131 663 4932; www.edinburgh-butterfly-world.co.uk. Entry: adult £5.95(summer)/£4.95 (winter), child £3.95, under 3s free; open daily, summer 9.30am–5.30am, winter 10am–5pm.

If you fancy staying on the outskirts of Edinburgh near these Midlothian attractions, **Dalhousie Castle Hotel** (Dalhousie Castle, Bonnyrigg EH19 3JB; ☎ 01875 820153, www.dalhousiecastle.co.uk) offers a historic setting, small spa and lovely parkland for a relaxing romantic stay.

Without having to head up to the Highlands for a real sense of wild countryside and fresh air, simply escape to the **Pentland Hills,** on the outskirts of Edinburgh. The Pentlands Hills regional park is a living, working, sheep-farming landscape of 10,000 hectares of countryside, woodland and 60 miles of paths for walking, hiking, biking and horse riding. There are good waymarked walks, such as from Flotterstone visitor centre to Glencorse reservoir, with interesting wildlife on the way. From Hillend there are fine views across Edinburgh. For full details of parkland walks and the natural environment, pick up a leaflet from tourist information or see www.pentlandhills.org.

Before you venture up any Perthshire mountains, you might like to experience climbing in a safe environment. The **Ratho Climbing Arena**, the world's largest, is built around the natural rock face of a disused quarry on the west side of Edinburgh. This five-star visitor attraction, for adults and children, houses a climbing arena, scrambles, and abseiling, as well as a gym, fitness studio, spa and children's soft play area. It is also home to the world's highest, longest aerial assault course: an adrenaline-fuelled challenge 100ft above the floor.

EDINBURGH INTERNATIONAL CLIMBING ARENA: Ratho EH28 8AA; ☎ 0131 333 6333; www.eica-ratho.com. Climbing arena prices: adult £8.75/£7.75 (off peak), children £5.50; scrambles £4; open Mon–Fri 10am–10pm; Sat–Sun 10am–7pm.

ⓘ Visitor Information

Tourist Information Centre: 3 Princes Street, Edinburgh EH2 2QP; ☎ 0845 225 5121; Edinburgh Tourist Board www.edinburgh.org; Scottish Tourist Board www.visitscotland.com; Edinburgh Festivals www.edinburgh-festivals.com.

Hospitals: Royal Infirmary of Edinburgh, 51 Little France Crescent, Edinburgh EH16 4SA, ☎ 0131 536 1000; Western General Hospital, Minor Injuries Unit open 7 days, 9am–9pm, Crewe Road South, Edinburgh EH4 2XU, ☎ 0131 537 1000; for children under 12: Royal Hospital for Sick Children, 9 Sciennes Road Edinburgh EH9 1LF, ☎ 0131 536 0000; Primary Care Centre, provides listsings of NHS services, ☎ 0131 537 8424, www.show.scot.nhs.uk.

Police: Lothians & Borders Police, Police Headquarters, Fettes Avenue EH1 1RB, ☎ 0131 311 3131; Gayfield Square Police Station (East End), 2 Gayfield Square EH1 3NW, ☎ 0131 556 9270; West End Police Station, 3–5 Torphichen Place EH3 8DY, ☎ 0131 229 2323; Leith Police Station, Queen Charlotte Street EH6 7EY, ☎ 0131 554 9350; Edinburgh Airport Police Station, Edinburgh Airport EH12 9DN, ☎ 0131 333 2724; South Queensferry Police Station 13 Hopetoun Road EH30 9RB, ☎ 0131 331 1798.

Internet Access: Edinburgh Internet Café (Old Town), 98 West Bow EH1 2HH, ☎ 0131 226 5400; Easy Internet Café (New Town), 58 Rose Street EH2 2YQ, ☎ 0131 226 5971.

Travel and Transport: Edinburgh Airport, ☎ 08700 400 0007, www.edinburghairport.com; Traveline, ☎ 0871 2002233, www.travelinescotland.com, www.traveline.org.uk; Lothian Buses and Airport Airlink, ☎ 0131 555 6363, www.lothianbuses.com; First Bus, ☎ 08708 72 72 71, www.firstgroup.com.

City Tours: Edinburgh Tour Guides, walking and coach tours, ☎ 0131 443 0548, www.edinburghtourguides.com.

Bike Rental: Biketrax, 11–13 Lochrin Place, Tollcross EH3 9QX, ☎ 0131 228 6633; Edinburgh Cycle Hire, 29 Blackfriars Street EH1 1NB, ☎ 0131 556 1212; Leith Cycle Co, 276 Leith Walk EH6 5BX, ☎ 0131 467 7775.

Taxis: Comcab ☎ 0131 225 9000; Festival City Cars ☎ 0131 552 1777; Central Radio Taxis ☎ 0131 221 2230.

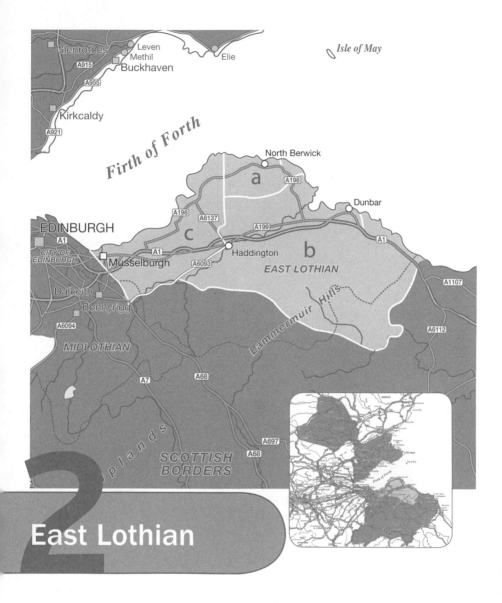

East Lothian

a. North Berwick
b. Dunbar to Haddington
c. Along the East Coast

Unmissable highlights

01 Dirleton Castle, one of the oldest medieval fortified castles with magnificent gardens featuring the world's longest herbaceous border, p.184

02 The Bass Rock, a geological wonder of the world and bird sanctuary for 100,000 gannets, p.159

03 John Muir Country Park, a beautiful stretch of coastline from Dunbar to Belhaven Bay, p.175

04 North Berwick, a traditional seaside resort with two long sandy beaches, Seabird Centre, golf, putting green and Luca's ice cream, p.158

05 The Museum of Flight, featuring vintage aircraft, wartime bombers and the chance to step on board Concorde, p.164

06 Aberlady Nature Reserve, Britain's first nature reserve covering woodland, seashore and marshland, p.190

07 Golf East Lothian Passport, 18 fabulous golf courses including the world-class Muirfield at Gullane, p.162

08 Glenkinchie Distillery, see how they make great whisky and sample a dram, p.184

09 Fenton Barns a co-operative steading for local farm food, café, arts, crafts and design studios, p.170

10 Gullane Bents, fabulous beaches for walking, windsurfing and picnics, p.189

EAST LOTHIAN

On a visit to Edinburgh, you must make time for a day trip to escape to East Lothian; or even better, stay for a few days to experience its 40 miles of fabulous coastline, white sand beaches, tiny islands, picture-postcard villages, rolling, rich green farmland, country parks and endless golf courses.

There are three separate signposted trails for motoring and cycling: the Coastal route along the seashore; the Saltire Trail to experience a sense of Scottish history visiting castles and old market towns; and the Hillfoots Trail for a rural journey over the Lammermuir Hills with its woodland walks.

Robert Louis Stevenson, the novelist and traveller, was born and brought up in Edinburgh and spent many family holidays during the 1860s in North Berwick – in fact the island of Fidra just offshore is said to have inspired *Treasure Island*. His memoir *The Lantern Bearers* describes very happy, carefree days as a boy:

He recalls: '*a smell of fish, a genial smell of seaweed, whiffs of blowing sand at the street corners; shops with golf balls and bottled lollipops; two sandy bays, a haven in the rocks, grey islets… a wilderness of hiding-holes, alive with popping rabbits and soaring gulls. The ruins of a mighty and ancient fortress, the air at the cliff's edge brisk and clean and pungent of the sea – in front of all, the Bass Rock.*'

The golf course, harbour, smell of seaweed, fresh sea air and soaring gulls are all just the same today as the 1860s – (and the 1960s when I spent idyllic, carefree summers here as a child). What more does a child need than a bucket and spade and rockpools for netting crabs?

For outdoor and sporting enthusiasts, you can enjoy watersports, sailing, kayaking, diving, golf, hiking, biking and horse riding. Right along the coastline the waves sweep in from the North Sea, a gentle roll at Gullane Bents or crashing over the rocks at Tantallon Castle.

East Lothian is serious farming country where at farmers' markets and farm shops you can sample the finest beef, pork and lamb, fresh lobster and crab, artisan cheese, organic mushrooms and sweet summer strawberries.

NORTH BERWICK

North Berwick is so easy to reach from Edinburgh: just take the train. The 30-minute journey travels through the golden arable farmland and coastal panoramas.

The name North Berwick comes from the Old English Bere for 'barley' and wic for 'farmstead'. The word North was added to distinguish this Berwick from Berwick-upon-Tweed.

This peaceful little harbour town has a long tradition of being a holiday resort (the 'Biarritz of the North') dating back over 150 years. The grand redstone Marine Hotel overlooking the seafront golf course was built in 1880 to cater for well-to-do families, golfers and health-conscious bathers who came for the benefit of the therapeutic sea water. Today the curving west and east bays of white sand beaches have Rural Seaside Awards for cleanliness. On the east bay, there's a wonderful tidal seawater pool for swimming, safe paddling and airbed 'boating' for children.

North Berwick is dominated by **Berwick Law**, a 613ft volcanic hill to the south of the town. It can be seen for many miles around and worth the climb for panoramic views of the surrounding countryside and coastline. Another iconic focal point is the **Bass Rock**, a massive 350ft volcanic crag of an island, home to over 150,000 gannets, cormorants, puffins and eider ducks.

The delightful High Street is full of independent boutiques, traditional sweet shops, an old-fashioned tea room, bars and bistros. Signposts on every street corner point you in the right direction for the harbour, beaches, car parks and visitor attractions. North Berwick is the perfect base to tour local castles, beaches, walking and biking trails, golf courses and the cute wee villages around East Lothian.

WHAT TO SEE AND DO

With whitewashed buildings, clean streets, good parking bays and an excellent tourist information office, there is a warm welcome to visitors. The town also has the best public toilets in Britain, well maintained and decorated with flowers. As you wander around you'll notice gardens, borders and baskets filled with colourful flowers; the town is a frequent Britain in Bloom winner. At the Britain in Bloom Awards September 2008, North Berwick was runner up in the coastal resort category, only second to the much sunnier Herm Island off the coast of Guernsey.

The prime draw to North Berwick is the natural unspoilt landscape and beautiful coastline for miles around. Think Big Sur on a small scale. On a fine day, head down to the beaches – there's the west and east beaches on either side of the harbour. You don't need children to enjoy a stroll along the sand, paddle in the waves, or clamber around the rocks. Sit on the wall and taste a creamy **Luca's Ice Cream**; the van is usually parked above East Beach near the Seabird Centre.

North Berwick is the perfect launch point for young sea kayakers, while beaches such as Tantallon provide waves for the enthusiastic surf kayaker. There is nothing

The town of North Berwick

better than sea kayaking in East Lothian, with plenty of hidden coves and rocky bays. Olympic champion David Florence learnt to canoe as a young boy off Seacliff beach, near Tantallon. Ed Smith, four-time British freestyle champion, is a member

> NORTH BERWICK KAYAK CLUB: ☎ 01620 880227. Sea kayaking season Apr–Sept. Visiting kayakers may join a club outing for £10.

and kayak coach of the **North Berwick Kayak Club**, which welcomes experienced kayakers through the summer season.

If you are feeling energetic, climb to the top of **Berwick Law**, with its whale jawbone sculpture at the summit. It's a reasonably easy walk, although steep in places up the winding path.

The **John Muir Way** (named after the founder of modern conservation who was born in Dunbar) is being developed by East Lothian Council to provide a continuous path linking East Lothian with the City of Edinburgh and the Scottish Borders. The signposted routes in this area are from North Berwick to the Law, Dirleton, and Yellowcraig beach along the shoreline, through glorious countryside, to heritage attractions and natural beauty spots. Leaflets and maps are available at the tourist information office.

An absolute must is to experience a boat trip out to the wonderful tiny islands on the Forth. The *Sula* and *Braveheart* boats are owned by a long-running local family business which now continues in the hands of the fourth generation of the Marr family. They run 90-minute cruises around Craigleith, Fidra, the Lamb and the Bass Rock. You can expect to see puffins, guillemots, kittiwakes and gannets, as well as various gulls, shags, cormorants, fulmars and also grey seals. Check the timetable at the Celtic Cross beside the Harbour. Departure is usually between noon and 1pm daily between May and September.

SEABIRD SEAFARI: Scottish Seabird Centre;
☎ 01620 890202; www.seabird.org.
Prices: adult £20, children £17, fee partly
funds the SOS Puffin project. Runs Mar–Oct,
several cruises a day for 12 passengers.

The **Seabird Seafari**, a new venture, is a high-speed boat ride suitable for children from aged eight. Kitted out with an oilskin jacket and lifebelt, it's safe, dry and exhilarating. The boat zooms out to Craigleith island, an important puffin colony, where a major environmental project is underway. SOS Puffin has a team of 250 volunteers (working with naturalist professionals and the Seabird Centre) who clear the island rocks from tree mallow. This thick non-native vegetation prevents the puffins from building their underground nests in order to rear the baby puffins. The Seafari then jets across to the Bass Rock

EAST LOTHIAN YACHT CLUB: 36–40 Victoria
Rd, North Berwick EH39 4JL; ☎ 0131
334 5951; www.elyc.org.uk. Dingy season
spring to Christmas, yacht season spring to
autumn. Dinghies for rent, sailing lessons
and courses for all ages.

where the engines are cut for a gentle cruise around the island, learning about and witnessing the extraordinary wildlife of gannets and seabirds and the former island abbey and prison.

East Lothian Yacht Club is based at the harbour and is a recognised RYA training establishment running club dinghy racing, keelboat racing and a variety of open events. The regatta days and races throughout the summer are amazing to watch.

As well as numerous yachts out at sea, you may even spot a bunch of surfing fanatics who regularly go out and test the waves along the coast on Sunday mornings.

Take a high-speed boat ride with Seafari

From the sea to the air: experience the thrill of flying in a microlight plane in the safe hands of an accompanying instructor. Fly over East Lothian's beautiful beaches and famous golf courses and see the world's largest gannet colony on the Bass Rock from a different perspective. You can take off over the Lammermuir Hills and down towards the Borders or over the Firth of Forth to Fife. Flights can be arranged through **East of Scotland Microlights** operated by Gordon Douglas, Chief Flying Instructor with over 25 years' experience of flying microlights. This is the longest established school and club in Scotland, located at East Fortune Airfield, East Lothian. On a 30 or 60-minute introductory Air Experience flight, after take off and full briefing of controls, you will be invited to try flying the plane yourself from the back seat – though the instructor will take over for the landing!

> **EAST OF SCOTLAND MICROLIGHTS:** East Fortune Airfield, near North Berwick EH39 5LE; ☎ 01620 880332; www.eosm.co.uk. Prices: 30 mins £60, 60 mins £99; 120 mins £180; open 7 days, year round.

Ancient castles

Just a few miles out of town is **Tantallon Castle**, an ancient fortress on a rocky headland surrounded by cliffs. The seat of the Douglas Earls of Angus, it has an amazing history of enemy attack and sieges, including Oliver Cromwell's army in 1651, yet it has survived for several centuries. For those with vertigo, you may not wish to climb up the steep winding stone stairs, but it's fun to walk around the old battlement walls and to the top of the Mid Tower. The castle is surrounded by beautifully kept grassland, covering the former ditch which was cut through the cliff rock to prevent invasion. The English Ambassador was based at Tantallon in November 1543 when he wrote a letter to Henry VIII about this formidable stronghold: '*Tantallon is of such strength as I nede not feare the malice of myne enymeys...*'

Scotland's music festival, the Fringe by the Sea

Direlton Castle and Gardens is just 3 miles west of North Berwick, and if you dont have a car, there's a local bus. This is one of the oldest surviving castles in Scotland and ancient seat of the De Vaux, Haliburton and Ruthven families. There are two fabulous gardens, one

> **TANTALLON CASTLE:** 3 miles East of North Berwick, off A198; ☎ 01620 892727; www.historic-scotland.gov.uk. Entry: adult £4.70 (summer)/£3.70 (winter), child £2.35; open Mar–Sept, 7 days, 9.30–5.30pm; 1 Oct– 30 Oct 9.30am–4.30pm; 1 Nov–31 Mar 9.30am–4.30pm; closed Thursday and Friday. Last entrance 30 minutes before closing. Local bus 120 from Quality Street, North Berwick to end of Tantallon Castle drive then 15-minute walk to Castle.

One of the oldest surviving castles in Scotland, Direlton Castle

with a formal design and a more typical country garden. This features the longest herbaceous border in the world as stated in the *Guinness Book of World Records*.

Play a round of golf

Visitors to East Lothian quickly realise that they can immerse themselves in the history of golf. It was here on the banks of the Firth of Forth that the game saw its earliest development, and some of the greatest events in golfing history have held centre stage only a few miles from Edinburgh. The ancient links of **Old Musselburgh** is still widely accepted as the oldest golf course in the world and has a fascinating history. Others in Gullane and North Berwick are just as historically important. The mighty links of **Muirfield**, which has hosted many exciting Open Championships, is home to the Honourable Company of Edinburgh Golfers, the oldest golf club in existence.

The **Golf East Lothian Passport** offers unbelievable value to visiting golfers, with a superb choice of links and parkland courses to choose from, including two in North Berwick: **Glen Golf** course, which has a seaside setting, with elevated tees and greens

> DIRELTON CASTLE AND GARDENS: Direlton Village EH39 5ER; ☎ 01620 850330; www.historic-scotland.gov.uk. Entry: adult £4.70 (summer)/£3.70 (winter), child £2.35; open 21 Mar–30 Sept, 7 days, 9.30am–5.30pm; 1 Oct–30 Oct 9.30am–4.30pm, 1 Nov–31 Mar 9.30–4.30pm; closed Thursday and Friday. Last entrance 30 minutes before closing.

LOCAL KNOWLEDGE

Kitty Douglas-Hamilton is a freelance writer, curator and exhibitions organiser. She has written for the *Scotsman* and *The Times* and worked with the National Galleries and National Museums. Her family home is next to the harbour at North Berwick, and her childhood was spent on the beach and in the freezing outdoor swimming pool.

Best seafaring excursion: Take a boat trip around the islands Craigleith, Fidra, the Lamb and Bass Rock. The Sula and Braveheart are the oldest family-run businesses, the boats of choice for the visitor.

Best natural icon: The Bass Rock owned by the Dalrymple family, formerly used as a prison, now houses the largest gannet colony in Europe, described by Sir David Attenborough as 'one of the 12 wildlife wonders of the world'. It's truly the most impressive natural landmark in Scotland.

Favourite takeaway: North Berwick Fry, Quality Street has the best fish 'n'chips. The best places to sit and eat are beside the Bass Rock mural, the beach or in the neighbouring Lodge Grounds and listen to the bird chatter in the Avery.

Best historic attraction: Tantallon Castle, former seat of the Douglas Earls of Angus. This dramatic backdrop has been used for various film shoots including Bollywood!

Best entertainment: Fringe by the Sea is Scotland's music festival by the beach in August when North Berwick is alive with great music and entertainment.

Best visitor attraction: the natural landscape and seascapes, Tantallon and Dirleton Castles. Come to the Seabird Centre to watch puffins hatching in the summer months, through the live live camera link on the Bass Rock.

Best pub: The Ship Inn at 7 Quality Street is a traditional, family-friendly pit stop with heart-warming fare on a windy day. Swing by for a quick nip of local whisky or Belhaven ale. It's also thought that Robert Louis Stevenson drank here.

for superb views of the Bass Rock and also **Whitekirk Golf Course** which has lush fairways and undulating contours for a challenging round. It's a regular venue for championship events on the PGA Europro Tour. With the passport, 12 East Lothian golf courses offer a 15%–30% reduction. The pass entitles visitors to purchase one round or day ticket at each club over five consecutive weekdays.

Many hotels in the area have created special golf packages offering the best possible value golf in East Lothian.

☂ Wet weather

The Museum of Flight is located about 15 minutes' drive from North Berwick in a former wartime RAF station at East Fortune, now an historic monument. In 1919 the airship R34 left from East Fortune to make the first east-to-west crossing of the Atlantic by air. The collection includes a number of R34 relics, as well as numerous aircraft, engines, rockets, photographs, a reference library, archives, models, flying clothing, instruments and propellers. The Museum traces the history of naval and military aircraft developed across two world wars, and the development of commercial passenger flights. One of the highlights is the **Concorde Experience**. In the giant Hangar 4, see the Concorde G-BOAA, the first of the British Airways fleet to fly commercially when she flew from London to Bahrain in January 1976. It's now preserved here for

The Concorde Experience at the Museum of Flight

all to see in its sleek streamlined glory. There are excellent exhibits on its engine and aircraft design, with images to show her final voyage by land and sea from Heathrow. And you can actually purchase a boarding pass and go aboard Concorde. An excellent hand-held audio guide relates the background aviation story, facts and figures on speed and the experiences of the famous passengers and crew who flew on this supersonic aircraft.

THE MUSEUM OF FLIGHT: East Fortune, near North Berwick EH39 5LF; ☎ 01620 897 240; Concorde booking line 0870 421 4299; www.nms.ac.uk.
Prices: adult £5.50, concession £4.50, children under 12 free. Concorde Boarding pass £8.50 (summer)/£6.50 (winter); children under 12 free; open daily Apr–Oct 10am–5pm (till 6pm Jul–Aug); Nov–Mar 10am–4pm weekends only.

What to do with children

The Scottish Seabird Centre, housed in a stylish wooden lodge building beside the harbour, is a state-of-the-art interactive wildlife attraction for families. There are live webcams, a cinema, an environmental zone, and kids' workshops and activities. Across the seasons, see nesting birds, diving gannets, baby chicks and seal pups close up. With over 1.5 million international visitors since opening in

SCOTTISH SEABIRD CENTRE: The Harbour, North Berwick EH39 4SS; ☎ 01620 890202; www.seabird.org. Entry: adult £7.95 (summer)/£5.95 (winter), children aged 4–15 £4.50, under 4s free; open daily Apr–Sept 10am–6pm; Feb, Mar, Oct, Mon–Fri 10am–5pm, Sat–Sun 10am–5.30pm; Nov–Jan, Mon–Fri 10am–4pm, Sat–Sun 10am–5.30pm.

The Scottish Seabird Centre

2000, the Centre won the Business Tourism of Scotland Award 2008 for their services to the community and as a wildlife conservation and educational charity.

For a great day out you can walk from North Berwick along the coast to **Yellowcraig Beach** opposite the island of Fidra with its impressive white lighthouse. Alternatively, it's a couple of miles drive and has a car park and visitor facilities. The sand dunes and grassy banks here are wonderful for playing and picnics, with a permanent barbecue grill station. The water is clean and safe for swimming. As Fidra is the island which inspired Robert Louis Stevenson to write his novels, there is the **Treasure Island Adventure Park** here with tree swings, ropes and climbing frames on the theme of a pirate ship. There is also a nature trail through the woodland.

Entertainment

As a lively community and seaside town, there are many local festivals and events throughout the year, with regular concerts held in the Blackadder Church and art exhibitions. The international **North Berwick Highland Games** (www.northberwickhighland games.co.uk) takes place in early August, and attracts around 15,000 people. There are pipe band contests, Highland dancing and other attractions.

There's also an annual **Raft Race** on a Saturday in August, where you can watch the locals (and perhaps a few brave visitors) in homemade rafts attempting to survive the tricky obstacles without capsizing. Peter Hammond, the enthusiastic organiser, tells the story: *'The Raft Race has been taking place for well over 30 years, its origin lost in the mists of time, to raise funds for the local RNLI and promote a community spirit. Everyone over 16 years of age is welcome to take part. The rafts must be made from scratch, adapted from suitable materials. A team found hiding a canoe inside boxes and tarpaulins, for example, is disqualified (this has happened) and keelhauled within a inch of their lives (this hasn't happened... yet). The event sets off from Elcho Slipway, West Beach to a buoy, then across to the Harbour Wall and back to the starting point. There are trophies for first raft, best dressed and first pub-team back to the beach.'*

While Edinburgh is enjoying its Arts festival in August, North Berwick has its own **Festival by the Sea** (www.fringebythesea.co.uk). The inaugural four-day festival in August 2008 presented a wide-ranging programme of well-known musicians and singers from jazz to opera. It was dreamt up by Eric Wales and friends with the aim of enhancing the cultural life in and around North Berwick. His idea was to 'pull a bit of the Festival Fringe buzz away from Edinburgh and down to North Berwick... a wee break down to the beach would be welcomed by the festival goers and for the local punters.'

The **Museum of Flight Airshow** (www.nms.ac.uk) at East Fortune Airfield each year in July (usually the last Saturday afternoon) is a spectacular world-class event for RAF veterans, aeroplane enthusiasts, families and children. Here you can witness aircraft soaring overhead with thunderous fly pasts and aeronautical displays. There is plenty to do on the ground too, with flight simulators, falconry displays, children's workshops and much more.

Performers at the Museum of Flight Airshow

🛒 Shopping

North Berwick High Street is great for a browse in and out of gift shops, fashion and accessory boutiques, art galleries, good-quality charity shops for second-hand books and bargains. Visit the **Sugar Mountain** to see the jars of soor plooms, gob stoppers, toffees and other traditional sweets.

The **Westgate Gallery** is a treasure house of artwork, jewellery, bags, soft toys, candles, cards and gifts. The **Green and Blue gallery** presents quality paintings by local artists.

A few miles away near Dirleton is **Fenton Barns** retail and leisure village. Originally a dairy and arable farm and also the wartime Drem RAF Station, now the buildings have been transformed into individual art, craft, design, furniture, clothing and farm food outlets creating a self-contained shopping village.

The best... PLACES TO STAY

BOUTIQUE

Nether Abbey

20 Dirleton Avenue EH39 4BQ
☎ 01620 892802
www.netherabbey.co.uk

Family-owned, small hotel featuring glamorous decor, contemporary fabrics and furnishings. Flat screen TVs, Frette linen, soft towels, very hot water. Ask for room 1 for super luxury. Start the day with a deluxe breakfast, scrambled egg, smoked salmon, classic Scottish with pork or vegetarian sausages.

Price: £60 B&B pp (sharing double rooms).

HOTEL

Macdonald Marine Hotel and Spa

Cromwell Road EH39 4LZ
☎ 0870 400 8129
www.macdonaldhotels.co.uk/marine

Well-established seaside resort with facilities for couples and families, featuring luxury spa, swimming pool and outdoor hot tub. Comfortable lounges with seaviews and excellent Craigleith Restaurant for fine dining. Hotel overlooks the golf course with short stroll to beach and harbour.

Price: £70–£100 B&B pp-double room.

Number 12 Quality Street

12 Quality Street EH39 4HP
☎ 01620 892529
www.no12qualitystreet.co.uk

Perfect location at the east end of High Street, a two-minute walk to harbour and beaches. Contemporary café bar-bistro (outdoor seating too) with 11 freshly decorated, smart bedrooms, in soft green and plum colours, plasma TV, shower-rooms.

Price: £35–£85 pppn.

B&B

The Glebe House

Law Road, North Berwick EH39 4PL
☎ 01620 892608
www.glebehouse-nb.co.uk

Beautiful aristocratic mansion house (1780) set in lovely gardens. Bedrooms have period furnishings, one with a four poster bed, TV and tea tray. Breakfast served at antique mahogany table, offering fresh fruit, croissants and full Scottish. Gwen and Jake offer warm hospitality and advice on local attractions.

Price: £50 pp B&B, £79 single.

SELF-CATERING

North Berwick Golf Lodge

18 Fidra Road, North Berwick EH39 4NG
☎ 02380 873007
www.eagleyerentals.com

This former coaching house offers luxurious accommodation for 8–12 people in six bedrooms (four bathrooms) featuring plasma TV, wireless broadband internet, fully fitted kitchen, outdoor 8ft arctic spa hot tub and putting green. Extra services include a chef housekeeping, chauffeured Mercedes Traveliner, concierge.

Price: £1,500–£3,000 per week. £18–£36 pp per night.

The Cottage on the Beach

9 Victoria Road, North Berwick EH39 4JL
☎ 01620 671966
www.coast-properties.co.uk

Modernised fisherman's cottage on two floors with three double bedrooms, two bathrooms, open-plan living/dining room (TV/DVD), and kitchen. There is also a patio with barbeque, table, chairs, croquet, cricket and table tennis equipment. The garden leads onto the beach through private gate.

Price: £550–£850 per week.

The best... FOOD AND DRINK

The rural farming and fishing community of East Lothian is renowned for its superior quality meat, fish, dairy produce, fruit and vegetables. The annual **East Lothian Food and Drink Festival** in September celebrates fine local food from coast to countryside (www.foodanddrinkeastlothian.com). Below, and in the following chapters which cover the villages and rural areas around North Berwick, there is information on the extraordinary range of farm shops, delis, farmers' market, breweries, whisky distilleries and food producers across East Lothian.

▶ Staying in

The **High Street, North Berwick** is ideal for people in self-catering accommodation needing supplies, or for visitors who want to sample some good food for a picnic or takeaway. Try **John Anderson Butcher** (36 High Street) for prime local meat and game, and the **Fisherman's Kitchen** (96 High Street) for East Lothian fish, lobster, eggs, groceries and a deli. Next door is the **Baguette Express** for fresh gourmet sandwiches. For all wines and alcoholic drinks, **Lockett Bros** off-licence (133 High Street) is reviewed as 'one of Scotland's most progressive wine merchants' and

Local hero: Cosmo Tamburo

Cosmo Tamburro is a well-known Italian-born chef in Scotland who founded the now legendary Cosmo's restaurant in Edinburgh in the 1960s. It was soon one of the leading places to wine and dine in the city. Celebrities visiting Edinburgh, including Burt Lancaster, Margaret Lockwood, James Last, Ronnie Corbett and Sean Connery (who was a great fan), would leave their luxury hotels and head to Cosmo's for dinner. It was in the basement of the Cosmo Ristorante where, from the 1970s, Cosmo began supplying homemade egg pasta to retailers. The success led the foundation of a family food company Cosmo Products with his son and son-in-law, which began making additive-free, healthy pizzas using traditional handmade dough and speciality homemade tomato sauce. Rather like the proverbial trading concept of selling coal to Newcastle, Cosmo Products export more than half a million Scottish pizzas to Italy each year. As well as classic toppings, Cosmo invented the haggis pizza which is very popular across Europe, as Cosmo himself said: 'We are well-rooted in Scottish life and we think the combination of haggis on an Italian margarita pizza reflects that.'

As well as managing director of his Pizza company, Cosmo was cofounder a couple of years ago of a seriously fine, intimate Italian restaurant *Osteria* on the High Street, North Berwick.

check out **Howdah Tea and Coffee Ltd** (42 High Street) for a deluxe range of fresh roasted coffee and quality tea.

Winner of the Best East Lothian café category at the Food Awards 2008, the **Fenton Barns Farm Shop and Coffee Shop** (☎ 01620 850 294; www.fentonbarnsfarmshop. com) is the ultimate foodie heaven for fresh, local and organic produce. Local potatoes, asparagus, mushrooms and seasonal fruit are delivered straight from field to shop; including fresh/smoked fish, local game, ostrich, wild boar, chicken. Homemade dishes such as Beef Bourguignon, fine cheese, free-range farm eggs, quail eggs, homebaking, bread, biscuits, preserves, honey and Luca's ice cream are all available. A true country store, it also stocks quality kitchenware, cook books and country gifts. The farm shop is at Fenton Barns Retail Village, just a couple of miles from North Berwick on the road to Dirleton.

Takeaway

North Berwick Fry (11 Quality Street) is regarded as the best fish and chips in town and is handily located next to Tourist Information Centre. Next door is the American-style **North Berwick Diner**. Along the High Street, you will find the usual suspects of Chinese and Indian takeaways.

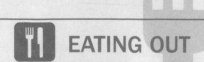

EATING OUT

FINE DINING

Craigleith Restaurant
Macdonald Marine Hotel, Cromwell Road, North Berwick EH39 4LZ
☎ **0870 400 8129**
www.macdonaldhotels.co.uk/marine

Head chef John Paul McLaughlin trained under Gordon Ramsay so you can expect exceptional, inventive, superior cuisine and dish presentation. Elegant dining room decorated with portraits and lush drapes with seaviews. Friendly knowledgeable staff. £35 for three courses.

Osteria
71 High Street,
North Berwick EH39 4HG
☎ **01620 890589**
www.osteria-no1.co.uk

This is seriously fine Italian cuisine including prosciutto, rocket and truffle oil, spaghetti frutti de mare, escalope of veal with aubergine and mozzarella, and roast rack of lamb with garlic. Superb wines, professional attention with a bill for two courses from £25.

EATING OUT

RESTAURANT

The Open Arms
Dirleton EH39 5EG
01620 850241
www.openarmshotel.co.uk

If you're visiting Direlton Castle, try
Deveau's Brasserie, which offers
Belhaven trout, chicken with haggis,
crab linguine; or try the intimate Library
Restaurant for a menu of pheasant, beef,
seabass. Deveau's £16 (two courses),
The Library £32 (three courses). The
Open Arms is also a small traditional
hotel with 12 rooms.

The Fly Half Bar and Grill
Nether Abbey Hotel, 20 Dirleton
Avenue, North Berwick EH39 4BQ
☎ **01620 892802**
www.netherabbey.co.uk

This bar and restaurant with outdoor
patio is very popular with local residents
and hotel guests. The lunch and dinner
menu offers something for all tastes;
with smoked salmon, langoustines,
Medierannean tapas platters, mussels,
Aberdeen Angus steak, 'catch of the
day', and fish and chips. Good value at
around £15 for two courses.

BISTRO

Number 12 Quality Street
12 Quality Street,
North Berwick EH39 4HP
☎ **01620 892529**
www.no12qualitystreet.co.uk

Expect to sample North Berwick lobster,
ribeye steak from Anderson's Butcher,
homemade soups, salmon fishcakes,
mushroom risotto, banana sticky toffee
pudding and Luca's ice cream, as this
places make sure it sources local, fresh
produce. Open for breakfast, coffee and
cake, tasty paninis, salads and pasta.
Two courses £10–£20.

Bass Rock Bistro
37 Quality Street,
North Berwick EH39 4HR
☎ **01620 890875**
www.bassrockbistro.co.uk

Seafood is a speciality, with local lobster,
octopus, crab, Eyemouth monkfish and
halibut, plus quality beef and game.
There is also a mussels and tapas bar.
They have a slow food philosophy of
high-quality local ingredients, simply
and expertly prepared. Lunch £10–£12,
dinner £20–£30.

EATING OUT

TEAROOM

Tea at Tiffany's
**21 High Street,
North Berwick EH39 4HH
☎ 01620 890057**

This charming old-fashioned tearoom serves tea in vintage floral bone china cups, with homemade pancakes, scones and cakes, including decadent chocolate fudge with ice cream. The décor features quirky Victorian collectables. Pot of tea and cake from around £5.

CAFÉ

The Orangery at Westgate Gallery
**39 Westgate, North Berwick EH39 4AG
☎ 01620 894 976
www.westgate-gallery.co.uk**

Browse around the art, accessories and gifts and then relax in the licensed conservatory café which serves teas, coffees, wines, beers, soft drinks, light lunches and a selection of homemade cakes, scones and pastries. Drink and snack costs £5–£10.

Fenton Barns Farm Shop and Café
**Fenton Barns Retail village, near North Berwick and Dirleton EH39 5BW
☎ 01620 850294**

Voted Best Café at the East Lothian Food and Drink Awards 2008. Serving the freshest local produce and homemade dishes, sample hearty soups, pies, savoury tarts, salads, fish and cheese platters, prosciutto, chicken, salmon or prawn sandwiches, children's meals, scones, and cakes. Expect to pay £4.95 for ploughman's lunch or roast beef roll.

Sunflower Café at Merryhatton Garden Centre
**East Fortune near Museum of Flight, nr North Berwick
☎ 01620 880278**

With fantastic views across the East Lothian countryside, this bright café makes everything from scratch. All cakes, bakes and scones are made in-house, right down to the impressive biscotti. Coffee is from The Howdah Tea and Coffee Company in North Berwick. Good soup and a sandwich will cost around £4.95.

🍷 Drinking

North Berwick is a small seaside town so you will have no difficulty trying out a few of the local pubs, all with a different atmosphere and style, with a short walk and staggering distance between them all. **The Ship Inn** (7 Quality Street) has a fine reputation for real ales including Belhaven Best from the local brewery.

Blenheim House Hotel bar (14 Westgate) offers local beers, whisky and live music from the North Berwick folk club (last Friday each month). At the **Quarterdeck** (1–5 Westgate) you will receive a warm welcome. This was the pub where Sam Torrance entertained John Daly and Fred Couples during the 1992 Open. The most popular beer amongst the regulars is the Belhaven 80/-.

And finally, a quiet setting, sophisticated manner, open log fires, armchairs and sofas can be found at the smart **Links Bar**, an elegant cocktail lounge bar at the **Macdonald Marine Hotel**, Cromwell Road.

ℹ️ Visitor Information

Tourist Information Centre: 1 Quality Street, ☎ 01620 892197, www.north-berwick.co.uk.

Hospitals: Edington Cottage Hospital, 54 St Baldred's Road, ☎ 01620 897040.

Doctors: Health Centre, 54 St Baldred's Road, ☎ 01620 892169.

Pharmacies: Boots chemists, High Street, ☎ 01620 892911.

Police: Police station, High Street, ☎ 01620 893585.

Supermarkets: Tesco, Tantallon Road EH39 5NF, ☎ 01620 642400.

Self-Catering Accommodation: NB Flats, 129 High Street, North Berwick, ☎ 01620 893204, www.nbflats.co.uk; Coast Properties, 27 High Street, North Berwick, ☎ 01620 67 1966, www.coast-properties.co.uk; Eagle eye, holiday homes near golf courses, ☎ 02380 873007, www.eagleyerentals.com.

Travel and Transport: First ScotRail trains, www.firstgroup.com/scotrail; North Berwick railway station, Station Road, ☎ 0845 601 5929; First Bus trips around East Lothian, ☎ 08708 72 72 71, www.firstgroup.com/scotlandeast.

Post Office: 7 High Street, North Berwick EH39 4HH, ☎ 01620 892165.

Sports Centre: North Berwick Sports centre, Grange Road, ☎ 01620 827810.

Garage: Bass Rock Garage 11–15 Station Hill, North Berwick EH39 4AN, ☎ 01620 894488.

Bike Rental: Law Cycle Hire, 2 Law Road, North Berwick EH39 4PL, ☎ 01620 890643, www.lawcycles.co.uk.

Taxis: Jim's Taxis, ☎ 01620 894900, four vehicles – two cars and two eight-people seaters for all transfers and golf excursions; Muirfield Private Hire, ☎ 01620 890083, private unbranded vehicles for train and airport transfers, golf, sightseeing trips and whisky tours.

DUNBAR TO HADDINGTON

With the wonderful John Muir Country Park, cliff walks, beaches for picnics, scuba diving, surfing, wind and kite boarding, the nature reserve, family leisure park, fishing, pony trekking, cycle rides, golf courses and tennis, there's plenty for the sporting enthusiast, nature lover and families with children to enjoy in and around Dunbar. What's more this south-east coast corner of East Lothian is renowned as the sunniest place in Scotland. According to the UK Met Office it enjoys an average of 1,523 hours of sun per annum, or four hours, 10 minutes daily.

The seaside resort town of Dunbar has a colourful, ancient history. It became a Royal Burgh in 1445 and was one of the most important Scottish fortresses in the middle ages. On rocks above the harbour stand the ruins of Dunbar Castle, where Mary Queen of Scots fled after the murder of her secretary Rizzio at the Palace of Holyroodhouse in Edinburgh.

Awareness of Dunbar today is widely international due to local hero John Muir, recognised as the father of the modern conservation movement. He spent his early life in Dunbar and a statue has been erected outside the Town House on the High Street. A large area around the estuary of the River Tyne to the north of Dunbar has been designated the John Muir Country Park. The John Muir Way is an extensive walking trail along the East Lothian coastline.

The visitor will find excellent accommodation, especially charming self-catering cottages; you can even stay in a lighthouse. And for seafood lovers, you'll find no fresher shellfish than from these coastal waters, with local lobster, langoustine and crab; while beer drinkers can visit Belhaven, Scotland's largest regional brewery. And nearby, explore the historic villages and attractions as well as a feast of outdoor adventures around the rural and rugged coastline of East Lothian.

WHAT TO SEE AND DO

In order to get a sense of the history of the town, have a walk around **Old Cromwell Harbour** (named after Oliver Cromwell's military attack on the town in 1650) and **Victoria Harbour**, created in 1842 beside the ruin of Dunbar Castle. Dunbar used to be a major herring fishing port and exported grain and potatoes. The Castle was excavated in the 1980s and was found to have been occupied in the Iron Age. It's not possible to visit the crumbling ruins as it's now home to a colony of 600 pairs of nesting kittiwakes. The harbour is also home to Sammy, the resident friendly seal, who waits patiently to be fed a fish supper by local fishermen.

The High Street features some interesting buildings, such as the 16th century **Town House**, (free admission), which includes an archaeological and local history exhibition and John Muir's birthplace. The Dunbar Tourist Information Centre is at 143 High Street and is a good place to stop to pick up brochures and maps.

There's no shortage of outdoor pursuits to enjoy, and where better to enjoy sunshine and fresh air than at the **John Muir Country Park**. Established in 1976 to commemorate the conservationist, the Country Park extends over 1,811 acres of coastline around Belhaven Bay to the west of Dunbar. Enjoy a walk along cliffs, dunes, woodlands, saltmarshes, scrub and grassland; the habitat of diverse wildlife including 12 species of butterfly. Birdwatchers and natural history enthusiasts will have numerous natural habitats to explore. The park stretches from Dunbar Castle to the Peffer Burn 5 miles to the north-west, along the Clifftop Trail with fine views of the Bass Rock and the long sandy sweep of Belhaven Bay to the mouth of the River Tyne. Visitor facilities include car parks, barbecue stoves and toilets.

For the more experienced walker, the **John Muir Way** is a world-class, signposted coastal and countryside trail being developed by East Lothian Council to provide a continuous path linking East Lothian with Edinburgh and the Scottish Borders. The John Muir Way is part of the international North Sea trail linking seven countries to establish a network of paths connecting heritage sites. There are several distinct sections in each area. For instance, you can follow the green John Muir Way signs along a shoreline path from Dunbar to Dunglass near Cockburnspath in the Scottish Borders. The 10-mile walk takes you along clifftops, beaches, a country estate and past a golf course and the Stevenson lighthouse. There are local buses between

Local hero: John Muir

John Muir was a Scottish-born American naturalist, author and pioneering advocate of conservation of wilderness. His writings and philosophy strongly influenced the creation of National Parks in the United States. He was born in Dunbar on 21 April 1838, the third of eight children, and as a child he developed a deep love of the surrounding countryside and seashore. He later recalled: *'When I was a boy in Scotland, I was fond of everything that was wild. I loved to wander in the fields to hear the birds sing and along the shore to gaze and wonder at the shells and the seaweeds, eels and crabs in the pools when the tide was low; and best of all to watch the waves in awful storms thundering on the black headlands and craggy ruins of old Dunbar Castle.'*

This interest grew into a lifelong journey, both spiritual and physical. His family emigrated to Wisconsin, USA in 1849, living on a farm where John had to work hard on the land, only allowed to read in the early hours of the morning. As a young man, after studying botany and science for a few years, he decided to enter the university of the 'wilderness and the inventions of God' and set off to walk to Florida, described in his memoir, *A Thousand Mile Walk to the Gulf*. He even reached Cuba. In 1868 he arrived in San Francisco, travelling around California working on a sheep ranch. His introduction to Yosemite Valley resulted in his campaign to preserve wilderness and the establishment of the National Park system, as he said *'No temple made with hands can compare with Yosemite... the grandest of all special temples of Nature.'*

Today he is internationally revered as the pioneer of the modern conservation movement, a passion which all began in the fields, woodland and beaches of his Scottish homeland in East Lothian. John Muir died on 24 December 1914.

Dunbar and Cockburnspath so that you only have to walk one way. Leaflets are available from the tourist office.

World-class watersports

East Lothian is home to beautiful beaches and open ocean, which create perfect conditions for the watersport enthusiast to enjoy surfing or kayaking in the waves, kite surfing with the wind, diving or sailing. Local kiter Andre and friends have set up **East Lothian Windchasers** and run a website, www.kiting.dunbar.org.uk. This will explain how you can join in and experience a thrilling ride or learn the basics.

Dunbar boasts the best surfable waves in the area, with wave faces as high as 12ft. **Belhaven** is the most exposed beach in East Lothian experiencing different swell directions and is the base for the **Belhaven Surf Club** (www.belhavensurf.com) currently the second top club in Scotland. With consistent softer waves, this is a perfect beach to learn to surf. The website gives daily sea, wind and weather conditions.

The **Coast to Coast Surf School** provides day and evening lessons throughout the year, as well as children's summer courses. It's a family-run surf school with three experienced British Surf Association (BSA) instructors. Courses are open to all ages from seven to 70, with events and competitions. The surfing takes place at Belhaven beach beside Linkfield car park.

COAST TO COAST SURF SCHOOL: ☎ 01368 869734; mobile 07971 990361; www.c2csurfschool.com.

Diving off Scotland's south-east coast has been described as world class, with a huge variety of ship wrecks and underwater cliff dives in and around the Forth, Bass Rock and the Isle of May. For further information, check out the **National Diving College** based at Dunbar to arrange a dive, a trial Scuba dive in the swimming pool or sea, and a full PADI course. The college offers high-quality diving experiences and training, as well as holiday courses and expeditions. The staff include expert advanced diving instructors and a marine biologist.

NATIONAL DIVING COLLEGE: ☎ 01368 869902; mobile 07876 547855, www.nationaldivingcollege.com.

Golf

East Lothian is renowned for its 21 (or so) golf courses, competing with the 17 Mile Drive on California's Monterey peninsula. The area boasts first-class courses, spectacular vistas and welcoming clubhouses. The local courses in this area are the **Dunbar Golf Club**, which was established in 1856 and is an Open Qualifying venue. It's one of the best seaside links courses in the country, with good facilities including a practice area, pro shop, tuition, buggy hire, and caddies. Also at Dunbar is the **Winterfield Golf Club** with seaviews out to the Bass Rock and Isle

- DUNBAR GOLF CLUB: East Links, Dunbar, ☎ 01368 862317.
- WINTERFIELD: St Margaret's North Road, Dunbar, ☎ 01368 863562.
- HADDINGTON GOLF CLUB: Amisfield Park, Haddington, ☎ 01620 822727.

Book through East Lothian Golf Passport, www.golfeastlothian.com.

of May, a pro shop, and club and trolley hire. And a few miles away is **Haddington Golf Club**, established in 1865, a treelined parkland course in quiet country estate.

Historical villages, castles and attractions

Take a drive, or cycle, around the delightful countryside to the charming, preserved little villages of **East Linton** and **Tyninghame**, which are both rather English in architectural style, with red pantile roof cottages and manicured village greens. You could imagine an episode of *Miss Marple* or *Poirot* being filmed here. East Linton lies to the west of a bridge built in the 1500s over the River Tyne, and was historically an important staging post on the Great North Road from London. This is reflected in the rather good choice of hotels and pubs in the village, including the **Bridgend Hotel**. The railway was built in 1846 and while the station has gone, the high-speed trains heading to and from Edinburgh zoom through the village right past the old ivy-clad stone pharmacy shop. The railway and the local water made East Linton an important farming community.

Nearby the picture-postcard village of Tyninghame (from an old name meaning 'dwellers of the village of the Tyne') has a strict conservation order to preserve its architecture. From the village, take a sideways seaside trip to Tyninghame Links beyond Tyninghame House. From the A198 (direction North Berwick) turn onto Limetree Walk down to the coast, where there is a car park, and from here a path through woodland leads down to a long sandy beach. Sheila, a local artist, waxes lyrical about this beach where she and her family spent all day on Boxing Day last year having a barbecue picnic. Well this is a warm, sunny place!

Preston Mill near East Linton is well worth visiting. This restored water-driven mill dates back to the 12th century. Now a National Trust for Scotland property, the mill worked commercially until 1959 and still operates to show visitors how water power produces flour. Set by a millpond with ducks and geese in a tranquil

The restored Preston Mill dates from the 12th century

Constable-painting landscape, the kiln building has a distinctive conical shape and is a popular subject for artists. Nearby is the unusual Phantassie Doocot. Cross the white footbridge over the River Tyne and along a narrow road beside a field on the Phantassie Estate to reach the beehive-shaped Doocot, another National Trust for Scotland property. Built in the 1500s it had 540 nesting boxes used to house hundreds of doves and pigeons, in order to provide a good source of eggs and meat over the winter.

PRESTON MILL AND PHANTASSIE DOOCOT: Preston Road, East Linton EH40 3DS; ☎ 01620 860426; www.nts.org.uk. Entry: adult £5, family party £14, one adult and children £10, National Trust members free; open 1 June–30 Sept, Thur–Mon 1pm–5pm.

Another fascinating old property to visit is the 13th-century **Hailes Castle**, a mile and a half south-west of East Linton, built on a rocky headland overlooking the River Tyne. Although very much a ruin, there's plenty to explore around the walls and interior including a chapel, kitchen and great hall. Mary Queen of Scots and her husband the Earl of Bothwell stayed here in May 1657 en route to Edinburgh.

HAILES CASTLE: 1.5miles south-west of East Linton, off the A1; ☎ 0131 668 8800; www.historic-scotland.gov.uk. Admission free; open daily 9.30am–6pm (summer), 9.30am–5pm (winter).

Chesters Hill Fort is one of the best preserved Iron Age fortified villages, dating back approximately 2,000 years. A Historic Scotland property, admission is free, and it's located one mile south of Drem off the B1377. There is a visitors car park.

Haddington and around

Haddington is a prosperous market town on the River Tyne, dating from the 12th century but mainly established in Georgian and Victorian periods when Haddington

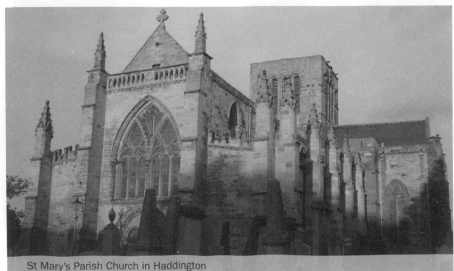
St Mary's Parish Church in Haddington

led the Agricultural Revolution which transformed farming in East Lothian. Haddington was the birthplace of the preacher **John Knox**, founder of the Presbyterian Church in Scotland, whose famous tract entitled *The First Blast of the Trumpet Against the Monstrous Regiment of Women* would not have inspired the three Queens who ruled Britain during his lifetime – Mary of Guise, regent of Scotland, Mary Queen of England or Elizabeth I.

When visiting the town, you must see **St Mary's Parish Church,** a magnificent pre-Reformation church, partially destroyed in the 16th century. It was fully renovated in 1970s with stained-glass windows by eminent artists. You can try your hand at brass rubbing (prior booking) and there's a tea room. Nearby at **Haddington House** are the peaceful medicinal gardens of St Mary's Pleasance, which are free and open during daylight hours. Buried in the churchyard is Jane Welsh (1801–1866), wife of essayist and historian Thomas Carlyle. The **Jane Welsh Carlyle House** was her home until her marriage, and part of it is open to the public.

> JANE WELSH CARLYLE HOUSE: 2 Lodge Street, Haddington; ☎ 01620 823738. Open Apr–Sept, Wed–Sat 2pm–5pm.

The village of **Athelstaneford** near Haddington may be of interest to historians as the birthplace of Scotland's flag. This is known as the Saltire based on St Andrew's Cross. The Parish Church has a fine stained-glass window of St Andrew and the **Flag Heritage Centre**, located in an old Doocot, has an audio visual film about the legendary Pictish origins of the flag.

The picturesque village of **Gifford** is just 4 miles from Haddington with a pretty village green, old pubs and a fine parish church. This is a great area for long rural walks and cycle rides. **Pedlars Way** (3 miles) follows a track through woodland and fields past an Old Mill to Bolton Church. The mother, brother and sister of Robert Burns are buried in the churchyard here. Walk route leaflets around Dunbar, Haddington, Gifford and East Linton are available at Dunbar Tourist Information Centre.

☂ Wet weather

After walking through John Muir Country Park on a fine day, visit **John Muir's Birthplace** when it rains. The 18th-century townhouse was purchased by the John Muir Trust and renovated through extensive fundraising and a Lottery grant, opening as a museum in 2003. The world-renowned naturalist was born here on 21 April 1838 and the exhibits document his childhood in Dunbar, world travels, life, work and legacy as the founder of the conservation movement. Muir is regarded in the United States as the 'greatest ever Californian, a man who changed the world'. His valuable environmental work continues today through the John Muir Trust which administers the national John Muir Award to encourage the exploration and preservation of the wilderness. The Birthplace

> JOHN MUIR BIRTHPLACE: 126 High Street, Dunbar EH42 1JJ; ☎ 01368 865899; www. jmbt.org.uk. Admission free, open Apr–Oct, Mon–Sat 10am–5pm; Sun 1pm–5pm; Nov–Mar, closed Mon–Tue.

LENNOXLOVE HOUSE: Haddington, East Lothian EH41 4NZ; ☎ 01620 823720; www.lennoxlove.com. Entry: adult £5, child £3; open Easter weekend; April until October, Wed, Thurs, Sun, 1.30pm, 2.30pm and 3.30pm. Opening times may change to accommodate functions, telephone to check before travel.

Museum is an inspiring place to visit for all ages, with 12,000 visitors a year. There are interactive, educational and fun activities for children, and the building is wheelchair and pushchair accessible with free parking for an hour on the High Street.

Near Haddington is the majestic old aristocratic castle of **Lennoxlove House,** dating from the 14th century and home

CELEBRITY CONNECTIONS

'Gian Carlo Menotti is by far the greatest of the living composers, and certainly one of the major composers of the 20th century', Nick Rossi, *Gramophone* magazine. The Italian composer **Gian Carlo Menotti** lived for over 30 years until his death in 2007 in Gifford at Yester House, his magnificent Palladian country mansion designed by Robert Adam. Born in Italy in 1911, he was a child prodigy and went to study music at the Curtis Institute, Philadelphia, where he studied with his great friend Samuel Barber. *The Consul*, Menotti's first full-length work, won the Pulitzer Prize and the New York Drama Critics Circle award in 1954. Menotti's best-known work is the Christmas classic *Amahl and the Night Visitors* which continues to be performed annually.

He moved to East Lothian having fallen in love with Yester House, surrounded by the 'peace and damp tranquility' of the Scottish countryside near the Lammermuir hills. Here he was able to compose and was also renowned as a most hospitable host, entertaining guests for lunch, house-party weekends and an Italian-style Christmas with his family. The Gifford villagers were rightly 'chuffed' to have a famous composer in their midst, affectionately known as 'Mr McNotty', the Laird of Yester House. There is a story that when a local shop owner won a considerable amount on the Lottery, a financial gift was given to the Laird to assist the funding for his musical projects.

Gian Carlo Menotti died in Monte Carlo aged 95 on 1 February 2007. His funeral at Yester Kirk, Gifford, was attended by a large congregation of villagers, neighbours, international musicians, friends and family. A message from Luciano Pavarotti was read during the service and the burial was given a fly past salute by the Duke of Hamilton. The Maestro is buried in the churchyard at Yester Kirk. *'Italy created me, America nourished me and Scotland will bury me'*, he once remarked with great pride.

of the Duke of Hamilton, surrounded by a 460-acre estate. The house has a superb art collection, with artefacts belonging to Mary Queen of Scots and memorabilia from Rudolph Hess's flight to Scotland and the 14th Duke of Hamilton's historic first flight over Mount Everest. Lennoxlove is available to rent for house parties, weddings and corporate events.

What to do with children...

This area of East Lothian is perfect for a family holiday with clean, safe, sandy beaches, leisure and sports, castles and clifftop walks. And they will enjoy the John Muir Birthplace Museum with its range of activities. The **East Links Family Park** is an amazing adventure playground, zoo and sports centre all in one and perfect for all ages, featuring an all-weather toboggan run, pirate ship playground, maze, pony rides, and a railway safari to see deer, llamas, rabbits, goats, pigs, cattle, sheep and donkeys.

> EAST LINKS FAMILY PARK: Near West Barns and John Muir Country Park, Dunbar EH42 1XF; ☎ 01368 863607; www.eastlinks. co.uk. Entry: adult £8, child £7, under 2s free, family ticket £28 (two adults, two children); open all year 10am–5pm, till 6pm summer holidays, till dusk in winter. Closed Christmas Day, Boxing Day, New Years Day.

Whether sun or rain, families will enjoy **Dunbar Leisure Pool**, a superb swimming pool with a wave machine for adults and children, and a sauna and steamroom.

> DUNBAR LEISURE POOL: Castlepark EH42 1EU; ☎ 01368 865456.

Lauderdale Park near Dunbar High Street has a sheltered walled garden, recreation activities and innovative children's play area and there's also a good child-friendly café.

... and how to avoid children

A visit to the local **Belhaven Brewery** on a chilly day will warm the blood. Book in advance for a two-hour tour around this historic brewery, established in 1719, to see how many of Scotland's best beers and lagers are produced: Belhaven

> THE BELHAVEN BREWERY: Sprott Road, Dunbar; ☎ 01368 869200; www.belhaven. co.uk. Prices: adult £5, ages 14–17 free when accompanied by adult; open Mon–Fri.

Best, 80 Shilling, Belhaven Scottish Lager and St Andrews Ale are just some brand names.

Entertainment

The long-running annual **Dunbar Traditional Music Festival** (www.dtmf.dunbar.org. uk) takes place around the last weekend of September featuring an eclectic mix of music from Scottish traditional, folk to jazz and blues; and **The Rossborough Hotel**, (Queens Road; ☎ 01368 862356) presents a regular series of music gigs and entertainment.

A first-class concert season takes place seasonally arranged through the **Lamp of Lothian** (☎ 01620 823738), presenting concerts mainly at St Mary's Church Haddington and other local venues. You can expect to see many of Scotland's top orchestras, such as BBC Scottish Symphony, Scottish Chamber Orchestra, as well as leading international singers and pianists.

Shopping

Dunbar has a charming High Street lined with many good shops for gifts, quality food and drink, souvenirs, art, crafts and antiques, including **Cromwell Antiques** (114 High Street), **Bass Rock Gallery** (Bayswell Road), and **The Bellevue Gallery** (8 High Street).

Due to the outstanding land and seascapes all around the area, many artists live and exhibit in towns and villages across East Lothian. The **Peter Potter Gallery**, Haddington, was established in 1976 by Peter Potter and Tom Criddle, prominent figures nationally in the theatre, opera and art world. It continues to follow the objective of its founders to 'increase the knowledge, understanding, practise and enjoyment of art.' It gives priority to exhibiting the work of professional artists and crafts people, as well as talented amateurs in a welcoming atmosphere. There is a café on first floor with views over the River Tyne and St Mary's Church.

PETER POTTER GALLERY: 10 The Sands, Haddington EH41 3EY; ☎ 01620 822080; www.peterpottergallery.org. Admission free; open Mon–Fri 10am–5pm, Sat 10am–5.30pm (café last orders 4.15pm).

The best... PLACES TO STAY

BOUTIQUE

Barns Ness Hotel

Station Road, Dunbar EH42 1JY
☎ **01368 863231**
www.barnsnesshotel.com

Two minutes walk from the train station, this is a smart and contemporary hotel. 16 bedrooms (kingsize, twin, family), each with TV/DVD. Dine well in the Lighthouse Restaurant and kids will love Retro's American Diner. Upgrade to VIP, Gold and Romantic packages. Great golf breaks.

Price: £80–£100 per room B&B.

Bayswell Hotel

16 Bayswell Park, Dunbar EH42 1AE
☎ **01368 862225**
www.bayswell.co.uk

Victorian, traditional house modernised with homely comfortable furnishings and facilities. Stay in en suite stylish bedrooms with TV and DVD library. Great views from Conservatory Bistro serving fresh seasonal produce. Lovely bar for wines and local Belhaven ale.

Price: £80–£86 double, £110 family room.

HOTEL

Maitlandfield House

24 Sidegate, Haddington EH41 4BZ
☎ **01620 826513**
www.maitlandfieldhouse.co.uk

Located opposite Haddington Golf Course, this whitewashed 18th-century mansion is set in lovely parkland with a walled garden. The contemporary interior design preserves the window drapes, wallpapers and fabrics of a traditional country house. Choice of standard rooms, luxury and honeymoon suites.

Price: £40–£90 pp B&B.

FARMHOUSE

Brandsmill Farmhouse

Dunbar EH42 1RU
☎ **01368 862447**
www.dunbar-bed-breakfast.co.uk

Brandsmill Farmhouse boasts a wonderful, peaceful setting near Dunbar, a stone's throw from the coast and local woodland walks. Friendly, traditional B&B. Cosy lounge with real fire to relax.

Price: £30 B&B pp.

Barnsness Lighthouse Cottage

Barnsness, By Dunbar EH42 1QP
☎ **01620 67 1966**
www.coast-properties.co.uk

This Lighthouse cottage is an exciting place to stay on the seashore, perfect for families, artists, walkers and bird watchers. With four bedrooms with twin beds, it sleeps eight. There is a walled garden with the beach just over the wall, two conservatories, sitting room, TV, and well-equipped kitchen.

Price: £700–£1,000 per week.

SELF-CATERING

Surfsplash

3 Fiddlers yard, Woodbush Brae, Dunbar EH42 1HB
☎ **01620 860374,** ☎ **07970 867089**
www.surfsplash.co.uk

Two-bedroom beach house (sleeps four) with open hearth fire and breathtaking sea views from the balcony, with the waves splashing below on the beach. It's a short walk to shops, restaurants, pubs, railway station, golf courses, tennis courts, and harbours.

Price: £260–£560 per week.

The best... FOOD AND DRINK

The **East Lothian Food and Drink Festival** (☎ 01620 827282; www.foodanddrink eastlothian.com) takes place annually throughout the region, to celebrate great local food and drink traditions. Restaurants, food outlets and visitor attractions stage a variety of events and offer a selection of dishes featuring East Lothian produce. Highlights may include the Glenkinchie Distillery's ceilidh, Haddington Farmers' Market, a Family Food and Fun Day at Dirleton Castle and the North Berwick Slow Food Fair.

▶ Staying in

Haddington has a wonderful **farmers' market** (☎ 01368 863593 www.haddington farmersmarket.co.uk) held on the last Saturday of every month outside the Corn Exchange on Court Street from 9am to 1pm. Local producers offer excellent quality from Muriel's homemade preserves to honey from heather-clad hills, as well as wild boar, game, beef, sausages and cured bacon from free-range pigs.

    Villeneuve Wines (82 High Street, Haddington) has an eclectic selection of wines from around the globe and over a 100 whiskies, including Glenkinchie, which is made less than 10 miles away. **Paul's Fish Shop** (7 High Street) provides good-quality fish. Clarissa Dickson Wright, the TV celebrity chef (one of the 'Two Fat Ladies') and leading food writer is a regular shopper at **Colin Peat & Son** (3 Court Street; ☎ 01620 823192), a traditional butchers. Game birds hang in the window during the season and Colin selects and buys locally sourced cattle, which is hung for four weeks. Bacon is cured in-house, smoked at Belhaven over whisky barrels and sliced to your preferred thickness. Pies and Scotch eggs are homemade and the cold meats are all home cooked.

    Food for Thought (13 Hardgate; ☎ 01620 823196) is one of the few places to sell loose organic flour and muesli, herbs and spices, nuts and dried fruit as well as local honey. You might even spot Ronnie Corbett shopping here. Jack-of-all-trades **Jaques and Lawrence** (37 Court Street; ☎ 01620 829829) has deli produce, homemade jams, chutneys, organic bread, cakes, soups, salads, sandwiches and carry-out evening meals to order.

    Over in **Dunbar**, the butcher, **Peter Whitecross** (96 High Street; ☎ 01368 865656) makes all their sausages, steak pies and cooks most of the cold meats. All the meat is from local suppliers but the black and white puddings comes from the award-winning Charles MacLeod's of Stornoway. Fruit and vegetables at **Crunchy Carrot** (43 High Street; ☎ 01368 860000) are locally sourced and organic wherever possible, with 10 types of the humble spud and the occasional grapes and peaches grown on the Dunglass estate. You will find meat, cheese and local drinks at **The Food Hamper** (124 High Street; ☎ 01368 865152) including damson gin and mead from Lindisfarne.

    Picking your own fruit can't get easier than **Belhaven Fruit Farm** (South Belton, nr Dunbar; ☎ 01368 863246). The fruit is grown in poly tunnels, just one metre off the ground. The season is from June to September but there's a shop and café open throughout the year. Nearby the **Belhaven Smokehouse** (Beltonford; ☎ 01368 864025) produces some of the finest smoked fish in East Lothian. Hot and cold smoked salmon; trout whole, filleted or smoked; Dunbar mackerel; Ballencrieff rare pedigree smoked bacon; and smoked Lammermuir cheese.

At **East Linton**, the greengrocers **Votadini** (9 High Street) is also a coffee shop, with a wood-burning stove, leather sofas and toy box. **The Bake House** (34 High Street) is the village bakery and has breads, rolls, cakes and homemade scones. The licensed deli **Millers Delicatessen** (18 High Street; ☎ 01620 860377) has a small stock of interesting wines, homemade chicken liver pâté, and a selection of cheeses and hams, local honey, smoked salmon and ice creams from Belhaven, Lucas in Musselburgh and Doddington Dairy. Buy home-grown farm produce, including 'Sun & Dung' vegetables and herbs and free-range eggs (see the chickens running around the paddock) at **Knowes Farm Shop** (☎ 01620 860010; www.knowes.com), near East Linton. Also sells homemade preserves, pâtés, local meat, fish, game, cheese, dairy, honey and breads.

Takeaway

The Town House Fish Bar (17 Market Street, Haddington; ☎ 01620 823293) is reputed to be the best chippie in town. In Dunbar, **Adriano's** (139 High Street) is a spotlessly clean chippie and **Umberto's** (121 High Street) Italian restaurant offers a takeaway service.

EATING OUT

FINE DINING

Creel Restaurant
25 Lamer Street, Dunbar EH41 4LN
☎ **01368 863279**
www.creelrestaurant.co.uk

Patron/chef, Logan Thorburn has an
excellent pedigree, working with the
likes of Rick Stein and the two-Michelin-
starred John Campbell. The ethos is
perfect simplicity, using good-quality,
ethically sourced and local ingredients.
The menu changes daily and can feature
Shetland salmon, Eyemouth haddock,
pork, Aberdeen Angus beef and a daily
veggie choice. Two courses cost about
£18.

RESTAURANT

The Avenue at the Victoria
9 Court Street, Haddington EH41 3JD
☎ **01620 823332**
www.theavenuerestaurant.co.uk

An inviting inn which offers an excellent
menu with a bias towards fish like
Eyemouth lobster – half or whole – and
bouillabaisse swimming with all types
of fish and seafood. The specials board
changes regularly and can feature
Shetland mussels, locally supplied meat
and game. Two courses cost about £21.

The Rocks
Marine Road, Dunbar EH42 1AR
☎ **01368 862287**
www.experiencetherocks.co.uk

Well-established restaurant run by Jim
Findlay and daughter Nicola. Beef is
smoked, seafood is always on the menu
– including whole lobster – and desserts
are decadent. There are rooms too; all
of which have panoramic views of the
sea. The sheltered terrace overlooks
Bass Rock and is perfect for an aperitif.
Two courses cost about £24.

Whitekirk Restaurant
**Whitekirk Golf & Country Club, nr East
Linton EH39 5PR**
☎ **01620 870300**
www.whitekirk.com

Open to everyone, with stunning views
towards Tantallon Castle. The menu
shows commitment to using produce
from local suppliers within the county
as much as possible. The Friday and
Sunday carvery is very popular and
excellent value at three courses for
£15.95.

BISTRO

Garvald Inn
**Main Street Garvald, nr Haddington
EH41 4LN**
☎ **01620 830311**

The hub of the community, the bistro
is home to locals and visitors alike.
The food is excellent and chef Peter
McQuade pays attention to detail. Of
particular note is the chicken liver pâté,
pheasant and a tangy lemon posset.
Two courses cost about £18.

EATING OUT

The Linton Hotel
3 Bridge Street, East Linton EH40 3AF
☎ **01620 860202**
www.lintonhotel.com

This small hotel near the river Tyne has a beautifully intimate dining room. The short menu is well rounded and has some interesting dishes like baked Pollock with lemon crumb or loin of pork with sweet potato pancakes. The cosy bar serves real ales and has an extensive selection of single malts. Two courses cost about £14.

CAFÉ

The Fullstop at Kesley's Book Shop
29 Market Street, Haddington
☎ **01620 826725**

Susan and Simon Kesley are certainly tuned to using local suppliers at their coffee shop. Milk is from Yester Farm at Gifford, cakes and scones are homemade and there is always a gluten free alternative. Homemade soup and filled roll for £5.75.

The Garden Path Café
Lauderdale Park, Bayswell Road, Dunbar
☎ **01368 865746**
www.gardenpathcafé.co.uk

This former bowling pavilion is now home to a charming award-winning café. The menu has several choices for vegetarians and vegans, gluten and wheat-free dishes and homebaking. Fully accessible to wheelchair users and very child friendly. £5 for soup and sandwich.

The Shoestring Café by the Station
Dunbar Station
☎ **01368 864824**
www.shoestringcafé.co.uk

Lennie Fawcett and her team provide commuters and regulars with first-class food. Her 'Track Snack Pack' promises a freshly made sandwich, homemade cake or crisps, fruit and a drink for only £3 (order the day before). She is very conscious of food miles and sources all her ingredients from within the local community.

Tyninghame Country Store & Coffee Shop
Main Street, Tyninghame
☎ **01620 860581**

This former smithy is now a rather nice coffee shop and country store. Brodies supply the coffee which is served in cafetieres, and all the cakes and scones are homemade. Coffee £1.50, cake £1.85, soup and bread £2.65.

Smeaton Nursery and Garden
Near East Linton
☎ **01620 860501**

The tearoom (open Wed–Sun only) in the walled garden boasts homemade soups, cakes and scones, to be eaten under parasols in the garden or, if the weather turns, the large conservatory is a peaceful place to potter. Coffee and cake £3.50.

⤴ Drinking

The largest regional brewer in Scotland, the **Belhaven Brewery** (Spott Road, Dunbar; ☎ 01368 869200) produces a leading draught ale, Belhaven Best, the cask-conditioned **80 Shilling** (described a few centuries back by the Austrian Emperor as 'the burgundy of Scotland') and crisp sweet Belhaven lager. Fully guided, two-hour tours (£5) end with a sampling session in the in-house bar, The Monks Retreat.

Haddington has a variety of pubs and inns: **The Mercat Hotel** (73 High Street) has a folk club every Wednesday, good atmosphere and the usual tap beers and lagers. **Tyneside Tavern** has cask ales, a good range of single malts, a roaring fire on cold days, live music every Friday and a Curry Club (curry and rice £5) all day Monday. Its bistro bar has a reputation for good food. A few miles out of town at Gifford is the **Goblin 'Ha** (Main Street) with a modern interior in a traditional coaching inn, three to four real ales, bright conservatory for food and a sunny beer garden with comfy seating.

Dunbar High Street is home to many traditional pubs and inns. The oldest, **The Black Bull**, is popular with locals and although they don't do food, it's worth popping in for a pint and enjoying the hospitable company. **The Volunteer Arms** (17 Victoria Street) down by the harbour, is a tiny inn with a good selection of real ales that change on a regular basis. Food is served upstairs in the restaurant, where children are welcome. **The Crown Hotel,** East Linton, has rooms, a snug bar with real ales and a bistro offering traditional Scottish food.

ⓘ Visitor Information

Tourist Information Centre: 143 High Street, Dunbar, ☎ 01368 863 353; East Lothian Tourism information, www.visiteastlothian.org.

Hospitals: Belhaven Hospital, Hospital Road, Dunbar EH42 1TR, ☎ 01368 862246; Roodlands General Hospital, Hospital Road, Haddington, ☎ 0131 536 8300.

Pharmacies: Lloyds, 25 High Street, Dunbar, ☎ 01368 862305; Boots, 35–36 High Street, Haddington, ☎ 01620 823 349.

Police: Dunbar Police Station, Queens Road, ☎ 01368 865646; Haddington Police Station, 39–41 Court Street, ☎ 01620 824101.

Travel and Transport: First Bus Company, bus journeys around East Lothian, ☎ 08708 72 72 71, www.firstgroup.com/scotlandeast; National Rail Enquiries, trains from Edinburgh to Dunbar, ☎ 0845 748 4950.

Taxis: Dunbar Taxi, ☎ 01368 862 822; Haddington and East Lothian private hire, ☎ 01875 852711.

ALONG THE EAST COAST

The beauty of living in or visiting Edinburgh is that you can escape the city and arrive at the seaside by car, bus or train in less than half an hour. For a day out, the stunning shoreline along the east coast between the city and North Berwick boasts fabulous sandy beaches, coastal walks, nature reserves and famous championship golf courses.

Travelling east from Edinburgh, the A198 begins just a mile from Musselburgh and continues along the coastal route through the pristine pretty villages of Longniddry, Aberlady and Gullane. Gullane beach is about a mile of golden sands, hidden below the village and flanked by tall dunes covered in marram grass. The rolling waves here attract surfers and other watersports enthusiasts. Longniddry beach nearby is perfect for picnics, family fun or even a bracing swim.

The coastline along this stretch of the Firth of Forth has been recognised as an important habitat for wildfowl and waders such as curlew and redshank and there are special protected and preserved nature reserves. The John Muir Way (the coastal parth linking Edinburgh, East Lothian and the Scottish Borders) in this section extends from Fisherow Harbour in Musselburgh to Gullane, a distance of 14 miles, offering the walker a wonderful nature ramble to observe the wildlife, flora and fauna, as well as the historic sites across this unique and unspoilt seashore and rural landscape.

WHAT TO SEE AND DO

Seaside and watersports

The beaches right along this coastline can be visited year round, a summertime picnic with the kids, fly a kite or a fresh air walk in the autumn and winter months. **Longniddry beach** (or Bents) is almost 2 miles in length – from Gosford Bay to the rockier Seton Sands. Longniddry is popular with families, holidaymakers, picnickers, horse-riders, ramblers, metal-detecting enthusiasts, dog walkers and the occasional kite buggy. This is the place for cockle-hunting in the shallow holes in the sand, digging down with your fingers. They are safe to eat but wash them well to remove the grit. You can boil them or even better roast them on a campfire.

Surfers and wind and kite surfers will more likely be seen further along the coast at **Gullane Bents**, another fabulous long sandy beach; you would be forgiven for thinking that you are holidaying along the Pacific Highway, California. Facilities are excellent for the visitor with car parking, toilets, picnic areas and barbecue grills. Even on a summer Saturday afternoon the beach rarely gets crowded, and in the spring you can have the whole place to yourself. Edged by grassy dunes, it has superb views west to Edinburgh and is a perfect spot for spectacular sunsets.

Aberlady Nature Reserve

The medieval conservation village of Aberlady is utterly picturesque with a charming main street with good country inns. The area is also a magnet for golfers as well as wildlife enthusiasts due to its nature reserve. **Aberlady Bay** was designated as Britain's first Local Nature Reserve in 1952 and continues to be a vital, well-preserved woodland, seashore and marshland habitat for local wildlife, plants, butterflies and wild deer. It is particularly popular with birdwatchers. There are good well-trodden paths throughout the reserve and you can enjoy a stimulating nature walk, rambling around here for a few hours. The marshlands are scattered with many colourful flowers such as water mint, yellow iris, meadowsweet, marsh marigold, bogbean and orchids.

Aberlady Bay is best known though for its ornithological interest. In the winter months, nationally important populations of waders and duck roost in the area, while at dusk, up to 15,000 thousand pink-footed geese fly in from the surrounding farmland. Spring sees the arrival of summer migrants and the start of the breeding season: with Skylark and Reed Bunting, Eider, Shelduck, Lapwing, Lesser Whitethroat, Redshank, Willow and Sedge Warblers. Ospreys may be seen in springtime and wild deer live on the reserve year round. For information on walks around Aberlady Bay, see www.walkeastlothian.co.uk.

A famous former resident of Aberlady was Nigel Tranter (1909–2000), a distinguished and popular novelist who lived at Quarry House near the nature reserve for the last 50 years of his life. His books include many historical novels on Scottish themes. His memoir *Footbridge to Enchantment* tells of his daily walks (with notebook and pen for literary moments) across the timber bridge to the nature reserve. There's a memorial cairn by the entrance to the car park at the reserve.

History and heritage

A magnificent mansion can be seen through the high gates on Gosford Bay on the coast road between Aberlady and Longniddry. **Gosford House** is the home of the Earls of Wemyss and March and was designed by Robert Adam in 1790. Later the Eighth Earl of Wemyss did not like the style of the wings and had them demolished, and additional renovation was designed by William Young, considerably extending the house. Young also created the stunn-

> GOSFORD HOUSE: Gosford Bay, Longniddry EH23 OPX; ☎ 01620 870201. Entry: adult £5, child £1; open mid-June to early August, Sat–Sun 2pm–5pm.

ing Italianate marble hall in pink alabaster with an enormous central dome. The house today has been painstakingly restored and refurbished to preserve the classical design. It contains a remarkable art collection, primarily due to the 10th Earl, a passionate and genuine collector who ignored the current fashion and bought what he actually liked. The collection includes works by Botticelli, Murillo and Rubens. The surrounding estate includes pleasure gardens, ponds, classic Adam stables, a mausoleum and ice-house; the parkland of wonderful trees is a natural habitat for wildlife and birds. The interior and exterior of Gosford House was used as the location for the film *House of Mirth* based on the novel by Edith Wharton. The house is open to visitors for a month during the summer.

Byres Hill sits at the end of a ridge of the Garleton Hills between Aberlady and Haddington. Its landmark is the **Hopetoun Monument**, which dominates the East Lothian skyline for miles around. A path winds up steeply through woodland of oak, ash, Scots pine, sycamore and sweet chestnut trees, past gorse bushes to the open hilltop. The short climb is worth it because the views can be superb: the Firth of Forth and Fife to the north; Edinburgh and Pentland Hills to the west; and Lammermuir Hills to the south. On a clear day, it's even possible to glimpse the Cairngorms in the far north. There is a car park at the foot of Byres Hill. Take the A6137 from Aberlady to Haddington, turn right, and then take the B1343 towards Athelstaneford.

Coastal walk

There are different sections of the **John Muir Way** for walking and cycling, all clearly signposted with green fingerposts. For instance, the Port Seton to Aberlady trail

CELEBRITY CONNECTIONS

John Bellany is one of the best known figurative painters in Scotland. Born in Port Seton, he was surrounded throughout his childhood by the seascapes and daily life of his family's work as boat builders and fishermen. Many of his paintings illustrate this fishing community: huge vibrantly colourful oil paintings of harbours with iconic fishing boats moored up, or his trademark portraits of the fisherfolk, women with red noses and flushed cheeks from the harshness of the environment in which they work.

This is John Bellany's personal view of his hometown: *'Port Seton has been the inspiration and the roots of much of my work from the formative years through to the present day. I find it the most inspiring place in the whole wide world. It is strange when I fly over the Firth of Forth, returning home from one of my Odysseys abroad, when I look down on this little village, snuggled in between Edinburgh and North Berwick, I wonder how on earth have I made so many paintings of this little bit of Enchanted Land and Sea.*

'All the knowledge and love of the people is a reflection of my life spent here – 60 years of joy, sadness and spiritual depth added to the sheer beauty of Port Seton overwhelms me: each and every time I see it, my heart skips a beat. Port Seton may have changed over the years but this still has not taken away the spirit of the fishing community which has dominated for two centuries.'

Today Bellany is internationally recognised as one of the greatest painters of the modern era, awarded the CBE in 1994. His work can be seen in many major national collections, including MOMA, New York, the Tate Gallery, London and the Scottish National Gallery of Modern Art, Edinburgh.

(5 miles/8km) follows the coastline to Longniddry and Gosford Bay (a spot for wading birds and divers), and past Kilspindie Castle. Aberlady to Gullane is 3 miles/5km one way. The trail passes Aberlady church, the 16th-century ruin of **Saltcoats Castle** and Aberlady Bay. If you walk one way, you can take the bus back again. Pick up a copy of the *East Lothian and North Sea Trail* and *John Muir Way* booklets at a Tourist Information Centre.

The John Muir coastal walk takes you to the harbour at Port Seton. Once a thriving fishing port, Cockenzie and Port Seton still have a fishing industry today but on a much smaller scale. Recent environmental improvements made to the coastal walkway and harbours have made Port Seton a popular place for day trippers and holidaymakers with a caravan park beside Seton Sands.

To learn more about the local art, visit **The Harbour Gallery** which shows the work of East Coast artists including the gallery owner, Alastair Hamilton, and the iconic fishing boat paintings by John Bellany with a fine display of regularly changing exhibitions of paintings, photography, sculpture and prints. The gallery has a lovely location with a panoramic view of the Firth of Forth.

> THE HARBOUR GALLERY: 9 Viewforth, The Harbour, Port Seton EH32 0DR; ☎ 01875 810798; www.portsetongallery.co.uk. No regular opening hours, just ring the bell or phone first to check what's on.

Golf

You are spoilt for choice when it comes to golf courses in this area. The quality of golf is world class with one of the highest concentration of links courses to be found anywhere. Even if you have never played golf, the name **Muirfield**, in the village of Gullane, is world famous.

> MUIRFIELD GOLF CLUB: Duncur Road, Gullane EH31 2EG; ☎ 01620 842123; www.muirfield.org.uk. Visitors welcome Tuesdays and Thursdays; max handicap 18 (men) 20 (women). Apply well in advance. Club and trolley hire available. Bar and dining room open to visitors.

Golf has been played in Gullane since 1854, and today there are three other courses offering fabulous scenic views. The best can be enjoyed from the number 7 green on Gullane number 1 course; a splendid 360-degree panorama across East Lothian, Edinburgh and the Forth.

This is serious golfing heaven: within a few miles you could also play at several fine courses, including Kilspindie, Craiglielaw, Longniddry and Luffness. Check out the East Lothian Golf Passport for great value packages to play a selection of 12 great local courses–. www.golfeastlothian.com.

> GULLANE GOLF CLUB: West Links Road, Gullane EH31 2BB; ☎ 01620 842255; www.gullanegolfclub.com. Visitors welcome (handicap certificate required). Club, trolley and buggy hire. Bar and restaurant open to visitors.

A day at the races

For something rather different, **Musselburgh Racecourse** is a popular sporting venue, great even if you have never been to a horse race before. Musselburgh has been a

CELEBRITY CONNECTIONS

Ronnie Corbett was born Ronald Balfour Corbett in December 1930 in Edinburgh and brought up in the leafy middle class suburb of Marchmont on the southside of the city. As a child he enjoyed the theatre and performing in amateur dramatics which led him, after National Service, to move to London to try his hand in the world of show business. As he recalls, *'I decided to come to London to follow my dream. I had £91 in my Post Office savings account and soon got two jobs: one in an actors' club called the Buckstone, the other doing cabaret at a club called Winston's.'* He soon made it as a successful actor and for several decades he has enjoyed a glittering career as a very popular comedic star, nationally beloved for the long-running BBC TV series, *The Two Ronnies*.

Now semi-retired, he and his wife Anne divide their time between their home in Surrey, south of England, and his house in Gullane, near the world-famous Muirfield and Gullane golf courses. Like Sean Connery, Ronnie is a keen golfer, which has been a long life passion. His father, in fact, died suddenly aged 75 while playing a game of golf on the course at Prestonfield Golf Club, Edinburgh. Corbett is a proud Scot and there is a rumour he is interested in presenting a TV series on malt whisky. *'I love the whole feel of Scotland. I love the place. Edinburgh is a treat to go to, a real buzzing city and it's so handsome. [In East Lothian] I love shopping for vegetables. "Is this a Seton Mains potato?," I ask my wife. She responds, "it's just a bloody potato!" For breakfast, I always make a pot of tea, Kenya Pekoe Highland, a loose-leaf tea we get from the Howdah Tea & Coffee Co in North Berwick.'*

As local residents, Ronnie and his wife are often seen around and about East Lothian and are great supporters of the Seabird Centre, North Berwick. He was invited to unveil the statues of an Arctic Tern and bronze penguins here in July 2008. As he said at the ceremony, *'It's wonderful to see so many people here today and it just goes to show how important maintaining the vibrant seabird centre is to the community here. My wife and I have a house in Gullane and we are big fans of the centre. I'm not an expert on sealife or birds but I would love to come here and use all the facilities so I could learn more. It's a wonderful place.'*

MUSSELBURGH RACECOURSE: Linkfield Road EH21 7RG; ☎ 0131 665 2859; www.musselburgh-racecourse.co.uk. Children are welcome.

venue for horse racing since 1816, and is a five-star Visit Scotland Visitor Attraction. The course hosts around 25 race days a year, both Flat racing and Jump meetings as well as other special entertainments, Ladies' Day and family days out events. Why not have a flutter on the horses?

Wet weather

Prestongrange, between Musselburgh and Prestonpans, is of major importance in the story of Scotland's Industrial Revolution. It was the site of a 16th-century harbour and later the development of glass works, potteries, coal mine and brick works. There are exhibitions, an audio tour by artist John Bellany, and original structures including the rare Hoffman Kiln built in 1937 and the Cornish Beam Engine.

PRESTONGRANGE MUSEUM: Morison's Haven, Prestonpans EH32 9RY; ☎ 0131 653 2904; www.prestongrange. org. Admission free; open daily Apr–Oct 11am–4.30pm.

The community of Prestonpans is extremely proud of their rich industrial and maritime heritage. Local artists are creating a painted Murals Trail to honour the memory of their ancestors and to illustrate the town's social and cultural history. This, of course, is the site of the **Battle of Prestonpans** when Bonnie Prince Charlie defeated the Hanoverian forces of King George II in Scotland on 21 September 1745. Each year on its anniversary a Battlefield Walk and a Battle Ceilidh is organised.

Prestoungrange Gothenburg (227 High Street, Prestonpans) is more than just an historic pub and brewery; it's also an art gallery and destination venue for regular music events and festivals.

The best ice cream in East Lothian, Luca's ice cream

What to do with children...

As well as the golden sand beaches right along this coast, where better to take the kids than the **Myreton Motor Museum**, located near Aberlady and established in 1966. The collection has cars, bicycles, motorcycles, and commercial vans, as well as toy pedal cars dating from 1899 to the 1970s. Associated automobilia includes period advertising, posters, and petrol pumps.

MYRETON MOTOR MUSEUM: Aberlady EH32 0PZ (signposted from A198 and B 1377); ☎ 01875 870288. Entry: adult £6 (summer)/£5 (winter), child £3, family of four £15; open Mar–Nov, daily 11am–4pm; Dec–Feb, weekends only 11am–3pm.

For the best ice cream in East Lothian visit **Luca's ice cream café** (32 High Street, Musselburgh), which was established over 90 years ago. Be prepared to queue!

... and how to avoid children

Glenkinchie Whisky Distillery is located in the glen of the Kinchie Burn, near Pencaitland, East Lothian. The name Kinchie is a corruption of 'De Quincy', the original owners of the land, and the distillery was founded around 1825. The standard 10-year-old Glenkinchie

GLENKINCHIE WHISKY DISTILLERY: Pencaitland EH34 5ET; ☎ 01875 342004; www.discovering-distilleries.com. Entry: adult £5 redeemable against purchase; children welcome but not admitted to production area; open Easter–Oct, Mon–Sat 10am–5pm; Sun 12–5pm; Nov, Mon–Sun 12–4pm; Dec–Easter, Mon–Fri 12–4pm.

The Glenkinchie Whisky Distillery

Edinburgh Malt is a fairly typical soft Lowland whisky. Its sweet nose and hint of peat is a good introduction to the world of single malts. The 14-year-old Distiller's Edition is double-matured in Amontillado sherry casks.

Entertainment

The **Three Harbours Festival** (☎ 07748 013042; www3harbours.com) takes place over 10 days at the end of May/early June. It celebrates the community and culture around the three harbours of Prestonpans, Cockenzie and Port Seton. Historically, this area was a thriving place for fishing, boat building, potteries, mining and salt making and it's this legacy which inspires

BRUNTON THEATRE: Ladywell Way, Musselburgh EH21 6AF; ☎ 0131 665 2240; www.bruntontheatre.co.uk.

the arts festival each year with the rugged coastline as a dramatic backdrop. Following the John Muir art trail, inspired art installations, street theatre, music, workshops, literature events and children's activities are all part of the fun.

For drama, music, dance, films, and a wonderful Christmas pantomime, the **Brunton Theatre,** Musselburgh has a lively year-round programme of entertainment for all ages and taste.

🛒 Shopping

The little coastal villages each have their own distinctive local arts, crafts and gift shops. **Lavender's Blue** (High Street, Longniddry; ☎ 01875 852500) sells French 'chateau chic' homeware and Lulu Guinness bedding, tableware and lighting. The **Merry Go Round** (Main Street, Gullane; ☎ 01620 842 222; www.the-merry-go-round. co.uk) boutique specialises in designer funky clothes and shoes for children.

LOCAL KNOWLEDGE

Malcolm Duck is a highly acclaimed and well known Edinburgh restaurateur who owns the Kilspindie House Hotel, Aberlady. This is a fine country roadside inn-featuring a cosy pub and Duck's at Kilspindie Restaurant which is recommended in the *Michelin Guide, Great Britain and Ireland 2008.*

Best walk: North Berwick to Aberlady. From the gannets diving off North Berwick in the spring to the chattering geese filling the fiery autumn skies over Aberlady, the views are quite spectacular, enhanced by the amazing East Lothian light. For some reason there seems to be more sky up there than anywhere else I have been.

Best place for children: The beach at Gullane where they can run, fish in the rock pools, play cowboys and Indians and get soaked accidentally falling into the sea. It's a quite excellent place for kids to have fun, mothers to fuss about drowning or sunburn and dads to work out whether they are kids or husbands.

Best tourist attraction: The Concorde experience at the Museum of Flight, East Fortune, is well worth doing; you really have to be on the plane to understand it.

Best shop: Mains the Saddlers in Haddington hasn't changed in years and is simply an Alladin's cave as saddler, ironmonger, fishing tackle and gift shop. There is little the staff can't help you with.

Best pub and restaurant: Duck's at Kilspindie House, Aberlady; the only East Lothian eatery in the *Michelin Guide.* Have a bar supper or dinner in the restaurant serving local lobster, asparagus, venison, cheese, wild boar, mussels, crab, mackerel.

Favourite farm shop: Fenton Barns Farm Shop has an excellent range of local produce and a lovely coffee shop. The Bothy in Aberlady sources wild boar from the forest nearby.

Best view: From the 6th tee on Gullane 1 golf course you can see forever; across to Fife, to North Berwick, to Edinburgh and the Forth Bridges; a very special place.

The best... PLACES TO STAY

HOTEL

Kilspindie House Hotel

Main Street, Aberlady EH32 0RE
☎ **01875 870682**
www.kilspindie.co.uk

This 17th-century townhouse and school is the setting for this attractive, homely hotel near beaches, nature reserve, Museum of Flight, and 19 golf courses within a 15-minute drive. Personally run by owner Malcolm Duck whose award-winning Duck's Restaurant specialises in local farm produce and seafood.

Price: £50 B&B sharing.

COUNTRY HOUSE

Green Craig

Aberlady, East Lothian EH32 0PY
☎ **01875 870301; www.greencraig.com**

Situated on a headland overlooking Aberlady Bay in a private woodland estate with direct access to beach. The house has six beautiful sea view (en suite) bedrooms, a lounge, beautiful dining room, 42" TV, iPod dock and PC, as well as meals catered and a housekeeping service.

Price: £6,000–£7,500 per wk. Short stays from £125 pppn.

SELF-CATERING

Kilspindie, Archerfield and Muirfield Cottages

West Fenton Court, West Fenton, East Lothian EH39 5AL
☎ **01620 842154; www.westfenton.co.uk**

Choice of one, two and three-bedroom cottages created within old stone courtyard buildings on West Fenton Farm. They are modernised with high-spec luxury yet homely furnishings. Private patio gardens.

Price: £280–£865 per week.

Sunset View

Quill House, Sea Wynd, High Street, Aberlady EH32 0RB
☎ **01875 870405; www.quillhouse.co.uk**

Two double-bedroom flat in old whitewashed house with romantic history of smugglers and a sea captain owner. View from sitting room over Aberlady Bay, TV (Freeview) with DVD/CD, fully fitted kitchen. With free parking and garden, it has a perfect location in Aberlady village near beach and golf.

Price: £315–£455 per week. £50–£65 per night (seasonal minimum three-night stay).

UNIQUE

Fenton Tower

Kingston, East Lothian EH39 5JH
☎ **01620 890089**
www.fentontower.com

Magnificent 16th-century, five-storey tower with turrets and battlements. Meticulously restored with luxury furnishings, five double and one single bedroom. Original vaulted dining hall, spiral staircases and open hearth fires. Bespoke service for catering, leisure and golf arrangements.

Price: £150 pp pn B&B.

B&B

Adniston Manor

West Adniston Farm, East Lothian EH33 1EA
☎ **01875 611 190**
www.adnistonmanor.com

Country house B&B run by Alan and Audrey Russell in their charming 19th-century mansion, formerly a farmhouse set in 1.6 acres of garden. Comfortable home-from-home offering graciously furnished bedrooms and suites with private facilities, tea tray, TV (Freeview).

Price: £40–£60 pp pn B&B.

The best... FOOD AND DRINK

▶ Staying in

Gullane, although a small village, has a diverse range of shops. **The Gullane Delicatessen** (40c Main Street) has a marvellous array of wines, whiskies, cheeses, cooked meats and other local and continental provisions. **Ramsay's** (23h Summerside Place) is a traditional family butcher selling local beef, lamb and pork. **Get Fresh** (23 Summerside Place) has an eclectic mix of flowers, fruit, vegetables, locally made chocolate and soft cuddly teddies and dolls. **The Village Coffee Shop** (10 Rosebery Place) has a quaint quirkiness, serving snacks, soups and specials, along with the normal assortment of homebaking. Port Seton has a small deli, **Morag's Larder** (16 Links Road), and next door is **Ramage Bakery**. Down by the harbour are several fishmongers selling local catches of fish and seafood.

For the best German bread and cakes visit **Falko:Konditormeister** (1 Stanley Road, Gullane; ☎ 01620 843168; www.falko.co.uk). They sell sublime Black Forest Gateau and Linzertort that can be either eaten in the coffee shop or taken home. They also offer dense but moist sourdough, seeded and rye breads, all baked to traditional recipes. There are always seasonal additions like stollen and gingerbread houses at Christmas. Falko is the only baker in Edinburgh and East Lothian who makes Callah and Kosher bread at his Edinburgh bakery on Thursdays and Fridays.

Northwood Wild Boar reared on the estate can be purchased from **Gosford Bothy Farm Shop and Café** (Gosford Estate, nr Aberlady; ☎ 01875 871234/870201; www.gosfordfarmshop.co.uk). Seasonal vegetables are sourced from within a 5-mile radius and are mostly organic. Jams, chocolate, juices, sauces, breads and condiments are also made locally. Award-winning bacon and sausages are available from **Ballencrieff Rare Pedigree Pigs** (Ballencrieff Gardens by Longniddry; ☎ 01875 870551). Gloucester Old Spots, Berkshires and Saddleback pigs snuffle freely on this farm. These free-range porkers are destined to become wonderful smoked and unsmoked bacon, sausages, chops and cutlets. Only open Tuesday to Sunday, 1pm–4pm.

Seasonal fruit and vegetables are grown in **Les Chalmers'** market garden and sold at **Seton East Farm Shop** (Fishers Road, nr Longniddry; ☎ 01875 815946). Summer heralds the arrival of salad leaves, soft fruit and herbs, with pumpkins, squashes and all sorts of root vegetables making an appearance during the colder months.

The seaside butchers **McKirdy Brothers** (21 Links Road, Port Seton; ☎ 01875 811726) has some of the best meat in the area: well-hung beef from Aberdeenshire, Borders lamb and homemade steak pies that come in five sizes, baby (1lb) through to grand-daddy (3lbs). They have also won prizes for their haggis and black pudding.

Down by Musselburgh harbour, **Clark Brothers Fish Merchant**, (220 New Street Musselburgh; ☎ 0131 665 6181) has an excellent choice of fish and crustacean, including live and cooked lobsters and crabs. Everything is displayed on ice-covered marble slabs. Salmon and trout are smoked in-house. And for wine and cheese, **The Fine Wine Company** (145 North High Street, Musselburgh; ☎ 0131 665 0088) has eclectic wines from across the globe, beers and single malts from Scotland and a small selection of **Ian Mellis's** cheeses.

Takeaway

There are just a couple of takeaways in the area: **The Gullane Super Fry** (3 Rosebery Place) has a varied menu from fish and chips to pizza and pasta, while **Adrian's of Aberlady** (33 High Street) has a good reputation for their fish and chips along with their ever-popular haggis pizza. In Port Seton there are numerous takeaways including two fish and chip shops down by the harbour. On the main street, Links Road, there are two Chinese carryouts.

🍴 Drinking

There are various pubs and inns in this area including the Longniddry Inn, the Old Aberlady Inn and the Kilspindie House, Aberlady.

The Golf Inn Hotel (Main Street, Gullane) has a vast collection of whiskies from the well known to some of Scotland's rarest. The public bar, with an open fire, is well stocked with ales, lagers and spirits. The restaurant has a good reputation for honest food. **The Prestoungrange Gothenburg** (227–229 High Street, Prestonpans) has its own microbrewery, carrying on the traditions of the original brewers and retaining the Fowler's name, a family who were brewing here since 1745. The beer is available in the James Fewell and Lord Mayor's Bars or you can take some home from the Jug Bar. **Staggs – The Volunteer Arms** (79 North High Street, Musselburgh; behind the Brunton Theatre) has been in the Stagg family for 150 years and has won many awards. There are always three or four real ales on pump at any one time and the atmosphere is homely, cosy and welcoming.

EATING OUT

FINE DINING

La Potinière
Main Street, Gullane EH31 2AA
☎ **01620 843214**
www.la-potiniere.co.uk

This award-winning restaurant is a member of the Scotch Beef Club and uses local and seasonal produce. The menu may feature slow-cooked haunch of Scottish roe deer or braised fillet of halibut. Their wine list may be short, but it's comprehensive suiting all tastes, without breaking the bank. Set menu £40.

The Glasshouse at Eskmills
Stuart House Eskmills, Station Road, Musselburgh EH21 7PQ
☎ **0131 273 5240**
www.theglasshouseateskmills.com

Chef Stevie Adair's award-winning, chic and contemporary restaurant is a hidden gem in the courtyard of the restored Eskmills and has gathered a plethora of awards. Food is exemplary with seasonal produce featured on the menu. Stevie has also had the pleasure of cooking for the Queen for her 80th birthday celebrations. Two courses cost about £20.

RESTAURANT

Ducks at Kilspindie House
Mains Street, Aberlady EH32 0RE
☎ **01875 870682**
www.ducks.co.uk

Eat either in the bar from the aptly named Duckling menu or in the restaurant itself. There's game, Buccleuch beef, the salmon is organic and the bread is homemade. Desserts are indulgent affairs. The wine list has been awarded with the much-coveted Le Routiers Wine List of the Year. Two courses cost about £23.

BISTRO

The Old Clubhouse
East Links Road, Gullane EH31 2AF
☎ **01620 842008**
www.oldclubhouse.com

A warm welcome and roaring fire for colder days make this pub a firm favourite. The blackboard menu covers all bases from Cullen skink to nachos. Ballencrieff sausages and gammon, with the free-range pigs coming from just outside Longniddry. Good range of cask beers as well as cask scrumpy. Two courses cost about £18.

EATING OUT

The Old Aberlady Inn
Main Street, Aberlady EH32 0RF
☎ **01875 870503**
www.theoldaberladyinn.co.uk

This quaint village pub opens up inside. The menu has some nice surprises like twice-baked cheese soufflé, venison with liquorice jus and shortbread mille feuille with strawberries and raspberries. Friendly service and well-cooked and presented food. Two courses cost about £15.

Restaurant 102
102 New Street,
Musselburgh EH21 6JQ
☎ **0131 665 3535**

Not far from the sea, this bistro offers a rounded menu with fish, chicken, meat and vegetarian dishes. Steaks come with a good selection of sauces and the cheeseboard is predominantly Scottish. Two courses for £15.95.

GASTROPUB

The Longniddry Inn
Main Street, Longniddry EH32 0NF
☎ **01875 852401**

This popular village inn is always busy due to the fact they serve good pub grub at a reasonable price. The menu is well rounded with dishes comprising of local produce and everything is cooked to order. Great for just a bowl of soup or a three-course meal. Two courses cost about £14.

CAFÉ

The Olympic Café (Luca's)
32–28 High Street,
Musselburgh EH21 7AG
☎ **0131 665 2237**
www.s-luca.co.uk

The queues out the door are testimony to the popularity of this café. The menu suits everyone, with soups and sandwiches to homemade burgers and lasagne. They make their own ice creams and it's a great place to have a knickerbockerglory or a banana split. Soup and sandwich £3.95.

The Tolbooth
63d High Street,
Musselburgh EH21 7BZ
☎ **0131 665 9072**

Café by day offers an excellent range of cakes, sandwiches and soup. A bistro by night, the simple menu is more sophisticated with homemade pâté, fresh fish and local chicken. Desserts are sinful temptations. Two courses cost about £15.

ⓘ Visitor Information

Doctors: Gullane Medical Practice, The Surgery Broadgait Green, Gullane EH31 2DW, ☎ 01620 842171.

Pharmacies: Fishers Pharmacy, 7 Rosebery Place, Gullane EH31 2AN, ☎ 01620 842248.

Travel and Transport: National Rail Enquiries, ☎ 08457 48 49 50, www.nationalrail.com; ScotRail, www.firstgroup.com/scotrail; First Buses, ☎ 08708 72 72 71, www.firstgroup.com; Lothian Buses, ☎ 0131 554 4494, www.lothianbuses.com.

Self-Catering Accommodation: Coast Properties, 27 High Street, North Berwick, ☎ 01620 67 1966, www.coast-properties.co.uk; Eagleye rentals, holiday homes near golf courses, ☎ 02380 873007, www.eagleyerentals.com.

Taxi: David Balfour, Aberlady; ☎ 01875 870711, offers modern four to eight-seater vehicles for eating out, golf outings, theatre and concert performances, holiday transport. Wheelchair access and children's seats available.

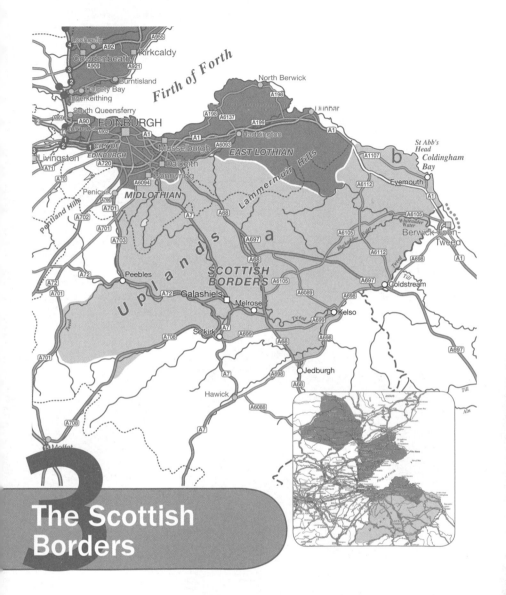

The Scottish Borders

a. Peebles and the Tweed Valley
b. The Berwickshire coastline

Unmissable highlights

01 Scott's View, probably the most graceful and tranquil spot in the Borders, p.215

02 St Mary's Loch, located in a lovely, tranquil valley, where travellers can eat and drink at Tibbie Shiels Inn, p.210

03 Lochcarron Waverley Mill for designer fashion cashmere, tweeds and tartan, p.220

04 Stobo Castle, a true destination spa, Zen-like sanctuary and oasis of calm, p.221

05 St Abb's village and St Abb's Head for spectacular craggy, wild coastline views, p.231

06 Melrose for its upmarket boutiques, antiques, bookshops and the Abbey, p.223

07 Floors Castle, home to the Duke of Roxburghe, rich in paintings, furniture and lovely gardens, p.238

08 Traquair, Scotland's oldest inhabited house, with a garden maze and home brewery, p.212

09 Manderston, a supreme historic house as seen on *Edwardian Country House* TV series, p.237

10 Mountain biking at Glentress, one of the best waymarked trails in the world, p.211

THE SCOTTISH BORDERS

'Yet was poetic impulse given
By green hill and clear blue heaven'

Sir Walter Scott

Border Country, Scott's beloved country, the site of centuries of skirmishes, cattle reivers and attacks between England and Scotland, has been described as a conundrum, not entirely part of either nation. It's an extraordinarily complex and colourful blend of breathtaking, gentle, green landscape, sheep hill farms, a dramatic sense of history, grand aristocratic mansions, castles and palaces, a rich literary heritage and also an adventure playground for outdoor sports and leisure.

Although just an hour south of Edinburgh, the Borders are often seen as a no-man's-land, ignored by visitors who drive straight up the A1, and forgotten even by those who live in the capital. The original railway line between Edinburgh and the central Borders was axed in 1969 as part of the infamous Beeching Report which did nothing to help the tourist industry. But nearly 40 years on, a Scottish Parliament Bill has been passed to resurrect the line from Edinburgh to Tweedbank. The 35-mile Waverley Line due to be completed by 2013 is viewed as 'historic, and the single most important economic and social decision to impact on the Borders and Midlothian communities for decades'.

There's a great deal going on, both to see and do, whatever your interests, across the vast expanse of rural landscape stretching from the forested glens to the fishing villages of Berwickshire on the east coast. It's a destination for all seasons, offering adventurous cross-country walks, cycle routes, world-class fishing on the Tweed and equally world-class mountain biking. The Border towns and villages create a close-knit rural community and preserve a tremendous sense of culture and heritage, which you can witness at annual fairs and festivals, and not forgetting their own sport, Rugby 7s.

This is the home of luxury textiles, fine tweed, soft cashmere and lambswool knitwear, a warm souvenir of your visit. With old coaching inns, pubs and romantic country house hotels, you'll sleep and eat very well with Scotland's finest lamb, salmon and seafood sourced from Border farms, rivers and fishing ports. In a nutshell, the Scottish Borders offers scenic tranquility and culture, activity and a taste of adventure.

PEEBLES AND THE TWEED VALLEY

The 18th-century Scottish Judge Lord Cockburn was said to have coined the phrase 'As quiet as the grave – or Peebles.' Probably meant as a slightly tongue-in-cheek witticism in his time, today we can use his comment in a much more positive light. **Peebles** is a delightfully welcoming and friendly short-break or day-trip town on the banks of the River Tweed with good arts, antique and crafts shops, restaurants, cafés, pubs and a theatre, as well as beautiful botanical gardens. Just an easy half an hour drive from Edinburgh (or you can take the bus), it's the perfect place to enjoy a combined 'city and country break', or you can stay longer to explore further afield.

Just as the region is distinct in its landscape, history and character, so too is each of the charming towns which are scattered across Tweeddale. **Melrose** offers another ideal base from which to tour around the vicinity to visit Walter Scott's home at Abbotsford, enjoy some healthy hill walking or delve into the local Roman archaeology. The town is the starting point for the St Cuthbert's Way, a 62-mile trek to Lindisfarne, the Holy Isle, an innovative venture which encourages people to walk in the countryside as well as recognising this ancient pilgrimage.

Take an inspiring journey around the Scottish Borders following the Tweed or through the Yarrow Valley to find traditional villages, ruined abbeys, castles and remote lochs. Take time to observe unspoilt scenic views and breathe in the almost tangible scent of ancient heritage across this proudly independent frontier land.

WHAT TO SEE AND DO

Peebles is a charming town, rather a hidden treasure of a place, surrounded by unspoilt scenery and character. Only 23 miles south of Edinburgh, it sits straddling the Tweed, the majestic river famed for its excellent salmon fishing, which gave Peebles its motto 'Against the stream they multiply.' In and around Peebles, there's something for everyone from outdoor pursuits, walking, golf, mountain biking and horse riding, and it has the distinction of being chosen as the best Independent Retailing Town in Scotland, (second in the UK) for traditional gifts, country clothing, books, arts and crafts, with each shop offering personal service. On a fine day, it's easy to explore Peebles with a stroll along the High Street, leading off into cobbled lanes and medieval closes. As a symbolic centre, the **Mercat Cross** of Peebles is situated in Eastgate where the old trading market was held, the Town Drummer announced royal proclamations, and criminals were punished.

The River Tweed flows through Peebles

River Tweed Walkway

The Peebles area is renowned for numerous woodland, forestry commission, hill and riverside walks. A moderate circular walk for a couple of hours along the River Tweed from Peebles town centre is certainly worth doing. The walkway begins from Hay Lodge Park, just round the corner at the west end of the High Street (with a public car park opposite). Heading right upstream after just a mile or so through

NEIDPATH CASTLE: Peebles EH45 8NW; ☎ 01721 720333. Open to visitors by arrangement only. Also available for wedding ceremonies and private events.

pretty wooded gorge, the path opens up beside a sandy beach and grassland below the impressive medieval stronghold, **Neidpath Castle**. The best viewpoint to photograph

Neidpath Castle

Neidpath Castle is a wonderful fairytale attraction best seen from below on the banks of the River Tweed. This authentic 14th-century castle located on a bend of the Tweed, 1 mile west of Peebles, dates from 1370 when it was built by the Hay family, who retained it for 300 years, before it was passed on to William Douglas, First Duke of Queensberry. From 1810 it became the property of the Earl of Wemyss whose family remain the private owners today. The castle was attacked by Oliver Cromwell, but withstood the longest assault on any stronghold south of the Forth, before being forced to surrender. Not surprisingly, the Castle has been used for film locations including *Merlin: the Quest Begins* starring Jason Connery. The castle, featuring a pit prison and Mary Queen of Scots' bedroom, was until 2009 open daily during the summer, but now tours are only available by arrangement in advance. On a fine day you can enjoy the prime picnic area beside the river beneath the castle. This was in fact my favourite place as a child for family summer picnics, where we bravely used to swim, and our dog chased sticks, in the briskly cold, strong currents.

the castle is further up river–and look out too for multicoloured kingfishers before reaching a 19th-century viaduct. The Tweed Walk signpost leads you onto the viaduct and along the old railway line towards **Manor Bridge** (built 1702). If you are feeling energetic, cross over the bridge and take a short but steep walk up **Manor Sware** hill, from the top are fantastic views over the Tweed valley. From here, walk back down through South Park Wood, with many paths leading back to the river which will take you along the opposite bank from the Castle, back to Peebles.

Walking in the Scottish Borders

The magical lure of the Scottish Borders is irresistible to serious ramblers, hikers and leisurely walkers. This is a walking destination, with 1,500 miles of dedicated walking routes such as the **Borders Abbeys Way**, linking Kelso, Jedburgh, Melrose and Dryburgh, including the towns of Hawick and Selkirk. Each section is 12 miles and the total circular route is 65 miles. Abbey Way leaflets are available from the local Tourist Information Centres. The **St Cuthbert's Way** is the path of pilgrims from Melrose, the site of St Cuthbert's early monastic life to his later ministry at Lindisfarne on Holy Isle. This is a popular route for dedicated walkers, following the River Tweed and the old Roman road with accommodation (featuring the Walkers Welcome logo) along the way. The walk offers an inspiring 60-mile adventure over hill and dale. It will take four days (three nights) if pushing the pace, or take it more leisurely over a week. Luggage can be transported between each B&B or country inn. For full information on how to plan your journey, see www.stcuthbertsway.fsnet.co.uk.

Another serious cross-country trek is the **Southern Upland Way** (from Portpatrick on the west coast of Scotland to Cockburnspath on the east coast) which follows an overland route right across the Tweed Valley for 82 miles, from St Mary's Loch to Traquair, Melrose and on to the Berwickshire coast.

Tweeddale offers the outdoor enthusiast the wonderful wilderness of the **Tweed Valley Forest Park** with numerous graded trails for hiking, cycling and horse riding. This Forestry Commission Park links several separate forests including Cardrona, Glentress, Cademuir, Thornilee, Cabertson, and Yair. It stretches from Peebles right along the Tweed, between the villages of Innerleithen and Walkerburn through rugged rolling hills and wooded valleys.

A network of waymarked paths also lead up to the summit of **Minch Moor** with views over the Tweed Valley, Yarrow Valley to the south and west towards Selkirk and Galashiels. The different forest areas offer not only exercise and fresh air but also historic sites and wildlife. This is the habitat for red squirrels and there are Osprey Watch Centres at Glentress and Kailzie Gardens. En route you'll find picnic tables and contemporary craftwork created by artists to commemorate local heritage and legends. The Tweed Valley Forest Park is open 365 days a year, featuring separate walking and biking trails with numbered posts – each marked easy, moderate or strenuous, so that all abilities, adults and children are welcome for a fun family day out. Pick up a Forestry Commission leaflet or contact Forestry Commission Scotland (☎ 01750 721120; www.forestry.gov.uk/scotland).

Mountain biking

Scotland is recognised as being home to the finest mountain bike trails in the world. The Forestry Commission has created challenging cross-country trails around Glentress Forest and Innerleithen, part of the internationally acclaimed 7stanes mountain bike trails (www.7stanes. gov.uk), which are spread right across the country from the Highlands to the south-west. The **Innerleithen Downhill Course**, for instance, offers thrills and a few spills on this heart-

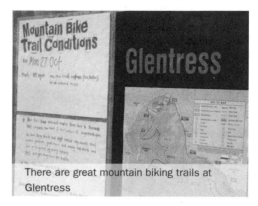

There are great mountain biking trails at Glentress

stopping steep route. Spectators can watch from special viewing spots when a championship race or event is staged.

The Hub in the Forest at Glentress offers bike rides for all ages and has superb facilities including a lodge hut, Hub Grub café, showers, toilets and bike hire. There are demo high-end bikes for adults and lightweight Islabikes and helmets for children. As well as colour-graded cycle routes from Green (easy) to Black (severe), there are short and more challenging routes with numbered checkpoints to keep you on the right track. The fascinating aspect of Glentress is that this was a prehistoric Iron Age settlement; historic sites include the ancient Shieldgreen tower and a reconstruction of a hut c.100AD. Bike trails are open 24/7, year round.

THE HUB IN THE FOREST: Glentress, near Peebles EH45 8NB; ☎ 01721 721736; www.thehubintheforest.co.uk. Facilities open Easter–Oct, Mon–Fri 10am–6pm, Sat–Sun 9am–6pm; end of Oct–31 Dec, Mon–Sun 10am–6pm; 1 Jan–Easter, closed Mon–Tues; bike hire bookable by phone, £20 per day. Car park fee £3.

The Scottish Borders has also created waymarked circular routes for **Cycle Tours**. The Border Loop runs for 250 miles from Peebles to Eyemouth on the Berwickshire coast, although you need only do a few sections! It runs through a landscape of rolling hills, moorland, and river valleys meandering along country lanes. The Tweed Cycleway is an 89-mile cycle route through the heart of the Borders. Borderloop and Cycleway guides and map are available at the Tourist Information Centre.

On a fine day enjoy a relaxing cycle ride or drive south of Selkirk along the meandering A708 beside the Yarrow Water to **St Mary's Loch**, and its sister, the **Loch of the Lowes**. This is a truly poetic and restful spot in a rather remote and desolate glen. **James Hogg**, the Scottish poet named the Ettrick Shepherd, worked all his life here on the sheep farms on the wild open moors. A spectacular waterfall, the Grey Mare's tail, plunges 200ft from an overhanging cliff-face and if you don't mind a precipitous drop beneath, you can climb up to the foot of the falls. In the summer, ospreys (fish-eating birds of prey) can often be seen 'fishing' in the lochs and reservoirs. St Mary's Loch is one of the most beautiful places in the Borders to get away from it all; it's so utterly secluded, surrounded by fields of sheep and mountains which are often shrouded in a shimmering morning mist. Visit **Tibbie Shiels Inn** (www.tibbieshielsinn.com) for a drink, lunch, supper or to stay the night. It's an authentic literary-themed 19th-century hostelry (probably haunted by Tibbie the Victorian landlady), which was regularly frequented by Sir Walter Scott, James Hogg and occasionally by Robert Louis Stevenson.

Historic houses and gardens

Traquair is the oldest inhabited house in Scotland dating back to 1107 and is still owned by the Maxwell Stuart family who have lived here since 1491. The house has been visited by 27 monarchs, including Mary Queen of Scots. The place is steeped in Jacobite history with some interesting furniture and memorabilia, including a cradle used by James VI, Mary Queen of Scots' bed, an 18th-century library, a collection of Jacobite glass and a set of secret stairs used by priests. One gate and drive to the house has been locked for centuries and will never be opened or used until the rightful Stuart King is back on the Scottish throne.

> TRAQUAIR: Innerleithen EH44 6PW; ☎ 01896 830323; www.traquair.co.uk. Entry: adult £7, child £4; family (two adults, three children) £20; open Easter weekend; daily 10 April–31 Oct; April, May and Sept 12–5pm; Jun–Aug 10.30am–5pm; Oct 11am–4pm; Nov, weekends only, 11am–3pm.

The house has magnificent gardens where you can wander through the woodland walk with some of the oldest yew trees in Scotland. Children especially will enjoy exploring the gigantic maze of tree hedging which is a real puzzle to reach the centre (a zig-zag walk of a quarter of a mile), where you can stand on a stone plinth and see over the top of the entire maze. Traquair organises several annual events, such as an Easter Egg hunt, a Medieval Fair on May Spring Bank Holiday featuring battle re-enactments, archery and falconry, and the Traquair Summer Fair in early August featuring live music, storytelling, arts and crafts. Traquair also has its own private Brewery where you can sample and buy their home-brewed Traquair ale.

In the Peebles area there are two superb gardens: **Kailzie**, an extensive, domestic garden on a grand scale, and **Danwyck Botanic Garden**, one of the

> KAILZIE GARDEN: Peebles EH45 9HT; ☎ 01721 720007; www.kalziegardens. com Entry: adult £2.50–£4.50 (seasonally varied fee), child 50p (under 5s free); open 7 days a week, year round; summer, end Mar to end Oct, 11am–5.30pm; winter end Oct–Mar, daylight hours and access to wild garden and woodland walks only.

world's finest aroboreta. Kailzie has been created over many years by Lady Buchan Hepburn near the River Tweed, featuring a walled garden of herbaceous borders, woodland walks, a wild garden and rose garden – from spring to autumn it's a riot

> DAWYCK BOTANIC GARDEN: Stobo EH45 9JU; ☎ 01721 760254; www.rbge.org.uk. Entry: adult £4/£3.50 (seasonal variations); child £1; family (two adults, four children), £9; open daily 1 Feb–30 Nov; Feb and Nov 10am–4pm; Mar and Oct 10am–5pm; Apr–Sept 10am–6pm.

The Border Ballads

From the early 14th to the 16th centuries, the Anglo-Scottish borderlands witnessed one of the most intense periods of warfare and disorder ever seen in modern Europe. Border Reivers began to criss-cross the farmlands between the Cheviots, Lammermuirs and Yorkshire dales, stealing cattle, sheep and horses from each other. Local commerce and international trade withered as the image of the Border region became one of notoriety and lawlessness. The legacy of this 300-year feud was that the Borderers held on tenaciously to a sense of identity and culture. Local poets wrote ballads about Borders life–from the shepherds, supernatural folklore, love and romance to the plundering and pillage by the Reivers. Oral history was very strong and strolling minstrels spread the word by singing these heartfelt ballads wherever they travelled.

'Last night a wind from Lammermuir came roaring up the glen,
With the tramp of trooping horses and the laugh of reckless men,
And struck a mailed hand on the gate and cried in rebel glee,
Come forth, come forth my Borderer, and ride the March with me.'

The story of the Borders people and their fight for survival has always been at the heart of their strong literary heritage. To this day the Border towns commemorate their local culture and tradition with annual Common Riding and Reivers Festivals. Hawick lies at the heart of Reiver country, and the town's annual festival brings to life the region's history and evokes the spirit of the Reivers through Border ballads, drama, music and fiery fireworks.

The heritage of the old Border ballads inspired two great writers, James Hogg and Sir Walter Scott. It's through Scott's epic novels and poetry as well as his own passionate love-affair with the Tweed valley which put the Borders firmly on the map. James Hogg was known as 'The Ettrick Shepherd',and his most famous work is *The Private Memoirs and Confessions of a Justified Sinner*, published in 1824, and today regarded as a masterpiece of Scottish literature. Hogg spent his entire life around the Ettrick and Yarrow valleys. Describing his love of the landscape in a letter to Scott in 1801, Hogg wrote: *'Having been born amongst mountains I am always unhappy when in a flat country. Whenever the skirts of a horizon come on a level with myself, I feel myself quite uneasy.'*

of colour. The gardens have a Tweed Valley Osprey webcam, an 18-hole putting green, a trout pond (fishing tackle to rent), children's play area, café and a gift shop.

Eight miles south of Peebles on the road to Stobo is Dawyck Botanic Garden, a five-star visitor attraction boasting some of the tallest trees in Britain and a lovely riverside walk, guided walks, a conservatory for teas and homebaking, and a plants and gift shop.

Border abbey towns

To gain a better understanding of the Scottish Borders, it's important to visit a few of the medieval abbey towns to gain a powerful insight into the area's history. During the flourishing, rich Renaissance period, the local, wealthy wool traders preferred to export from Berwick directly to Europe rather than over the border to England.

The 14th-century Melrose Abbey

Magnificent monasteries were built by entrepreneurial monks in Melrose, Dryburgh, Selkirk and Jedburgh. But the golden age was short-lived following the death of Alexander III in 1286, when the wars of independence between England and Scotland brought devastation across this debatable land.

MELROSE ABBEY: Abbey Street, Melrose TD6 9LG; ☎ 01896 822562; www.historic-scotland.gov.uk. Entry: adult £5.20/£4.20 (seasonal varations), child £2.60; open daily, 21 Mar–30 Sept 9.30am–5.30pm; 1 Oct–31 Mar 9.30am–4.30pm.

The 14th-century **Melrose Abbey**, at one time the richest abbey in Scotland, is particularly stunning architecturally; you can stand in the central nave under the towering arches and also climb the spiral staircase to the roof. It retains a proud elegance in its weather-beaten, worn grey stonework and carved sculptures, most notably the bagpipe-playing pig. The chapter house is where the heart of Robert Bruce is believed to be buried. Try to witness its graceful beauty when illuminated at night or in a wintry mist which adds a spooky glow.

Melrose is a most attractive and tranquil Border town with a strong sense of literary and cultural heritage. Surrounded by the Eildon hills, one of which is named the Magic Mountain and was believed to be a sacred place by the Celtic priests who performed fire festivals to ward off evil spirits and offered human sacrifice to the vengeful sky gods. The hills are believed to have been created by an alchemist wizard Michael Scott and it was here that Thomas the Rhymer was given the gift of prophecy by the Faerie Queen. You can visit the Rhymer's Stone marking the site of the Eildon Tree where he met her. The location is on the old road linking Melrose and Newtown St Boswells with the viewpoint accessible at all times. Magic and mysterious legends aside, the hills are perfect for an energetic walk, easily reached from the town centre.

A few miles away **Dryburgh Abbey** sits on the banks of the Tweed and its remarkably complete medieval ruins are fine examples of gothic ecclesiastic architecture. It was originally founded in 1150 and burnt down in 1322 by English troops. The burial places of Sir Walter Scott and Field-Marshal Earl Haig are in the north transept. The gardens are very peaceful and give an idea of the original enclosed monastery. To truly experience the delights of this attractive abbey, by day and night, stay next door at the Dryburgh Abbey Hotel.

DRYBURGH ABBEY: St Boswells TD6 0RW; ☎ 01835 822381; www.historic-scotland. gov.uk. Entry: adult £4.70/£3.70 (seasonal variations); child £2.35; open daily, 21 Mar–30 Sept 9.30am–5.30pm; 1 Oct–31 Mar 9.30am–4.30pm.

Scott's View

A couple of miles from Dryburgh Abbey at Bermersyde is one of the most exquisitely painterly scenic views in the Scottish Borders and one of the area's unmissable highlights. **Scott's View** is so called because this was Sir Walter Scott's favourite place to stop and meditate. The scene will hardly have changed one iota since his day, looking out across the valley towards the Eildon Hills, over a patchwork of green fields, clumps of thick woodland and the curving River Tweed. As the wind sweeps upwards against the steep sides of the valley, it creates a great lift for birds of prey such as

Scott's View, where the poet liked to stop and meditate

buzzards, who ride the breeze to gain height and reach the open country behind. Even on a fine day, the weather can shift in a few minutes as clouds sweep over the summit of the Eildon peaks and mask them in mist and rain, but equally rain clouds can drift away in an instant. It's a beautiful view at any time. Scott's View is signposted from St Boswells and Dryburgh off the B6356.

On the day of Scott's funeral en route to Dryburgh Abbey, his horses pulling the hearse immediately stopped at this viewpoint as they always had done on regular journeys. A plaque on the stone wall here commemorates this literary spot with a few lines from Scott's patriotic poem, *The Lay of the Last Minstrel*:

'Breathes there the man, with soul so dead,
Who neer to himself hath said,
This is my own, my native land.'

Just 10 miles north of the Scottish/English border is the Royal Burgh of **Jedburgh**, where King David I founded the red-sandstone **Jedburgh Abbey** on the banks of the Jed Water in 1138, as a priory for Augustinian canons. Given Jedburgh's close proximity to England, David I saw his new abbey as a way to demonstrate his power and authority over of the Border country. Inevitably it was attacked and rebuilt several times over the centuries but has survived war and weather and still preserved are the original transepts, arcades, cloisters and gothic nave. The visitor centre has a small collection of artefacts such as the ivory Jedburgh Comb (dated c.1100) found during excavations.

JEDBURGH ABBEY: Abbey Bridge End, Jedburgh TD8 6JQ; www.historic-scotland. gov.uk. Entry: adult £5.20/£4.20 (seasonal variations); child £2.60; open daily, 31 Mar–30 Sept 9.30am–5.30pm; 1 Oct–31 Mar 9.30am–4.30pm.

Jedburgh, the 'Jewel of the Borders', is locally known as 'Jethart', and with its architectural treasures from centuries past it has an almost timeless quality. Follow the Town Trail to explore with a series of plaques marking historic houses, churches and the market place; or take the riverside walk passing by the Piper's House in Duck Row and the 16th-century Canongate Bridge. The Trail is about 2 miles starting and finishing at the Tourist Information Centre, Abbey Place, where you can collect the free Trail map.

MARY QUEEN OF SCOTS VISITOR CENTRE: Queen Street, Jedburgh TD8 6EN; ☎ 01835 863331. Entry: adult £3/ £2 (seasonal variations); children free; open 5 Mar–30 Nov, Mon–Sat, 10am–4.30pm; Sun, 11am–4.30pm.

Mary Queen of Scots stayed in Jedburgh in 1566 after an arduous journey to meet the Earl of Bothwell. After a 40-mile wet moorland ride, she arrived here very ill and close to death and when later, her fate was sealed, she is said to have remarked 'Would that I had died in Jedburgh'. You can visit the Queen's former house here, now a visitor centre, which has a well-presented exhibition about her tragic life. In the gardens are several pear trees, a fruit for which the town was once rather famous.

Fishing on the River Tweed

Fishing

The **River Tweed** has always been internationally renowned for salmon fishing, with keen anglers travelling from far and wide to fish here. After three record-breaking years, not only does the Tweed catch more Atlantic salmon than any other EU river, it also now ranks among the best salmon rivers in the world. The fishing season is long, from 1 February to 30 November, Monday to Saturday, with the best fishing often in spring when salmon are moving freely, and in autumn, when the river is packed with migratory fish heading to spawn in the upper river. There's also Brown and Sea Trout fishing, but whatever your interest, do book ahead through the various angling associations and dozens of salmon beats on the bottom, middle and upper Tweed, to arrange your permit and allocated dates. Try **Fish Tweed** (☎ 01573 470612; www.fishtweed.co.uk) or **Tweed Guide** which offers fly fishing packages including instruction, waders, equipment and experienced guides for a three-hour session, a day's fishing or fishing holidays (☎ 07962 401770; www.tweedguide.com).

Golfing

The Scottish Borders area is fast emerging as a golfer's paradise, with two championship courses at **The Roxburghe Country House Hotel** near Kelso already enjoying an international reputation, and local courses such as at Peebles, offering magnificent holiday golf in the finest setting. **The MacDonald Cardrona Hotel**, just outside Peebles, is the latest addition to the splendid choice of courses in the south-east.

    The Freedom of the Fairways is a golf pass that operates in the Scottish Borders from April until the end of October and is Scotland's best-selling golf pass. The scheme

FREEDOM OF THE FAIRWAYS GOLF
PASSPORT: VisitScotland Borders, Shepherds
Mills,Whinfield Road, Selkirk TD7 5DT;
☎ 0870 608 4040; www.visitscottishborders.
com. Golf Pass £88–£120.

is ideal for individuals or groups and provides golfers with different options for all ages. A three-day passport is valid for up to six rounds on consecutive weekdays for a fixed fee of just £88 or there is a five-day passport for £120 with junior and senior passes available.

Wet weather

Abbotsford on the banks of the Tweed, west of Melrose is the house built and lived in by Sir Walter Scott, the 19th-century novelist, author of epic poems and classic novels such as *Rob Roy*, *Ivanhoe* and *The Lady of the Lake*. The house has been preserved just as it was in his lifetime, containing his extraordinary library of 9,000 rare books, and a collection of weapons and armoury. Visitors can see Scott's study, drawing room, dining room, all furnished with fine antiques and memorabilia. The house has real character and warmth and you can imagine just how contented Scott was here (until his own personal credit crunch) in his beloved country house in the Borders.

ABBOTSFORD: Melrose TD6 9BQ; ☎ 01896
752043; www.scottsabbotsford.co.uk.
Entry: adult, £7; child £3.50; family
(two adults, two children) £16.

The home of Sir Walter Scott, Abbotsford

LOCAL KNOWLEDGE

Vicky Davidson is a councillor for Selkirkshire on the Scottish Borders Council where she has responsibility for Economic Development, Regeneration and Tourism. She lives in the scenic Ettrick Valley and in previous lives has been a radio producer, event manager and shepherdess!

Favourite afternoon tea: I always love to collapse into the comfy sofas of the Tontine Hotel on the High Street in Peebles. It's just the right mix of grand elegance, attentive staff and three-tier cake stands!

Favourite kids' outing: The salmon viewing point at Philiphaugh in Selkirk has something for everyone: a healthy walk to the old cauld to watch the salmon leaping out of the water, an indoor education centre and a café with huge sunny windows. The salmon run in the spring and the autumn but the centre is open all year round.

Favourite ice cream: It was always unthinkable in my family to pass through Innerleithen without stopping at Caldwells,

a tradition I'm very happy to continue with my daughter. It's highly addictive stuff.

Favourite picnic spot: St Mary's Loch on the Selkirk-to-Moffat road must be one of the most inspiring places in the Borders. Artists have long tried to capture the reflection of the hills in the water and writers used to gather here to mull over their lines in the lochside pub, Tibbie Sheils. You can walk up into the hills or along the shore and if you don't want to carry a picnic, the home-cooking in the Glen Café is a treat.

Favourite drive: If you turn off the A708 at Cappercleuch (before you reach the picnic site at St Mary's Loch) the road climbs up into the hills past the Meggat Reservoir created to serve Edinburgh. The road winds higher and higher before a breath-taking descent into Tweedsmuir with the historic Talla reservoir laid out below you on the valley floor. There's a magical quality to the light reflected from the hills in this area at dusk which makes the journey seem even more out of the ordinary.

SIR WALTER SCOTT'S COURTROOM: Market Square, Selkirk TD7 4BT; ☎ 01750 20096; admission free; open end Mar–30 Sept, Mon–Fri 10am–4pm; Sat 10am–2pm; May–Aug, also Sun 10am–2pm; Oct, Mon–Sat 1pm–4pm.

ROBERT SMAIL'S PRINTING WORKS: 7–9 High Street, Innerleithen EH44 6HA; ☎0844 493 2259. Entry: adult £5, child £4, family £14; open April–31 Oct, Thurs–Mon 12–5pm; Sun 1pm–5pm; closed Tues and Wed.

ST RONAN'S WELL VISITOR CENTRE: Wells Brae, Innerleithen EH44 6JE; ☎ 01896 833583. Admission free; open Apr–Oct, Mon–Fri 10am–1pm, 2pm–5pm; Sat–Sun 2pm–5pm.

The neighbouring town of **Selkirk** above the Ettrick and Yarrow valleys is also closely associated with Sir Walter Scott, as it was here at the Courthouse that Scott served as Sheriff of Selkirkshire for 30 years.

A good friend of Scott's was **Mungo Park**, the famous 18th-century explorer of the Gambia and the River Niger, who was born in 1771 on his family farm near here, the seventh of 13 children! There's a fine statue of him in the centre of town.

Continuing the literary theme, an interesting attraction is **Robert Smail's Printing Works** at Innerleithen, near Peebles, established in 1866, and which continued until the retiral of Cowan Smail after 120 years of the family business. Now owned by the National Trust for Scotland, visitors can see an impressive archive of vintage books, slates, sealing wax, ink and printing press machine room.

Innerleithen is also well known for the **St Ronan's Well Spa**. This historic spa was a magnet for the Victorians in need of curative mineral waters, which had become popular after a visit by Robert Burns in 1787. Walter Scott also came as a boy and later wrote a novel about St Ronan's Spa. Today you can sample the healthy spring water which is still on tap at the museum.

On a cold or wet day, where better to head than **Lochcarron Waverley Mill,** the home of the finest and fashionably designer Scottish cashmere, tweed and knitwear. On most weekdays you can take

LOCHCARRON VISITOR CENTRE: Waverley Mill, Selkirk Riverside TD7 5DZ; ☎ 01750 726 100; www.lochcarron.com. Admission free, open year round, Mon–Sat, 9am–5pm. Mill tours, Mon–Thur, 10.30am, 11.30am, 1.30pm, 2.30pm (or by appointment).

a tour around the mill to find out about the production process, from spinning the yarn to the finished woollen sweater. The visitor centre has a café and a shop to buy the perfect souvenir.

What do with children...

The impressive **Jedburgh Castle Jail** at the top of the Castlegate Hill will appeal to children, with a kids guide, activities and dressing-up centre. The prison cell blocks today give an atmospheric glimpse of harsh life behind bars in the 19th-century. Here you can meet some inmates and sample the local mint sweets, Jethart Snails, which were said to be made in the town by the Napoleonic prisoners of war held at Castle Jail.

Five miles south of Jedburgh is **Jedforest Deer and Farm Park**, featuring not only a large herd of deer, but also rare breeds of sheep, pigs, chickens and ducks. Children can help to feed the animals, there are ranger walks, birds of prey demonstrations and tuition and a children's playground.

North of Jedburgh towards St Boswells, is **Harestanes Countryside Visitor Centre**, an outdoor natural history attraction offering wildlife trails, country walks, seasonal events and activities, playpark and a sandpit for children.

Bowhill House and Country Park is the home of the Duke of Buccleuch and family. As well as seasonal guided tours of this aristocratic house, the Country Park offers a great day out for the family with woodland and river walks, Ranger Wildlife and Tree trails through the estate learning about the flora and fauna, while children can hide in a badger den. The Adventure Playground is an exciting place to play, with beech trees acting as natural umbrellas during a sudden shower. The top of the big slide reaches up into the woodland canopy and the flying fox zips through the trees, with slides and swings to suit all ages.

> JEDBURGH CASTLE JAIL: Castlegate, Jedburgh TD8 6BD; ☎ 01835 864750; www.scotborders.gov.uk. Admission free; open late Mar–31 Oct, Mon–Sat 10am–4.30pm, Sun 1pm–4pm.

> JEDFOREST DEER PARK: Camptown, Jedburgh TD8 6PL; ☎ 01835 840364; www.jedforestdeerpark.co.uk. Prices: adult £5, child £3, under 5s free, family ticket, (two adults, two children) £14; open daily Easter–August 10am–5.30pm; Sept–Oct 11am–4.30pm.

> HARESTANES COUNTRYSIDE VISITOR CENTRE: Ancrum, near Jedburgh TD8 6UQ; ☎ 01835 830306. Admission free, open end Mar–31 Oct 10am–5pm.

> BOWHILL HOUSE AND COUNTRY PARK: Bowhill Selkirk, TD7 5ET; ☎ 01750 22204; www.bowhill.org. Country Park and adventure playground prices: adult £3, child £2; open Easter weekend, 10am–5pm; May–June, weekends and Bank Holidays, 10am–5pm; Jul–Aug, open daily 10am–5pm.

 ## ... and how to avoid children

Stobo Castle Health Spa near Peebles is an oasis of calm and contentment, a hideaway place for 'me time' pampering and a quiet space to revive the spirit. At Stobo you will not encounter children, and also very few men. This is a country house residential spa attracting a clientele of 95% women, mainly girlfriends, mothers, daughters and sisters, but men are more than welcome and don't know what they are missing! Set within a redstone Victorian mansion, surrounded by Japanese Zen

> STOBO CASTLE HEALTH SPA: Stobo EH45 8NY; ☎ 01721 725300; www.stobocastle. co.uk. So Indulgent two-day spa break, from £165 pp pn.

gardens and peaceful parkland, this £5 million state-of-the-art spa has full leisure facilities, including a swimming pool and steam rooms. Glamorous bedrooms (including the So Divine Cashmere Suite) fine dining, daily walks, yoga and aerobic classes are all part of an all-inclusive package.

📽 Entertainment

Melrose Wynd Theatre (☎ 01896 820028; www.thewynd.com) is a charming village community theatre showing regular drama productions, music concerts, cabaret evenings, children's shows and films. This is the place to see some fine Borders arts companies such as the local Gilbert and Sullivan Society musicals and productions by the Rowan Tree Theatre. **Bowhill House** (www.bowhill.org) near Selkirk has a theatre with seasonal plays and music events and on Peebles High Street is the **Eastgate Theatre and Arts Centre** (www.eastgatearts.com), presenting year-round drama, music, films, dance and art exhibitions.

Events

Melrose is the birthplace of the **Rugby 7s** (1883) featuring seven-a-side teams, and the town is crowded out during **7s Week**. The game of Rugby 7s is now played on an international stage from Hong Kong to Scotland and is testimony to its founder Ned Haig in the Scottish Borders. The annual Rugby 7s festival takes place across the Borders – Galashiels, Melrose, Hawick, Berwick, Langholm, Peebles, Jedforest, and Earlston – week by week through April and May.

Common Riding, Reiver festivals and other village fairs and music festivals take place around the Borders from Easter to Christmas, so whenever you visit there is sure to be some event taking place. Visit Selkirk in June to witness one of the most traditional pageants. The **Selkirk Gathering** is the largest of the Border Common Ridings, and dates back to the Battle of Floddon in 1513. The famous **Hawick Reivers Festival** takes place in late March. For Rugby 7s, events and festivals, see www.visitscottishborders.com.

The Peebles Beltane Festival (www.peeblesbeltanefestival.co.uk) is a festival of local legend, history and tradition to mark the return of summer with the lighting of fires. Taking place over a week at Midsummer in June it includes the Riding of the Marches, the crowning of the Beltane Queen, music, and a fancy dress parade.

The Borders Book Festival (☎ 07929 435575; www.bordersbookfestival.org) is an international, star-studded event held around Midsummer at the end of June in Melrose with a programme of best-selling novelists, poets, travel writers, politicians and TV entertainers and children's events. Tickets sell like hot cakes for this inspiring event in Harmony Garden where festival-goers can meet authors face to face in a friendly, intimate setting.

The historic **Traquair House** (www.traquair.co.uk) near Innerleithen presents entertaining seasonal events for all the family including the Summer Fair, Mediaeval Fayre and a Halloween festival.

Shopping

The best things to buy in the Scottish Borders are authentic, locally crafted, beautifully soft woollens, tweed and cashmere. In **Hawick** you'll find several fine knitwear shops, such as **Hawick Cashmere** (Trinity Mills, Duke Street), **Peter Scott Factory shop** (11 Buccleuch Street), and **Wiltonburn Country Farm** (www.cashmerescotland.com) selling designer cashmere in a converted barn. **Selkirk** is home to the **Lochcarron Waverley Mill Shop** (www.lochcarron.com) for tweeds, tartans and cashmere knitwear.

For a broad range of men and women's fashions, accessories and gifts, Melrose is full of smart, attractive boutiques such as **Finlay Grant** (14 High Street), a modern gentleman's outfitters selling an exceptional range of designer clothes by top labels Mulberry, Hacket and Dunhill. Owned by Blair Finlay and Gordon Grant, it's all rather upmarket and glamorous (clothing and staff) and is Melrose's mini Harvey Nichols.

Also on the High Street you'll find women's fashion at **Sarah Thomson**, **12 Boutique** and **Lochcarron** cashmere. The town centre is small and easy to wander round to find some hidden shopping gems. For collectors, there's **The Book Room** for browsing second-hand books, **Michael Vee** for decorative furniture and design, and the **Whole Lot** antique shop. A couple of miles away at St Boswells, visit a wonderful treasure house of a bookshop, **The Main Street Trading company**, also selling crafts and gifts with a good café too.

Across the Borders, every town and village has an art gallery or crafts studio, so many that there is a brochure published called *Crossing Borders Art Trail* (www.crossing-borders.org.uk) listing dozens of galleries and studios to buy paintings, prints, glassware, pottery, accessories and textiles.

The best... PLACES TO STAY

BOUTIQUE

Townhouse Hotel

Market Square, Melrose TD6 9PQ
☎ 01896 822645
www.thetownhousemelrose.co.uk

Traditional, whitewashed townhouse in the heart of Melrose. Featuring contemporary furnishings and a fashionable city style, there are 11 bedrooms dressed in warm tweedy colours of walnut and oatmeal, arty lamps and some superior rooms have a jacuzzi bath.

Price: £50 pp B&B; £75 pp dinner, B&B.

COUNTRY HOUSE

Cringletie

Edinburgh Road, near Peebles EH45 8PL
☎ 01721 725750; www.cringletie.com

This four-AA-red-star turreted redstone Victorian shooting lodge has lovely gardens and 14 contemporary bedrooms (one wheelchair accessible) all with views over the valley. Homely and tranquil for a cosy romantic break, with the log fire and local golfing, fishing and mountain biking.

Price: £100–£190 pp B&B; £175–£225 pp dinner, B&B. Short-break packages.

HOTEL

Castle Venlaw

Peebles EH45 8QG
☎ 01721 720384; www.venlaw.co.uk

This chic, boutique chateau has cosy country-style rooms and four-poster suites oozing romantic charm. The huge family room has a vintage bath and kids' bunk bed den in a castle turret! A warm, friendly place to enjoy the Borders' seriously good food and a dram or two in the Library bar.

Price: £70–£145 pppn.

Dryburgh Abbey Hotel

St Boswells TD6 0RQ
☎ 01835 822261; www.dryburgh.co.uk

Unique location on the River Tweed and beside the stunning ruins of Dryburgh Abbey. Traditional shooting and fishing hotel with contemporary design, comfortable lounge bar and exceptional fine dining restaurant: salmon is delivered direct from the river to kitchen. Complimentary (seasonal) trout fishing, swimming pool and bike hire for relaxing countryside break.

Price: £75–£170 pppn.

Peebles Hydro

Innerleithen Road, Peebles EH45 8LX
☎ 01721 720602
www.peebleshydro.co.uk

Scottish Family Hotel of the Year 2008–2009. Guests can enjoy fantastic range of sport and leisure with swimming, tennis, putting, horse-riding, a supervised playroom, games, lunch and supper for kids, while parents can relax all day and dinner a deux by night. There's also a spa for facials/massages.

Price: from £75 pp dinner, B&B.

UNUSUAL

Barns Tower

3.5 miles south of Peebles, c/o Vivat Trust
☎ 0845 090 0194; www.vivat.org.uk

This utterly unique, miniature 16th-century Scottish castle offers modern cosy comforts with a farmhouse kitchen, leather sofa, TV/video, roll-top bath, and Scrabble. Enjoy country walks before returning to the Great Hall with crackling log fire to warm up afterwards, and then a clamber up the ancient turnpike stair to bed.

Price: £590–£755 per week, £335 short break.

The best... FOOD AND DRINK

▶ Staying in

Driving through Tweeddale, you can't fail to notice the sheep and cattle that graze on the undulating hillsides. With produce this close to the towns, it's no wonder the local suppliers can claim that their meat comes from within a 15-mile radius.

Peebles is a thriving market town with a regular farmers' market on the second Saturday of each month, 9.30am–1.30pm in Eastgate Car Park. You're spoilt for choice for places to buy and eat good food. **Forsyth Butchers and Bakers** (21–25 Eastgate) has an old-fashioned courtesy, and money in the butchers is handled at the till rather than by the butchers. Next door, the bakery sells bread and cakes made on the premises. For wholefoods, fruit and vegetables **Petals, Peelings and Pips** (25 High Street) offers a variety of fresh produce. For cheeses, meats, pasta and preserves, then **Riley's** (57 High Street) will fulfil your requirements.

Melrose has some fine food shops such as **Martin Baird Butchers** (2 Market Square) or **Miller Butchers** (2 High Street) who have a blackboard outside listing where their beef, lamb and chicken are from. **Maid by Marion** (1 High Street, Melrose) is where you can find freshly made sandwiches, hearty, homemade soups and gooey cakes and bakes, all made by Marion. **Rhymers Fayre and Abbey Fine Wines**

The farmland in the Borders offers great local produce

(17 Market Square) sells local cheeses (like the wonderfully named Fatlips Blue Castle made by Standhill Cheesery just outside the little hamlet of Lilliesleaf), and Scottish beers as well as a diverse selection of wines from around the globe.

Jedburgh Farmers' Market is held in Market Place from 9am–1.30pm on the first Friday of the month. Jedburgh High Street has several excellent shops; from the two butchers **J & J Davidson** (3 High Street) and **A J Learmouth** (13 High Street) to a delightful little chocolate shop, **Jedburgh Chocolate House** (23 High Street), run by Beverley Turner, who is passionate about all her wonderful products. She is especially proud of the chocolates sourced from the Cocoabean Company based in Dumfries and Galloway. You can find local artisan cheeses, chutneys and preserves as well as a good cup of coffee at **Parlies Fine Foods** (9 Market Place).

Cameron's Bakery (40 High Street, Selkirk) professes to be the only place in Selkirk to make the famous Bannock (a sweet bread packed full of juicy sultanas) and there is always a queue out the door of this small shop. Further down the street is the **Selkirk Deli** (17 High Street, Selkirk) which has an unusual variety of stuffed vegetables to cook at home. There are some rather nice rustic tarts and salads too. **Alex Dalgetty and Sons** (21 Island Street, Galashiels) also make Selkirk Bannocks, freshly baked rolls, loaves, cakes, buns, tarts and pies.

At Traquair, after wandering around the house and gardens, sample the home-brewed ale at **the Traquair House Brewery**. Nearby in the village of Innerleithen you must stop off to taste the superb ice cream at **Caldwells** (88 High Street) made traditionally to an old family recipe with fun teddy cones for the kids.

🍷 Drinking

Exploring the borders, you will discover town pubs and country inns in unexpected places, like the **Cross Keys** in the tiny hamlet of Lilliesleaf. **The Royal Hotel** (21–23 Canongate, Jedburgh) offers its guests a good choice of over 30 whiskies in the aptly named Whisky Bar, a friendly spot for a wee dram. **Burts Bar** at Burts Hotel, Melrose, is a popular with locals and visitors who throng the town year round. There's a log fire, good pub grub and a friendly atmosphere.

The **County Inn** (35 High Street, Peebles) has a good selection of cask ales and single malts, while **Tibbie Shiels Inn** (St Mary's Loch) is worth a detour to sample local ales and 50 whiskies and the quaint ambience of this historic Victorian pub. **Buccleuch Arms** (St Boswells) has a cosy bar with log fire and was voted Scottish Inn of the Year. **Castle Venlaw Hotel** has a charming Library bar focusing on good single malts, and **Dryburgh Abbey Hotel** has a lively lounge bar with good food and good banter on the best catch of the day by the fisherfolk.

EATING OUT

FINE DINING

Cringletie
**Edinburgh Road,
nr Peebles EH45 8PL
☎ 01721 725750
www.cringletie.com**

A Baronial mansion with a conservatory for family lunch and elegant Sutherland room for glamorous dinner. Chef Craig Gibb creates supreme cuisine featuring best Borders produce. The eight-course tasting menu might include crab with avocado ice cream, foie gras, halibut, pork belly, chocolate jaffa cake. Dinner £39.50; tasting menu £55.

RESTAURANT

Hoebridge Inn
**Gattonside, Melrose TD6 9LZ
☎ 01896 823082
www.thehoebridgeinn.com**

Originally a 19th-century bobbin mill, the Hoebridge Inn was voted the best 'Borders formal meal 2008' for its garden herbs and country-coast menu to savour, featuring oven-baked whole partridge, roast guinea fowl, rack of lamb, seabream, lobster. Two-course set lunch £10, dinner (average) £20.

Dryburgh Abbey Hotel
**St Boswells TD6 0RQ
☎ 01835 822261
www.dryburgh.co.uk**

Traditional country house serving all day homely good food in the Abbey Bar: such as seafood chowder, lamb burger, and pumpkin risotto. In the elegant restaurant, chef Mark Greenaway presents Michelin-star-quality eight-course menu (£35) with scallops, confit duck, roast pheasant, monkfish, and exemplary service; worth travelling far for this dinner experience.

Halcyon
**39 Eastgate, Peebles EH45 8AD
☎ 01721 725100
www.halcyon-restaurant.co.uk**

Chef/patron Shona Thomson's menu shows the diversity of local produce. Dishes are robust and fragrant like Borders lamb with okra, lentils coconut and coriander. Puddings are moreishly sinful like the pecan slice with chocolate ice cream. Two courses cost about £20.

BISTRO

The Nightjar
**1 Abbey Close, Jedburgh TD8 6BG
☎ 01835 862552
www.thenightjar.co.uk**

This intimate little bistro just behind the Jedburgh Abbey may have a small menu but is diverse enough to suit all palates and vegetarians are well catered for. The menu changes on a regular basis and on the last Tuesday of every month they host a Thai evening. Two courses cost about £17.

EATING OUT

Marmion's Brasserie
5 Buccleuch Street, Melrose TD6 9LB
☎ **01896 822245**
www.marmionsbrasserie.co.uk

Marmion's has a popular reputation with locals and visitors alike. They have a menu for every taste with homely soups and fishcakes, classics like mussels, beef stroganoff, Thai green chicken curry and beer battered haddock, Cumberland sausages and mustard mash. Two courses cost about £16.

The Sunflower Restaurant
4 Bridgegate, Peebles EH45 8RZ
☎ **01721 722420**
www.thesunflower.net

Visit the sunny Sunflower for coffee and cake, lunchtime soup or dinner (Thur–Sat) with a colourful fusion menu inspired by Val Brunton's world travels: sweet potato fritter with spicy curry dip and then pink-rare roasted rack of lamb, fig and almond pastry. Two courses £15–£20.

The Horseshoe Inn
Eddleston EH45 8QP
☎ **01721 730225**
www.horseshoeinn.co.uk

This former blacksmith's shop is a welcoming roadside inn serving classic French cuisine under chef patron, Patrick Bardoulet. Dine on John Dory with spiced pig's tail risotto, foie gras and quince terrine, wild grouse fillet soufflé, pear belle helene; (two courses, £25–£30). And then stay overnight in one of eight contemporary-style bedrooms.

Windlestraw Lodge
Tweed Valley, Walkerburn EH43 6AA
☎ **01896 870636**
www.windlestraw.co.uk

This magnificent Arts and Crafts mansion is owned by Alan and Julie Reid presenting gastronomic cuisine such as organic leek espresso, saddle of roe deer on pearl barley risotto, wood pigeon with black pudding, pan-fried monkfish in parmesan batter. Four-course dinner, £42. You can stay overnight in one of six lovely guest rooms.

GASTROPUB

Buccleuch Arms Hotel
The Green, St Boswells TD6 0EW
☎ **01835 822243**
www.buccleucharms.com

Winner of Scottish Inn of the Year 2008, in recognition of welcoming staff and traditional pub food. Serves good home cooking of local provenance – Buccleuch beef, artisan cheeses, Berwickshire seafood with wide menu of chargrilled ribeye and sirloin steaks (£16.50), homemade beef burgers (£8.25) and Teviot smoked salmon (£4.95).

Tibbie Shiels Inn
St Mary's Loch, Selkirkshire TD7 5LH
☎ **01750 42231**
www.tibbieshielsinn.com

Atmospheric historic inn owned by Tibbie the famous hostess (1824–1878) attracting literary visitors, Scott, Stevenson and Hogg. Traditional Scottish food served from 12 to 8pm, lunch, high tea, supper, children's menu. Speciality Yarrow trout and Tibbie's mixed grill, local ale and 50 whiskies. Great food, two courses for £15.

EATING OUT

The Black Bull
Market Place, Lauder TD2 6SR
☎ **01578 722208**
www.blackbull-lauder.com

Situated on the main road through Lauder, this town centre inn has a fine reputation for quality food served in the Bar or Georgian dining room. Featuring Border beef, chicken liver pâté, Black Bull burger with port salut melted cheese, vegetarian tarts and crêpes. Two courses cost about £15.

CAFÉ

Russell's
28 Market Square, Melrose TD6 9PP
☎ **01896 822335**

Lovely tearoom with speciality teas and coffees served in Wedgwood china. Offers homebaking, platters of fresh and smoked salmon or for the more ravenous the substantial 'high tea' may just hit the spot. High tea costs £11.95 with main dish, toast, homebaking and a pot of tea.

The Glen Café
St Mary's Loch, Selkirk TD7 5LH
☎ **01750 42241**
www.glencafé.co.uk

Enjoy an exhilarating walk around the Grey Mare's Tail waterfall and then relax at the Glen Café for a slap-up breakfast, coffee, tea, hot chocolate, cakes, lunch or evening meal (summer). Menu includes Yorkshire pudding with chilli con carne, ham sandwich baguettes, beans on toast, and jacket potatoes. A homely snack costs £5–£10.

COFFEE SHOP

Main Street Trading Company
Main Street, St Boswells TD6 0AT
☎ **01835 824087**
www.mainstreet books.co.uk

A wonderful destination bookshop run by former London publisher, Rosamund de la Hay, with a chic, organic café alongside for happy browsing. Coffee and homemade cakes and muffins and even little ones can enjoy a *babycino* (£1.50). Menu includes soup, salads and Loch Fyne smoked salmon sandwich (£4.95).

Jammy Coo Gallery and Coffee Shop
**The Green, Lilliesleaf,
nr Melrose TD6 9JB**
☎ **01835 870 537**
www.jammycoo.co.uk

This little gem is worth taking a detour for. Food and art sit side by side and everything is made by Delia Job, including some of the art on the walls. Large bowls of soup with warm and very cheesy scones (£3.50) sets you up for an afternoon of exploring.

(i) Visitor Information

Tourism Information Centres: Open all year: Peebles, High Street EH45 8AG; Melrose, Abbey House, Abbey Street TD6 9LG; Jedburgh, Murray's Green TD8 6BE; Hawick, Tower Mill TD9 0AE; open April to October, Selkirk, Halliwells House TD7 4BL. Excellent brochures available on accommodation, walks, sport, historic attractions festivals and events, ☎ 0870 608 0404, www.visitscottishborders. com.

Hospitals: Scottish Borders General Hospital, Melrose TD6 9BS, ☎ 01896 826000; Hay Lodge Community Hospital (Minor Injuries Clinic), Neidpath road, Peebles EH45 8JG, ☎ 01721 722080.

Police: Peebles Police Station, Rosetta Road Peebles EH45 8HH, ☎ 01721 720637; Melrose Police Station, High Street Melrose TD6 9RY, ☎ 01896 822602; Jedburgh Police Station, Castlegate Jedburgh TD8 6AR, ☎ 01835 862264; Hawick Police Station, Wilton Hill Hawick TD9 8BA, ☎ 01450 375051.

Travel and Transport: First Group bus company, ☎ 08708 727271, www. firstgroup.com; Travel Line, ☎ 0871 200 2233, www.travelline.org.uk; One Ticket, bus and train travel across Edinburgh and east Scotland, www.one-ticket. co.uk.

Self-Catering Accommodation: Historic country houses, ☎ 0845 090 0194, www.vivat.org.uk; National Trust for Scotland holiday homes, ☎ 0844 493 2108, www.ntsholidays.com; Eildon Holiday cottages, ☎ 01896 823258, www.eildon.co.uk; converted farm steading, ☎ 07876 377671, www. luxuryletborders.com.

Useful websites: www.borderstraditions. org.uk; www.peebles.info; www.jedburgh-online.org.uk; www.melrose.border-net. co.uk.

Activities: Walking: for guided walks, accommodation and information, www. stcuthbertsway.fsnet.co.uk; Walking Support, ☎ 01896 822079, www. walkingsupport.co.uk; **Fishing:** www. tweedguide.com, www.fishtweed.com; **Mountain Biking:** www. thehubintheforest.co.uk, www.7stanes. gov.uk; **Golf:** Peebles Golf Club, Kirkland Street, Peebles EH45 8EU, ☎ 01721 720197, www.peeblesgolfclub. co.uk; Macdonald Cardrona Hotel Golf & Country Club, Cardrona, Peebles EH45 8NE, ☎ 0844 879 9024, www. macdonaldhotels.co.uk/cardrona.

THE BERWICKSHIRE COASTLINE

The geography of the Scottish Borders contrasts sharply between the forested hills and valleys of Tweeddale, the flat arable lands of Berwickshire, over to the dramatic cliffs of the south-east coast and down to the English border at Berwick upon Tweed. The Berwickshire coastline is a designated heritage environment of outstanding beauty and a natural habitat for abundant bird, sea and wildlife, protected as a European Marine Site. This is a wild and wonderful destination for visitors for breathtaking clifftop walks, bird watching, diving and fishing as well as exploring the traditional seafaring harbours of St Abbs and Eyemouth.

A few miles inland the pretty, picturesque countryside around Berwickshire features several of Scotland's most magnificent country houses, Manderston and Mellerstain and their glorious gardens and estate parks, nature reserves, museums, art galleries, in between a myriad of tiny villages. Further west, where the two great Border rivers, the Tweed and the Teviot, meet is the rather majestic town of Kelso, the location of the grand and gracious Floors Castle, home of the Duke and Duchess of Roxburghe.

Across the whole region, local rural and maritime heritage is kept alive in annual music, maritime and fishing festivals, agricultural shows, the famous Kelso Races and horse trials at Thirlestane, Lauder.

Whatever your interests, be it scuba diving around the coastal coves and caves, visiting aristocratic castles or playing golf, there is accommodation from country house hotels, and village B&Bs to 'badger watching' self-catering cottages. Everywhere you go, the farmland and coastline of the Scottish Borders provides you with a natural larder of supreme-quality meat, game, vegetables and fine seafood, straight from the fisherman's catch to your plate. On your travels around this south-east corner of Scotland, you are sure to sample the freshest fish you will ever taste.

WHAT TO SEE AND DO

St Abb's Head

Above the quaint little village of St Abbs, the headland formed by long extinct volcanoes, known as **St Abb's Head** is a scenic landmark and major attraction for walkers. The high cliffs here mark the join where Scotland and England crashed into each other 420 million years ago. This breathtaking geological sweep of steep cliffs, stacks and narrow gullies make it look like huge chunks and wedges of cheese were cut out of the landscape where it reaches the North Sea. Although best known as a seabird colony, this National Nature Reserve includes 200 acres of grassy clifftop and a freshwater Mire Loch and woodland. The cliffs, rocky reefs and sandy shores support large colonies of breeding kittiwakes, fulmars, guillemots, razorbills, shags

St Abb's Head

and puffins (in the summer the nesting colonies number thousands) while a carpet of spring flowers colour the coastal grasslands.

St Abb's Head is owned by the National Trust for Scotland and is a prime vantage point for birdwatchers to see nesting birds at close hand, as well as giving nature lovers the chance to explore this unspoilt, wild environment. Visit from May to July for seabirds, July to August for flowers and butterflies and spring and autumn for migrant birds. From the clifftop you may spot whales, dolphins, seals and porpoises out at sea and within the reserve, foxes, red squirrels and roe deer. The NTS Visitor Centre has an exhibition about the geology and natural history of the whole maritime site along the Berwickshire coast. A Ranger Service operates all year round with guided walks available. A good 3-mile circular walk goes along the cliff path to the lighthouse and back again around Mire Loch. Note that the pathway runs beside the cliff edge, so children should be watched and dogs kept on a lead. Beside the Visitor Centre is a café and art gallery and craft shop, well worth a visit. To get to St Abb's Head, from the A1 follow the A1107 signposted Berwickshire Coastal Trail, at Coldingham take B6438 signposted to St Abbs and follow signs for the Nature Reserve. There's a car park at Northfield farm.

ST ABB'S HEAD NATIONAL NATURE RESERVE: Northfield, St Abbs TD14 5QF; ☎ 018907 71443; admission free, (£2 car park charge); Visitor Centre open daily 1 April–31 Oct 10am–5pm; Nature Reserve open daily all year.

St Abbs, below St Abb's Head cliff walk, is a tiny old fishing port with just a few cottages and where it's great fun to watch as the sea water crashes over the harbour wall in a storm. You can drive down the steep hill to the harbour where there is limited parking (due to popular diving sites here) and you'll find refreshment in a couple of village cafés.

The stretch of coast between Eyemouth and St Abbs is split between the rocks of Linkim Shore and the sandy shores of Coldingham Bay. This whole area is very interesting to geologists; it was only a few miles further north at Siccar Point that **James Hutton**, the father of modern geology, did much of his fieldwork investigations during the late 18th century and realised the impact of unconformities on the geology of the Earth. With his work he challenged Creationist beliefs well before Darwin. Around Fort Point at Eyemouth, the geology shows red sandstone, a pattern which changes by the time you reach Linkim Shore, where Silurian mudstones and siltstones are thrown up into jagged patterns as they have been folded and lifted and banded across the centuries. As you approach St Abbs, the geology reflects the ancient volcanoes active in the area, with cast cliffs of igneous rocks forming the nesting places for seabirds. For those particularly interested in James Hutton's life and work, an exhibition is displayed a few miles from Eyemouth at **Reiver Country Farm Foods**, at Reston TD14 5LN.

St Abb's Head is not accessible by public road, but **Clifftop Discovery** offers a unique opportunity to explore the natural history and coastal scenery of Berwickshire's sea cliffs sitting in a comfortable and secure Landrover. This exclusive, guided safari trail drives across the clifftop wilderness over the rugged terrain of seven coastal farms through woodland and forestry, past historic forts, rivers and lochs. Tours are half-day or full-day with special-interest geological excursions to James Hutton's Siccar Point available by arrangement.

CLIFFTOP DISCOVERY: St Abb's Head; ☎ 01890 771838; www.clifftopdiscovery. co.uk. 90-minute trip, four adults £10 pp, two adults £15 pp; half day, four adults £20, two adults £35, children under 16 £9; full day, four adults £35, two adults £49, children £15.

The harbour at Eyemouth

The Berwickshire Coastal Path

For the adventurous rambler, the cliff path along the Berwickshire Coast stretches for 15 miles from Berwick upon Tweed through Burnmouth, Eyemouth to St Abbs and then curves inland down to Coldingham. It is waymarked and easy to follow and while some strong walkers can tackle it in one day, as there is so much to explore, the walk can be taken in bitesize stages, stopping off along the route. The coastal environment is a wonderful seascape of cliffs, sandy shores, mudflats, shallow inlets and bays, sand dunes, farmland and woodland all with conservation status as a natural habitat for wildlife. Look out for herons, oystercatchers, sandpipers and curlews. Plantlife is rich and varied, with pink thrift, yellow gorse, primroses, cowslip and purple orchid in spring and meadowsweet, willow herb in summer.

Between Burnmouth and Eyemouth at **Fancove Head** the cliffs reach a height of 340ft, so watch your step. Take care crossing Eyemouth Golf Course and be observant on the path just south of Burnmouth where the east coast rail line runs close to the trail with Intercity trains speeding past at 100mph. Pick up a Berwickshire Coastal Path booklet and map, available at local Tourist information centres.

Scuba diving

'St Abbs was the place that converted me to diving for pleasure. Coral reefs may offer warmer water and better visibility but they lack the ever-shifting, sensuous forms of the kelp forest.' David Bellamy

The Berwickshire coastline is renowned for superb windsurfing, surfing and diving. The seashore is an amazing treasure trove of sea caves, shallow inlets and rocky reefs which support a wonderfully varied marine life. St Abbs is one of the most popular dive sites in the UK due to its status as a European Marine Site and a voluntary marine reserve with distinctive flora found here. The whitewashed house in the centre of St Abbs Harbour is the **Rock House Dive Centre**. It's run by Paul Crowe, who has worked on a fishing boat here for 10 years, so he must surely know the seas, waves,

ROCK HOUSE DIVE CENTRE: St Abbs TD14 5PW; ☎ 01890 771945; www. rockhousediving.com. Daily dive trips year round for pairs and groups; £20 pp (up to two dives); diving and accommodation packages also available.

rocks and currents pretty well. The dive sites around here sound wonderful, such as Weasel Loch, Leeds Bay, Hairy Ness, Conger Reef, Anemone Gully (where guillemots swim down to check out divers); crazy names which make you want to get a wetsuit on. One of the most popular dives for the experienced is the *Glanmire* wreck, a ship which sank in 1912, crashing on rocks, ironically, below the lighthouse. Divers are advised to book well in advance with weekends often sold out; holiday midweek dives are ideal.

AQUASTARS DIVE CENTRE: Guns Green Basin, Eyemouth; ☎ 01890 750904; www. acquastars.co.uk. Supervised shore/ boatdive £25/£30; Discover Scuba £35; Scuba course £100; PADI open-water course £350.

Along the coast at Eyemouth is **Aquastars**, located at the New Harbour with free parking, watersports shop and café. This dive centre offers supervised orientation-guided dives (suitable for beginners and visitors), boat dives, introductory training and PADI open-water courses. All wetsuits, equipment, air and underwater cameras can be hired and bought.

Up the coast at Coldingham is the **Scoutscroft Holiday Centre** (St Abbs Road, Coldingham TD14 5NB; ☎ 018907 71338). The dive centre has a dive shop for all equipment for the visiting diver, fishing tackle, clothing and also children's wetsuits. There is a self-service compressor for Nitrox fills and O2 refills as well as an air fill station at St Abbs. Scoutscoft offers dive equipment hire, suit repairs as well as chalet accommodation, restaurant, beach and children's play area.

Coldingham Bay

The waves off the Berwickshire coastline area ideal for surfing and if you are not proficient on the board, the **St Vedas Surf School** at Coldingham Bay offers two-hour beginners lessons for age eight and above. You will have 15 minutes on the beach learning about the safety aspect of surfing and an hour and 45 minutes in the water learning to surf. All you need to bring with you is your swimming costume

> ST VEDAS HOTEL/SURF SHOP: Coldingham Bay, Coldingham TD14 5PA; ☎ 018907 71679; www.stvedas.co.uk. Surf lesson two hours £35 (children must be over eight).

and towel as wetsuits, surf boots and surfboards are provided. For experienced surfers and body boarders, you can hire all the equipment you need.

Coldingham beach has been popular with visitors since Edwardian times when the first beach huts were erected. There is disabled parking, toilets and over the summer season, lifeguards make the beach a safe, clean place for families to enjoy, with the **St Vedas Hotel** and beach café nearby. Trout fly-fishing is popular on Coldingham loch as well as deep-sea fishing off-shore for mackerel.

Coastal villages and country walks

You may prefer to view the sea from dry land, and the villages along the coast, St Abbs, Eyemouth and Coldingham are worth visiting for a stroll around. The busy fishing port of **Eyemouth** takes its name from the River Eye which flows through the town to reach the sea, creating the perfect harbour. As Roy Brett mentions in his foreword to this book (see p.5), the harbour is jam-packed with fishing boats, creels and boxes and the fishmarket here is a magical sight while the sea air smells are captivating to the senses.

Eyemouth was a smuggling haven during the 18th century, when a tax was paid not only on luxury goods like silk and tobacco, but on everyday essentials, such as coal, salt, soap and tea. As one of the few safe landing places along the rocky shoreline, and with the nearest custom house at Dunbar, 20 miles north, the port flourished as a destination for contraband. The grand **Gunsgreen House** beside the harbour is said to have underground passages and cellars in which to hide hundreds of kegs of brandy while the owner, John Nisbet, reputedly used his position as a wealthy merchant to cover up the smuggling business. Gunsgreen House is owned by a Trust, currently going through a £2 million refurbishment, and is due to be opened to the public

Gunsgreen House, site of the smuggling at Eyemouth

in summer 2009. Visitors will enter at cellar level to learn all about the smuggling in Eyemouth and the Berwickshire coast. The main floor will be furnished as it would have been in the 18th century complete with the infamous tea chute where non-duty-paid tea was hidden from the authorities.

The small village of **Coldstream** is situated where the River Tweed forms a natural boundary between Scotland and England. Smeaton's seven-arched bridge spans the Tweed and connects Scotland to the north and England to the south. Much of the town's history arose because of its location on the border and the continual feuding between the two nations. It is probably best known for the second oldest Regiment of Foot Guards, The Coldstream Guards. To this day the Regiment sends representatives to the annual civic week Common Riding festival in August.

Near Coldstream is **Hirsel Country Park** which offers something of interest to the ornithologist, zoologist, historian and archaeologist through several colour-coded walks through the gardens, woodland and riverside within the farming estate of Lord Hume of the Hirsel. For bird watchers, 170 species have been identified as resident or migrant here and the flora changes from spring snowdrops to the colourful rhododendron and azalea wood in June. There are Highland cattle and geese, moorhens, ducks and swans on the lake. Several museums show the heritage of the estate, and there is an arts and craft studios and a tearoom.

THE HIRSEL: Coldstream TD12 4LP; ☎ 01573 224144; www.hirselcountrypark. co.uk. Admission £2.50 per car, open year round in daylight hours.

Many visitors may believe that **Berwick upon Tweed** is on the Scottish side of the Border, but for several centuries it's been an English town. During the battles of independence across the debatable lands of Border country, the frontier town of Berwick changed hands between England and Scotland about 14 times between 1147 and 1482. Today many residents feel more part of Berwickshire than Northumberland in this hidden corner of the UK which seems too north for England and too south for Scotland; they think their economy would be better understood and better looked after by the Scottish Government than by Westminster. In 2008, a television programme organised a local referendum in Berwick upon Tweed and those in favour of becoming part of Scotland again won by a margin of 60% to 40%.

Thirlestane Castle

Near Lauder on the A68 is **Thirlestane Castle,** dating from the 13th century but rebuilt as the Maitland family home in 1590 and greatly enhanced by the Duke of Lauderdale, later extended with two new wings. Its architectural significance comes from the numerous Cinderella fairytale-style rose pink curved turrets topped with grey slate conical roofs. Guided tours between 10am and 3pm take visitors around the wonderful state apartments, Bonnie Prince Charlie's room (the Prince stayed here in 1745 after victory at the Battle of Prestonpans), the Duke's Grand bedchamber, the billiard room, nurseries

> THIRLESTANE CASTLE: Lauder, Berwickshire TD2 6RU; ☎ 01578 722430; www.thirlestanecastle.co.uk. Entry: adult, £8/£7, child £6, family £20, grounds only £3; open Easter weekend; 15 Apr–28 June on Sun, Wed, Thur, May Bank Holidays; July–Aug, Sun–Thur; Sept, Sun, Wed and Thurs; 10am–3pm (last admission); grounds close 5pm.

(with a collection of Edwardian, Victorian and Georgian toys) and the grand kitchen where in its heyday, the Castle burned a ton of coal every day and had a resident staff of 40. Today visitors can have tea and scones, sandwiches, the Butler's Special and the Gardner's salad in the Old Servants' Hall.

The Castle is set in extensive parklands overlooking the Lammermuir Hills and the Leader Water, a tributary of the River Tweed. The Southern Upland Way stretching from the west coast to the east coast runs through the park and walkers stop to admire the castle and visit the tea room. An adventure playground has been created on the site of a Borders artillery fort where Scottish and English troops fought 450 years ago. The playground features tunnels and walkways for toddlers and exiting activities for older children.

Historic houses

A few miles inland from Eyemouth, within the gentle countryside is the village of **Duns**, which offers a number of historic attractions. **Manderston House** (2 miles to the east of Duns) is a spectacular and supreme country house open to the public. The historical and cultural

> MANDERSTON: Duns; ☎ 01361 882686; www.manderston.co.uk. Entry: adult £8.50, children over 12 £4.50, under 12s free; open mid-May to the end of September, Thurs and Sun 1.30pm–5pm. Last entry at 4.15pm. Gardens open from 11.30am until dusk.

preservation of the house, park and gardens is regarded as unique in Britain. Channel Four's recent series *The Edwardian Country House* was filmed here. The interior decoration, woodwork, original architectural features and furnishings illustrate Edwardian extravagance to the letter. The mansion was built by architect John Kinross for Sir James Miller and no expense was spared with opulent staterooms, silk-lined walls, Italian crystal chandeliers, painted ceilings and a magnificent silver staircase. The upper class lifestyle in stark contrast to the staff working downstairs is still carefully preserved and is of particular interest when you walk around and learn about the history of the house. And with a Huntley and Palmer connection to the house, there's also a biscuit tin museum.

Mellerstain House is the home of the Earl and Countess of Haddington and is a superb Georgian house designed by William Adam in 1725, and expanded and completed by Robert Adam in 1778. Exquisite ceilings are preserved in the original colours complemented by hand-printed wallpapers, fine period furniture and a marvellous art collection; including work by Van Dyck, Gainsborough, Ramsay, Aitken and Nasmyth. The great gallery windows overlook the Italian-style terrace gardens, lovely lawns, a lake and the surrounding landscape.

MELLERSTAIN: Gordon TD3 6LG; ☎ 01573 410225; www.mellerstain.com. Entry: adult £7, children under 12 free; open Easter weekend, May, June and Sept, Sun, Wed and Bank Holiday Mondays; Jul–Aug, Sun, Mon, Wed, Thur; Oct, Sun only; 11.30am–5.30pm.

For another spectacular historic house, visit **Floors Castle** near Kelso, which is Scotland's largest inhabited castle. This has been the home of the Duke of Roxburghe since 1721 and has been continuously lived in by each successive generation. A guided tour of the spectacular state rooms is recommended to hear the history of the family through the centuries and their extraordinary collection of paintings, tapestries and furniture. Floors also has lovely walled gardens to visit if the sun comes out.

FLOORS CASTLE: Kelso TD5 7SF; ☎ 01573 223333; www.floorscastle.com. Entry: adult £7.50/£6.50 (seasonal variations); children aged 5–16 £.3.50; open Easter weekend; 1 May–31 Oct 11am–5pm, last admission 4.30pm.

Paxton House, which is part of the National Galleries of Scotland, is a superb example of Palladian country houses dating from the 18th century in Britain. It's home to fine decorative art and a collection of Chippendale furniture. For families with children the gardens offer an adventure playground, picnic tables, putting green and squirrel and bird-viewing hide. Children are especially welcome to visit with organised events such as a house activity guide, Paxton Ted games and races and a nature detective trail. There's also the Paxton Music Festival in July.

PAXTON HOUSE: near Berwick upon Tweed and Duns TD15 1SZ; ☎ 01289 386291; www.paxtonhouse.com. House tour and garden, adult £7; children aged 5–15 £3.50, under 5s free, family £18; gardens only, adult £4, children £2. Open Easter–31 October.

Golf

Eyemouth Golf Club is the only seaside golf course in the Scottish Borders and at over 6,500 yards in length is one of the longest. A superb 18-hole layout featuring some spectacular holes such as the 3rd Par 3 'Paddocks Pond' played across water, the 6th Par 3, played across the North Sea and the 13th Par 5 'The Hawk Ness Monster' offer a unique challenge. Visitors are welcome.

The Championship **Roxburghe Golf Course** at the Roxburghe Hotel is home to the Charles Church Scottish Seniors Open and regarded as the fifth best inland course in Scotland. The Duke of Roxburghe, an avid golfer, commissioned Dave Thomas to design this challenging course on the Roxburghe estate which opened in 1997. Expect deep challenging bunkers and large rolling greens with wide fairways following the natural contours of the land. The 'Viaduct' hole is an elevated tee beside the River Teviot with its magnificent towering arched viaduct.

> EYEMOUTH GOLF CLUB: Gunsgreenhill, Eyemouth, Berwickshire TD14 5SF; ☎ 018907 50004; www.eyemouthgolfclub.co.uk. Weekday/weekend green fees, adult £28–£33 (round), £38–£43 (day), junior £11–£15 (round), £15–£17 (day).

> ROXBURGHE GOLF COURSE: Roxburghe Hotel, Helton, By Kelso TD5 8JZ; ☎ 01573 450331; www.roxburghe.net. Green fees £35 (winter) to £70 (summer), four-ball fee £140–£220. Accommodation and golf packages available.

Wet weather

A tour around **Eyemouth Museum** will reveal the history of Eyemouth and Berwickshire coastline and how its people lived through the ages by land and sea. There are exhibitions on fishermens' cottages, farming, milling and blacksmiths. One of the displays is a tapestry to commemorate the tragic seafaring disaster of October 1881 when the Eyemouth community suffered the loss of 189 local fishermen at sea. The visitor information centre is located at the museum.

For those interested in boats and shipping, the **Eyemouth Maritime Centre** has a fantastic location in the old fishmarket beside the harbour. The building has been designed to create the exterior of an 18th-century Frigate. The centre houses the 'World of Boats,' a collection of nearly 400 boats and 300 models with archive information on their history, from fishing boats to pleasure yachts. There are regularly changing major exhibitions such

> EYEMOUTH MUSEUM: Auld Kirk, Market Place TD14 5HE ☎ 018907 50678; Admission free to second floor exhibits; prices: adult £2.50 for special exhibitions, children free; open end Mar to end Sept, Mon–Sat 10am–4.30pm, Sun 12am–3pm; end Sept to end Oct, Mon–Sat 10am–4pm.

> EYEMOUTH MARITIME CENTRE: Harbour Road TD14 5SS; ☎ 01890 751020; www.worldofboats.org. Entry: adult, £3, children £2.50, family of four £8, under 5s free; open, summer, Mon–Sun 11am–6pm; winter, Wed–Sun 11am–4.30pm.

as *The Mutiny of the Bounty*, Second World War ships and modern-day transatlantic rowers. Audio visual presentations, interactive displays and nautical adventure trails, are geared towards adults and children.

What to do with children

WHITEADDER SAILING CENTRE: Cranshaws, Duns TD11 3SW; ☎ 01361 890397. Sunday boat hire, £6 per hour; 1-day sailing course, £30; fishing, adult £8, junior £6.

The Whiteadder Sailing Centre near Duns is a Royal Yachting Association training centre offering a range of courses. All equipment, wetsuits, helmets and lifesavers are provided. If you are proficient in sailing, you can rent a boat here on Sunday afternoons and fishing is available too.

Entertainment

The Scottish Borders are famous for the traditional fairs and festivals commemorated in many towns and villages. It is impossible to list them all, but the main annual events are in the *Scottish Borders Essential Guide* for visitors, or see www.borderstraditions. org.uk.

The Eyemouth Herring Queen Festival (www.ehq.org.uk) is a local community event which aims to symbolise the ideals and everyday life of a fishing community. The festival owes its origins to the 'Peace Picnic' or 'Fisherman's Picnic' first organised by the late Mr Chrystie to celebrate the end of the First World War. This day came to be celebrated throughout the following years and to be looked upon as a local holiday for the fishermen of the town. It takes place over a couple of days in mid-July with a programme of entertainment and events for all the family.

Duns has a summer music festival in July (www.borderstraditions.org.uk), the town's most important event which originated in 1949. The festival principals, the Reiver and Reiver's Lass, lead the Riding of the Bounds to the summit of Duns Law. There are also sports, concerts and parades, and the Grand March marks the start of the Reiver's Ball.

Lauder celebrates its **Common Riding Festival** (www.laudercommonriding.co.uk) on the first Saturday in August and the ceremony has remained the same since 1911, featuring the election of the Cornet and Cornet's Lass, with music concerts, dances and a gymkhana. The **Kelso Races** take place regularly from October to May at Kelso Racecourse, and attract big crowds whatever the weather. For race dates, see www. kelso-races.co.uk. **Floors Castle** (www.floorscastle.com) organises annual local fairs and festivals such as the Easter Extravaganza and Christmas Winter Wonderland.

The **Border Agricultural Show** (www.buas.org) is regarded as a great visitor attraction held on the last Friday and Saturday of July each year in Springwood Park, 46 acres of parkland near Kelso. The show includes competition for ponies, horses,

The best of... COAST AND COUNTRYSIDE

THE SOUTH EAST CORNER OF SCOTLAND OFFERS A PAINTERLY PANORAMA OF WILD,
NATURAL LANDSCAPE FROM QUIET GLENS, FORESTED HILLS, LOCHS AND FAST FLOWING
RIVERS TO RUGGED SEACLIFFS AND SANDY BEACHES. NO WONDER IT'S THE PERFECT
PURE FRESH AIR DESTINATION FOR ADVENTURE SPORTS, GOLF, MOUNTAIN BIKING,
WALKING HOLIDAYS OR A RELAXING, CHILL OUT BREAK.

Scott's View

Top: Melrose Abbey; Middle: Scottish Crannog Centre; Bottom: Kenmore

Top: Leith Shore Evening; Middle: Puffin, Craigleith Island; Bottom: St Monans

Top: St Andrews Old Course; Middle: Portobello Beach; Bottom: Greencraigs

dairy goats, poultry, alpacas, shepherds' crooks, horse shoeing, stands for clothing, equestrian goods, Flavours of the Borders Food Fair, and a children's funfair.

Kelso is a very traditional village with a community event held every year in early September, the **St James' Fair** in the Market Square. There was originally a St James' fair held in Friars Haugh, in the old town of Roxburgh on the first Monday of every August as far back as the 11th century, and was a market for the sale of linen, cheese, wool as well as for livestock. Today, Kelso's St James' Fair is a two-day festival of music and entertainment, children's funfair, market stalls for crafts and local food produce as well as antiques and bric-a-brac. Another prime Kelso event is the **Riding of the Marches** in July.

🛒 Shopping

In **Eyemouth,** a highly recommended bookshop is **Crossing The Bar** (Market Place; ☎ 01890 751997; open Tuesday to Saturday, 9.30am–5pm), run by Susan Shepherd, which sells new and second-hand books, greetings cards and post cards. It's well worth a browse after a blustery walk around the harbour.

Kelso is an ideal town for men to buy Borders tweed jackets and outdoor clothes for fishing and shooting. Archie Hume is in charge of the traditional gentleman's outfitter, **A Hume** at 46 The Square (☎ 01573 224620; www.ahume.co.uk), which first opened its doors for business in 1929 and has been owned and run by the family over three generations. You'll find traditional and contemporary clothing, formal and casual wear, made-to-measure tailoring, quality-brand shirts, ties, trousers and knitwear. **Forrest of Kelso** (1 Bridge Street; ☎ 01573 224687; ww.forrestofkelso. co.uk) has provided a specialist service to the country enthusiast since 1837, stocking a wide range of fishing, shooting and walking equipment, fishing rods, guns and gifts. **Tweedside Tackle** (36 Bridge Street; ☎ 01573 225306; www.tweedsidetackle.co.uk) is the place for the fisherman or woman. Based on the banks of the Tweed this Kelso shop caters for all anglers' needs for trout, salmon and saltwater fishing.

If you're looking for locally produced knitwear, either to take home as a souvenir or as a way to keep warm, check out **Hawick Cashmere** (20 Bridge Street; ☎ 01573 226776) or **The Mill Warehouse** (2 Roxburgh Street; ☎ 01573 226835). **The Horseshoe Gallery** (22 Horsemarket; ☎ 01573 224542) exhibits an ever-changing range of affordable watercolours, oils and prints. More paintings and sculpture can be found at **The Art House** (35 The Square; ☎ 01573 228666) and **Vennel Gallery** (9 Bridge Sreet; ☎ 01573 224003).

The best... **PLACES TO STAY**

COUNTRY HOUSE

Roxburghe Hotel and Golf Course

Helton, by Kelso TD5 8JZ
☎ **01573 450331; www.roxburghe.net**

This enchanting, homely, ivy-clad country mansion is surrounded by wooded parkland and gardens. Enjoy a classic luxurious bedroom the library bar, log fires, exceptional food, a spa, private championship golf course and fabulous landscape.

Price: £185–£210 per room B&B.

Ednam House

Bridge Street, Kelso TD5 7HT
☎ **01573 224168**
www.ednamhouse.com

Owned and run by the Brooks Family since 1928, Ednam House (1761) is now managed by Ralph and Anne, the fourth generation and features some wonderful original woodwork, ceilings and fireplaces. Accommodation ranges from luxurious Orangerie suite (two four-poster rooms and lounge), to the Attic rooms.

Price: £110–£200 per room B&B; £160–£210, per room dinner, B&B.

BOUTIQUE

Churches Hotel

Albert Road, Eyemouth TD14 5DB
☎ **018907 50401**
www.churcheshotel.co.uk

Privately owned by Lesley and Lawson, this seaside hotel has a prime site just up the hill from the harbour. There are sea views from the conservatory seafood restaurant and the pretty garden. The six en suite rooms have a fresh, contemporary décor and you can sample local smoked cod with a poached egg for breakfast.

Price: £80–£120 per double room B&B.

Edenwater House

Ednam, near Kelso TD5 7QL
☎ **01573 224070**
www.edenwaterhouse.co.uk

Highly recommended delightful house with lovely gardens beside Eden Water is owned by Jeff and Jacqui Kelly. There are four beautifully furnished rooms and a warm, welcoming drawing room with log fire to relax before and after a first-class dinner and fine wine.

Price: £40–£50 pppn B&B.

B&B

Courtburn House

School Road, Coldingham TD14 5NS
☎ **01890 771266**
www.courtburn.com

This charming country house offers three comfortable, homely bedrooms with private bathrooms, TV and guest lounge. Start the day with porridge, bacon and eggs, vegetarian breakfast, omelette or scrambled egg with smoked salmon before a bracing walk along the cliff at St Abb's Head.

Price: £70 double; £45 single.

SELF-CATERING

Press Main Cottages

Coldingham TD14 5TS
☎ **01890 771310**
www.watchbadgers.co.uk

Watch badgers from inside one of four environmentally friendly cottages (sleeping two, four or six) for a relaxing, romantic nature lover's holiday. Luxury accommodation ideal for families and couples featuring spa baths, four-poster beds, open fires with local webcams to see swallows, owls, badgers, red squirrels and bats.

Price: £295–£330 (Nov), £400–£595 (July) per week. Short breaks available.

The best... FOOD AND DRINK

▶ Staying in

On the banks of the River Teviot, halfway between Jedburgh and Kelso is the **Teviot Game Fare Smokery and Water Gardens** (Kirkbank House, Eckford TD5 8LE). For the fishing and shooting fraternity, you can leave your spoils to be smoked and when ready, they will deliver them to you. Alternatively, pop into the well-stocked shop and pick up freshly smoked whole trout, sliced smoked salmon and a variety of local victuals. The conservatory restaurant serves tea, coffee and homebaking all day.

Kelso has a bustling farmers' market held in the Town Square on the fourth Saturday of each month, offering a wide choice of local fresh produce and and Alpaca wool straight from a local farm. **Lees Butcher** (40–44 Bridge Street) doubles as a deli with homemade soups and casseroles and a variety of local cheeses. For fresh fish, head to **DR Collin and Son** (34–36 Harbour Road) for the catch landed at Eyemouth. **Mitchell & Son** (44 Bridge Street; ☎ 01573 224109) are a family butchers and delicatessen with 40 farmhouse cheeses, pastas, olive oils, pâtés and new-world wines. They also offer a freshly prepared range of ready meals from their own kitchen. **Jackie Lunn Bakers** (Horsemarket; ☎ 01573 224139) is a family-run bakery selling all kinds of bread from Selkirk Bannock to the Berrymeal loaf.

Reiver Country Farm Foods at Reston, near Eyemouth (TD14 5LN; ☎ 018907 61355; www.reiver-foods.co.uk) sells everything – beef, lamb, cheese, eggs, bread, groceries, homebaking, vegetables, wine–and will supply a hog roast or large joints of beef for your barbecue direct from their own farm.

The small town of Duns is cosseted in the heart of the Berwickshire countryside and offers a good selection of foodie places to buy local produce. Fruit and vegetables are displayed with loving care at **Borders Fayre** (3 South Street) and when you leave **Prentice**, the butchers (4 Golden Square), it's not just meat you'll come away with; they have an eclectic range of wines too at very reasonable prices

Eyemouth Fishmarket unfortunately isn't open to the public, but award-winning fish merchants, DR Collin and Son has a fantastic selection of fish on sale, from local crab and lobster, scallops and mussels along with wild salmon and sea trout, to the more traditional cod, haddock and various flat fish. The board outside the shop also displays the best fish in season. For mature beef that has been hung for four weeks, a trip to **RG Foreman and Son** (4 Chapel Street) is in order. They are members of the Rare Breeds Survival Trust so the lamb and pork are from traditional stock.

Takeaway

Eyemouth is bracing with its wide stretch of beach and the sea (depending on the weather) can be dramatic with waves crashing into the sea wall or gentle enough to paddle in. Having built up an appetite, head to **MacKay's of Eyemouth** (20–24 High

Street) fish and chip shop for a takeaway or sit in the back room overlooking the beach and enjoy freshly cooked, golden fish and chips, with or without mushy peas! Alternatively drop in to the award-winning **Giacopazzi's** (18–20 Harbour Road). Not only do they make good fish and chips good, but pizzas too. Not that hungry? Then have a dollop of their wonderful, made-on-site ice creams.

In **Kelso** sample a hot haggis or Mexican chicken baguette from **Central Baguette** (52 The Square), which you can have to sit in or takeaway.

Drinking

The Cobbles Inn (7 Bowmont Street, Kelso) is an inviting freehouse with cask ales, open fires and good food. It's listed in the *Good Beer Guide 2009* and every Friday night the Kelso folk and live music club meets here for their weekly jamming session. In Lauder, **The Black Bull** on Market Square is an award-winning pub for beer, food and atmosphere. Winner of the AA Scottish pub of the Year 2006, it's still good!

Duns has numerous pubs, with **The Black Bull**, **the Plough Inn** and the **White Swan** all in and around Market Square. For something a little different, there's always the kinky-sounding **Whip and Saddle** on the corner of Castle Street and Market Square in Duns. Two rural local pubs are **The Red Lion** in Reston, which has a cosy atmosphere serving bar food (children welcome) and **The Craw Inn**, Auchencrow, which has won the Camra Best Scottish Pub of the Year Award several times, so you can expect cask-conditioned ales, as well as excellent food and beer garden.

There are plenty of atmospheric pubs and bars in Eyemouth; **The Tavern** (High Street) is situated 20 yards from the seafront and enjoys the breathtaking view over Eyemouth Bay, with family lounge, beer garden and live entertainment on Saturday nights. **The Contented Sole** is also a harbour side pub and restaurant on the Old Quay and **The Ship Hotel**, Harbour Road, serves local Hadrian and Border ales. **Oblo Bar** is a city-style contemporary and classy joint for drinking and eating.

EATING OUT

FINE DINING

Roxburghe Hotel and Golf Course
Helton, by Kelso TD5 8JZ
☎ **01573 450331**
www.roxburghe.net

In this elegant dining room, dine on game and salmon from the estate, mushrooms and fresh herbs from the garden. Other specialities include lobster risotto, breast of corn-fed duck, raspberry tart. With canapés and coffee dinner is £39.95. The superb lunch menu features soup (£3.50) salad bar, fishcakes or rump of lamb (£8.95).

Ednam House Hotel
Bridge Street, Kelso TD5 7HT
☎ **01573 224168**
www.ednamhouse.com

Settled on the banks of the River Tweed, this county house hotel is where you can enjoy a relaxing meal with great views. The menu includes fresh salmon fishcakes, homemade carrot soup, smoked salmon, Tweeddale lamb and steak, monkfish and delicious desserts. Four-course dinner £27.50; two courses £21.50. Sunday lunch and bar lunches also available.

BISTRO

Cobbles Inn
7 Bowmont Street, Kelso TD5 7JH
☎ **01573 223 548**
www.thecobblesinn.co.uk

Winner of Best Informal Meal at the Scottish Borders Eating Out Awards 2008 for a menu of Borders steak, mushroom and ale pie, smoked haddock fishcakes, king prawns on Thai cucumber salad, slow-roasted belly of organic pork, local cheese and whisky chocolate torte, plus traditional Sunday roasts. £15 for two courses.

Oblo Bar and Bistro
**18–20 Harbour Road,
Eyemouth TD14 5HU**
☎ **01890 752527**

This stylish, laidback bistro situated on the harbour's edge with a balcony terrace, serves breakfast, lunch, snacks and dinner. The fish is spankingly fresh (as you'd expect) and the menu also features Oblo's beef burger, Eyemouth haddock with hand-cut chips, and daily fishmarket specials. Two courses cost £10–£20.

GASTROPUB

The Craw Inn
**Auchencrow, Reston,
Berwickshire TD14 5LS**
☎ **01890 761253**

There are crab sandwiches at the bar as well as a first-class restaurant menu of local Lammermuir lamb, seasonal game and seafood, Assiette de fruits de mer (48 hours notice), steaks, chicken, guinea fowl and a vegetarian dish of the day. Huge portions, with starters around £6 and mains £15.

EATING OUT

PUB

The Black Bull
Market Place, Lauder TD2 6SR
☎ **01578 722208**
www.blackbull-lauder.com

Situated on Lauder's Market Square, this popular inn has a fine reputation for quality food served in both the bar and smart Georgian dining room. Sample for instance Border beef, chicken liver pâté, Black Bull burgers, vegetarian tarts and crêpes, local cheese and ice cream. Two courses cost about £15.

The Contented Sole
3/4 Old Quay Harbour Road, Eyemouth TD14 5HS
☎ **01890 750268**

Situated at the end of the picturesque harbour in a converted sail loft with low beamed ceilings. There is bar food available and a restaurant upstairs serving good fresh seafood. Fish and chips in the bar £6.35; restaurant steak £14.

CAFÉ

Giacopazzi's
18 Harbour Road, Eyemouth, TD14 5HU
☎ **01890 750317**

The best fish and chips in town, pizzas and also gold-medal ice cream. The bill will not be too expensive with children's meal packages (from £3) and gourmet lemon sole fish and chips (£7.50). The perfect place for lunch or supper, open year round.

Flat Cat Gallery
2 Market Place, Lauder TD2 6SR
☎ **01578 722808**
www.flatcatgallery.co.uk

This café is a must for those who love good home-baked cakes. Don't miss the amazing brown sugar, crunchy yet gooey, soft-centred, cream-filled meringues and sit at original carved wood tables and chairs made by the late furniture maker Tim Stead. Soup and bread £2.90, cappuccino £1.50.

Springbank Cottage Tea Garden
St Abbs Harbour, TD14 5PW
☎ **018907 71477**
www.springbankcottage.co.uk

The café offers delicious scones, crab rolls and other seafood delights, which they will bring to your car if the weather is wild. If you're there on a day when the sun shines, from the terrace you can watch the seabirds dip and dive in the surf. Open daily April to September, March and October, weekends only. Fishy snack lunch or tea and scones £5–£10.

ⓘ Visitor Information

Tourist Information Centres: Eyemouth: Auld Kirk, Manse Road TD14 5JE (open April to October); **Kelso:** Townhouse, The Square, Kelso TD5 7HF (open all year). Excellent brochures available on accommodation, walks, sport, historic attractions festivals and events, ☎ 0870 608 0404, www.visitscottishborders. com.

Hospitals: Scottish Borders General Hospital, Melrose TD6 9BS, ☎ 01896 826000; Minor Injuries Clinic, Kelso Hospital, Inch Road, Kelso, ☎ 01573 224591; Coldstream Cottage, Hospital, Kelso Road, Coldstream TD12 4LQ, ☎ 01890 882417.

Police: Coldstream Police Station, Lennel Road, Coldstream TD12 4AX, ☎ 01890 882402; Duns Police Station, 10 Newtown Street Duns TD11 3DT, ☎ 01361 882222; Eyemouth Police Station, 28 Coldingham Road, Eyemouth TD14 5AW, ☎ 01890 750217; Kelso Police Station, Coal Market Kelso TD5 7AH, ☎ 01573 223434; Lauder Police Station, East High Street Lauder TD2 6RP, ☎ 01578 722222.

Travel and Transport: Train timetables and information to Berwick upon Tweed, www.nationalexpresseastcoast. com, www.nationalrail.co.uk; Bus and transport services, www.firstgroup. com, www.travelinescotland.com, www. traveline.org.uk; Scottish One Ticket, bus and train travel across Edinburgh and east Scotland, www.one-ticket. co.uk.

Self-Catering Accommodation: Press Castle, Coldingham, 17th-century property of apartments and suites, www.presscastle1.co.uk; Spital House, three cottages on private country estate at Paxton, ☎ 01289 386139, www. spitalhouse.co.uk; Courtburn cottages, ☎ 01890 771266, www.courtburn.com.

Useful Websites: www.eyemouth.com; www.kelso.border-net.co.uk; www.lauder. border-net.co.uk.

Activities: Diving: for information on Berwickshire Dive centres, training and events, www.divestabbseyemouth.co.uk; **Golf:** Roxburghe Hotel and Golf Course, www.roxburghe.net; Eyemouth Golf Course, www.eyemouthgolfclub.co.uk.

4
The Kingdom
of Fife

a. St Andrews
b. The rest of Fife

Unmissable highlights

01 Walk along the West Sands **at St Andrews,** p.253

02 Explore the East Neuk **fishing villages,** p.271

03 Find out about the **original Robinson Crusoe in Lower Largo,** p.278

04 Experience divine cuisine **at the Seafood Restaurant (St Andrews and St Monans),** p.267

05 Visit the Secret Bunker, **if you dare step deep inside!** p.280

06 Experience a thrilling drive **at Knockhill motorsport centre,** p.278

07 Watch a cricket match **on the sands of Elie Beach,** p.277

08 The Pittenweem Art Festival, **over 100 artists exhibit in gardens, garages and studios,** p.282

09 Non-golfers can play 18 holes **at the Himalayas Putting Green, right beside the Old Course,** p.259

10 See Europe's largest collection **of sharks at Deep Sea World,** p.281

THE KINGDOM OF FIFE

Fast Scotland is so distinctive, with wild and wonderful landscapes, coastline and countryside, all within a short journey from Edinburgh. That's what makes exploring around and beyond the city so easy, accessible and attractive. Cross the Forth Bridge and turn right along the coastal route and within half an hour you've arrived in the historic county of the Kingdom of Fife.

Fife is particularly distinctive geographically; it's spread out in the shape of an elongated peninsula bordered by the Tay estuary to the north, the Forth to the south and North Sea to the east. The historical name of 'Kingdom' dates back to the Pictish realm of the 12th century when '*Fif*' was named one of seven kingdoms. The town of Dunfermline was also an ancient capital of Scotland and a royal residence.

The eastern stretch of coastline towards St Andrews is called the East Neuk ('neuk' meaning corner). Here you'll find a continuous row of timeless old fishing ports – Crail, Anstruther, Pittenweem, St Monans – virtually unchanged for centuries with their tiny harbours, whitewashed quayside houses and cobbled alleyways. Each village has its own particular character and charm, recalling times as thriving sea-ports trading with Europe which influenced the Dutch and Flemish architecture found here.

There's a proud sense of maritime history, cultural heritage and a strong artists' community with galleries galore in this area. This is the place for an active holiday; breathtaking clifftop walks, cycling, motorsports, and the crème de la crème, a round of golf or two at St Andrews. But it's not all about energetic, sporting and family fun. The glorious countryside, miles of white sand beaches, quaint old fishing villages, castles, music festivals and fabulous fresh seafood, makes Fife a relaxing and peaceful 'get-away-from-it-all' destination.

ST ANDREWS

'St Andrews by the Northern Sea
A haunted town it is to me.
The grey North Ocean girds it round,
The long sea-rollers surge and sound ....'

Andrew Lang

The picturesque, medieval, greystone town of St Andrews, located in the easternmost corner of Fife, is perched on steep cliffs where the North Sea waves crash against the rocks and sweep in giant rollers up the long curving beach. The spires of the once-majestic cathedral and the castle ruins tower above the old harbour below. The town's world-famous status is due to its significant place in the history of religion, its fine 15th-century university and, of course: golf. St Andrews, home to the Royal and Ancient Golf Club, is the undisputed international Mecca for golfers, known as *the* Home of Golf. Serious golfing enthusiasts come here on a rite-of-passage pilgrimage to play on the venerated Old Course. The game has been played on the sandy links by the seashore for over 500 years and today there are four championship courses, including the famous Old Course which has hosted no less than 27 Open Championships, including millennium year, and the championship will return again in 2010.

But you don't have to play golf to enjoy a visit to St Andrews. The bracing, fresh North Sea air provides a naturally beneficial and refreshing environment, while the never-ending sea and sky create a painterly landscape. Today St Andrews is a contemporary, colourful and cultural wee place due to an eclectic year-round mix of residents (bustling with university students who enjoy its lively pub scene!) and international tourists. There are superb seafront hotels and inns, bars and bistros, shops, galleries, an aquarium, leisure, sports and so much else to see and do for all ages.

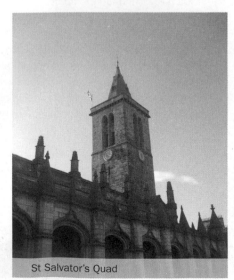
St Salvator's Quad

WHAT TO SEE AND DO

St Andrews was a market town for centuries and the centre is laid out just as it was when the wide streets were lined with traders stalls, featuring huge stone cobbles, narrow wynds and the original town gateways such as Mill Port and Sea Yett. The **University of St Andrews** was founded in 1412 (although some records claim it was 1411 and others 1413), the first in Scotland and the third oldest in Great Britain. The university soon celebrates its 600th anniversary, starting in 2011 and continuing until 2013 (to allow for the debate over the date of foundation). Amongst its famous alumni over the years, graduates include several Scottish Kings who attended up until the 16th century; John Napier, inventor of logarithms, who entered college age 13 In 1563; Elizabeth Garrett, the first female student in Britain; Sir James Black, who won the Nobel prize for Medicine in 1988; the novelist Fay Weldon; Alex Salmond, First Minister of the Scottish Parliament; and Prince William who graduated with a degree in Geography in 2005.

As you walk around you'll see the names of the colleges, libraries and residences as the university buildings are dotted all over town, mixing old with new. The university, like Oxford and Cambridge, is steeped in tradition. One of the colourful customs is after Sunday church when students, dressed in their red gowns, walk around the harbour walls; another is the **May Dip** when after staying up all night, a few hundred brave souls plunge into the North Sea at sunrise on May Day to ensure they pass their exams! There is also the popular **Kate Kennedy Procession**, which takes the form of a procession through the town with many historic characters represented. A first-year student takes on the role of Kate Kennedy, the niece of the founder of St Salvator's College, founded in the 15th century. This is a popular event for both town and gown. The students run festivals, fashion shows and cultural events during the year.

St Andrews town centre is very compact, so you can explore everywhere on foot. From the promenade above the West Sands walk along the clifftop road,

The May Dip, a student tradition of taking a swim in the North Sea at sunrise

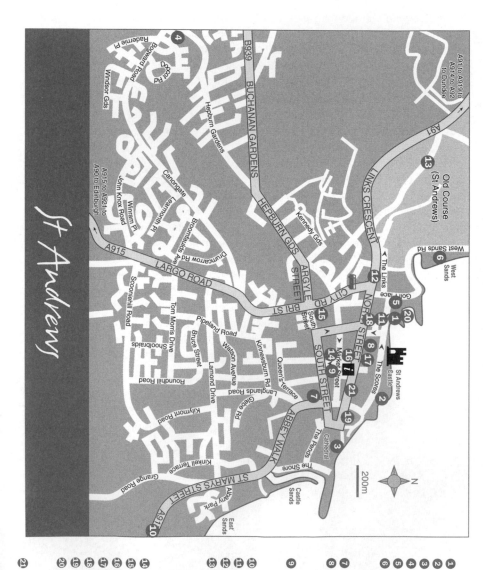

St Andrews

Things to see and do
1. Aquarium
2. Castle
3. Cathedral
4. Craigtoun Park
5. Golf Museum
6. West Sands Beach

Entertainment
7. Byre Theatre
8. New Picture house

Shopping
9. J&G Innes, Booksellers

Places to Stay
10. Fairmont Golf Resort
11. Golf Hotel
12. Macdonald Rusacks
13. Old Course Hotel, Golf Resort and Kohler's Spa

Eat and Drink
14. Doll's House
15. Drouthy Neebors
16. Glasshouse
17. Harbour House
18. The Inn on North Street
19. North Point
20. Seafood Restaurant

Visitor Information
21. Tourist Information Centre

The Scores to the **castle** ruins on a craggy headland. The castle was the ancient residence for the Bishops and Archbishops of St Andrews, the focal point of the church in medieval Scotland. You can explore the 16th-century underground siege mine and the bottle dungeon hollowed out of solid rock from which a prisoner could never escape. The castle visitor centre has a fascinating exhibition about the history of the town and the role of Church and State. The castle is also a great observation point for seabird watching.

ST ANDREWS CASTLE: The Scores KY16 0AR; ☎ 01334 477196; www.historic-scotland.gov.uk. Entry: adult £5.20/£4.20 (seasonal variations), children £2.60; open all year 9.30am–4.30pm/5.30pm, depending on season.

The ruins of the 16th-century castle

A short stroll around the corner stand the remains of St Andrews **Cathedral** built in the 12th and 13th century, beside the ruins of **St Rules Tower**, part of an older Augustinian priory. St Andrews became a

ST ANDREWS CATHEDRAL AND ST RULES TOWER: The Pends KY16 9QU; ☎ 01334 472563; www.historic-scotland.gov.uk. Entry: adult £5.20/£4.20 (seasonal variations); children £2.60; open all year 9.30am–4.30pm/5.30pm, depending on season.

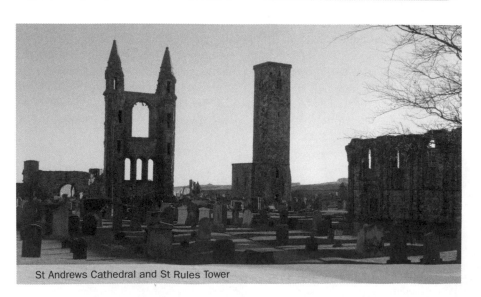
St Andrews Cathedral and St Rules Tower

The expanse of the West Sands

major religious settlement, or so the legend goes, when a Greek monk brought relics of St Andrew here and Celtic monks then built St Mary's church on the Rock beside the harbour. Pilgrims visited the shrine of St Andrew here who became Scotland's patron saint. His cross inspired the design of the Saltire, Scotland's national flag. The cathedral museum has a collection of medieval sculpture and you can climb to the top of St Rules Tower (108ft) for a great view over the town and seashore.

The beaches

The famous **West Sands** beach at St Andrews stretches for 2km and is popular with kite flyers as well as surfers tackling the big breakers. This beach, which won the Blue Flag Seaside Award for family safety and cleanliness, is where scenes for the multi-Oscar-winning movie, *Chariots of Fire* was filmed, starring Ian Charleson as the Scottish Olympic runner Eric Liddell, known as 'the Flying Scotsman'. But watch out for the kite buggies which whirl along at great speed with the driver waving madly, trying to steer out of your path.

ST ANDREWS TRACTION KITES: Balmullo, St Andrews; ☎ 07714 214667; www. standrewstractionkites.co.uk. Introductory lessons or tailor-made courses available to learn landboarding or to go on a kite buggy.

There's a growing passion for Power Kiting. **Kite landboarding** involves the use of an oversized skateboard with large pneumatic wheels and foot-straps. You can also try kiting with a traction buggy, and there are a few places which can provide you with lessons. No wonder West Sands is perfect for the sport with its hard-packed sand, a large expanse of empty space up to 0.5 km wide at low tide, with the surface going from soft to hard, rippling to bowling green flat and favourable wind conditions. A specially flagged off safe area is used for kiting as the beach is extremely popular with walkers, horse-riders, picnickers and families with kids building sandcastles.

Also check out **Castle Sands** with the ruins of the medieval castle towering on the cliff above, or walk along the Scores to **East Sands** near the harbour, which tends to be less crowded than the iconic West Sands but still has plenty of golden sand and a great view of the harbour.

Golf

St Andrews is regarded as the Cradle of Golf; its geographic and cultural centre where golf has evolved; where the spirit and traditions of golf have been safeguarded for over six centuries; where its laws and conventions are made and preserved; and where everyone who plays the game wants to visit in their golfing lifetime. This is because the **Royal and Ancient Golf Club**, founded in 1754, exercises legislative authority over the game worldwide (except in the USA and Mexico) and because **the Links** is the most frequent venue for the Open Championship.

The world-famous **Old Course** is, therefore, a place of global importance and is managed by **St Andrews Links Trust** (www.standrews.org.uk), through which you can plan your golf trip and book tee-times well before your visit. The seven golf courses of the St Andrews

FIFE FAIRWAYS DISCOUNT CARD: Wilkinson Golf and Leisure; ☎ 01383 629940; www.wilkinsongolf.com/golfpass.
Price: £149 midweek (£5 supplement on weekends at each course).

The Royal and Ancient Golf Club

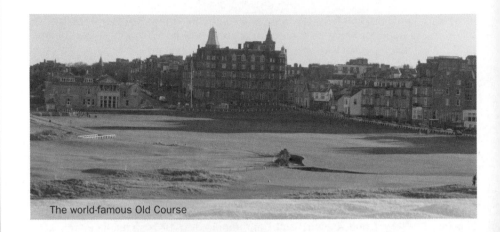

The world-famous Old Course

Links, which include the Old Course and The Castle Course, are open to all, as are the golf practice centre and the three clubhouses. There is a ballot system in operation to play on the Old Course. To enter phone ☎ 01334 466666 or hand in a ballot card by 2pm on the day before you want to play. Golfers can now enjoy golf on a choice of Fife's finest golfing challenges, including the Duke's Course and the Torrance, the magnificent new links course at Fairmont St Andrews Hotel and Spa. Saving up to 50% on the individual green fees, the three courses have joined together to offer a combined course pass which can be used over any seven-day period, the Fife Fairways Discount Card.

Wet weather

The British Golf Museum will tell you everything you always wanted to know about the game but were afraid to ask. Find out about the history of golf, how a golf ball is made, learn more of the story of great players past and present, and wander around interesting exhibitions.

THE BRITISH GOLF MUSEUM: Bruce Embankment, The Scores KY16 9AB; ☎ 01334 460046; www.britishgolfmuseum. co.uk. Entry: adult £ 5.50/£4.50 (seasonal variations), children under 15 £2.90, under 5s free; open Mar–Oct, Mon–Sat 9.30am–5.30pm, Sun 10am–5pm; Nov–Mar, Mon–Sun 10am–4pm.

The Museum of the University of St Andrews, the first of its kind in the UK, opened in October 2008 and displays over 112,000 artefacts, paintings, medals and rare books to commemorate the 600-year history of the university, its students, staff and rectors – from playwright JM Barrie to Olympic cyclist Chris Hoy. The museum was opened by

THE MUSEUM OF THE UNIVERSITY OF ST ANDREWS: 7a, The Scores KY16 9AR; ☎ 01334 461660; www.st-andrews. ac.uk/musa. Admission free; open Apr–Oct, Mon–Sat 10am–5pm, Sun 12–5pm; Nov–Mar, Thurs–Sun only 12–4pm.

crime writer Ian Rankin who came face to face with the death masks of 18th-century murderers Burke and Hare which were previously treasures of the university's anatomy museum.

What to do with children...

St Andrews Aquarium, a five-star visitor attraction, has a perfect location on the waterfront with a fascinating range of sealife – seals, sharks and seahorses, weird and wonderful catfish, poisonous dart frogs and deadly piranhas. You can visit the **Catch Beach** restaurant for something to eat and there's also a gift shop, talks and fish feeding.

> ST ANDREWS AQUARIUM: The Scores KY16 9AS; ☎ 01334 474786; www. standrewsaquarium.co.uk. Entry: adult £6.80/£5.50 (seasonal variations), children £ 4.90; open daily 10am–4.30pm. Check Dec–Feb times.

The East Sands beach south of the harbour has activities for children with rock pools and has won the Blue Flag Seaside Award. **Craigtoun Country Park** (☎ 01334 473666) has a range of family activities, such as crazy golf, boating, and trampolines.

The **Himalayas Putting Green** is beside the Links Clubhouse, adjacent to the 2nd Tee of the Old Course; and at around £1 a round, it's reasonable entertainment for the family.

Finally, on a fine day, we recommend that you take a lovely woodland walk along **Lade Braes** which follows the Kinness Burn to reach a large children's play park with swings, slides and a football field.

... and how to avoid children

The outdoor hot tub at the **Old Course Hotel Kohler's Water Spa**. The spa has a thermal suite, luxury treatments, swimming pool and a rooftop jacuzzi which is a sophisticated, calm and peaceful environment for adults only. Alternatively, you could settle in next to the fire for a pint of traditional ale at **The Central**, one of the town's most popular old pubs.

> KOHLER'S WATER SPA: Old Course Hotel KY16 9SP; ☎ 01334 474371; www. oldcoursehotel.kohler.com. Open daily, Apr–Sept 6.30am–9.30pm; Oct–Mar 6.30am–9pm.

The rooftop jacuzzi at the Kohler's Water Spa in the Old Course Hotel

🎭 Entertainment

The Byre Theatre (Abbey Street; ☎ 01334 475000; www.byretheatre.com) is a highly acclaimed local company offering exciting, accessible theatre for adults and children. Also check out the Byre bar and bistro.

There's a cute little cinema called the **New Picture House** (117 North Street, ☎ 01334 474902; www.nphcinema.co.uk), an old theatre with all the mod cons, showing a selection of the latest movies, live opera and old classics. They also offer VIP packages with drinks.

Events

The Lammas Market was traditionally the local Harvest Festival. It continues today as a funfair for all the family when Market Street closes to traffic for a few days in early August. The last Sunday in July is the **Highland Games** featuring such traditional activities as caber tossing and tug of war.

At the end of November, **St Andrews Week** is the local festival with music, drama, and art exhibitions all around

The New Picture House cinema

LOCAL KNOWLEDGE

Debbie Taylor is the managing director of the luxury Old Course Hotel, Golf Resort & Spa, St Andrews. As one of Scotland's most prominent hoteliers, she is a leading figure in the Scottish tourism industry, Chairman of the British Hospitality Association Scotland Committee and a Master Innholder.

Best beach walk: West Sands beach is the setting of the opening scene from the film *Chariots of Fire*, with its long, broad sandy beach which stretches as far as the eye can see. It's superb for a gentle stroll, power-walk and also great to take the children to fly kites.

Best visitor attraction: My sons love visiting the Scottish Deer Centre, just outside Cupar. There are nine different species of deer, a treetop walkway, feeding time in the wolf wood, and birds of prey demonstrations in the outdoor theatre.

Best pub: The Jigger Inn, next to the Old Golf Course is fondly referred to as the 'town's best 19th hole' and much loved by the many celebrities who visit.

Best gift shop: I love the 'Ness' shop, 84 Market Street, as it has a fantastic range of wellies and stylish handbags, bedecked in contemporary tartan: Scottish style at its best.

Favourite clothes shop: I love the stylish clothing range in Sam Thomas (137 South Street) which attracts the fashion-conscious students from the university.

Best place to spot some wildlife: Tentsmuir Forest is a popular, extensive pine forest planted on the sand dunes at the mouth of the River Tay and is a popular spot to watch the curious seals basking on the beach.

Best place for relaxation: It can only be Kohler's Waters Spa, Old Course Resort. Enjoy a Highland Fling, chill out in the rooftop hot tub, and take a dip in the 20m swimming pool.

261

CELEBRITY CONNECTIONS

The Scottish singer-songwriter **KT Tunstall** was born in 1975 to a Chinese/Scottish mother and Irish father in Edinburgh, and then brought by her adoptive parents, both academics in St Andrews: her father was a Professor of Physics at the university and her mother was a teacher. She was interested in drama and enjoyed theatre performance as a child. Aged 16 she taught herself guitar from a busker's book, later studying music at the Royal Holloway College. She quickly developed her own individual style, inspired by her love of 'eccentric music,' Lou Reid, Billie Holiday and Tom Waits.

After several years perfecting her style and gaining experience (including gigs around Edinburgh bars and restaurants, earning £20 a night), KT then burst as a breath of fresh air onto the music scene in 2005 with her debut single, *Black Horse and The Cherry Tree*, followed by a multi-platinum-selling album, *Eye to the Telescope*. The title song is a personal reflection on her father who took her and her brothers to the university's observatory in St Andrews at night to show them Halley's comet. As she has described, her songs *'explore little specific emotions or situations or stories. They're kitchen table songs, like a conversation between me and one other person.'*

She was thrilled to be invited to perform at Edinburgh Hogmanay (2006/2007); *'As a Scots lass it's the gig of a lifetime'* she admitted. *'I've spent a few Hogmanays at the Edinburgh Street Party over the years and have always dreamt of playing it one day'.*

Living in the small town of St Andrews clearly influenced her music and poetic, romantic song lyrics. Her home town she describes as *'beautiful but sheltered, a little bubble.'*

town. A major poetry festival, Stanza (www.stazapoetry.org), takes place in March each year with a programme of international poets and writers.

🛒 Shopping

St Andrews has an inspiring range of independent family-run shops and boutiques for quality golf sportswear and equipment, tweeds, scarves and woollens, homeware, gifts, arts and crafts. The main shopping streets are **South Street**, **Church Street** and **Market Street**, all of which are within a block of each other for an easy stroll around. A distinctive Tudor-style old building on South Street is **J&G Innes**, booksellers.

The award-winning **Bonkers** gift shop on Market Street is full of distinctive and quirky cards, gifts and homewares. They even offer a free gift-wrapping service.

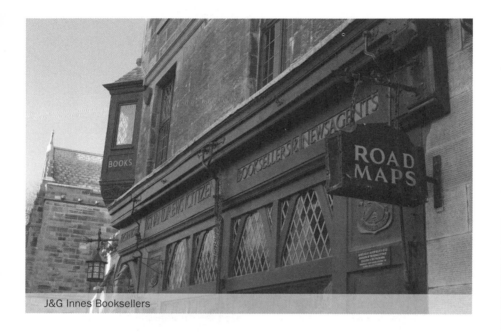
J&G Innes Booksellers

MacGregors further along Market Street is another popular gift shop, with a café tucked up the back serving homemade sandwiches and cakes. For those must have St Andrews souvenirs, try the **Gift Gallery** next to Tesco or the student shop **Bess** which sells a range of university-branded clothing and gifts. For a guide to all shops see www.visit-st.andrews.co.uk.

The best... PLACES TO STAY

GOLF RESORTS

Old Course Hotel Golf Resort and Spa

St Andrews KY16 9SP
☎ **01334 474371**
www.oldcoursehotel.co.uk

World-renowned, leading five-star resort and spa located on 17th green of Old Course, a short walk to beach. With 144 sumptuously stylish bedrooms and suites, the Road Hole bar (with the best golfing view), two restaurants, the private Duke's golf course and the luxury Kohler's Waters Spa with thermal suite and rooftop jacuzzi.

Price: from £96pp sharing; two-night short breaks from £225 pp dinner, B&B.

Fairmont St Andrews

St Andrews KY16 8PN
☎ **01334 837000**
www.fairmont.com

Contemporary American golf and leisure resort built on a grassy headland a few miles out of town, surrounded by the Torrance and Kittocks golf courses. With stunning seaviews, 217 rooms and suites featuring elegant design, cashmere throws and local art. There's the atrium lounge, cocktail bar, two restaurants, golf clubhouse, spa, and swimming pool. The hotel also runs a free shuttle bus for guests to and from the town.

Price: short-break offer from £170 B&B for two.

BOUTIQUE

St Andrews Golf Hotel

40 The Scores KY16 9AS
☎ **01334 472611**
www.standrews-golf.co.uk

City, boutique hotel beside the sea. A quiet location near promenade and beach with glorious views, 22 chic, sexy bedrooms, glamorous cocktail bar, patio garden, lively Ma Bells pub downstairs (Prince William student haunt) and an exceptional fine-dining restaurant. Enthusiastic, friendly staff, and traditional hospitality with a contemporary smart look.

Price: from £200 pr B&B. Special offers available.

The Inn on North Street

127 North Street KY16 9AG
☎ **01334 473387**
www.theinnonnorthstreet.com

Superb town centre location with the slogan 'Meet-Eat-Drink-Sleep – all the necessities of life under one roof.' Contemporary rooms with DVD, satellite TV (for an early night, you may wish a room away from the lively Lizard bar!). Downstairs is the Oak Rooms for drinking and eating, featuring inspiring modern Scottish cuisine.

Price: from £80 single, double from £120 B&B.

The best... **PLACES TO STAY**

HOTEL

Macdonald Rusacks Hotel

Pilmour Links KY16 9JQ
☎ 0870 400 8128
www.macdonaldhotels.co.uk/rusacks

Wilhelm Rusack, an entrepreneurial farmer keen to promote golf tourism, created the Rusacks Hotel in 1887. With comfy cosy rooms in crimson, green or touch of tartan, every bedroom is named after a famous golfer. Book the superior Tom Morris or Turret suite. Located in a prime site overlooking the Old Course, there's a bar and restaurant (with seaviews), and hearty breakfasts.

Price: £65–£175 pp B&B.

B&B

Little Carron Cottage

Little Carron Gardens KY16 8QN
☎ 01334 474039
www.littlecarroncottage.co.uk

Gorgeous, traditional country cottage (built 1800) on the west side of town with two ground-floor suites, both with private lounge. There's also a fridge, tea tray, DVDs, extra children's bed and toys, pretty garden and a parking area. Enjoy a pretty riverside walk to town centre. Offers porridge and full Scottish breakfast.

Price: £30–£45 pp B&B.

SELF-CATERING

Old Admiralty House

24 East Scores KY16 9BE
☎ 02380 873007
www.eagleyerentals.com

Stunning location just 10 minutes' walk from the Old Course, a clifftop vista overlooking the sea near the castle and harbour, it could not be more dramatic. Three bedrooms (double or twin), two en suite, a third bathroom, lounge (with TV/DVD), well-equipped kitchen and dining for six guests. An added extra is the private garden.

Price: £550–£875 per week for 2009.

UNUSUAL

The Old Station

Stravithie Bridge,
St Andrews KY16 8LR
☎ 01334 880505
www.theoldstation.co.uk

Country house guest house located in refurbished Victorian railway station. Six en suite bedrooms (garden room wheelchair accessible); two luxury suites in railway carriage, each with double room, private lounge and outdoor deck. Fresh local produce for breakfast. Beautiful landscaped garden has putting green with bunker for golf practice.

Price: £90 standard double, £130 suite B&B per room.

The best... FOOD AND DRINK

▶ Staying in

Depending on the season you are visiting the area, the **Allanhill Farmshop** offers the chance to pick your own strawberries, blueberries, gooseberries and brambles. The farmshop has fresh produce, jam and homebaking. Children can see farm animals and explore the mini maze and swing park.

ALLANHILL FARMSHOP: Allanhill Farm, St Andrews KY16 8LJ; ☎ 01334 477999. Open from May to September.

On the first Saturday of each month in the main St Andrews car park, there is a **farmers' market**. St Andrews has been awarded Fairtrade status for its excellence in selling and serving fairly traded products, sugar, tea, coffee, chocolate. **Fisher & Donaldson** (13 Church Street) is a fine foodie boulangerie and patisserie, with its famous fudge doughnuts and coffee towers. **Luvians Bottleshop** (66 Market Street) is the place for wine, and just up the road is **Luvians** (84 Market Street) ice cream parlour. Another famous ice cream shop is **Janetta** (31 South Street), which has been here for 100 years and offers 52 flavours of award-winning ice cream. **Cherries**, a sandwich shop on South Street is a handy place to pick up a picnic on your way to the beach.

Luvians Bottleshop

Visit the **Scottish Deer Centre**, a few miles from St Andrews (near Cupar KY15 4NQ, ☎ 01337 810391); it's both a visitor attraction, bird of prey centre with picnic area but is also home to the Highland Smokehouse for quality Scottish provisions, venison, preserves, shortbread, wines, beers and a large selection of single malts and blended whiskies.

EATING OUT

FINE DINING

Road Hole Grill
**Old Course Hotel,
St Andrews KY16 9SP
☎ 01334 474371
www.oldcoursehotel.co.uk**

Awarded three AA rosettes you can expect inventive cuisine under head chef Paul Hart. Elegant, romantic dining room with floor-to-ceiling windows overlooking the Old Course. Dine on spicy parsnip cappuccino, West Coast scallops, Aberdeen Angus beef, roasted wild seabass, lemon meringue pie soufflé (two courses £38) or the eight course gourmet tasting menu (£65).

Esperante
**Fairmont St Andrews,
St Andrews KY16 8PN
☎ 01334 837000
www.fairmont.com**

Mediterranean-inspired cuisine and design with colour scheme of rich terracotta, rustic browns and olive green. Candlelit cocktail bar (fabulous armchairs) for aperitif before dinner with a menu featuring seared sea scallops, lobster and prawn risotto, slow-braised pork belly, chocolate fondant, and Italian cheese. Impeccable service. Two courses £38.

Balaka
**3 Alexandra Place KY16 9XD
☎ 01334 474 825
www.balaka.com**

Award-winning Bangladeshi and Indian restaurant offering traditional curry dishes and specials such as a Bengali dish, Mas Bangla, salmon fillet marinated in lime juice, turmeric, green chili and other spices. Also offers a takeaway menu. Good value prices: pakoras £3.50, chicken or vegetarian kurma or madras curry £8.50.

RESTAURANT

Number Forty
**St Andrews Golf Hotel,
40 The Scores KY16 9AS
☎ 01334 472611
www.standrews-golf.co.uk**

First have a cocktail in Number Forty, the plush cocktail bar with garden terrace then move on to dinner in the Number Forty restaurant. With wood-panelled walls and brown leather banquette seating, white linen, sparkling glasses, single-flower vase. Offers delectable Scottish produce such as pan-fried Sea Bass, confit duck leg, Pittenweem crab, local cheese. Two courses cost around £20.

The Seafood Restaurant
**Bruce Embankment
☎ 01334 479475
www.theseafoodrestaurant.com**

Giant glass box above the harbour wall with waves pounding beneath. Lives up to its slogan, 'Fish, pure and simple'. Menu includes oysters, mussel veloute, fillet of cod, confit potatoes, crushed truffle peas (their gourmet fish and chips), lemon sole, and basil risotto. Exquisite cooking! Three-course lunch £26, dinner £45. Seasonal offers: £15 lunch/£25 dinner.

EATING OUT

Ziggy's
6 Murray Place KY16 9AP
☎ 01334 473686
www.ziggys.fslife.co.uk

This happy American and Mexican diner with funky rock'n' roll memorabilia adorning the walls is beloved by visitors from celebrity golfers to families. Fantastic lunchtime menu of 30 gourmet burgers (£5.25–£8.95). For dinner, classic fajitas, steaks and ice cream sundaes. Average two courses cost £16–£20.

BISTRO

The Doll's House
3 Church Square
☎ 01334 477422
www.dolls-house.co.uk

City-centre eatery aiming to cater for all, 'ladies who lunch, golfers, tourists and child friendly'. Well-priced seasonal fresh local food, such as warm mushroom salad with poached duck egg; chicken and smoked bacon quiche, mackerel, pork chop with celeriac puree, steak, and butternut risotto. Two-course lunch £6.95, dinner £20.

The Glass House
80 North Street
☎ 01334 473673
www.houserestaurants.com

This modern glass and ancient redstone architecture (within a former church) is impressive and unmissable, with an open-air terrace. Offers a contemporary Italian menu, with tiger prawn and squid risotto, roast chicken, garlic butter, spinach and mozzarella pizza. Set lunch from £7.95, two-course dinner around £12.

CAFÉ

Harbour House,
5 Ellice House, North Street
☎ 01334 474689

The perfect pit stop for breakfast, morning coffee and cake, lunchtime soup, panini, pasta dishes, teatime scones, ice cream. Everything is freshly made and there's a great value children's menu. Open seven days, 8.30am–5pm. Soup £2.95, panini £4.95.

The North Point
24 North Street
☎ 01334 473887

Welcoming café with comfy seats and the ideal pitstop after a sightseeing walk around the castle nearby. Breakfast bacon roll, bone china cup of tea, speciality hot chocolate and homebaking (coffee and cake under a fiver). Popular with students for its happy hour deal (£1 for a large hot drink).

▣ Drinking

As a student town, you can be assured of lively banter and party atmosphere around the pubs and bars. **Ma Bells** (basement of the St Andrews Golf Hotel) was a popular haunt of the royal couple 'William and Kate' and is a still a cool fashionable place, as is the **West Port** on South Street, which does great cocktails and pub food.

At the Inn on North Street, **The Oak Rooms** is a popular drinking hole with a cosy whisky bar upstairs or head down to the **Lizard**, a cavern of all-day entertainment with sports TV, live music and DJ sounds. For a glass of wine or a dram in five-star comfort, visit the **Road Hole Bar** at the Old Course Resort, which also offers alternative drinking ambience at the **Jigger Inn**, an old pub beside the golf course. For a more traditional pub experience try the **Central** or **Drouthy Neebors** on South Street.

ⓘ Visitor Information

Tourist Information Centres: 70 Market Street, St Andrews 01334 472021; www.visit-standrews.co.uk; www.visitfife. com.

Doctors: St Andrews Health Centre, 68 Pipeland Road, St Andrews KY16 8JZ, ☎ 01334 476840.

Pharmacies: Boots the Chemist, 113–117 Market Street, St Andrews KY16 9PE, ☎ 01334 474306.

Police: St Andrews Police Station, 100 North Street, St Andrews KY16 8AE, ☎ 01334 418900.

Travel and Transport: Train travel to St Andrews: Alight at Leuchars Station on the main east coast Edinburgh-to-Aberdeeen line. From there, St Andrews is a 10-minute drive by taxi or bus ride. First Scotrail, www.firstgroup. com/scotrail; National Rail Enquiries, ☎ 08457 48 49 50, www.nationalrail. co.uk; Traveline, ☎ 0871 200 22 33, www.travelinescotland.com; **Bus travel**

around Fife: www.stagecoachbus.com; St Andrews Bus Station, City Road, St Andrews KY16 9HW, ☎ 01334 474238.

Accommodation: **Self-Catering:** www. astayinfife.co.uk; www.eastfifelettings. co.uk; www.standrewsletting.com; www.fifecottages.co.uk; **B&B:** Murray Place is a small street full of great B&B guest houses; www.places2stay. co.uk; www.stayinstandrews.co.uk; www. standrewsopen.com/guest-houses.

Activities: **Golf:** www.linksgolfstandrews. com; official website for the Home of Golf, www.standrews.org.uk; Calluna Tours, small group special interest tours, golf, scenic walks, ☎ 01334 656500, www.callunatours.com.

Taxis: Club Cars, ☎ 01334 479900/ 01334 838555, www.clubcars-standrews.com; Golf City Taxis, ☎ 01334 477788, www.golfcitytaxis. co.uk; Town and Country Taxis, ☎ 01334 840444, www. townandcountrytaxis.co.uk.

THE REST OF FIFE
THE EAST NEUK TO NORTH QUEENSFERRY

The Kingdom of Fife is scarcely 50 miles at its widest point but there are surprisingly diverse scenic changes across the landscape as you travel around. The north and central area is predominantly rural, featuring a patchwork of golden fields full of oats, vibrant yellow rape and harvest-time hay bales, dairy farms, fruit orchards and soft rolling Lomond Hills.

Heading south of St Andrews, you are greeted by rugged windswept cliffs and silver sand beaches which line the undulating coastline from Crail to Lower Largo. This is the East Neuk (meaning 'eastern corner') which is dotted with picturesque fishing villages, featuring the trademark harbour cottages which arose during the Middle Ages through trade with European and Baltic countries. Fife used to be very poor until the discovery of coal, while the East Neuk became a thriving fishing community prompting King James VI to describe the area as a 'Beggar's mantle fringed with gold'.

Today this golden fringe of Caribbean-style white sand beaches and a string of fishing ports with their whitewashed houses, red pantile roofs and crow-step gables is wonderfully preserved, reflecting the character and heritage of the fishing industry centuries ago. The natural beauty of the seashore and wide expanse of open skies is a great attraction for artists who live and work here; the villages of Pittenweem, Anstruther and Crail have dozens of galleries, jewellery and crafts studios. The East Neuk is buzzing in the summer with a series of lively community, cultural festivals.

There's so much to see and do, wandering around these exquisite little towns each with their own history and age-old tales of fisherfolk and smugglers. And one of the best known adventure stories ever written was inspired by a local sailor, Alexander Selkirk from Lower Largo, the original Robinson Crusoe.

WHAT TO SEE AND DO

The East Neuk fishing ports along the coast from Crail to Elie are all just a couple of miles apart and perfect for exploring by car, bike or on foot. On a fine day, walking is the ideal option. There's a specially waymarked **Fife Coastal Path** linking all the villages along this coastline. You can choose one or two sections for a good

Part of the Fife Coastal Path

afternoon hike along a spectacular seascape of dramatic cliffs, sandy beaches and grassy dunes. It's a real nature trail, where you may spot seals basking on the rocks or dolphins out in the Forth.

The Pittenweem-to-Elie coastal trail was voted the number one coastal walk in Britain by the *Guardian* as it takes you on a journey beside idyllic coves and rockpools, strolling past windmills and castle ruins. And all around the scenic seashore, hear the shrieking call of gulls, crashing waves and breathe in the pure, fresh salty air. Each corner along this coastline holds another secret place to discover, with caves, beach combing, cliffs, wildlife reserves and of course a pitstop drink in a village pub en route; with so much on offer, walking just a few miles along the Fife Coastal Path is a fabulous experience. In fact, if you are extremely energetic, the complete Fife Coastal Path runs from North Queensferry stretching 90 miles to the Tay Bridge. Walking route maps and information are available from www.fifecoastalpath. co.uk.

Crail

Crail is probably the most historically well preserved of these unique villages, and noted for its fine architecture of merchant houses in the Marketgate and Nethergate, along with the old fishermen's lofts in the narrow alleyways leading down to the medieval harbour. This is one of the most attractive, and frequently photographed, harbours in Scotland.

The 'piano leg'-design pier wall dates from the 12th century, and was developed further over the years when the west pier was added in 1826 by Robert Stevenson. Sit and watch the crab and lobster boats come and go and simply drink in the atmosphere. You might be lucky enough to be able to buy some cooked lobster from the tiny wooden hut in the harbour.

The harbour at Crail

There's a strong Dutch influence in the town from ancient trade with the Low Countries, illustrated today by the old **Tolbooth** (1520) and its Dutch-cast Curfew bell in **Marketgate** beside the Town Hall. A real sense of history echoes up and down the hilly cobbled wynds with traditional 'fairytale' red-roof white cottages. Browse the art galleries, craft shops and Crail pottery workshop, or, to learn more about Crail's seafaring tradition, visit the **Crail Museum and Heritage Centre**.

The Old Tollbooth in Crail

CRAIL MUSEUM AND HERITAGE: 62/64 Marketgate, Crail; ☎ 01333 450 869.

Anstruther

A few miles down the coast is the Royal Burgh of **Anstruther**, (the local pronunication is 'Ainster'), another ancient fishing village which was for generations the capital of Scotland's herring industry. Up to 50 years ago, the port was so busy it was possible to walk from one side of the huge harbour to the other by stepping from one fishing boat to the next.

Again you'll see the typical Dutch design gable-front white houses and a rabbit warren of narrow winding streets unchanged for centuries. As a busy commercial port, trade was not always legitimate and wine, tobacco, cloth and sugar were smuggled up the Dreel Burn river to the **Smugglers' Inn**, from where linen and coal were smuggled out. This is the largest seaside resort in the East Neuk with many gift shops, galleries, restaurants and cafés, including its famous fish and chip shop, in a long row along the promenade overlooking the harbour.

The world-famous Fish and Chip Bar

ISLE OF MAY PLEASURE TRIPS: Ticket desk, middle pier, Anstruther; ☎ 01333 310054; www.isleofmayferry.com. Prices: adult £17/£15 (seasonal variations); child £8, under 3s free, family tickets available; sailing season runs from mid-Apr–end Sept. One return trip per day according to tide.

From Anstruther you can take a pleasure boat trip out to the **Isle of May** aboard the *May Princess*. The island is a nature reserve in the mouth of the Firth of Forth. Between April and September there is one departure to the island daily, though departure times vary depending on weather and tides. Allow four or five hours for the round trip.

Take a trip on the *May Princess* out to the Isle of May

There are impressive vertical cliffs along the west coast, teeming with seabirds, such as kittiwakes, razorbills, and guillemots from early summer. Good paths (some of which are very steep) make it possible to explore this unique wildlife and bird sanctuary. Visitors will also experience its human history dating back to Viking times, with the ruins of an old monastery, the oldest lighthouse in Scotland and shipwrecks on the rocks.

THE SCOTTISH FISHERIES MUSEUM: St Ayles, Harbourhead, Anstruther; ☎ 01333 310628; www.scottishfishmuseum.org. Entry: adult £5; children free (if accompanied); open daily Apr–Sept 10am–5.30pm, Sun 10am–4.30pm; Oct–Mar 10am–4pm, Sun 12–4pm.

Anstruther's association with the fishing industry has not been forgotten; **The Scottish Fisheries Museum**, located beside the harbour, has numerous displays including a recreated fisherman's cottage, paintings, model boats and fishing gear charting the important fishing heritage of the village.

Pittenweem

Pittenweem is the next port of call along the East Neuk coastal route and continues its tradition as a shellfish market, landing

The Scottish Fisheries Museum

CELEBRITY CONNECTIONS

Edith Bowman, the BBC Radio 1 DJ and TV presenter, was born in Anstruther in 1975 and as a child her parents worked in The Craw's Nest in Anstruther, a hotel owned by her grandfather. Her mother had worked in hotels since she was 14. It therefore seemed a normal way of life, and, as a teenager, Bowman worked weekends in the family business. Her interest in show business was perhaps sparked by her mother who performed in local amateur dramatic productions, including the role of Nancy in *Oliver Twist* at the Anstruther Town Hall. Edith then studied media and communications at Queen Margaret University in Edinburgh during which time she began working at local station *Radio Forth*, the start of her very successful broadcasting career.

Iain Banks, the novelist was born in Fife in 1954 and is a long-time resident of North Queensferry. He came to widespread and controversial media and public attention with the publication of his first novel, *The Wasp Factory*, in 1984. As well as mainstream novels he writes popular science fiction under the name Iain M Banks. He is now acclaimed as one of the most innovative and exciting writers of his generation.

Another celebrity in town is **Gordon Brown**. He was brought up in Kirkcaldy, Fife, and at the age of just 16 entered Edinburgh University to study history, gaining his PhD in 1982. He has been an MP since 1983, firstly for Dunfermline East and since 2005 for Kirkcaldy and Cowdenbeath. When not in residence in Downing Street, Gordon Brown lives with his family in North Queensferry, in a redbrick house on the crest of a hill looking east down the Firth of Forth, a beautiful panorama of sea, the islands of Inchcolm and Inchkeith, and the distant hills.

lobster, prawns, crab and surf clams. The traditional little village is similar to St Ives in Cornwall with a fine reputation as an artists' community featuring a plethora of galleries and studios. The artist John Lorimer (brother of Robert the architect), lived here and this began a long tradition of arts and crafts.

Pittenweem Kirk, the Parish church, is worth visiting, featuring a 17th-century Swedish bell. Next door is the **Tolbooth Tower**, a focal point of the High Street. Its dungeon is alleged to be the old prison for witches awaiting trial.

Two miles from Pittenweem is **Kellie Castle**, managed by the National Trust of Scotland. This is a superb (reputedly haunted!) 14th-century castle, latterly restored by the Lorimer family with furniture designed by Sir Robert. Highlights include a Victorian nursery and kitchen,

KELLIE CASTLE AND GARDEN: Near Pittenweem KY10 2RF; ☎ 01333 720271; www.nts.org.uk. Entry: adult £8, child £5, family £20, free to National Trust members; open 31 Mar–31 Oct 1pm–5pm.

The traditional fishing village of Pittenweem

an organic walled garden, woodland walks and a children's adventure trail in the grounds. There is also a gift shop and a tearoom.

St Monans

As mentioned above, you can walk along the Fife coastal path from Pittenweem to Elie, through the tiny hamlet of **St Monans** huddled close by the seashore. The attractions here are the **Auld Kirk**, located strategically on the cliff edge, an old

Auld Kirk at St Monans

windmill (which you can visit) and the **Seafood Restaurant**. The **St Monans Windmill** is a reminder of the 18th and 19th century salt industry here which used iron pans placed along the shore to evaporate sea water. The salt was then transported by horse drawn wagon to Pittenweem harbour for export.

ST MONANS WINDMILL: Coastal path Pittenweem to St Monans; ☎ 01333 730240. Admission available on payment of deposit for entrance key at Post Office, west shore.

Elie

The East Neuk journey continues to **Elie**, the quintessential British seaside resort which has welcomed day trippers and holidaymakers since Victorian times. Many Scottish families to this day own a holiday home here. It boasts a mile-long sandy beach which has been awarded an EU blue flag, denoting clean water ideal for bathers and windsurfers.

St Monans Windmill

ELIE WATERSPORTS: Elie Harbour KY9 1BY; ☎ 01333 330962; www.eliewatersports. com. Hire and instruction of windsurfs, dinghies, canoes, water-skiing, inflatables, pedaloes and mountain bikes; open end May–early Sept.

The area of the beach right beside the beachfront terrace of the fabulous old **Ship Inn** is the location for regular 'infamous cricket matches' which take place through the summer. The pub team take on cricket teams from around Scotland and beyond. For match dates see www.ship-elie.com.

Lower Largo, a tiny fishing village in the East Neuk

The harbour is a haven for yachts and motor boats, while the sailing club has equipment for hire, including inflatable dinghies and canoes.

Lower Largo

Another must-visit destination on your tour of the East Neuk is **Lower Largo**. It was once a prosperous fishing village, manufacturing nets and knitwear, with trains running right through it over the high pillared viaduct. This tiny village, with fishermens' dwellings jostling irregularly for space along the main street, has a certain nostalgic appeal. The small harbour, now virtually empty, was once home to dozens of herring boats. Although the fishing and trains have long gone, this charming place is designated as a conservation area to preserve the lifestyle and character of the village.

Alexander Selkirk, the inspiration for *Robinson Crusoe* was from Lower Largo

And it's no wonder, as Lower Largo is the birthplace of **Alexander Selkirk**, the inspiration for Daniel Defoe's novel, *Robinson Crusoe*. At 101 Main Street is a statue marking the thatched cottage where Selkirk was born in 1676. The son of a shoemaker, he left for a life at sea. On one voyage in the South Pacific, he had a quarrel with the captain about the state of the ship and he was put ashore on the deserted island of Juan Fernandez, where he survived alone for four years until he was rescued. The ship he left later sank. As well as the statue, his legacy in Lower Largo is also marked by the **Crusoe Hotel** which has an enviable spot beside the harbour and a fabulous terrace for al fresco drinking and eating. There's even a signpost made out of driftwood pointing out to sea with the inscription: 'Juan Fernandez Island 7,500 miles.'

Other attractions

For car enthusiasts and lovers of *Top Gear*, the place to visit is **Knockhill Motor Sport centre** near Dunfermline. This is a superb day out whether as a spectator or if you fancy trying a fast spin around the track. Knockhill is famous for hosting the top events in the UK, such as British Touring Cars, British Superbikes and The Scottish Motorshow. As well as racing days, visitors can a book a Driving Experience, Karting or Trackday. The Driving Experience gives you the chance to drive a racing car, take the wheel of a Ferrari, slide a rally car or get muddy in a Jeep 4x4. The 500m Karting circuit is fun for a family outing or group of friends;

KNOCKHILL RACING CIRCUIT: Saline, Dunfermline KY12 9TF; ☎ 01383 720044; www.knockhill.com. Racing events, Sundays, Apr–Oct. Check racing events and book Driving Experiences, Karting or Trackdays online.

CELEBRITY CONNECTIONS

Born in St Andrews and brought up near Leven, in Fife, **Jack Vettriano** left school at 16 to become a mining engineer. For his 21st birthday, a girlfriend gave him a set of watercolour paints, and from then on he spent much of his spare time teaching himself to paint. In 1989, he submitted two paintings to the Royal Scottish Academy's annual exhibition; both were accepted and sold on the first day. His new life as an artist had begun. Over the last 20 years, interest in Vettriano's work has grown consistently with sell-out solo exhibitions in Edinburgh, London, Hong Kong and New York. His best-known painting is perhaps *The Singing Butler* (set on the beach in St Andrews), as well as other iconic, film noir images of mysterious men and seductive women. His early life in Fife plays a defining part in the sense of nostalgic romanticism in his work, like memories of teenage nightlife amidst the faded glamour of Kirkcaldy ballrooms and his childhood a time when he describes having 'the idea you can't remember a summer that wasn't sunny. That's where the beach paintings come from.'

you can even challenge the Knockhill Stig to the best laptime. There are also Kids Karting events. On Trackdays, bring your own car or bike to test the twists and turns of the racing circuit.

Near Knockhill is the village of **North Queensferry**, opposite South Queensferry on the other side of the Forth. The old car and passenger ferry would arrive here from its sister port. Its location is spectacular, on a rocky promontory, right underneath the Forth Bridge, and you'll find different views of the two bridges side by side as you wander around. There's an unusual hexagonal lighthouse on the old Ferry Pier and a popular visitor attraction near here is Deep Sea World aquarium (see What to do with children, p.281).

Another place worth visiting is **Falkland Palace,** which was built by James IV and James V between 1450 and 1541 and was a country residence of the Stuart monarchs of Scotland for over 200 years. It features wonderful furnishings, Flemish tapestries and paintings, lovely gardens with herbaceous borders and is home to the world's oldest tennis court. The tennis court is known to be the earliest surviving court in Britain, having been built around 1540 for King James V. It is a rare example of the *jeu quarré* court

FALKLAND PALACE: Falkland, near Auchterarder KY15 7BU; ☎ 0844 493 2186; www.nts.org.uk. Entry: adult £10/£7 (seasonal variations), child £5, family £25; open daily 1 Mar–31 Oct, Mon–Sat 10am–5pm, Sun 1pm–5pm; 1 Nov–28 Feb, Mon–Sat 11am–4pm, Sun 1pm–4pm.

which was common in France, a square court with some key design differences from the *jeu à dedans* court which is played on today. The Falkland court is still in use today

Falkland Palace is home to the oldest surviving tennis court in Britain

Myres Castle

A couple of miles from Falkland Palace is Myres Castle, not an ancient palace which you can visit by day, but a luxury, 16th-century, restored, turreted mansion where your family and friends can stay for a few days. Myres Castle was the home of the Fairlie family from 1887 to 1999 before being sold by Captain David Fairlie to become an exclusive-use property. The beauty is that the castle remains intact like a living museum, featuring the antique furniture, personal belongings, ornaments, china, crystal, silver, paintings, golfing ephemera, childhood books and vintage toys dating back 100 years. It is simply thrilling, and rather moving, to find an old battered copy of the AA Milne poetry book, *When We Were Very Young*, inscribed to David Fairlie as a Christmas present in 1928.

using a heavy asymetric wooden racket shaped like a hand. Given advance notice, you may also play on this court. Interestingly the French warning of *'Tenez'*, meaning 'Look out' when serving a ball, is the origination of the name Tennis. Mary Queen of Scots was a frequent visitor, enjoying the peace and tranquility of Falkland away from the intrigues and politics of Holyrood in Edinburgh.

Wet weather

The ideal place to go on a rainy day is to go and hide 100ft underground beneath a farmhouse in Fife. **The Secret Bunker** is a fascinating visitor attraction, a vast

A control room at the Secret Bunker

subterranean complex that remained hidden until 1993. During the Cold War it served as the British government civil defence centre in the event of a nuclear war. When it was disbanded, the rooms, with all the original equipment, radar, computers and furnishings, were sealed off, completely frozen in time. Since 1994 it has been open as a most exciting museum revealing the true story of a major government military campaign. The bunker contains cinemas showing original newsreel, an RAF control room, staff dormitories, a BBC studio, canteen and many other fascinating original authentic exhibits. This is no Disney theme park: this is the real (rather unnerving) nuclear defence base.

SCOTLAND'S SECRET BUNKER: Troywood, near Crail and Anstruther KY16 8QH; ☎ 01333 310301; www.secretbunker. co.uk. Entry: adult £8.60/£7.10 (seasonal variations), child £5.60, family £26.30; open daily mid-March to early November, 10am–5pm. Shop and café on site.

⚡ What to do with children

A major visitor attraction for all the family is **Deep Sea World,** located near the seashore beneath the Forth Bridge at North Queensferry. It's a well-designed, accessible, long tunnel of aquaria featuring Europe's largest collections of sharks, and piranha fish. There's an Amazon river

DEEP SEA WORLD: North Queensferry KY11 1JR; ☎ 01383 411880; www. deepseaworld.com. Entry: adult £11.25, child £ 7.75, under 3s free; open weekdays 10am–5pm; weekends 10am–6pm. Last entry one hour before closing.

experience, and you can even touch live creatures in the rock pools.

For a day of activity and sport, the **East Neuk Outdoors Centre** offers the chance to try canoeing, kayaking (for beginners, in the river and sea), rock climbing and mountain biking.

EAST NEUK OUTDOORS CENTRE: Cellardyke, Anstruther KY10 3AX; ☎ 01333 311929; www.eastneukoutdoors.co.uk. Prices: £28pp for half day; £20 for groups of four and more; open daily during the summer 10am–5pm.

Entertainment

Many of these seaside villages along the East Neuk of Fife offer seasonal festivals. **Crail Festival** is a community fair which takes place around mid-July with many events for children, sandcastle contests, mask making and drama workshops, as well as an art exhibition in the Town Hall. Pittenweem, as the arts capital of Fife, has an annual festival, the **Pittenweem Arts Festival** (www.pittenweemartsfestival.co.uk), for 10 days from early August. This is a unique celebration of local artists, with over 80 exhibitions in artists' houses, studios, gardens and galleries. There is also music and children's entertainment. Kids will also enjoy the summer fairground which comes to Burntisland from May to August.

The East Neuk Festival is a feast of classical music which takes place over the first week of July, with performances by leading orchestras, pianists and singers. And in late July to early August the **Aberdour Festival** offers music events, sports and children's shows.

Shopping

The Fife villages are all great for browsing for souvenirs, gifts, arts and crafts. A special place to visit is **Wemyss Ware**, makers of the famous and very collectible Scottish pottery, first produced in Fife in 1882. Every porcelain cat, pig and piece of decorative tableware is hand painted and unique.

The Coach House (School Wynd; ☎ 01333 313700) in Pittenweem is an art gallery, fashion boutique, jewellery and craft studio. Pay a visit to see locally designed and handmade wool and tweed jackets and coats.

WEMYSS WARE: Kirkbrae, Ceres; ☎ 01334 828273; www.wemyss-ware.co.uk.

The Coach House art gallery and shop in Pittenweem

The best... **PLACES TO STAY**

BOUTIQUE

Crusoe Hotel

The Harbour, Lower Largo KY8 6BT
☎ **01333 320759**
www.crusoehotel.co.uk

Set in a wonderful dramatic location right on the water's edge in the *Robinson Crusoe* village of Lower Largo, with a nautical-themed design relating to the local fishing history. Single, double, twin rooms and two penthouse suites available with painterly seaviews. The Castaway restaurant serves fresh lobster from pier to plate.

Price: from £85 per room B&B.

HOTEL

Balbirnie House

Markinch Village KY7 6NE
☎ **01592 610066; www.balbirnie.co.uk**

Georgian country mansion set within a 400-acre parkland. Small luxury hotel (four AA red stars), with fine dining. Thirty individually designed bedrooms (some palatial suites) with lavish fabrics and furnishings. Guests can also enjoy the gorgeous gardens, local Balbirnie Park golf course and woodland walks.

Price: from £75 pp B&B.

COUNTRY INN

The Inn at Lathones

Largoward, (between Cupar and Anstruther) KY9 1JE
☎ **01334 840494; www.theinn.co.uk**

Atmospheric, 400-year-old coaching inn featuring 21 contemporary rooms and deluxe suites (some with real fires, four-poster bed, jacuzzi and patio) in former stables and Blacksmith forge. With a cosy pub and bistro serving slow food cuisine.

Price: Standard £80–£150 pp.

Peat Inn

nr Cupar and Upper Largo KY15 5LH
☎ **01334 840206; www.thepeatinn.co.uk**

Winner of the Restaurant with Rooms Award 2008, this food lovers' country inn is run with sheer perfectionism by Geoffrey and Katherine Smeddle. Exceptional hospitality, exquisite luxury suites and gourmet food. With a log fire in the stone-walled lounge, in-suite, TV and morning papers.

Price: from £195 per room dinner, B&B; luxury break £290 pp for six-course tasting menu, champagne and flowers.

SELF-CATERING

Kilconquhar Castle Estate and Country Club

nr Elie KY9 1EZ
☎ **01333 340501;**
www.kilconquharcastle.co.uk

Former aristocratic mansion set in 130 acres of gardens offers one to four-bedroom self-catering castle suites and estate cottages. Sports facilities include swimming pool, squash, tennis, gym, cycling riding, play park, golf range, putting, snooker etc. Bistro and Restaurant on site.

Price: High season, from £715 (one bed), £1,630 (four bed).

Skippers Rest

Anstruther KY10 3DD
☎ **01333 330241; www.eastfifeletting.co.uk**

Idyllic setting on the harbour front, this historic seaman's cottage (1650) is fully modernised to sleep eight or for a romantic retreat for a couple. Isla Dewar wrote her novel *Women Talking Dirty* here. Includes deluxe facilities, rolltop bath, Sky TV, DVD, and courtyard. Local restaurants and famous fish bar nearby.

Price: £525–£975 per week. Three-day short breaks also available.

The best... FOOD AND DRINK

▶ Staying in

The Lobster Store (34 Shoregate, Crail KY10 3SU; ☎ 01333 450476) is the place to buy freshly caught lobster and crab at the harbour wall; have it cooked for you to munch on the beach or take it back to your holiday cottage.

The oldest bakery in the UK is **Adamson's Bakery** in Pittenweem (☎ 01333 311336), selling award-winning oatcakes.

The Pollock family has been farming at Ardross for over a century using the traditional five-year rotation of crops, and specialising in ethically farmed beef. Buy superb quality home-grown and homemade produce at the **Ardross Farm Shop** (Elie KY9 1EU ; ☎ 01333 330415 ; www.ardrossfarm.co.uk), including Rob Pollock's beef, meat cuts, daily picked potatoes and vegetables, as well as rhubarb-infused vodka, raspberry jam, homemade stews, pasta bakes, puddings and pies, and other local farm produce.

Some fresh produce at the Ardross Farm Shop in Elie

Anster cheese is handmade on the farm to a traditional recipe by Jane Stewart, using unpasteurised milk from her husband Robert's herd of home-bred Holstein Friesian cows. This new cheese is fresh and dry, with an almost crumbly texture, which dissolves in the mouth to leave a full-flavoured finish. At the **Cheese Dairy** (St Andrews Cheese Company, Falside Farm, Pittenweem, nr Anstruther KY10 2RT; ☎ 01333 312580; www.standrewscheese.co.uk), you can sample a bowl of soup and an 'Anster' cheese scone, whilst enjoying fantastic views down towards Anstruther and the sea.

Venison humanely reared by vet John Fletcher and food writer Nichola Fletcher was featured on Rick Stein's *Food Heroes,* and they were runners up in BBC Food and Farming Awards. Their products are sold through mail order and at the farm shop, **Fletchers of Auchtermuchty** (Reediehill Deer Farm, Auchtermuchty KY14 7HS; ☎ 01337 828369; www.seriouslygoodvenison.co.uk). The **Pillars of Hercules farm** (Falkland, nr Auctermuchty KY15 7AD; ☎ 01337 857749) grows fruit and vegetables and stocks wholefoods, dairy and meat produce. There is a café here too to enjoy coffee and delicious homemade food.

Takeaway
Anstruther Fish Bar (42 Shore Road, Anstruther; ☎ 01333 310518; www.anstrutherfishbar.co.uk) is regularly voted the best fish and chip shop in Scotland,

if not the UK. Prince William was occasionally spotted standing in the queue while a student at St Andrews. **Pittenweem Fish and Chips** is also highly rated; it's at 5 High Street, a tiny red door next to Clock Tower.

🍺 Drinking

The Ship Inn in Elie is a traditional old pub with a terrace above the beach for lazy days with a drink in hand, a jug of Pimms, Deuchars, Belhaven Best or a sunny South African wine. Sit in or out at **The Crusoe Hotel** in Lower Largo with its great seafront patio; and the **Waterfront** (20 Shore Road) in Anstruther is an attractive pub overlooking the harbour. For a rural setting the **Inn at Lathones** offers authentic country pub ambience, log fires and first-class food.

EATING OUT

FINE DINING

The Peat Inn
nr Cupar and Upper Largo KY15 5LH
☎ **01334 840206**
www.thepeatinn.co.uk

Winner of the Best Rural Restaurant Award 2008. Offering a la carte, tasting and daily set menus emphasising East Neuk food, including Anstruther lobster, halibut with watercress gnocchi, slow-braised daube of beef, confit potatoes and bacon, and mandarin parfait. The service is gracious and sophisticated yet not fussy or formal. Lunch £16, dinner £32–£48.

Seafood Restaurant
St Monans, 16 West End,
nr Elie KY10 2BX
☎ **01333 730327**
www.theseafoodrestaurant.com

Harbourside smart-casual seafood diner with seaviews to die for. Minimalist yet classy menu featuring oysters with Bloody Mary, pan-seared monkfish, halibut, cod, duck confit and beef. Have a summer glass of Chablis and crab salad on the terrace or stay in the cosy bar for clam chowder and Islay malt in winter. Table d'hote menu costs £21–£35.

RESTAURANT

The Wee Restaurant
17 Main Street,
North Queensferry KY11 1JG
☎ **01383 616263**
www.theweerestaurant.co.uk

This whitewashed cottage is certainly wee and has a simple café style. Craig Wood cooks exciting Michelin Bib Gourmand cuisine such as Perthshire lamb, plump juicy scallops, halibut, baby squid, langoustine bisque, roast loin of venison and sage gnocchi. For dessert there's pear frangipane tart or artisan cheeses. Lunch £14, dinner £22 (two courses).

Sangsters
51 High Street, Elie KY9 1BZ
☎ **01333 331001**
www.sangsters.co.uk

Scottish AA Restaurant of the year 2007, this is a serious foodie's kind of place (there's no kids menu) and bookings imperative. Taste crab from Kyle of Lochalsh, organic Scottish salmon, Gressingham duck, Glen Isla venison, apples and herbs from the back garden. Lunch £18.50, dinner £30 (two courses).

The Cellar
24 East Green, Anstruther KY10 3AA
☎ **01333 310378**
www.cellaranstruther.co.uk

Located behind Fisheries Museum through the cobbled courtyard, this 17th-century building has old beams, a real fire, and candlelit tables. Since 1982 Peter and Susan Jukes have offered an intimate setting, impeccable service and star-quality food including East Neuk smoked fish stew, seared tuna and chocolate terrine. Lunch £19.50, dinner £33.50 (two courses).

EATING OUT

GASTROPUB

The Inn at Lathones
**Largoward (between Cupar and
Anstruther) KY9 1JE**
☎ **01334 840494**
www.theinn.co.uk

This welcoming bar and bistro (with
chunky farmhouse pine tables) presents
an extensive slow food menu based
on local Fife produce such as slow-
braised Lamb shank, roast partridge
and seabass. There's also a bar
menu (fishcakes, game casserole,
steakburger) for a lazy cosy lunch or
supper beside the log fire. There are
rock/blues music gigs in the Stables.
Main course costs £8.95–£19.

The Ship Inn
Elie KY9 1DT
☎ **01333 330246**
www.ship-elie.com

Heston Blumenthal came here as part
of his *In Search of Perfection* BBC
series, to check out the Cullen Skink
and the perfect seafood pie. This is a
well-established beachfront pub serving
good grub with a great choice from steak
and Guinness pie, smoked haddock
crêpe, to an avocado and crayfish
sandwich. Main course costs from £9.
Sunday barbecues on the terrace.

CAFÉ

The Honeypot Guest House and Tearoom
6 High Street South, Crail KY10 3TD
☎ **01333 450935**
www.honeypotcrail.co.uk

This homely guest house (£33 pppn
B&B) runs a licensed café serving tea,
coffee, and breakfast till noon. There is
an extensive menu of homemade soups,
cheese toasties, sandwiches, baked
potatoes, homebaking, as well as beer,
cider and wine. Full breakfast £3.95,
bacon roll £1.90, toastie/baked potato
£2.95.

Heron Bistro and Coffee Shop
15a High Street, Pittenweem KY10 2LA
☎ **01333 311014**
www.herongallery.co.uk

Experience the true Pittenweem culture
and browse the superb landscapes,
crafts and artwork by local artists as you
sample fine tea, coffee, good food and
wine. Open on Saturday night for evening
meals, this is a licensed bistro and
coffee shop with homebaking. Soup and
sandwich £5.95, daily lunch specials
£8.95.

ⓘ Visitor Information

Tourist Information Centres: Kingdom of Fife Tourist Board, Haig Business Park, Balgonie Road, Markinch, Fife KY7 6AQ, ☎ 01334 472021; **Anstruther (seasonal),** Scottish Fisheries Museum, Harbourhead, Anstruther KY10 3AB, ☎ 01333 311073; **Crail (seasonal),** Crail Museum & Heritage Centre, 62–64 Marketgate, Crail KY10 3TL, ☎ 01333 450869; **Kirkcaldy,** The Merchant's House, 339 High Street, Kirkcaldy KY1 1JL, ☎ 01592 267775; Visit Fife, ☎ 0845 22 55 121, www.visitfife.com.

Hospitals: Victoria Hospital, Hayfield Road, Kirkcaldy KY2 5AH, ☎ 01592 643355; Queen Margaret Hospital, Whitefield Road, Dunfermline KY12 0SU, ☎ 01383 623623.

Police: Fife Police (non emergency), ☎ 0845 600 5702; Anstruther Police Station, March Crescent, Anstruther KY10 3AF, ☎ 01333 592100.

Travel and Transport: Fife is very well served by mainline rail and express coach services and it is close to the airports in Edinburgh and Dundee, with a good road network. **Train:** First Scotrail, www.firstgroup.com/scotrail; National Rail Enquiries, ☎ 08457 48 49 50, www.nationalrail.co.uk; **Bus companies:** www.citylink.co.uk; www.nationalexpress.com; Traveline, ☎ 0871 200 22 33, www.travelinescotland.com; Stagecoach Bus, Esplanade, Kirkcaldy, Fife KY1 1SP, ☎ 01334 474238, Timetable advice line ☎ 0870 608 2 608, www.stagecoachbus.com; **Ferry:** From Spring 2009 Norfolk line will operate a new car and passenger ferry service between Rosyth, Fife and Zeebrugge, three times each week in each direction, www.norfolkline.com.

Self-Catering Accommodation: www.astayinfife.co.uk; www.eastfifelettings.co.uk; www.fifecottages.co.uk.

Tour Operators: Calluna Tours, small group special-interest tours, golf, scenic walks, ☎ 01334 656500, www.callunatours.com; Cycling tours, www.visitfife.com/guide/cycling.

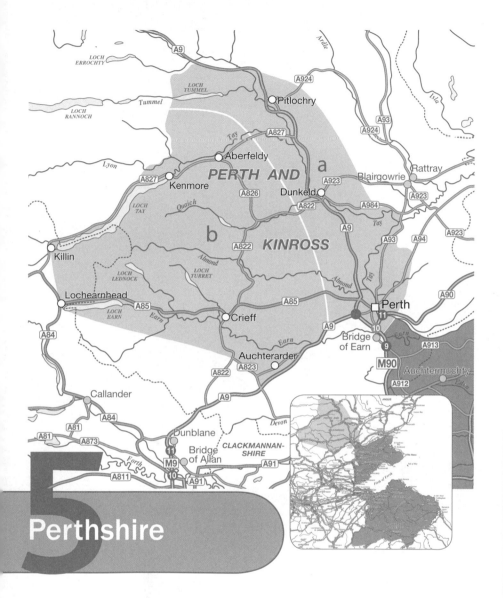

5 Perthshire

a. Perth to Pitlochry
b. Aberfeldy to Loch Tay

Unmissable highlights

01 The whitewashed conservation village of Kenmore at Loch Tay, p.313

02 T in the Park, the best music festival in the UK, p.302

03 A walk through the woodland at the Hermitage, Dunkeld, p.294

04 Experience a wild outdoor adventure sport, p.298

05 Moulin Inn, a quaint 17th-century country pub, p.306

06 House of Bruar country store and the Falls of Bruar, p.303

07 Loch Tummel and the Queen's View, p.299

08 The trees in autumn along the Pass of Killiecrankie, p.296

09 Kinnaird, a relaxing, homely country house and sporting estate, p.304

10 The Watermill, Aberfeldy, an art gallery, music and bookshop, p.319

PERTHSHIRE

The city of Perth is known as the Gateway to the Highlands, surrounded by awe-inspiring, artistic landscape, which bridges the soft gentle Lowlands to the south and the rugged mountain peaks to the north. Perthshire is the true heart of the country and has been given the epithet 'Scotland in microcosm', as you can experience everything here.

Travel through breathtaking scenery of heather-smothered glens, tranquil lochs, pretty villages, fast-flowing rivers and spectacular woodlands and forests. Visit ancient kirks and castles, gardens and golf courses, arts events and sample fine local produce and Scotch whisky.

Perthshire is known as 'Big Tree Country', home to some of the most remarkable, tallest and ancient trees in Europe. Most of the credit for this accolade is due to the early 19th-century local gardener, David Douglas, regarded as 'the greatest plant and seed collector to walk the earth'. His most visible marks on the county are the Spruce and Firs; the Douglas Fir is proudly named after him, along with new garden plants, including the lupin and sunflower. Perthshire boasts a long list of record-breaking champion trees. These include the yew at Fortingall, estimated to be 3,000–5,000 years old and the Meikleour beech hedge standing 100ft high and a third of a mile long, now officially recognised in the *Guinness Book of Records* as the highest hedge in the world.

Perthshire is a sporting paradise, especially for golfers, with around 40 golf courses for both the novice and the expert, found in idyllic parkland settings, scenic Highland backdrops and including the world-famous Gleneagles Resort. Perth stands on the Tay, one of the finest salmon fishing rivers and this whole region is a Mecca for the keen angler. And for the sports enthusiast there are wild and wonderful activities for all ages to experience adrenaline pumping, white-knuckle trips: mountain biking, canoeing, hang-gliding, river rafting, rock climbing, Munro Hill bagging, water-skiing, off-road driving as well as gentle walks, hikes and horse riding. Perthshire is an outdoor adventure playground for everyone.

PERTH TO PITLOCHRY

Standing at the crossroads of Scotland, pulling together Lowland and Highland cultures, Perth is located 'where city meets country – at the heart of things'. It has always been a focal point in the country's history as the Scottish Kings were crowned at Scone Palace until the Union of the Crowns with England and Wales. It's a very accessible city, easily reached by road and rail and is the ideal starting point to tour the surrounding countryside of Perthshire.

Around Perth and on the journey up the A9 to Pitlochry, there are some fascinating places to visit, such as Scone Palace, Kinnoul Hill, Dunkeld Cathedral, Birnam Wood (of *Macbeth* fame), the Beatrix Potter Gardens and The Hermitage woodland walk. You can try your hand at microlight flying at Scone, white-water kayaking on the River Tay at Stanley and white-water rafting on the Rivers Tay and Tummel. Dunkeld is where you can experience quad biking, off-road driving and wildlife tours. Located a few miles north at Ballinluig, a company called Nae Limits organises the adventure sport of Sphereing (also known as zorbing): literally throwing yourself down a hill inside a huge round ball!

Pitlochry is a popular holiday destination, with its Festival Theatre, great shopping, scenic views and woodland walks. The autumn months are when Perthshire is looking its golden best and to explore further there are 250 miles of waymarked paths for countryside walks, many of which are also suitable for mountain biking.

Whether you plan to enjoy outdoor sports, visit castles, shop for tweed and cashmere or relax by a quiet lochside, Perthshire offers the visitor a world of unique leisure attractions, rich heritage, country house hotels and superb places to eat and drink.

WHAT TO SEE AND DO

Perth

Perth is a small, vibrant modern city with a traditional rural heart. Known as 'the ancient capital of Scotland' it has been a Royal Burgh since the 13th century. The city was formerly known as St Johnstoun after the magnificent **St John's Kirk** was built in 1126, although most of the present cathedral dates from the 15th century. In keeping with tradition, St Johnstone is also the name of the local football team.

Surrounded by verdant countryside it's a thriving market town with an array of typical British fashion stores, coffee shops and restaurants. The compact town centre with its traffic-free high street, can safely be explored on foot. The **North and South Inch public parks** – with their glorious floral displays – and the mighty **Tay** (the longest river in Scotland) frame the picture.

Perth has a fine museum and several art galleries (see Wet weather, p.300) and on North Port is **Fair Maid's House**, the fictional home of Sir Walter Scott's heroine from his novel *The Fair Maid of Perth*, later inspiring Bizet's opera of the same name.

For those interested in military history, the **Black Watch Museum** at Balhousie Castle, north of the Perth town centre, explores the 250 years of the ancient British regiment's history with weapons, uniforms, medals and paintings. The Black Watch continues to be a major regiment in the British army and a recent play, *Black Watch* by Gregory Burke for the National Theatre of Scotland focuses on the life, work and emotional hardship of young men fighting in Afganistan. The play has toured the world to great critical and public acclaim.

THE BLACK WATCH MUSEUM: Balhousie Castle, Hay Street, Perth PH1 5HR; ☎ 0131 310 8530; www.theblackwatch. co.uk. Admission free; open May–Sept, Mon–Sat 10am–4.30pm; Oct–Apr, Mon–Fri 10am–3.30pm.

Perth Theatre has a fine reputation as one of Scotland's top repertory theatres, and the classic 1930s cinema, **The Playhouse**, still retains its Art Deco façade but is now a seven-screen multiplex. Perth's state-of-the-art concert hall presents a year-round programme of music and entertainment. (For Perth theatre and concert hall events, see www.horsecross.co.uk.)

Pitlochry

Just 20 miles up the A9, **Pitlochry** has long been recognised as an attractive Highland holiday town, the perfect base for visitors touring Perthshire, to go hill walking or fishing, as well as enjoying the superb summertime **Pitlochry Festival Theatre.** 'The Theatre in the Hills' was founded in 1951, first housed in a temporary marquee, but now boasts a superb, purpose-built theatre at Port-na-Craig on the banks of the River Tummel. From May until October, six plays

PITLOCHRY FESTIVAL THEATRE: Port-na-Craig, Pitlochry PH16 5DR; ☎ 01796 472680; www.pitlochry.org.uk.

The Pitlochry Festival Theatre

are performed in repertoire, with the slogan 'stay six days, see six plays', covering the classics, comedy, drama and thrillers. As well as the summer festival, there are year-round music, theatre and literary events such as Winter Words in January.

With attractive shops selling tweed, woollens, walking sticks, boots, jewellery and gifts, complemented by good hotels, restaurants and pubs, Pitlochry is an extremely popular holiday destination for all ages. In the height of the summer season, coaches, cars, cyclists and wandering pedestrians are sure to block the high street. The best time to visit is spring and the glorious golden months of autumn.

Big Tree Country

A good introduction to truly appreciating the natural beauty of Perthshire is to climb **Kinnoull Hill,** which dominates the eastern side of the city, rising steeply from the banks of Tay. The summit is only around 700ft (222m) and an easy walk. This is a tranquil haven with miles of woodland paths and nature trails. On a clear day there are magnificent views of the Carse of Gowrie farmland to the east, Lomond and Ochil hills to the south and the Cairngorms to the north.

Kinnoull Hill is a favourite scenic spot of the actor Brian Cox, which he visited with his father as a young boy: '*My dad was so transfixed by the view that we just sat there in wonderment. I remember a great sense of literally being above it all and my dad said to me "you'll never see a finer view in your life, Brian".*' Access to Kinnoull Hill is just 1 mile from Perth town centre, heading to the Jubilee car park on the A90 Perth-to-Kinfauns road. A waymarked woodland trail leads through the beech woods along the edge of a cliff path to **Kinnoull Hill Tower**, a folly created by Lord Gray in 1829, an imitation of the castles along the Rhine. The woodland is rich in Scots pine, birch and oak, the natural habitat for red squirrels and roe deer. There are an estimated 120,000 red squirrels in the UK, 75% of which are in Scotland, particularly native in the Perthshire forests.

Another great day out is to head to the stunning woodland park of **The Hermitage** near Dunkeld and Birnam. This spectacular beauty spot along the River Braan takes you on a walk past tumbling waterfalls, rapids and swirling pools and through a forest of rowan, oak and Douglas Firs. Beside the Black Pool a majestic fir tree measures a height of 212ft, one of the tallest in Britain. In autumn you may witness the amazing sight of the salmon jumping up the falls on their way to spawn. The forest glen features an 18th-century folly, **Ossian Hall**, perched on the rocky promontory above the dramatic Black Linn Falls, built in tribute to the legendary third-century blind bard who wrote heroic

THE HERMITAGE: National Trust of Scotland/ Forestry Commission PH8 0AN; half a mile north of Dunkeld on the A9; www.nts.org.uk. Open year round; begin from car park (pay and display charge) or take river bank walk from Dunkeld and Birnam; picnic tables; dogs allowed on lead.

verses. The circular pagoda-style building is open to the public – turn the handle of the outer door and step inside the stone chapel-like space. Then slide the inner door to venture outside on to the glass-windowed balcony with an unbelievable sight of the thundering waterfall in front of you. A poem inscribed around the wall reads '*Sit in

The Hermitage in Dunkeld

this tranquill recess with your friend, your lover, your spouse hear the harp of the deep entice the verses from memory'.

The forested gorge with the folly and tiny bridge were all created by the Dukes of Atholl as a mystical 'wild tree garden'. With trees clothed in dense green moss and a carpet of abundant snowdrops in springtime, The Hermitage has a misty, magical atmosphere; no wonder it was a popular destination for Romantic poets like Blake and Wordsworth. The attraction of The Hermitage is that there are different paths and routes with fairly accessible terrain to suit all abilities and even children's buggies.

Perthshire is proud of its high and mighty trees and lush green landscape. No wonder this is Big Tree Country. The long, tall hedge at **Meikleour** near Dunkeld forms an incredible living wall of beech trees measuring 100ft high and a third of a mile long. The trees were planted in 1745 and are now officially recognised in the *Guinness Book of Records* as the highest hedge in the world. The hedge is on the A93 approximately 10 miles east

The highest hedge in the world, the Meikleour hedge

of Dunkeld and the best time to see it is in the autumn, between the end of September and November. The story goes that the men who planted it were called away to fight in the Jacobite Rebellion and not one of them returned alive. To pay tribute to their memory, the trees were allowed to grow to the heavens.

KILLIECRANKIE: B8079, 3 miles north of Pitlochry OG16 5LG; ☎ 01796 473 233; www.nts.org.uk. open daily 21 Mar–2 Nov, 10am–5.30pm; woodland site open all year; free admission to visitor centre; car park (pay and display charge), shop, café and picnic areas.

Another fabulous woodland walk is through the **River Garry** gorge at the **Pass of Killiecrankie,** a few miles north of Pitlochry. A National Trust of Scotland visitor centre provides information on the local natural history and the story of the battle fought here in 1689. There's wonderful wildlife to see including red squirrels, otters and pine martins. The visitor centre also has a remote camera link to watch nesting birds in the trees. The best time of year to visit is the autumn when the trees are ablaze in rich crimson, gold and bronze painterly colours.

Scottish history

A fine day might be best time to visit **Scone Palace** to explore the beautiful gardens. This palace has held a unique position in the history of Scotland from the 6th century when Scone was the capital of the Pictish Kingdom. Scotland was later united as a nation in 838AD

SCONE PALACE: Perth PH2 6BD; ☎ 01738 552300; www.scone-palace.co.uk. Entry: adult £8/£7 (seasonal variations), £4.50 gardens only, child £5, £3 gardens only; open 21 Mar–31 Oct, Sun–Fri 9.30am–5.30pm; Sat 9.30am–4.30pm; winter opening: mid-Nov–mid-Dec, Fri, Sat, Sun, guided tours at 11am, 1pm and 3pm. Restaurant, gift shop and free parking.

and the Stone of Scone was placed on the Moot Hill opposite the palace entrance. This became the crowning place for all 42 Scottish kings on the fabled Stone of Destiny, including Robert the Bruce and Macbeth. In fact the final words of Shakespeare's 'Scottish play' are, *'So, thanks to all at once, and to each one, whom we invite to see us crown'd at Scone.'*

The **Stone of Destiny** was removed and taken to Westminster Abbey by Edward I in 1296 and it has only recently been returned to Scotland, now preserved at Edinburgh Castle. The film, *Stone of Destiny* (2008), starring Billy Boyd and

Scone Palace

Robert Carlyle tells the true account of a group of students in 1950 who planned a daring raid to steal the stone from Westminster.

Today, as the family home of the Earl of Mansfield, Scone Palace has magnificent State rooms, collections of art, porcelain, needlework and furniture. The extensive gardens are full of roses, rhododendrons and bluebells, strutting peacocks and Highland cattle, as well as an adventure play park and a maze for children.

Visitors should spend a few hours touring around **Blair Castle**, the ancestral seat of the Dukes of Atholl located at Blair Atholl, 7 miles north of Pitlochry. This magnificent whitewashed, turreted, fairytale castle is surrounded by parkland (with grazing Highland cattle) and a back-drop of forested hills behind. Highlights are an impressive display of arms and armour in the entrance hall, portraits, paintings, antique furniture, porcelain and family memorabilia. The story of Blair Castle and the Dukes of Atholl covers the period from Mary Queen of Scots to the English Civil War; from Lord George Murray and the Jacobite cause to the disaster of Culloden; and from the Isle of Man to Queen Victoria's love affair with the Scottish Highlands which led to the castle being presented with the privilege of a private army, the Atholl Highlanders.

> BLAIR CASTLE: Blair Atholl, Pitlochry PH18 5TL; ☎ 01796 481207; www.blair-castle. co.uk. Entry: adult £8.25/£7.20 (seasonal variations), gardens only £2.70, child £5.10, £2 gardens only; open Mar–Oct, 9.30am–4.30pm (last admission); Nov–Mar, Tues and Sat only, 9.30am–12.30pm. Restaurant and shop.

Blair Castle, the ancestral seat of the Dukes of Atholl

Adventure sports

In this area you'll find over 35 different outdoor activities on land, sea and air that are guaranteed to get the heart pumping and adrenaline levels soaring; but perhaps not for the faint hearted or those suffering from vertigo. From fun quad biking and off-road driving to the more exhilarating and mind-blowing pursuits of white-water rafting and microlighting, you can experience it all, and much more, around Perthshire.

At the **Pegasus Flight School** at Scone you can take a flight in a **microlight plane**, described as a hang-glider with a motorbike engine. This will give you a true bird's eye view of the world below and captures the pioneering spirit of early aviation and the 'magnificent men in their flying machines'.

PEGASUS FLIGHT SCHOOL: Perth Airport, Scone PH2 6PL; ☎ 01738 550044; www.scottishaeroclub.org.uk. Trial flights £50–£60 for 30 minutes. Tuition £85 per session.

And now for something completely different. **Sphereing** (or **zorbing**) is a sport which developed in New Zealand and now has a cult following having featured in TV programmes such as *I'm a Celebrity, Get Me Out of Here*. Now this madcap rural activity has come to Scotland and you can try it yourself at **Ballinluig**, a small village between Dunkeld and Pitlochry. Nae Limits will provide you with all the equipment, training and venue to throw yourself off a hill inside a 12ft rubber ball. Participants are strapped in with a safety harness though! Sphereing is not a sport for children and the minimum age is 16.

Other adventure sports run by Nae Limits include white-water rafting in six-to-eight-passenger river crafts, racing down the rapids on the Tay, the Tummel and the Braan. Each trip is graded for the beginner to the brave with different rides for kids or adults only. Nae Limits offer safe summertime family rafting for parents and younger children and also evening trips with BBQ. The latest craze for the very experienced is black-water rafting, which takes place at night time. Canyoning is a real adventure, with a combination of white-water river swims, rock climbs, rock slides and scrambles. Check the Nae Limits website for information on a fantastic choice of outdoor sports to experience the art of adventure and to give you an absolute buzz and a truly memorable holiday in Perthshire.

NAE LIMITS: Ballinluig PH9 0LG; ☎ 08450 178177; www.naelimits.co.uk. Adventure sports run all year; prices range from £25 per sphere roll to £50 for white-water rafting trip; family rafting £35 pp. Nae Limits booking and information also at Dunkeld Tourist Information Centre, The Cross, Dunkeld PH8 0AJ.

Many visitors come to Scotland to enjoy hill walking and mountain climbing. **The Munros** are the highest of Scotland's mountains (over 3,000ft), named after Sir Hugh Munro who first catalogued them. Serious climbers aim to climb all 284 of the Munros, called 'Munro bagging'.

Corbetts are mountains with altitudes between 2,500ft and 3,000ft, and many can rival Munros for the walking and climbing experience. Around Pitlochry there are superb hill and mountain landscapes including **Ben-y-Vrackie** (2,757ft), offering a good moorland walk followed by a stiff, steep climb to the summit. From Pitlochry take the Braemar road for a mile or so to the village of Moulin and the whitewashed Moulin Inn (an excellent gastropub, by the way). Turn left behind the inn and follow the signs to 'Ben-y-Vrackie' uphill to the car park. From here walk along the pine-needled forest track for about half a mile to the foot of the hill. For other hills and mountains see www.munromagic.com

Biking

For a slightly less adventurous outdoor pursuit, why not hire a bike for the afternoon to enjoy a gentle ride along the country roads or woodland trails. If you haven't brought your bike, hire a mountain bike, tandem or kid's bike from **Escape Route,** Pitlochry, a cycle and outdoor specialist.

> ESCAPE ROUTE: 3 Atholl Road, Pitlochry PH16 5BX; ☎ 01796 473859; www.escape-route.biz. Open 7 days; half/full-day bike hire, hybrid/kid's bike £10/£18; mountain bike £12/£18; tandem £15/£25.

Queen's View

A must-visit attraction in the Pitlochry area is the **Queen's View** on Loch Tummel. This viewpoint presents a photogenic panorama of classic Highland loch and mountain scenery featuring the 3,547ft-high peak of Schiehallion, one of Scotland's most famous Munros. The Queen's View is open year round with a seasonal visitor centre.

Queen Victoria came to this beautiful scenic spot in 1866, according to her journal entry for Wednesday 3 October. After a long coach drive from Dunkeld to Kenmore for lunch, the party returned over a wild moor below Schiehallion and down to Tummel Bridge. The Queen recorded: *'we then drove along the side of Loch Tummel high above the loch, through birch wood which grows along the hills. Here it was again very clear and bright. At the end of the loch – on a highish point called after me "The Queen's*

Queen's View

THE QUEEN'S VIEW: Loch Tummel, B8019, 6 miles from Pitlochry; ☎ 01796 473123. Visitor centre open March to mid-November; car park charge, tea room, shop; public transport route, bus from Pitlochry.

View" – we got out and took tea. But the fire would not burn, the kettle would not boil... and the tea was not good.' Although Queen Victoria did visit this spot, it is also suggested it is named after Queen Isabella, the wife of Robert the Bruce.

Wet weather

Galleries

Perth has two fine art galleries both with free admission. **The Perth Gallery and Museum** (78 George Street) has exhibits on local history, archaeology and whisky. **The Fergusson Gallery,** located in an imposing Victorian sandstone water tower, is dedicated to the work of **JD Fergusson** (1874–1961), the leading figure in the famous Scottish Colourists group, working with fellow artists Peploe, Cadell and Hunter. Inspired by French Impressionism, they grafted their knowledge of contemporary French Art (Monet, Matisse, and Cezanne) onto the painterly traditions of Scotland, redefining the qualities of light and colour in their still life, landscapes, figurative

THE FERGUSSON GALLERY: Marshall Place (corner of Tay Street) Perth PH2 8NS; ☎ 01738 441944. Admission free; open year round from early May to end August, Mon–Sat, 10am–5pm; Sun, 1pm–4.30pm.

paintings and drawings into their own individual style. Fergusson was perhaps the most versatile and experimental of the Scottish Colourists; his love of vibrant colour and depiction of the human form leaving a lasting impression on the viewer.

What to do with children...

The natural world always seems to inspire kids and is both educational and fun. The **Nature Reserve at Loch of the Lowes** has a pair of ospreys, red squirrels, woodpeckers, pine marten, roe deer and 2,000 geese in the winter. There are observation hides and HD cameras to watch the osprey eyrie (their nest) at nesting time and all sorts of wildlife activity. The visitor centre has exhibitions, interactive displays and a coffee shop.

SCOTTISH WILDLIFE TRUST, LOCH OF THE LOWES: off the A923, 2 miles north-east of Dunkeld; ☎ 01350 727337; www.swt.org. uk. Prices: adult £3.50, children free; open daily, 10am–5pm.

Beatrix Potter, the children's writer and illustrator (1866–1943) developed her interest in wildlife, drawing and painting during her childhood summers spent at Dalguise House near Dunkeld. In 1893 she wrote a letter to a little boy in which she introduced him to Flopsy, Mopsy, Cottontail and Peter, the little rabbits later loved by generations of children all over the world. The first story was *The Tale of Peter Rabbit* published in 1902. The Birnam Institute houses a

Beatrix Potter exhibition as well as a lovely garden with bronze statues of her famous animal characters.

Pitlochry is famous for its hydro-electric **Dam and Salmon Ladder** on the River Tummel. The ladder was specially constructed to enable salmon to bypass the dam and make their way upstream to Loch Faskally. The ladder consists of 34 chambers, linked together by tunnels that the salmon can swim through. It enables around 5,000 salmon to return to their spawning grounds each year, a journey of some 6,000 miles. A fascinating viewing chamber gives a close up view of the travelling wild salmon. Open all year, access is on Armoury Road just off Pitlochry High Street (☎ 01796 473152 for further information).

> THE BEATRIX POTTER GARDEN: Birnam Institute, Birnam, by Dunkeld PH8 0DS; ☎ 01350 727674; www.birnaminstitute. com. Admission free; exhibition open daily, 10am–5pm; closed Sun, end Nov–mid-March. Garden open dawn to dusk. Café, shop; disabled access.

 ## ... and how to avoid children

The best idea would be a visit to **Edradour distillery**, 2 miles east of Pitlochry. This is Scotland's smallest distillery, the only original farm distillery, and the whisky is handmade today just as it has been for over 150 years, with only 12 casks produced a week. Free distillery tours are given throughout the year.

> EDRADOUR WHISKY DISTILLERY: Pitlochry PH16 5JP (on the A 924); ☎ 01796 472095; www.edradour.co.uk. Admission free; open Jan–Feb, Mon–Sat 10am–4pm; Mar, Apr, Nov, Dec, Mon–Sat 10am–4pm; Sun 12–4pm; May–Oct, Mon–Sat 10am–5pm; Sun 12–5pm.

Scotland's smallest distillery, the Edradour whisky distillery

🎭 Entertainment

Perth is a prime centre for theatre and music events at the **Perth Theatre** (185 High Street), and the **Perth Concert Hall**, (Mill Street), with a year-round programme of plays, comedy, concerts, bands, singers, children's shows, dance and a Christmas pantomime. What's On listings are available at www.horsecross.co.uk.

Pitlochry Festival Theatre (☎ 01796 484 626; www.pitlochry.org.uk) is a much-loved summer repertory theatre which draws hundreds of visitors each year to the town for a week's holiday to enjoy as many as six plays in six days. The theatre was a dream of John Stewart, a Glasgow theatre director. In 1944 when visiting Pitlochry he made himself a promise, *'when peace is declared I shall return to this spot to give thanks to God and to establish my Festival'*. In 1951 a wood, steel and canvas tent was built as a temporary theatre, which was slowly developed and improved over the years. In 1981 a superbly designed 540-seat auditorium with a restaurant, bar and art gallery was opened at Port-na-Craig, a short stroll from the town centre, with grassy lawns sweeping down to the river Tummel. The annual summer season of six plays is staged between May and October. During the winter there are regular music and literary events.

Events

T in the Park (www.tinthepark.com) has been held annually since 1994 and in recent years has been voted Best Music Festival in the UK. It's named after its sponsor, Tennents, and held at a disused airfield in Balado, near Kinross, over a weekend in early July. Aimed at young music fans it's rowdy, happy and hedonistic, full of 80,000 festival goers from all over Britain who come to drink, laugh and see world-class bands.

Perth Festival of the Arts (www.perthfestival.co.uk) is a well-established 10-day annual music, theatre, comedy, literature and entertainment showcase which takes place in mid-to-late May. It was was founded in 1972 by three members of the Perth Junior Chamber of Commerce in response to a comment by music critic Conrad Wilson, who had remarked that 'Perth was the perfect festival city without a festival'. Since then the event has grown in stature and broadened its base with the intention of offering 'something from everyone'.

The Enchanted Forest (www.enchantedforest.org.uk) is a spectacular outdoor *Son et Lumiere* (a sound and light show) at Faskally Wood near Pitlochry, presented annually between mid-October and early November. The event takes place at night as a magical sensory experience for adults and children, attracting over 20,000 visitors each year. There's a different dramatic theme each year and in 2008 the festival was entitled 'A Journey through Space'.

To coincide with the Enchanted Forest, the **Pitlochry Autumn Festival** (www.pitlochryautumnfestival.co.uk) takes place from mid-October to early November, when many visitors will visit the glorious golden-tinted woods around Faskally and Killiecrankie. The programme includes live music concerts, Halloween ghost tours, story telling and street theatre.

Faskally Wood near Pitlochry

The autumn is also when the **Perthshire Amber Festival** (www.perthshireamber. com) tours all around this area, with performances by fine Scottish and international musicians featuring traditional and contemporary tunes, toe-tapping jigs, romantic songs and ballads.

🛒 Shopping

Perth town centre is easy to walk around with a pedestrianised precinct lined with pavement cafés. The long-established independent department store, **McEwens** on St John Street was established in 1868, and along the road is **Cairncross,** which is great for unique jewellery featuring Scottish pearls.

The tiny historic conservation village of **Dunkeld** has an inviting selection of shops located up and down the three main adjoining streets leading up from the river, Bridge Street, Atholl Street and High Street, all within a five-minute stroll.

The High Street (Atholl Road) running through the centre of **Pitlochry** has many attractive clothing, gift and souvenir shops all in a row. **McNaughtons** is the place for tweed country clothing, walking sticks, rainwear and hats. **The House of Bruar** (Blair Atholl PH18 5TZ) 9 miles north of Pitlochry is the known as the home of country clothing.

The home of country clothing

If you were asked what one of the most-popular visitor attractions in Scotland is, you might suggest Edinburgh Castle, the National Gallery or Royal Yacht Britannia but you may not think of a country clothing store in rural Perthshire.

First opened in 1995, The House of Bruar, 'the Home of Country Clothing', welcomes more than one million visitors through the door every year. This is not just a shop but a delightful and deluxe emporium, where you are positively encouraged to spend the day. The House of Bruar specialises in their own high-quality branded classic tailoring, tweed jackets and coats as well as the best of British clothing, shoes and Wellington boots, including Jermyn Street Tattersall shirts, Aquascutum, Viyella, Barbour. There's a cashmere and knitwear hall, fashion accessories, handbags and luggage; and a Country Living department for homeware, garden shop and gifts moving on to children's clothing, books and toys. The Food Hall promotes the best Scottish food and drink with fresh, organic produce, such as bread from the Dunkeld bakery, Carse of Gowrie berries, seasonal asparagus, Orkney crab, Highland venison, foie gras, Inverawe smoked salmon, Brodies tea and Blackwood gin, and artistically labelled H of B French wines and Champagne. After shopping for hours, stop for coffee, lunch or afternoon tea in the restaurant and then visit the Rural Art Gallery. If the weather turns fine, take time for a stroll nearby to the Falls of Bruar to see this spectacular series of pools and waterfalls, where the Bruar water river cuts a dramatic gorge through the rugged and forested landscape.

THE HOUSE OF BRUAR: Blair Atholl, near Pitlochry PH18 5TZ; ☎01796 483236; www.houseofbruar.com. Open 7 days year round (except Christmas and New Year), 9.30am–6pm.

Kinnaird mansion is situated on a 7,000-acre estate

LOCAL KNOWLEDGE

John Durnin is Artistic Director of the **Pitlochry Festival Theatre**. He trained as a director with Manchester's Library Theatre Company and after working with several leading companies in London and Chichester he joined the Festival Theatre in 2003 and has since directed many PFT productions including *The Shop At Sly Corner*, *To Kill A Mockingbird*, *Chimneys*, and *Hamlet: The Actors' Cut*.

Favourite pub: No competition, it has to be the 17th-century Moulin Inn near Pitlochry. Roaring fires, good food, great company and outstanding home-brewed beer, and they let my greyhounds behave as disgracefully as only greyhounds can.

Favourite restaurant: I would have to say that the Festival Theatre restaurant is excellent, with great views: straight through the famous glass wall, across the River Tummel, to Ben-y-Vrackie beyond. But I'm also partial to the Old Armoury, the historic Port-na-Craig Inn.

Favourite woodland walk: The Faskally, the Killiekrankie circular walk has all the attractions of any dark, dense forest walk. Your thoughts quickly turn Grimm, with Loch Faskally wildlife, Killiecrankie gorge and the spell cast by the fierce flowing Linn of Tummel. 11-and-a-bit miles of extraordinary natural beauty.

Favourite river view: The view of the mighty Tay. From Jubilee Bridge on the A9 near Dunkeld: the vista south is breathtaking as it curls darkly into the mysterious, wooded Pass of Birnam; to the north it's a silver ribbon winding through the glen towards Ben Lawers and Schiehallion. My heart lifts every time.

Favourite food shop: Provender Brown in Perth is an outstanding deli, and in Pitlochry, MacDonald Brothers is an excellent family butchers offering wonderful game, pies and the best haggis in Perthshire, while The Scottish Deli has Scottish cheeses, breads, cured meats and exotic fare.

Favourite town: It has to be Pitlochry; a real community, set in a landscape that thrills, inspires and humbles. Its unique theatre attracts audiences from across Scotland and beyond. To be honest, whenever I'm not here, I can't wait to get back.

The best... PLACES TO STAY

BOUTIQUE

Killiecrankie House Hotel

Killiecrankie, by Pitlochry PH16 5LG
☏ **01796 473 220**
www.killiecrankiehotel.co.uk

Hidden in a tranquil setting beside the Killiecrankie river gorge, and owned and personally managed by Henrietta Fergusson, this whitewashed mansion (1840) with pretty garden has 10 traditional homely bedrooms, conservatory bar and smart intimate restaurant.

Price: £94–£115 per room

Kinnaird

Dalguise, Dunkeld PH8 0LB
☏ **01796 482440;**
www.kinnairdestate.com

Distinguished mansion on 7,000-acre estate creates a tranquil rural retreat. Nine romantic bedrooms and homely self-catering cottages for families with children (sleep two to eight). Shooting, fishing, tennis, and lochside picnics can be arranged on the estate. Be pampered with exemplary fine dining, gourmet breakfast and old-style service.

Price: £140–£240 pp dinner, B&B; self-catering cottages £560–£1,050 per week.

HOTEL

Ballathie House Hotel

Kinclaven, Stanley, (nr Perth) PH1 4QN
☏ **01250 883268**
www.ballathiehousehotel.com

Victorian country house on River Tay, named Scottish Sports Hotel 2008. Expect old-fashioned hospitality, drawing room, log fires, antiques, chintzy bedrooms and Riverside Lodge suites. Dining is an elegant white linen/crystal glass affair with exemplary cuisine and service.

Price: £130–£155 pp dinner, B&B.

COUNTRY INN

East Haugh House Hotel

East Haugh, nr Pitlochry PH16 5TE
☏ **01796 473121; www.easthaugh.co.uk**

The McGown family own this 17th-century inn, with head chef Neil assisted by his wife and daughter. Traditional, warm, homely bedrooms, flat screen TV/DVD, bathrobes, superior four-poster rooms with fire, and jacuzzi bath. Bistro and restaurant serve organic game, meat, fish. Landrover driving, shooting, fishing, and biking available on local estates. Family facilities and seasonal breaks on offer.

Price: £99–£129 pp dinner, B&B. £39–£95 B&B.

Moulin Hotel,

11–13 Kirkmichael Road,
Moulin, nr Pitlochry PH16 5EH
☏ **01796 472196**
www.moulinhotel.co.uk

This 17th-century village inn is a destination place to sleep, eat and drink. Fifteen attractive, tartan-draped bedrooms have a classic Clan theme (single, double, family). Three-bed self-catering cottage also available nearby. The Moulin Inn was Scottish Pub of the Year 2007 serving Braveheart ale from their own brewery.

Price: £30–£45 pp B&B; £50–£65 pp dinner, B&B. Special seasonal offers available.

The Loch Tummel Inn

Queens View, Strathtummel,
Pitlochry PH16 5RP
☏ **01882 634272; www.lochtummelinn. co.uk**

Tom and Amanda's 19th-century coaching inn on the lochside offers rustic charm, warm hospitality, log fires, good food and ale for the weary traveller. Seven bedrooms have historic character (rolltop bath), soft duvets and quality toiletries.

Price: £75–£150 dinner, B&B

The best... FOOD AND DRINK

▶ Staying in

Perthshire is the green heart of Scotland, and the land, rivers and climate provide the best meat, fish, fruit and vegetables as well as Highland spring water and several malt whiskies. In March 2007, **Perth** became the first town in Scotland to join *Cittaslow* an international network of 100 European towns where good food, local produce and traditional production methods ensure high quality. Cittaslow is Italian for Slow Cities developed from the Slow Food Movement.

The **Perth Farmers' Market** (www.perthfarmersmarket.co.uk), is held on the first Saturday of each month, from 9am to 2pm on King Edward Street with dozens of stalls and cookery demonstrations. **Provender Brown Delicatessen** (23 George Street) stocks cheeses, meats and all groceries, and the **Smart Good Food shop** (8 Bridge Lane) sells just what the name suggests.

Home produce, such as eggs, oatcakes, jams, cakes, quiches, vegetables, meat, fish, bacon, and wild boar sausages are available at **Gloagburn Farm shop** (Gloagburn Farm, Tibbermore, Perth PH1 1QL; ☎ 01738 840864). Open daily 9am to 5pm, the café is open from 9am to 4.30pm and is highly recommended. In Dunkeld the **Springwells Smokehouse** (Brae Street, Dunkeld; ☎ 01350 727639) is a traditional, artisan, Gold Medal-winning smokehouse for wild salmon, gravadlax and hot smoked salmon. The **Country Bakery** (26 Atholl Street; ☎ 01350 727343) has wonderful homebaking, bread, pies, and cakes and along the road, **The Scottish Deli** (1 Atholl Street; ☎ 01350 728028) sells local game, fish, groceries and wines.

In **Pitlochry** buy your meat at **MacDonald Brothers** (6 Bonnethill Road), which also sells homemade ready-to-cook pies and spare ribs, burgers and sausages for barbecues. For local artisan cheeses, smoked fish and meat, jams and groceries, try **The Scottish Deli** (8 West Moulin Road). A few miles up the road near Blair Atholl is **The House of Bruar** (☎ 01796 483236). Their Food Hall is the place to stock up on fine food and drink, including fish, meat, game, cheese, eggs, vegetables, bread, cakes, preserves and alcohol.

You can visit the **Blair Atholl Water Mill**, a short walk from Blair Atholl village, and signposted (Ford Road, Blair Atholl PH18 5SH; ☎ 01796 481321), to see how wheat and oats are stoneground in the traditional manner for pinhead, coarse and fine oatmeal and wholemeal bread flour. The flour and oatmeal are used in homebaking in the café and bakery shop. Open daily from 10am to 5.30pm, from 1 April to 31 October.

For real foodies, **Atholl Estates** (www.atholl-estates.co.uk) at Blair Atholl offers **Organic Breaks in Highland Perthshire**, a choice of five Highland Lodges which offer a unique Organic Highland Experience. The Estates' farms form part of the Atholl Glens Organic Meat cooperative. Delivery of organic beef and lamb, reared on the estate,

EATING OUT

FINE DINING

Kinnaird
**Kinnaird Estate, Dalguise,
Dunkeld PH8 0LB**
☎ **01796 482440**
www.kinnairdestate.com

A classic, romantic setting for the modern
French cuisine of Jean Baptiste-Bady.
Garden fruit, vegetables, herbs, Estate
game, fish and home smokery provide
a seasonal menu which will start with
delectable canapés, and then perhaps
roast quail, John Dory, prune and
armagnac soufflé, cheese. A sublime,
inspirational experience worth travelling
far to experience. Lunch £20–£30; dinner
from £59.

RESTAURANT

Keracher's
168 South Street, Perth PH2 8NY
☎ **01738 449 777**
www.kerrachers-restaurant.co.uk

Well-established fish restaurant above
what was formerly the family fishmongers
(established 1925, now a tailors). Menu
includes seafood chowder, North Sea
halibut and Skye scallops with potato
dauphinoise, market seafood specials,
Aberdeen Angus beef, mustard mash, and
sticky toffee pudding. Two courses £17.50,
house wines from £13.90.

Deans at Let's Eat
77 Kinnoull Street, Perth PH1 5EZ
☎ **01738 643377**
www.letseatperth.co.uk

Winner of two AA rosettes, this is a popular
Perth restaurant run by husband and wife
team Willie and Margo specialising in
vibrant modern, seasonal Scottish food.
Menu includes filo parcel of black pudding
and haggis, Blairgowrie beef with streaky
bacon, mustard potato cake, and shellfish
tagliatelle. Daily changing carvery lunches
(£13.95), dinner £25 (two courses).

The Two Sisters and Snug Bistro
**East Haugh House Hotel, East Haugh,
nr Pitlochry PH16 5TE**
☎ **01796 473121**
www.easthaugh.co.uk

The Two Sisters set dinner menu
celebrates local seasonal food for the
gourmand, with wild mountain hare
and chorizo cassoulet, monkfish with
pancetta and home-grown leeks. Daily
specials (served in restaurant and Bistro)
may include west-coast lobster; grouse,
pheasant or venison shot by the chef!
Dinner menu £34.95, bistro main £12.95–
£18.

BISTRO

Port-na-Craig Inn
Portnacraig, Pitlochry PH16 5ND
☎ **01796 472777**
www.portnacraig.com

Take a short stroll from town centre across
footbridge over the Tummel to this peaceful
riverside spot for coffee, drink, lunch and
dinner. Quality Scottish dishes, such as
Cullen Skink soup, roast beef sandwiches,
mussels, slow-roast lamb, organic salmon,
rhubarb crumble, and cheese. There are
also children's and pre-theatre menus.
Average price £15–£20 (two courses).

The Old Armoury
Armoury Road, Pitlochry PH16 5AP
☎ **01796 474281**
www.theoldarmouryrestaurant.com

On the way to the Salmon Ladder, this
cottage restaurant and tea garden
offers a delightful setting day and night.
Restaurant-style fine dining beside roaring
log fire, with home-smoked salmon,
Perthshire venison, spinach ravioli, and
Drambuie ice cream. Lunchtime light
dishes, afternoon tea and pre-theatre
suppers. Dinner (two course) average £25.

EATING OUT

The Loch Tummel Inn
Queens View, Strathtummel, Pitlochry PH16 5RP
☎ **01882 634272**
www.lochtummelinn.co.uk

With new owners, chef and décor, this traditional coaching inn offers a couthy bistro bar and smart restaurant. Welcoming ambience, log fires and rustic pine settle seats. Eat Arbroath smokie and salmon fishcake, homemade burgers, wild mushroom risotto, blackberry bread pudding, and drink Scottish ale. £14 for two courses.

GASTROPUB

Killiecrankie House
Killiecrankie, nr Pitlochry PH16 5LG
☎ **01796 473220**
www.killiecrankiehotel.co.uk

This pretty, whitewashed country house hotel has both a conservatory bistro and an intimate candelit restaurant. The bar menu is extensive and enticing with classic fish pie, game pie and chicken pie with mash, Aberdeen Angus steak, and sticky toffee pudding. There's a good children's menu too. Lunchtime menu includes Ploughman's cheese platter and sandwiches. Starter/dessert £5, main course £10.

The Moulin Inn
11–13 Kirkmichael Road, Moulin, nr Pitlochry PH16 5EH
☎ **01796 472196**
www.moulinhotel.co.uk

This 1685 country inn is a hidden gem. Homemade, wholesome food is served all day every day from noon through to evening meals. Menu includes mussels from Skye, steak and ale pie, lamb shank with rosemary gravy, Angus sirloin steak, game casserole, and (very fresh) fish and chips. To drink? Home-brewed Moulin beers. Two courses around £15.

DINER

Paco's
Mill Street, Perth PH1 5HZ
☎ **01738 622290**
www.pacos.co.uk

Phenomenal favourite with locals and visitors queuing out the door, especially at weekends. Freshly made pasta, pizzas, burgers, steaks, seafood and chicken. Jazz music on the soundtrack; families more than welcome. Dishes from £7.95.

CAFÉ

The County Bakery and Coffee Shop
26 Atholl Street, Dunkeld PH8 0AR
☎ **01350 727343**

As well as being a busy baker's shop selling bread, pies and cakes there are a few comfortable diner tables and a wide menu for tea, coffee, breakfast, sandwiches and cakes. After a good walk around the town enjoy a bacon roll (£2.95), soup and bread (£2.60) or panini (£5). Friendly service.

Café Biba
40 Atholl Road, Pitlochry PH16 5BY
☎ **01796 473294**

Centrally located on Pitlochry's main street, this quaint terraced cottage building houses a spacious conservatory coffee shop and bistro. Open May to 2 November 10am–9pm; winter 10am–5pm. Sandwiches, paninis, burgers (£5–£7); dinner menu, steak, chicken, fish (main course £7–£14).

can be arranged for guests on their arrival, along with organic Scottish-grown fruit and vegetables from a local supplier. Visitors can also experience a taste of Estate life through one of the Estates' many activities: 'talking and stalking' with a gamekeeper, discovering the workings of organic cattle and sheep farming, trekking the hills on a Highland pony or taking a Landrover tour with the Estate ranger.

🍸 Drinking

The Moulin Inn (1695), at Moulin near Pitlochry (☎ 01796 472196) has its own microbrewery producing light ale, **Braveheart Ale** and rich and smooth **Old Remedial**. A lively, popular village pub for a few drinks perhaps *after* climbing the local hill, Ben-y-Vrackie nearby. With two log fires and cosy nooks, you'll be hard pressed to find a more traditional hostelry.

The **Tummel Inn** (☎ 01882 634272) is a traditional couthy pub with outdoor beer garden offering a fine selection of draught ales, Belhaven, bottled real ales from Scottish Highland and island microbreweries, 80 Scotch malt whiskies, both local and regional favourites, such as Edradour, Laphroaig, Talisker, Lagavulin and cask strength. Live traditional music entertainment is performed at weekends at **McKays pub** (138 Atholl Road, Pitlochry).

The original Moulin Inn

ⓘ Visitor Information

Tourist Information Centres: Perth, Lower City Mills, West Mill Street, Perth PH1 5QP, ☎ 01738 450600, perth@visitscotland.com; **Dunkeld,** The Cross, Dunkeld PH8 0AN, ☎ 01350 727688, dunkeld@visitscotland.com; **Pitlochry,** 22 Atholl Road, Pitlochry PH16 5BX, ☎ 01796 472215/472751, pitlochry@visitscotland.com; **visitor guide website,** www.perthshire.co.uk; **Perth city guide,** www.perthcity.co.uk.

Hospitals: Perth Royal Infirmary, Taymount Terrace, Perth PH1 1NX, ☎ 01738 623311; **Pitlochry,** Irvine Memorial Hospital, Pitlochry PH16 5HP, ☎ 01796 472052.

Police: Tayside Police, non-emergency number ☎ 0845 600 5705, Tayside Police station, Barrack Street, Perth PH1 5SF, ☎ 01738 892650.

Travel and Transport: Traveline, ☎ 0871 200 2233, www.traveline.org.uk; **Train:** www.nationalrail.co.uk.

Self-Catering Accommodation: Kinnaird Estate Cottages, ☎ 01796 482440, www.kinnairdestate.com; Squirrel Cottage, ☎ 01796 473335, www.squirrelcottage.net; Dalshian Chalets, ☎ 01786 473080, www.dalshian-chalets.co.uk; Woodland Lodges, ☎ 01796 472843, www.selfcatering-in-scotland.co.uk.

Activities: Perthshire Adventure Sports: ☎ 01577 86 11 86, www.perthshire.co.uk/adventure; **Golf:** www.perthshire.co.uk/golf.

Bike Hire: Escape Route, 3 Atholl Road, Pitlochry, ☎ 01796 473859.

ABERFELDY TO LOCH TAY

This is the heart of Highland Perthshire where the soft forested hills around Dunkeld transcend into wild, heather-clad mountains, fast-flowing rivers and majestic endless lochs. The pretty little town of Aberfeldy, situated on the River Tay, is a great holiday base to explore the villages and enjoy the sports activities around Loch Tay from walking, fishing and sailing to white-water rafting and mountain climbing.

Loch Tay is stunningly beautiful in all seasons; at one end is the conservation whitewashed village of Kenmore and 14 miles away at the other end is Killin, perched on the swirling rapids of the Falls of Dochart. The loch remains unspoilt, uncommercialised and tranquil as there's no monster and less noisy watersports, such as waterskiing or jet skis, as found on other lochs. As a child I spent many Easter holidays and weekends during the summer at Kenmore Hotel or self-catering holidays as my father had a motor boat moored here. I learnt to row a dinghy here (getting into difficulty on River Tay's strong current!), and loved pony trekking or cycling along forest trails and quiet country lanes.

Perthshire's highest mountain Ben Lawers (3,984ft) towers over the loch and Glen Lyon offers a picturesque drive. Near Kenmore is the village of Fortingall where legend dictates that Pontius Pilate was born, and it's also home to the Fortingall Yew, a tree between 3,000 and 5,000 years old, believed to be the oldest living thing in Europe. But it's simply the breathtaking natural landscape all around which will attract the active family for a great outdoor sporting experience and the leisure traveller for a chance to unwind for the enrichment of the soul.

WHAT TO SEE AND DO

Aberfeldy and around

The villages all around here are well worth a visit with some fascinating heritage attractions as well as whisky distilleries and gardens. **Aberfeldy** is a handsome market town on the south bank of the River Tay, and was the first Fairtrade town in Scotland. The **Wade Bridge** was built here in 1733 as part of the network of military roads built by General George Wade following the 1715 Jacobite uprising. The old bridge has stood the test of time and is still used by traffic today. Overlooking the river and the Wade Bridge is an imposing statue of a Black Watch soldier standing on a rocky cairn (erected 1887). The Black Watch, the most senior of the Scottish Regiments, was raised in 1739/1740 on this actual site. After the Jacobite Rebellion, George II needed a loyalist army in Scotland to literally 'watch out for' Jacobite rebels.

Cluny House Gardens, about 5 miles from the Wade Bridge, is a Himalayan and North American woodland garden. A feature of Cluny is its natural appearance, with many woodland plants regenerating and expanding freely beneath a canopy of rhododendrons, rowans and birches. See exotic blue poppies, giant lilies and an 11m-girth Sequoia. No chemicals are used in the garden and weeding is carried out by hand to avoid disturbing interesting seedlings and allowing some native plants their place in the garden. From spring to autumn, it's an explosion of scent and colour, with local wildlife, red squirrels and woodland birds.

Another lovely garden in the area is **Bolfracks**, 2 miles outside Aberfeldy with views over the Tay Valley. It was created by Douglas Hutchison, a plantsman, specialising in rhododendrons and azaleas in a woodland setting. It is beautiful to visit in spring time, with orchids and primulas, or in autumn to see the cyclamen and bronze leafed trees. There is no café at the gardens, but you may bring a picnic to enjoy in a tranquil spot.

CLUNY HOUSE GARDEN: 3 miles from Aberfeldy. Cross Wade's Bridge on the B8446, then turn right towards Strathtay at the Ailean Chraggan Hotel. After 2.5 miles turn off left and go up hill for half a mile. Entry: adult £4, children free; open 1 Mar–31 Oct, 10am–6pm. Free entry in winter from 10am to dusk, although donation for bird feed welcome.

BOLFRACKS: 2 miles west from Aberfeldy on A827, PH15 2EX; ☎ 01887 820344; www.bolfracks.com. Entry: adult £3, children free; open 1 Apr–31 Oct;

Kemore

The pretty whitewashed village of **Kenmore** stands on the confluence of Loch Tay and River Tay, where the river flows out of the loch. It was built in 1760 as a model village by the local landowners, the Campbells of Breadalbane. Many of their policies were forward thinking with cottages provided for local people free of charge as long as they brought a skill to the area. Today you will find a plaque on one of the cottages which was dedicated to the village nurse. The church with elegant clock tower is at one end of the village square directly opposite the imposing archway leading to **Taymouth Castle**, the Campbell's former family seat. Queen Victoria and Prince Albert spent part of their honeymoon here and scenes from the film *Mrs Brown* (1997) was filmed here. The **Taymouth golf course** (see p.317) surrounds the castle, now empty and in need of repair, but plans are underway to redevelop it as a six-star resort. Kenmore has remained virtually unchanged in architectural layout for over 250 years and as a result it has unique character and charm. **The Kenmore Bridge** (1774) which crosses the River Tay beside the village is a lovely scenic view.

The Falls of Dochart

At the other end of Loch Tay, 14 miles away, is **Killin** and the **Falls of Dochart**. While perhaps not quite as spectacular a destination as the Niagara Falls, there is an attraction in the rushing water crashing and splashing over the rocks. Visitors have travelled here for generations due to the fact that guide books in the 19th century reported that the Falls were painted by more artists than any other scenic spot in Scotland. In the summer the rocks act as a magnet to those who fancy having a picnic beside the roar of the water. There is a deep pool below the falls, which is popular with fishermen because salmon returning to the river to spawn rest there before the strenuous effort of swimming up the rushing water. The Falls are particularly ideal for white-water rafting which has developed into a very popular adventure sport.

BEN LAWERS: ☎ 01567 820397; access: Minor Hill Road off A827. Visitor centre open May–Sept,

A landmark, towering above Loch Tay at a height of 3,984ft (1,214m). is **Ben Lawers,** the highest mountain in Perthshire. The wild, open landscape all around is an important nature reserve administered by the National Trust for Scotland. There are ranger-led nature walks in summer and it's a popular climb for hill walkers.

Fortingall

It's well worth driving or cycling 6 miles from Kenmore to visit the historic village of **Fortingall.** It's so utterly cute you wouldn't think anyone actually lives here, with the neat old-fashioned houses out of a child's fairytale. It was designed by Arts and Crafts architect James MacLaren, featuring a row of cottages with thatched roofs and crow-stepped gables. And it is here that you can see the oldest living organism in Europe, if not the world. In a corner of the churchyard is the **Fortingall Yew**, estimated to be 3,000 to 5,000 years old. This is the offspring of the original tree, measured in 1769 as having a girth of 56ft. Today the precious roots and branches are protected behind a locked gate. Yew trees are vitally important today for medicinal research, the bark of which can be harvested for taxol, an anti-cancerous drug. To preserve the endangered yew species, clippings from this ancient Fortingall Yew have been taken to the Royal Botanic Garden in Edinburgh to create the world's first DNA yew hedge combining 2,500 specimens of yew tree.

It is said that Fortingall village was the site of the Caledonian Chieftain Metellanus when he was visited by Roman envoys in about 20BC. It seems one of them fathered a child with a local girl. The child was taken back to Rome and grew up as **Pontius Pilate**.

Fortingall is at the start of Glen Lyon, described as '*the longest, loneliest and loveliest glen in Scotland*' by Sir Walter Scott. This single-track road through the valley, featuring small lochs, ancient pine forests and the habitat of pine martens and stags, is a place of remote wilderness popular with hill climbers and bikers.

The Birks of Aberfeldy

Follow in the footsteps of Robert Burns to **The Birks of Aberfeldy** on a wonderful circular trail through this forested river gorge on the outskirts of Aberfeldy. Visit the scene by the **Falls of Moness** which inspired Burns to write his romantic ballad after a visit here on 30 August 1787. The poem certainly captures the natural light, colour and sounds of this glorious glen through dense Birch (Birks) woodland and along the riverside to the powerful tumbling waters of the Falls. The circular route follows a nature trail and a path alongside the Moness Burn, reaching the highest point where it crosses the bridge above the white-water falls. There are seats and scenic points along the way, with winter views down the Tay Valley. Legend has it that Burns wrote the song after resting on a hollowed seat on the rock just at the side of the Birks where a plaque now marks the site.

The Birks of Aberfeldy by Robert Burns
'Now simmer blinks on flowery braes,
And o'er the crystal streamlet plays;
Come, let us spend the lightsome days
In the Birks of Aberfeldy.
Bonnie Lassie, will ye go,
Will ye go, will ye go,
Bonnie Lassie, will ye go
To the Birks of Aberfeldy?'

A tree trail sign posts a number of species, such as birch, oak, ash, elm and willow. As remnants of the ancient Caledonian Forest have been found within the steep gorge, the origins of this woodland are believed to date back 5,000 years. There are also exotic trees and shrubs planted in the early 1960s by a local horticulturalist with an interest in Himalayan plants, as well as wildflowers in summer such as red campion, yellow pimpernel and the aromatic smell of wild wood garlic. This is the habitat of great bird life, including warblers, flycatchers, woodpeckers, pied and grey wagtails as well as dippers searching for food in the stream.

The path is rough in places along steep slopes, so young children should be kept in sight at all times. The best times to visit are in springtime when the rivers are running high and the waterfall cascades in dramatic torrents down the rocks, or in autumn when the leaves are changing from green to gold. The 2.5-mile circular walk is accessible from the centre of Aberfeldy or from the Birks Car Park off the A826. Walking tour maps are available from the Aberfeldy Tourist Information Centre.

Adventure Perthshire

Perthshire is the irrefutable 'adventure capital' of Scotland and as well as the traditional activities of walking, cycling, angling and golf, the region boasts an unrivalled range of unique outdoor experiences. Around Aberfeldy, Kenmore and Killin on the River Tay and Loch Tay, there's the opportunity to try out some amazing outdoor watersports as well as mountaineering, gorge jumping and mountain biking.

Paddle your way around Perthshire waterways on canoeing and kayaking trips in a one/two-man kayak or open Canadian canoe. Canyoning is an awesome, wet and wild experience for the adrenaline junkie. Swim through rapids, cliff jump into deep clear pools, abseil through waterfalls and slide down natural stone 'flumes'. The minimum age is 12 years and under 18s must be accompanied by a parent or guardian.

Duckies are inflatable open canoes which are extremely manoeuvrable and great fun on either white-water or flat-water trips. Again the minimum age is 12 years and under 18s must be accompanied by a parent or guardian. Perthshire's lochs and rivers are ideal for white-water rafting and an unforgettable experience with a group of friends or family. The minimum age is eight years, depending on route and water conditions.

LEGEND @ LOCH TAY HIGHLAND LODGES: nr Killin, Perthshire FK21 8TY; ☎ 01567 820051; www.legendsailing.co.uk. Prices range from gravity-assisted downhill cycle trips from £12, to sailing boat hire from £45.

Outdoor activity providers

This is a just a selection of numerous specialist outdoor adventure activity providers in the area:

- **Activ8s**: The Coachyard, Aberfeldy PH15 2AS; ☎ 01887 829292; www.activ8s.com. White-water rafting, canyoning, gorge descents, quad bikes. From £30 half day.
- **Dunolly Adventures**: Taybridge Drive, Aberfeldy PH15 2BP ; ☎ 01887 820298; www.dunollyadventures.co.uk. River rafting, duckies, off-road biking, gorge ascent and cliff jumping. From £12 per person.
- **Killin Outdoor Centre**: Main Street, Killin, Perthshire FK21 8UJ; ☎ 01567 820652; www.killinoutdoor.co.uk. Canadian canoes, kayaking, children's activities, mountain biking. See website for prices.
- **Splash White-Water Rafting**: Dunkeld Road, Aberfeldy PH15 2AQ; ☎ 01887 829706; www.rafting.co.uk. Rafting, river bugs, duckies, canyoning, splash ultimate white-water kayaking. From £25 half day.

For more information contact Adventure Perthshire Hotline on ☎ 01887 829010 and check out www.visitscotland.com/adventure.

Loch Tay is a beautiful calm and majestic loch and perfect for sailing, boating, cruising and fishing. Learn to rig a sail and pilot a single-hander yacht safely. This is a real challenge but a lot of fun to learn. Seasonal motor boat hire and loch cruises are also available. **Legend Sailing** is one of the best places to learn to sail in Scotland, and it also offers activities from quad biking and mountain biking to archery and kayaking.

Horse riding
Mains of Taymouth Stables is situated by the shoreside of Loch Tay just over the bridge from Kenmore. Pony trekking and horse hacking is available for all ages and abilities along forest trails and mountain tracks.

Golf
If you are a keen golfer and plan to tour around and wish to play on several courses, check out the Perthshire Green Card (www.perthshire.co.uk/golf) for discounted fees. One of the most celebrated 18-hole courses in the area is **Taymouth Castle**, Kenmore near Loch Tay. Surrounding the magnificent, baronial Taymouth Castle, (former family seat of the Campbells of Breadalbane), the course is laid out through a mature

Horse riding on the shores of Loch Tay

MAINS OF TAYMOUTH STABLES: Kenmore PH15 2HN; ☎ 01887 830226; www.taymouthstables.co.uk. Open all year round, 10am–5pm every day, excluding Tuesdays; one-hour trek (beginners) £26; one-hour hack (experienced rider) £30.

parkland with gentle slopes and water features to add a challenge and bunkers to catch the unwary. The club advises to 'keep it straight, stay out of the rough and don't push too hard and you will have a braw day'. The course offers a shop, clubs and trolley hire, practice green and a welcoming 19th hole clubhouse with log fire.

As well as many premier 18-hole golf courses, Perthshire has a range of **9-hole courses** suitable for beginners and families. The 9-hole **Kenmore Golf Club** welcomes visitors, encourages women to play, has discounts for junior golfers, hires out buggies and clubs, and offers the use of the Courtyard bar and restaurant nearby.

At the other end of Loch Tay, **Killin Golf Club** established in 1911, is one of the most scenic courses in Scotland.

TAYMOUTH CASTLE GOLF CLUB: Kenmore PH15 2NT; ☎ 01887 830 228; www.scotland-golf.co.uk. Round of golf £25–£30, day fee £40–£50.

KENMORE GOLF COURSE: Mains of Taymouth, Kenmore PH15 2HN; ☎ 01887 830226; www.kenmoregolfclub.co.uk. Prices: £15–£17, juniors half price; winter season £11.

KILLIN GOLF COURSE: Killin FK21 8TZ; ☎ 01567 820312; www.killingolfclub.co.uk. Prices: £12, junior golfer £8; winter season £5. Visitors welcome.

☂ Wet weather

As you drive into Kenmore you will see the **Kenmore Hotel** on the village square with its traditional gable roof and attic dormer windows. Established in 1572, it's regarded as Scotland's oldest inn. The story goes that Sir Colin Campbell of Breadalbane granted a lease to his servant Hay and his wife Christian to run their 'honest hostelrie'. The location beside the bridge was an important crossing point where accommodation and refreshments were often required by travellers. One such visitor in 1787 was Robert Burns. Visit the Snug bar where a poem by Burns hangs in a picture frame:

'The Tay, meand'ring, sweet in infant pride,
The Palace, rising on its verdant side.'

From *Verses written with a pencil over the chimney piece in the parlour of the Inn at Kenmore, 1787.*

Julie Woolgal, a visitor to the hotel in summer 2008 was similarly inspired after dining here:

'Swallows dive from cloudy Skies
Rippled Loch beneath them lies
A tranquil evening, calm and fresh
Embraces us, our hearts enmesh.
A pleasant evening over dinner

Such times as these are such a winner,
The Tay beneath us flowing by
Reflects the grandeur from on high
Dancing ripples twinkling bright
The evening here is sheer delight.
As daylight closes we can say
This was such a perfect day.'

The Scottish Crannog Centre

This award-winning heritage attraction features guided tours of a Celtic loch-dwelling. A 'Crannog' was a wooden dwelling built on stilts offshore from the banks of a loch and reached by a narrow walkway. They were built around 2,500 years ago to provide a method of defence from intruders as the walkway could be destroyed. The Scottish Crannog Centre was created to promote the study and preservation of these ancient loch dwellings. A replica of one of the Crannogs has been built on Loch Tay and is based on excavations from a 2,600-year-old site here, where the locations of another 18 Crannogs have been discovered. The centre has an exhibition room with videos, original artefacts and 'hands-on' crafts, gift shop, refreshments and seasonal events.

Castle Menzies

Where better to spend a few hours on a wet day than a 16th-century castle. **Castle Menzies** has been the seat of the chiefs of Clan Menzies for over 400 years, an important historic site where Bonnie Prince Charlie stayed on his way to Culloden in 1746. Architecturally it's a splendid example of an ancient rugged fortress developed over the centuries into a country mansion. As well as seeing the Prince's bedroom, there are fascinating artefacts and paintings and also a walled garden.

SCOTTISH CRANNOG CENTRE: Kenmore, Loch Tay, ☎ 01887 830583; www.crannog.co.uk. Prices: adult, £6.25, child; £4.50;open daily 15 Mar–31 Oct, 10am–5.30pm, last entry 4.30pm; Nov, Sat and Sun, 10am–4pm, last entry 3pm.

An example of a Celtic loch-dwelling at the Scottish Crannog Centre

CASTLE MENZIES: Weem, Aberfeldy PH15 2JD; ☎ 01887 820982; www.menzies.org. Entry: adult £5, children £2; concession £4, family ticket £12; open 1 April (or Easter) to mid-October 10.30am–5 pm, Sun 2pm–5pm.

What to do with children...

Experience the beauty of Highland Perthshire exploring 250,000 acres of wild moorland, forests and hills, on foot, by mountain bikes or 4x4 Landrover. **Highland Adventure Safaris** offer a range of wildlife safaris, led by a kilted ranger and offering the opportunity to see red squirrels, wild roe deer and other Highland wildlife. The safaris operate under a sustainable tourism policy to preserve the environment and protect wild places.

> HIGHLAND ADVENTURE SAFARIS: Aberfeldy PH15 2JQ, follow the B846 for 2.5 miles past Castle Menzies until you see the Highland Safaris sign at Dull Village; ☎ 01887 820071; www.highlandsafaris.net. Prices: forest safari, adult £20, child £10, group discounts available; mountain safari, adult £65, teenager £45, child £30. Off-road driving, 90 mins, £90, passengers £25; gold panning £4.

The visitor centre has the only gold panning activity in Scotland, where you can try your luck to pan for gold and semi-precious gem stones. There's also a children's playground and café for a great day out.

... and how to avoid children

Find out all about how a local Perthshire family created a global brand name at **Dewar's World of Whisky**. Since 1898 the stills at Aberfeldy have produced a fine single malt which is distinctive for its heather honey sweetness. Sir Thomas Dewar, the son of John, the founder, was a pioneer in modern marketing to promote

> DEWARS WORLD OF WHISKY: Aberfeldy PH15 2EB; ☎ 01887 822010; www.dewarswow.com. Prices: adult £6.50, concession £4.50; open Apr–Oct, Mon–Sat 10am–6pm, Sun 12–4pm; Nov–Mar, Mon–Sat 10am–4pm.

Dewars to the world. He was an expert public speaker and his famous comments became known as 'Dewarisms'. Experience a guided tour to learn all about the whisky-making process and then sample a few drams in the Dramming bar.

Entertainment

The Watermill (www.aberfeldywatermill.com) at Aberfeldy has regular art exhibitions and also organises author readings and music events.

The **Heartland Film Society** (www.heartlandfilmsociety.org.uk) was founded to give local residents and visitors to the area the opportunity to see big-screen movies. The Society presents old films, new films, Scottish films, foreign films, and art house films in the Locus Centre, The Square, Aberfeldy–the same building as the Tourist Information Centre. Films are shown (normally) at 7.30pm (£5 a ticket) on the first Thursday and Friday of each month, between September and June.

Events

A colourful occasion takes place on 15 January each year when the annual **Fishing Season** on the **Kenmore Beat** starts on the River Tay at Kenmore Bridge. The opening ceremony begins at 9am in the village square, witnessed by locals, ghillies, lairds, landowners, visitors, a celebrity or two, and officials There's pipe band music, a few speeches and the dramming (sipping a wee dram). A quaich of whisky is poured over the first boat to wish the fishermen 'tight lines' and the salmon fishing begins in earnest.

The Heartland Film Society organises an annual **Film Festival** in October with films shown at various local venues including Watermill and Dewars World of Whisky. There are guest speeches by film directors and prizes for the best films.

🛒 Shopping

The **Mains of Taymouth Courtyard,** Kenmore, featuring a restaurant, gift shop and deli, has been constructed around an open-decked area beside the River Tay. There is free car-parking for 80 vehicles. **The Courtyard Shop** (☎ 01887 830756) is crammed full of homeware from cosy blankets and cushions to kitchenware. In May 2005 Michael Palin opened the **Watermill Book Shop** which has been such a success it was voted UK Independent Bookshop of the Year 2008. It's located in an amazing setting within an old watermill in Aberfeldy, a rambling, ramshackle three-storey stone building housing a coffee shop, extensive bookshop, CD music department and gallery. On the top floor among former mill machinery, **The Watermill Gallery** (The Watermill Mill Street, Aberfeldy; ☎ 01887 82896) features a changing exhibition of abstract modern and contemporary paintings as well as limited-edition prints by post-war artists such as Miro, Lichtenstein, Warhol, Hirst and Hepworth.

Loch Tay Pottery (Village of Fearnan, nr Kenmore PH15 2PF; ☎ 01887 830251) is also worth a visit with a showroom of wonderful hand-crafted ceramics, bowls and jugs.

The best... PLACES TO STAY

BOUTIQUE

Fortingall Hotel

Fortingall, nr Aberfeldy PH15 2NQ
☎ **01887 830367**
www.fortingallhotel.com

Winner of the Small Country House Hotel of the Year award (2007), this pretty village inn matches tradition with contemporary luxuries; with satellite TV, CD, whisky decanter, and soft towels. Surrounded by rivers, fields and mountains. There is also a bar, two-AA rosette restaurant, library and free Wi-Fi.

Price: £190–£235 dinner, B&B per double room.

HOTEL

Kenmore Hotel

The Square, Kenmore PH15 2NU
☎ **01887 830205; www.kenmorehotel.com**

Reputedly Scotland's oldest hotel founded in 1572. Located beside the River Tay and Loch Tay, it's ideal for a relaxing or sporting holiday. With comfortable accommodation in Standard, Executive and family rooms. The Tay salmon fishing season is launched here every January. Drink and dine in cosy Poet's Bar and riverside restaurant.

Price: £54–£74 B&B pp; Suite £220 pp dinner, B&B.

COUNTRY INN

The Inn on the Tay

Grantully PH9 0PL
☎ **01887 840760; www.theinnonthetay.co.uk**

The 'Best Posh Pub with Rooms' said The Sunday Times. Geoff and Jodie's wee village inn has five family-size rooms, cosy bar (pool table, outdoor decking) and smart restaurant beside the River Tay. A paradise for canoeists and rafters and a homely place to relax and unwind.

Price: £40 pp B&B.

Ailean Chraggan

Weem, Aberfeldy PH15 2LD
☎ **01887 820346**
www.aileanchraggan.com

Small, whitewashed country house (owned and personally run by Mr Gillespie for 40 years), surrounded by a two-acre estate by the River Tay with pretty garden. With just five rooms (two family), expect friendly personal service, excellent food.

Price: £59–£95 pp dinner, B&B. £42–£50 pp B&B.

B&B

Coshieville House

Coshieville, by Aberfeldy PH15 2NE
☎ **01887 830319**
www.aberfeldybandb.com

This 300-year-old inn is a charming place to stay with excellent breakfast, and dinner by arrangement. Lounge with wood-burning stove. Guests can experience wildlife safaris, deer stalking, biking, white-water rafting.

Price: £28–£30 pp B&B.

SELF-CATERING

Bell Tower Cottage

Mains of Taymouth, Kenmore PH15 2HN
☎ **01887 830226; www.taymouth.co.uk**

This is one of several historic cottages converted from Taymouth Castle Farm courtyard buildings. Sleeping two, this is the perfect hideaway for a romantic weekend. Beautifully designed over, featuring four-poster bed, leather and oak furnishings, BBQ patio, wood stove, spa bathroom, and Finnish sauna. Sheer luxury.

Price: Three-night break £675; week £900–£1,350.

The best... FOOD AND DRINK

▶ Staying in

Aberfeldy is Scotland's first Fairtrade town and wherever you may eat, drink or buy food throughout the area, shops and businesses do their best to promote Fairtrade, organic and environmentally friendly products. Visit **Lurgan Farm**, Aberfeldy (☎ 01887 820808; www.luganfarmshop.co.uk) for home-produced beef and lamb, home-cooked ready meals, organic fruit and vegetables, organic dried goods and dairy produce.

If you plan to eat in, order food supplies or tailor-made meals from **Dows** (13 Dunkeld Street, Aberfeldy; ☎ 01887 829616) and it will be personally delivered. As well as selling a wide range of produce, such as pâté, smoked meat and fish, homemade cakes, jams, biscuits and Fairtrade tea and coffee, Dows offers a fully catered facility of freshly prepared quality cuisine (curries, pies, soups, pasta) ideal for self-caterers.

At Kenmore, the **Mains of Taymouth Courtyard Delicatessen** has an eclectic mix of the finest products sourced from Scotland, Italy and even New Zealand. For something different for dinner there's a wide variety of Scottish, Chinese and Italian ingredients for an authentic meal. There's also local Rannoch game and meat, bread, cheese, fruit and vegetables, quality pâtés, chutney and preserves.

At the **Highland Safari Visitor Centre**, near Aberfeldy, you'll find **The Scottish Deli** (☎ 01887 822821; www.scottish-deli.co.uk) selling local beef, lamb, game and fish, ready-made meals for self-catering visitors, organic fruit and vegetables and deli counter produce. Order online and food will be delivered to your holiday cottage. There are also branches of The Scottish Deli in Dunkeld and Pitlochry.

Takeaway

The **Quaich Coffee Shop** (21A Dunkeld Street, Aberfeldy; ☎ 01887 822621) sells homebaking, quiche, baked potatoes, sandwiches, soup, tea and coffee.

⌣ Drinking

A focal point in the village of Kenmore is the **Courtyard Bar and Brasserie**. The long, sleek glass-panelled bar offers good wines, beers and 96 malts, with comfy leather sofas, central BBQ stove, bar meals and snacks. There are two bars at the Kenmore Hotel round the corner: **Poet's Bar** is certainly a cosy wee place with roaring log fire and named after the visit by Robert Burns in 1789. There's a good selection of whiskies and several Scottish draught beers. **The Boar's Head** offers a Highland atmosphere with a veranda overlooking River Tay just where it leaves the mouth of Loch Tay, with views of Drummond Hill and the majestic Ben Lawyers in the distance.

EATING OUT

RESTAURANT

Brasserie and Bar
**Mains of Taymouth Courtyard,
Kenmore PH15 2HN
☎ 01887 830763
www.thecourtyard-restaurant.co.uk**

Contemporary café, bar and brasserie owned by Jake and Kim, young and energetic South Africans. Serving 'Estate to Plate' beef, venison and blackface lamb slow cooked on indoor barbecue. 'Foodies' menu features scallop and sweet potato chowder, homemade burgers, crabcakes, ciabatta sandwiches, and pizza. £15–£20 for two courses; full breakfast £7.50.

Aileen Craggan
**Weem, Aberfeldy PH15 2LD
☎ 01887 820346
www.aileanchraggan.com**

This tiny, whitewashed country house hotel specialises in West Coast oysters and langoustines, scallops, local lamb, venison, and woodpigeon. A guest writes 'Superb hospitality, top grub, try the venison and shittake mushrooms'. £20 for two courses.

Kenmore Hotel
**The Square, Kenmore PH15 2NU
☎ 01887 830205
www.kenmorehotel.com**

This dark-wood furnished restaurant with full-length picture windows has outstanding views over the River Tay and the quaint old bridge. The cosy bar serves lunchtime snacks and sandwiches beside the fire. The restaurant at this historic country inn has a traditional menu of local beef, duck and salmon. Dinner £20 for two courses.

Weem Hotel
**Weem, Aberfeldy PH15 2LD
☎ 01887 820381
www.weemhotel.com**

Small friendly country inn (13 rooms), near Aberfeldy offering the traveller traditional Scottish hospitality and informal dining, including lamb shank, steak pie, mussels, sirloin/ribeye steaks, haddock and hand-cut chips, fruit crumble and sticky toffee pudding. Vegetarian and special diets catered for. Good-value menus at £15–£18 for two courses.

GASTROPUB

The Inn on the Tay
**Grantully PH9 0PL
☎ 01887 840760
www.theinnonthetay.co.uk**

Gourmet bar offers lunch and supper, while the restaurant presents a dinner menu of locally sourced food and classic dishes, such as Loch Tay salmon, venison, Italian roasted chicken, steaks, and apple tarte tatin. In the bar, choose from mussels, haggis, handmade sausages and mash, game pie, and clootie dumpling. There's a children's menu and Sunday roasts. Dinner £20–£25 for two courses, bar meal £15.

CAFÉ

The Quaich Coffee Shop
**21A Dunkeld Street, Aberfeldy
☎ 01887 822621
www.quaichaberfeldy.co.uk**

The menu is amazing, with delicious breakfast dishes, coffee, tea, homebaking, soup, sandwiches, paninis, baked potatoes, quiche, tortilla wraps and smoothies. Good healthy home cooking at reasonable prices: soup and bread £2.25, baked potato £3.95, bacon sandwich £1.90, latte, £1.70.

The Boar is on the Campbells of Breadalbane clan crest, the original founders of this Inn.

The **Weem Hotel Bar** is renowned for real ales and beers featuring local brewers and a real ale specially brewed for the Weem by Inveralmond Brewery as well as a good old 'scrumpy' cider. Extensive list of 60 wines, six house wines served by the glass, and selection of rare malt whiskies.

The **Inn on the Tay** at Grantully near Aberfeldy, located right beside the river, is the place to enjoy a range of malt whiskies and local cask ales, while sharing stories with local ghillies, golfers and fables of 'the one that got away'. They serve good bar food all day.

ⓘ Visitor Information

Tourist Information Centre: The Square Aberfeldy PH15 2DD, ☎ 01887 820276, www.perthshire.co.uk.

Doctors: Aberfeldy Medical Practice, Taybridge Road, Aberfeldy PH15 2BH, ☎ 01887 820366.

Pharmacies: Aberfeldy Pharmacy, 7 Bank Street, Aberfeldy, ☎ 01887 820324.

Police: Kenmore Street, Aberfeldy, ☎ 01887 820338.

Travel and Transport: www.travelline. org.uk

Self-Catering Accommodation: Aberfeldy cottages, 7 cottages in and around Aberfeldy, Loch Tay and

Glen Lyon, 33 Appin Place, Aberfeldy PH15 2AH, ☎ 01887 820478, www. aberfeldycottages.co.uk; **Loch Tay Highland Lodges,** Milton Morenish Estate by Killin FK21 8TY, ☎ 01567 820581, www.lochtayhighlandlodges. co.uk, www.lochtay-vacations.co.uk; **Castle Menzies Home Farm,** Aberfeldy PH15 2JD, ☎ 01887 820260, www. castlemenzies.com.

Activities: Perthshire Outdoor and watersports: www.perthshire.co.uk/ adventure; **Fishing:** www.fishingnet. co.uk; **Aberfeldy Recreation Centre:** pool, gym and squash, Crieff Road, Aberfeldy PH15 2DU, ☎ 01887 820922.

Garage: Girvan's Of Aberfeldy, Dunkeld Street, Aberfeldy, ☎ 01887 820254.

FURTHER AFIELD

South of Loch Tay, the Lowland area around **Strathearn, Loch Earn** and **the Ochills** is on the geological fault line which divides the Scottish Lowlands and Highlands. This scenic and tranquil area has much to offer the visitor with hill and woodland walks, golf, watersports, all complemented by some seriously good hotels–from country inns to a famous five-star golf and spa resort.

The Gleneagles Hotel

The **Gleneagles Hotel** is undoubtedly a world-class, premier golf and spa resort, known as the 'Palace in the Glens' within an 850-acre estate in the Strathearn valley. The very name itself, Gleneagles, is synonymous with luxury living reflecting an image of old-fashioned style and elegance. And it is that image of a grand country house surrounded by stunning landscape and especially the three golf courses which have enticed many famous names here; Bob Hope, Bing Crosby, Jackie Stewart, Sean Connery, Steven Spielberg, Harrison Ford, Jack Nicklaus and Lee Trevino have visited over the years to take part in pro-celebrity, charity and major golfing championships. First opened in 1924, Gleneagles has had the ingenuity to keep up to date, with smart new restaurants and a spa a to ensure it remains a contemporary, rural resort for everyone.

The Gleneagles Hotel

Gleneagles history

The foundations of Gleneagles date back to the summer of 1910 when Donald Matheson, the general manager of the Caledonian Railway company, was enjoying a well-earned holiday in the Strathearn valley in Perthshire. With its soft landscape and the forested Ochil hills he realised this would be the perfect location for a grand hotel. Up until the 1960s the railway ruled supreme for all travel across the UK. He believed that once he had 'the traveller in his pocket' on the train then he should aim to look after the traveller at the end of the journey. With this vision in mind he developed several city-centre railway hotels, including the prestigious Caledonian Hotel in Edinburgh, built in 1902 beside the Caledonian Station. Matheson could see the great potential of a different kind of resort hotel, offering first-class service and hospitality as well as golfing and sports facilities. With the design plans in place, construction began, only to be halted with the outbreak of the First World War in 1914. Nine years later Donald Matheson completed his dream project and in June 1924 his Highland Palace celebrated its gala opening. The architectural design was fashioned on the style of a French chateau and the celebrated 18th-century landscape gardener Capability Brown was the inspiration for the landscaped gardens. Five-time British Open winner and leading course architect of his day, James Braid, designed two of the golf courses.

The first visitors were able to travel by train to Gleneagles Station just down the road, from where chauffered cars would transport guests and their luggage to the hotel. This custom continues today and is a popular and comfortable way to arrive from Glasgow, Edinburgh and London. The opening of Gleneagles was a major event, with newspaper articles appearing with headlines such as 'A Riviera in the Highlands' and 'The Playground of the Gods'. The first-night dinner dance, with Henry Hall and his band, was broadcast live on the BBC, a broadcast which was a technical feat of genius for its time. Hall composed a special piece of music for the opening night entitled *Glen of Eagles,* and to this day the hotel has a Golden Eagle as its symbol.

The Gleneagles Hotel is a place where great things happen; Gleneagles hosted the G8 Summit of world leaders in July 2005, and has been selected as the venue for the 40th Ryder Cup Matches in 2014. Gleneagles also has an important Golf Academy and three golf courses. The King's and Queen's courses follow the contours of the natural landscape, the woodland, lochs, streams and a rich habitat for wildlife. The Monarch course was designed by Jack Nicklaus in the 1990s, and with wide fairways it is more suitable for the less-experienced with five tees per hole, on offering variety and flexibility for every handicap.

The brand-new £8million spa was voted by *Conde Nast Traveller* as the favourite Hotel Spa in the UK in September 2008. This is the first ESPA-branded Spa in the UK and was designed by Amanda Rosa. Wining and dining at Gleneagles is also an experience to savour, with a choice of restaurants for all tastes: Deseo, for Mediterranean cuisine; Strathearn restaurant for classic Scottish cuisine; Dormy clubhouse for light lunches and grills; and the **Andrew Fairlie Restaurant** for the ultimate two-

THE GLENEAGLES HOTEL: Auchterarder PH3 1NF, ☎ 01764 662231; www.gleneagles.com.

Michelin star experience. Choose from the Menu Degustation, a la carte and seasonal Du Marche menu all based on classic French cuisine with a Scottish accent.

Glendevon

A few miles south from Gleneagles, the village of **Glendevon** is surrounded by gorgeous scenery and brilliant motoring country. **An Lochan Tormaukin** is a fabulous old country inn, tastefully refurbished with 12 warm, homely rooms, a bar and gourmet restaurant. Dine on prime beef, wild boar, venison and lamb from local farms and fish and shellfish from Loch Fyne, not forgetting home-baked bread. A member of Camra, the bar stocks locally brewed ales and fine whiskies. This welcoming rural residence (owned and run by the entrepreneurial McKie family, featuring several award-winning chefs), is in the heart of the Perthshire countryside and only an hour's drive from Edinburgh.

> AN LOCHAN TORMAUKIN: Glendevon, Perthshire FK14 7JY; ☎ 01259 781252; www.anlochan.co.uk.

Crieff

Once an ancient market town from around 1700, **Crieff** is where the wild Highlander Drovers would bring 30,000 cattle a year for the tryst sales. During the Jacobite rebellion, General Wade was in charge of military road-building and assisted the growth of Crieff by placing it on the main route from Perth to Stirling, with a road north to Aberfeldy.

Today this quiet, rather genteel country town is the second largest in Perthshire. It is now a place for retired people and has been a popular holiday resort since Victorian times after the railway opened in 1857; unfortunately for visitors, the station has long gone. In 1868 a Hydropathic Establishment was founded by Dr Henry Meikle as an original spa. He believed that water was the best cure for all ills and that Crieff had 'one of the purest and finest waters ever examined'. The health spa had a strong religious element and a fine of one penny was levied on any guest who was late for grace at meal times, daily cold baths were compulsory and alcohol consumption was banned. Today **Crieff Hydro** is a popular family resort with impressive sports and leisure facilities; and there's now also a bar!

The town straddles around the Knock, a forested hill at the top, and the streets descend steeply down to the River Earn. There are numerous tweed, knitwear, gift shops and art galleries for browsing, but beware, you have to be pretty energetic to walk up and down the hilly streets! Located centrally between the Highlands and Lowlands, Crieff makes a great centre for exploring Perthshire between Perth to the east, Loch Earn to the west and Loch Tay and Pitlochry to the north.

> CRIEFF VISITOR CENTRE: Muthill Road; ☎ 01764 654014.

CELEBRITY CONNECTIONS

'The Knock hill in Crieff is a very special place to me. It reminds me of childhood holidays of freedom and getting up to no good! I especially like the view looking over to Comrie.'

The actor and motor cycle enthusiast **Ewan McGregor** was brought up in Crieff, of which he is very proud, 'a great wee town' which sits on a forested hill, known as the 'Knock of Crieff' (911ft). Knock derives from the Gaelic 'cnoc' which means hill. The lower slopes are cloaked in woodland with numerous paths for walking. The top of the hill is open, heather moorland with a view indicator explaining the vista in every direction, the farmland of Strathearn and wilder country stretching away to the west.

In recognition of being an ambassador for Crieff and Scotland, Ewan was given the honour of the role of Chieftain of the Crieff Highland Gathering in 2001. As a boy he and his brother always came to the Gathering, playing the drums with the pipe band and having 'a great laugh'. Ewan has admitted that he never imagined he would be given the accolade of Chieftain. It's a great community event every August and loved by visitors too, who enjoy the music soundtrack all day of the pipes, track races, tossing the caber, Highland dancing and a funfair. See www.crieffhighlandgathering.com for details.

The **Crieff Visitor Centre** has extensive grounds with a children's play area to keep them amused, while parents spend time in the garden centre, crafts and gift shop featuring pottery and Caithness glass.

Innerpeffray is the oldest free lending library in the country, founded about 1691 by David Drummond, Third Lord Madertie, with a valuable collection of old bibles.

INNERPEFFRAY LIBRARY: Located is on the B8062, 5 miles from Crieff towards Auchterarder, look out for road signs; ☎ 01764 652819.

The oldest books are Barclay's *Ship of Fools* dated 1508 and the Paris edition of Hector Boece's *Chronicles* printed in 1527.

Two miles south of Crieff on the A822 are **Drummond Castle Gardens**. The castle is not open to the public but you can visit the Italianate parterre gardens, one of the finest formal gardens in Europe. The gardens were originally laid out in 1630 by John Drummond, Second Earl of Perth, and embellished with fine statues in 1830. Features include an ancient yew hedge, a long avenue of beech trees and a 17th-century sundial. The gardens are open daily in the afternoons from May to end of October. **Glenturret Distillery** (Crieff PH7 4HA; ☎ 01764 656565) offers The Famous Grouse Experience where you can learn how The Glenturret Single Malt is produced and also the blended Famous Grouse whisky.

The best...places to stay

Knock Castle Hotel and Spa offers an oasis of tranquility in the 19th-century baronial home of Scottish shipping magnate Lady McBrayne, with uninterrupted views across the beautiful Perthshire countryside and the historic town of Crieff. As well as a leisure centre with pool and sauna, the hotel's 21st-century spa offers a full range of treatments in a tranquil environment, for a single treatment or a whole day of pampering.

KNOCK CASTLE HOTEL & SPA: Drummond Terrace, Crieff PH7 4AN; ☎ 01764 650088; www.knockcastle.com.

For families, the **Crieff Hydro Hotel** is arguably the most comprehensive family resort in Scotland with lots of facilities for children. There are also 40 on-site activities, two swimming pools, tennis courts, horse riding and quad biking so that parents can escape while the kids can play together in a safe environment.

CRIEFF HYDRO: Crieff PH7 3LQ; ☎ 01764 655555; www.crieffhydro.com.

Loch Earn

Perthshire could almost be renamed the Lake District due to its many glorious lochs. In the Strathearn valley is the freshwater **Loch Earn**, just over 6 miles long from east to west. The village of **St Fillans**, the popular holiday destination sits at the eastern corner, from where the River Earn flows out of the loch, through the glen to join the River Tay Estuary. The loch is famous for its watersports, sailing, waterskiing and canoeing; it is also stocked regularly with brown and rainbow trout and fishing by permit is possible from the shore and by boat. To the south of the loch lies **Ben Vorlich,** a steep-sided pyramid-shaped mountain peak. At 3,230ft, this is a popular climb and the views from the top are spectacular.

At the west side of the loch is the village of **Lochearnhead,** a major destination for watersports. Waterskiing and wakeboarding are organised by Active Scotland, the outdoor sports provider at Lochearn Watersports centre on the loch's edge. They also offer kneeboarding (kneeling on a board and a good start before waterskiing) and towables, such as a banana rides.

ACTIVE SCOTLAND: Lochearnhead watersports centre, Lochearnhead, Perthshire FK19 8PU; ☎ 01567 830321; www. activescotland.com.

The best... places to stay

The **Four Seasons hotel** at St Fillans (PH6 2NF; ☎ 01764 685 333; www.fourseasons hotel.co.uk), is a homely, whitewashed country inn, featuring a gastropub, fine-dining restaurant (with excellent food) and cosy lounges where you can curl up and read. Superb views down the loch capture superb sunsets, snow-covered hills and the changing colours through the seasons. The hotel won, quite appropriately, the Good for the Soul award 2008. There are 12 rooms in the main house and six Swiss-style hillside chalets.

In the quaint wee village of **Comrie** a few miles from Loch Earn is the **Royal Hotel** (PH6 2DN; ☎ 01764 679200; www.royalhotel.co.uk). The name was bestowed on this handsome 18th-century coaching inn by Queen Victoria after her visit here. Today the traveller will find four-poster suites, lush fabrics, antiques, log fires, comfy sofas and a library of books in the lounge. During the summer, the walled garden with its al fresco tables is a sunny spot for a leisurely Pimms and lunch. The hotel can arrange fishing on Loch Earn, golf and suggest activities and attractions nearby.

INDEX

E

F

S

This first edition published in Great Britain in 2009 by
Crimson Publishing, a division of Crimson Business Ltd
Westminster House
Kew Road
Richmond
Surrey
TW9 2ND

A catalogue record for this book is available from the British Library

ISBN: 978 1 85458 464 9

The author and publishers have done their best to ensure that the information in *The best of Britain: Edinburgh and East Coast Scotland* is up-to-date and accurate. However, they can accept no responsibility for any loss, injury or inconvenience sustained by any traveller as a result of information or advice in this guide.

Printed and bound by Mega Printing, Turkey

Series editor: Guy Hobbs
Layout design: Nicki Averill, Amanda Grapes, Andy Prior
Typesetting: RefineCatch Ltd
Cover design: Andy Prior
Picture editor: Holly Ivins
Production: Sally Rawlings
Town map design: Linda M Dawes, Belvoir Cartographics & Design and Angela Wilson, All Terrain Mapping, using source material from Ordnance Survey.
Regional map design: Linda M Dawes, Belvoir Cartographics & Design and Angela Wilson, All Terrain Mapping, using source material: © Maps in Minutes™/Collins Bartholomew, 2009.

This product includes mapping data licensed from Ordnance Survey® with the permission of the Controller of Her Majesty's Stationery Office. © Crown Copyright 2009. All rights reserved. Licence number 150002047.

Permissions
The author would like to thank the following publishers for permission to quote literary extracts from: **Moral Causes**, Ian Rankin (Orion Books); **Dead Souls**, Ian Rankin (Orion Books); "**We cultivate literature on a little oatmeal**" for a quotation on Edinburgh's literary heritage from J. K Rowling, (The Edinburgh World City of Literature Trust); **The Right Attitude to Rain**, by Alexander McCall Smith (Little Brown); **44 Scotland Street** by Alexander McCall Smith (Polygon); Quotations from Ian Rankin and Brian Cox from **A Sense of Belonging to Scotland** edited by Andy Hall (Mercat Press).

Help us update
While every effort has been made to ensure that the information contained in this book was accurate at the time of going to press, some details are bound to change within the lifetime of this edition: phone numbers and websites change, restaurants and hotels go out of business, shops move, and standards rise and fall. If you think we've got it wrong, please let us know. We will credit all contributions and send a copy of any *The Best of Britain* title for the best letters. Send to: The Best of Britain Updates, Crimson Publishing, Westminster House, Kew Road, Richmond, Surrey TW9 2ND.

Acknowledgements

This book could never have been completed without the personal and professional support, dedication and enthusiasm from my partner, Ken Scott. He assisted me hugely with inspirational fact-finding and research and wrote the History, Geography & Geology, Wildlife & Habitats and Local Heroes sections for The Background. He also undertook proof reading, indexing, and most importantly, the photography. All this work has been invaluable and I cannot express my appreciation enough for his tireless commitment to this project.

I thank Lea Harris, restaurant editor of Instant magazine and foodie guru, for contributing the Staying In and Eating Out lists for East Lothian and the Scottish Borders. Julia Oliveira researched Edinburgh Writers and New Town bars and Kit Gilchrist wrote the section on Cramond. Author and broadcaster, John Ritchie contributed his personal commentary on Rosslyn Chapel on which he has written his own book, *Rosslyn Revealed*.

The national tourism agency, VisitScotland provided me with topical, seasonal news and stories. I am especially grateful to Martha Bryce for information on Scottish food producers, Fiona Carruthers for visitor statistics, Kirsty Innes, Fiona Stewart and Gayle Wilson for details on festivals, events and Homecoming 2009, Helena Kopecka and Rebecca Smith for brochures on golf and sports.

Tourism media offices around the region have been most helpful, namely Claire Dutton and Jackie Gardiner of East Lothian Council, Lynn McMath, City of Edinburgh Council, Mark Murray of VisitScotland Perthshire, and Amanda Goller at Visit Scottish Borders. I would also like to thank the following PR companies: Crimson Edge, Elaine Howie, Mango, Niche Works, Emma Offord, Porter Novelli, Profile Plus, Stripe Communications and 3x1.com.

I am indebted to Gary McLean, Director of Food Review Scotland and Scottish Hotel Awards and I was delighted that Roy Brett took up the challenge to write the Preface – a truly personal commentary on Scotland and Scottish food. Finally I would like to thank all the writers of the Local Knowledge pages - Alexander McCall Smith, Claire Askew, Susanna Beaumont, Tony Borthwick, Glyn Farrer, Kitty Douglas-Hamilton, Malcolm Duck, Vicky Davidson, Debbie Taylor and John Durnin for their time and interest to contribute their favourite places.

Photo credits

Front cover: Queen's View, Ken Scott; **Inside flap:** Tolbooth, Ken Scott; **Back cover:** Edinburgh Castle, Ken Scott; St Andrews Pier, Holly Ivins; **Inside cover:** Big Wheel, Ken Scott; **Contents:** Portobello beach, Ken Scott; **Introduction:** Dunkeld, Ken Scott; Princes Street, Edinburgh, Ken Scott.; **Colour Section: City of Edinburgh:** Victoria Street: Ken Scott; Edinburgh sunset: www.britainonview.com; Ramsay Garden from Princes Street: Ken Scott; Scott Monument and Gardens: Ken Scott; Edinburgh Winter Skyline: Ken Scott; Ramsay Statue and Castle: Ken Scott; Hogmanay Fireworks: Ken Scott; Stockbridge: Ken Scott; Arthur's Seat: Ken Scott; High Street Fringe performers: Ken Scott; Dean Gallery: Ken Scott; **Colour Section: Countryside and coastline:** Scott's View: Ken Scott; Melrose Abbey: Ken Scott; Faskally: Ken Scott; Scottish Crannog Centre: Ken Scott; Leith Shore Evening: Ken Scott; Puffin: Ken Scott; St Monans: Ken Scott; St Andrews Old Course: Ken Scott; Portobello beach: Ken Scott; Greencraigs: Ken Scott; **All other photos by Ken Scott,** except **p.77:** Holly Ivins; **p.79:** Graham Clark; **p.103:** Ken Scott/Claire Askew; **p.117:** Ken Scott/ Susanna Beaumont; **p.133:** Ian Bruce; **p.151:** Ken Scott/ Glyn Farrer; **p.163:** Ken Scott/ Kitty Douglas-Hamilton; **p.219:** Vicky Davidson; **p.252:** Holly Ivins; **p.253:** Holly Ivins; **p.260:** The Old Course Hotel, Golf Resort and Spa; **p.260:** Holly Ivins; **p.261:** Debbie Taylor/ Ken Scott; **p.266:** Holly Ivins; **p.296:** www.britainonview.com; **p.297:** www.britainonview.com; **p.305:** Ken Scott /John Durnin.

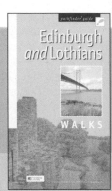